AF796015

॥ श्री सुपर्णाध्यायः ॥

(ऋग्वेदीयखिलात्मकं काव्यरूपकम्)
पदपाठसंवलितः श्रीजयस्वामिकृतभाष्योपेतश्च

दुर्लभं जयस्वामिभाष्यमैदम्प्राथम्येन सुसंपाद्य,
संहितापाठं समीक्षात्मिकाभिष्टिप्पणीभिश्च संयोज्य

आंग्लभाषया–हिन्दीभाषया चानूदितः

त्रिपाठ्युपाह्वेन गयाचरणेन

NATIONAL MISSION FOR MANUSCRIPTS
New Delhi

and

DK PRINTWORLD
Publishers of Indian Traditions

Suparṇādhyāyaḥ

(A Metrical Play of the Late Vedic Age)

With Padapāṭha and a Hitherto Unknown Commentary by Jayasvāmin

Edited the Commentary for the first time and embellished the text with an Introduction, text-critical notes and translations into English and Hindi

by

Gaya Charan Tripathi

National Mission for Manuscripts

NATIONAL MISSION FOR MANUSCRIPTS
New Delhi

and

DK PRINTWORLD
Publishers of Indian Traditions

Cataloging in Publication Data — DK

[Courtesy: D.K. Agencies (P) Ltd. <docinfo@dkagencies.com>]

Suparṇādhyāya

Suparṇādhyāyaḥ: (a metrical play of the late Vedic age) : with padapāṭha and a hitherto unknown commentary by Jayasvāmin / edited the commentary for the first time and embellished the text with an introduction, text-critical notes and translations into English and Hindi by Gaya Charan Tripathi.

pages cm (Prakashika series; no. 25)

In Sanskrit; translation, commentary and introductory matter in English and Hindi.

Added t.p. title: Śrī Suparṇādhyāyaḥ.

Includes index.

ISBN: 9789380829371

1. Garuḍa (Mythical bird) — Drama. 2. Verse drama. 3. Suparṇādhyāya. — Criticism, interpretation, etc. I. Tripathi, Gaya Charan, translator. II. Jayasvāmi, writer of added commentary. III. National Mission for Manuscripts (India) publisher. IV. Suparṇādhyāyaḥ. Hindi. V. Suparṇādhyāyaḥ. English. VI. Title. VII. Title: Śrī Suparṇādhyāyaḥ.

BL442.S87 2016 DDC 294.513 23

ISBN: 978-93-80829-37-1

First published in India, 2016

© National Mission for Manuscripts, New Delhi.

All rights reserved. No part of this publication may be reproduced or transmitted in any form or by any means, electronic or mechanical, including photocopying, recording or any information storage or retrieval system, without prior written permission of both the copyright owner, indicated above, and the publisher.

Published by:
National Mission for Manuscripts
No. 11 Mansingh Road
New Delhi - 110 001
Phone: (011) 2338 3894; *Fax:* 2307 3340
e-mail: director.namami@nic.in
Website: www.namami.nic.in

Co-published by:
D.K. Printworld (P) Ltd
Regd. Office: Vedaśrī, F-395, Sudarshan Park
(Metro Station: Ramesh Nagar), New Delhi - 110 015
Phones: (011) 2545 3975; 2546 6019;
e-mail: indology@dkprintworld.com
Website: www.dkprintworld.com

Printed by: D.K. Printworld (P) Ltd., New Delhi.

Foreword

We have great pleasure in presenting to the scholars of Indology, especially to the scholars interested in the history of performing arts, a rare Vedic text which is not yet so widely known to the researchers working on the historical tradition of Indian dramatic literature and its paramount importance. This is the first dramatic text of India that has not yet come to light.

The text of *Suparṇādhyāya* or *Suparṇākhyāna* presents the script of a short play in a verified format, interspersed with occasional prose-pieces. The play was used to be enacted most likely during the celebration of Indradhvaja festival in early autumnal months (September–October). The text is composed in later Vedic Sanskrit which forms a sort of intermediate stage between Vedic language and classical Sanskrit. It is thoroughly marked with Vedic accent which follows the system of *Ṛgveda Saṁhitā*. At some places the marks of accents differ from the traditional Vedic usages which may either be due to the further development in Vedic chanting, regional variation or even due to faulty transmission of the textual tradition. The *adhyāyas* of the text are usually arranged according to scenes. As the action develops and the scene changes, a new section is introduced.

The above text of *Suparṇādhyāya* in Roman transcript was presented to the scholars as early as 1875 by Elmar Grube with a precise introduction in Latin as partial fulfilment of his doctorate under Albrecht Weber of Berlin. But no commentary or English translation of the work is available to the scholars till date which mainly accounts for its relative unfamiliarity to the Indian scholars.

Prof. Ulrich Schneider of the University of Greiburg, the *guru* of Prof. G.C. Tripathi instructed him to prepare a good critical edition of *Suparṇādhyāya* with some Sanskrit commentary if available. Prof. Tripathi frantically searched for manuscripts of the text and its commentary. Luckily one single, although damaged, manuscript of its commentary by one Jayasvāmi was found. Prof. Tripathi painstakingly supplemented the lacunae wherever it was incomplete and in the process he managed to present the traditional interpretation of the text as it was available a few centuries ago.

Since the text has not come down to us in a correct form due to faulty manuscript tradition, Prof. Tripathi has also tried to restore the text with the help of higher textual criticism and has given due justification for his amendment. The scholar has presented the text with translation in English and Hindi especially for the readers who are not conversant with Sanskrit.

Prof. Tripathi is a erudite scholar of Indology trained both in India and in Germany by best hands. His researches encompass various disciplines of Sanskrit language which includes Vedic Studies, Literature, Āgamas and Manuscriptology. He has been associated with the IGNCA as the Professor and Head of its Kalakosh Division for many years.

I feel confident that the publication of this text shall definitely open up new vistas of our dramatic tradition.

Veena Joshi
Director
National Mission for Manuscripts

Preface

I AM happy to present hereby to the readers an ancient text with its commentary, annotations and a bi-lingual translation which is not yet so widely known or utilized by the Indian Vedic scholars. The "text" is rather, what we now call, a "script" of a post-Vedic, but pre-classical, folk play which was probably enacted in ancient times during the occasion of Indradhvaja festival (celebrated mostly after the rainy season in or around September, later also in spring, etc.) mainly in honour of Indra, but also of Garuḍa. The plot of the play is woven around the story of the incredible dexterity and strength of Garuḍa and his wondrous deed of bringing *soma,* viz. *amṛta* from Indra's heaven for the sake of Snakes, after subduing Indra's unique guards and ridiculing his divine weapon, an anecdote which is later elaborated and expanded in the Ādiparvan of *Mahābhārata*, most probably on the basis of this very text.

It is certainly the most ancient versified play of India that has come down to us and is much more archaic than any form of Sanskrit *rūpakas*, which we know of, from our texts on dramaturgy. It takes us back to a time when the classical form was still absent, the Indian drama was in its infancy, was still forming itself and taking shape on the basis of various types of folk presentations in honour of gods or for celebrating the seasons. It is this rich communal and regional variety of performances which leads to the development of multiple kinds of *rūpakas* in the classical age.

Anybody who has been witness to a dramatic event, which is being performed by the common folk, knows that here the ongoing dramatic action of the characters is intercepted and complemented by the musical narration given by a chore group between scenes from time to time. Both are integral parts of a dramatic performance. No Rāmalilā performance would be delectable without the recitation of the *caupāīs* from *Rāmacaritamānasa*. These metrical recitations take the story further, bridges over the events which cannot be shown on the stage and stop at the point when the next important scene is going to be enacted. Same is the case with our text which contains both narrative and performative elements in its body and makes up for a perfect dramatic script.

This small, but excessively important Vedic text, which goes under three different names *Suparaṇādhyaya, Suparṇākhyānam* and simply *Sauparṇam,* is relatively less known to Indian scholars and is hardly available in the libraries of Indian universities. There are at least two apparent reasons to account for this situation, besides, of course the main reason of the rarity of its manuscripts: the first is that no full-fledged work on the text was ever attempted in the English language; whatever work has been done, is available only in Latin, German or Swedish and that too stopped around 1920; the second reason is perhaps its quasi "apocryphal" nature because of which it was denied inclusion even in the collection of the Vedic *khilas* (cf. *Die vedischen Apokryphen* of Sheftelowitz). Add to that is the fact that the work has been composed in a younger Vedic language with certain doubtful accents and with obvious additions (or, should we term them as "interpolations"?) in the original. The text has also not come down to us in its pristine form and the long chain of copyists has left the imprint of ignorance and carelessness at several places.

But in spite of these shortcomings the text has been treated with honour by such eminent scholars as Johannes Hertel, Sergei Oldenburg and Alfred Weber. Weber was incidentally the first to realize its importance and who inspired his student Elmar Grube to work on the text along with a short introduction for his doctoral dissertation.

I have been working on *Suparṇādhyāya,* along with my other academic and administrative commitments, leisurely and by fits and starts, for the last many years or so, although in a more concentrated manner for the last three years. It has been a long journey since the mid-1980s when I was foraging for manuscripts of the text, especially its commentaries and finally chanced upon a partially mutilated and defective one at Jammu along with the other two, containing the text and the *padapāṭha*. I humbly bow to the Almighty for granting me physical strength and also long enough a life to complete the work and to see it in print.

I first offer my respectful obeisance on this occasion to my venerable *guru* (late) Prof. Ulrich Schneider of the University of Freiburg (later Muenster) who gave me a new vision to understand the Vedas, taught me the *sūktas* of *Ṛgveda* on the robbing of *soma* and kindled my interest in the legend of Garuḍa through his book *Der Somaraub des Manu*.

Sincere thanks are then due to the authorities of the National Mission for Manuscripts (NMM), especially to Mrs Veena Joshi, IRS, the Member Secretary of the Indira Gandhi National Centre for the Arts, New Delhi, who is presently also looking after the NMM, and its learned and very cooperative publication officer Dr Sanghamitra Basu, due to whom the work is seeing the light of the day in their Prakashika series.

Grateful thanks are next due to Dr Raghav Prasad Chaudhary, ex-Principal of the Jammu Vidyapeeth of the Rashtriya Sanskrit Sansthan, who procured copies of the *Bhāṣya, Padapāṭha* and the text of *Suparṇādhyāya* from the Raghunatha Sanskrit Manuscripts Library for me.

I further give my sincere blessings and thanks to my learned disciple Dr Prakash Pandey, presently Principal of the Jaipur Campus of the Rashtriya Sanskrit Sansthan, who copied out the text of *Suparṇādhyāya* as presented by Grube and also the entire *Bhāṣya* of Jayasvāmin. This has been of immense help to me in preparing the finally edited version of the text.

I am further beholden to my dear wife Suman for bearing the boredom of loneliness patiently to which I subjected her while remaining engaged in finishing this work and for her constant insistence to finish the work as early as possible.

The challenging task of typesetting the Vedic text has been carried out with a masterly precision by Mr Raju Verma of D.V. Printers for which he deserves my thanks. I am also thankful to Shri Laxmi Kant, the Computer Operator of the B.L. Institute of Indology, who has greatly helped me in correcting and laying out pages of the English material.

That the work is appearing in this beautiful, correct and perfect form, is entirely due to the untiring efforts of Shri Susheel K. Mittal of the D.K. Printworld who is a perfectionist. Not only did he make his editors read the work twice, but also himself went through the entire script discovering a few misprints and, in addition, gave valuable suggestions for its improvement.

Finally, I hope that the work should inspire the younger generation of scholars to produce further critical studies on the subject.

I dedicate this work affectionately and with hearty blessings, to my younger siblings : **'Ramā'** [Prof. R.C. Tripathi, MA, PhD (Michigan)], former Professor and HoD of the Department of Psychology, University of Allahabad and later Director, G.B. Pant Institute of Social Sciences, Allahabad as well as **'Munni'** [Dr Aparna Shukla, MA, PhD (BHU)], former Associate Professor of Psychology, Basant (Annie Besant) College, Varanasi, both of whom have continuously been pillars of strength for me, and from whom I have constantly received a lot of love, respect and support. How true really are the sentiments of Śrī Rāma for his younger brother Lakṣmaṇa expressed in Yuddhakāṇḍa (101.14) of the *Vālmīki Rāmāyaṇa*, taking cue from where, I may add:

देशे देशे तु मित्राणि देशे देशे तु बान्धवाः ।
तं तु देशं न पश्यामि यत्र सन्ति सहोदराः ।।

— **G.C. Tripathi**

विषय-सूची

Pl. 1: Performance of Indradhvaja as a part of the dance drama based on Bharata's *Nāṭyaśāstra* (*Adhyāya* 1) at Indira Gandhi National Centre for the Arts in 2009 by Prof. R. Sathyanarayana of Mysore and his family members. Performers coming to deliver the *dhvaja* to the organiser of the Event (Prof. G.C. Tripathi, HoD, *Kalākoṣa*).
In the pictures are seen: Shri Nanda Kumar (son of Prof. Sathyanarayana), his mother, wife Ms. Radha and the son Sumukha

Pl. 2: Prof. R. Sathyanarayana, his family members and Prof. G.C. Tripathi

Pl. 3: Prof. G.C. Tripathi offering flowers to the Indradhvaja

Pl. 4: Inhabitants of a village trying to erect a debarked birch tree which shall later function as a May Pole of the village when decorated properly. (Source: Ottmar Schuberth, "Maibäume: Tradition und Brauchtum")

Pl. 5: A modern May Pole in the city of Munich in Germany (2011)

Pl. 6: A stone statue of Adler (Garuḍa), the state emblem of Germany, erected in a war memorial at Goerlitz, Germany

Pl. 7: A wooden statue of Garuḍa from Bali, Indonesia, showing him in his *ugra* form attacking the enemies.
(Photo courtesy: Indonesian Embassy, Delhi)

Pl. 8: *Parāṅ gacchad garuḍo vainateyaḥ*. The Garuḍa flying away. The Golden Eagle of America, the like of which has given rise to the imagination of our extinct Garuḍa (*sauvarṇavarṇam*)

Pl. 9. Arrangement of bricks in the form of Śyena/Garuḍa in the Vedic altar as the carrier of sacrifice to gods.

Pl. 10: The classical sculptural depiction of Garuḍa in the Viṣṇu Temples

Pl. 11: A bronze statue of Vaiṣṇavite Garuḍa
at Salarjang Museum, Hyderabad.
(Photo courtesy: Samiksha Bajpai)

Introduction

What Is Suparṇādhyāya ?

THE text that you have in your hand, dear reader, is a metrical dramatic work composed in the late-Vedic period, the oldest in India of this genre, possibly even in the entire world. The plot of the work is woven round the Vedic myth of fetching the drink of immortality, the Soma, by Garuḍa from Indra's heaven for the sake of snakes in order to liberate his enslaved mother, Vinatā/Suparṇī, from the bondage into which she has inadvertently fallen due to losing a bet to her co-wife Kadrū. Both of these, along with eleven others, are wives of Prajāpati/Kaśyapa who is also a *ṛṣi*. Kadrū is the mother of snakes and Vinatā of the birds. Vinatā lays three eggs, out of first emerges *vidyut* (lightning), from the second Aruṇa, the legless charioteer of the sun-god and from the third finally the mighty Garuḍa with the inherent energy of the *tapas* (austerities) of the Bālakhilyas. When he observes his mother serving Kadrū as a slave-girl performing the function of an *ancilla*, he asks his mother the reason and upon being told it, wants to know the means of redemption. Snakes put the condition of fetching Soma for release of Vinatā. Thereupon, after strengthening himself with proper food, Garuḍa flies to heaven, receives the blessings of Bṛhaspati underway and reaches the spot where Indra has hidden his Soma under unusual heavy surveillance and protection. He kills the guards, conquers the gods, defies Indra's thunderbolt and successfully robs the Soma.

However at the end Indra and Garuḍa reconcile with each other. After showing the vessel of Soma to the snakes and thus fulfilling the condition of "bringing" the Soma from heaven, Garuḍa returns it to Indra. Both become friends. Garuḍa lauds Indra and recognizes his authority as the overlord of the world.

The story is, in fact, an elaborately worked out and extended version, enriched with new motifs, of certain vague references found in the *Ṛgveda*, the Saṁhitās of the Black Yajus school and in the *Śatapatha Brāhmaṇa*. In these texts, the myth still has a symbolic character. Various Vedic metres are "sent" to bring Soma from heaven, but they fail and lose their syllables. Gāyatrī is then finally dispatched who assumes the form of a falcon and brings down the Soma (cf. *Maitrāyaṇī Saṁ*. IV.1.1) which is again symbolic of the fact that the majority of the *mantras* during the time when Soma is pressed out and made ready for being offered are in the Gāyatrī metre (cf. the *sūktas* 1-65 of the Maṇḍala IX of the *Ṛgveda*). In the *Vājasaneyī Saṁhitā* XII.4, however, the sacrificial fire itself is addressed as Suparṇa and is identified with the metres and the *sāmans*. Our Garuḍa is later also described in the text as a physical embodiment of the totality of the metres (*chandāṁsi*), the sacrificial formulae (*yajūṁṣi*) and melodies (*sāmāni*).[1] We shall come back to this point again in the following pages (cf. p. 21).

The Earth (Kadrū) revolts against Heaven for the callous treatment of its beings. The humans, represented by priests, are capable of depriving gods of their Soma, gods relent and concede to the wishes of humans, but ask humans in return to restore their Soma. With this act both earthly and divine

---

1 For further details, vide Jarl Charpentier, 1920, *Die Suparṇasage*, Uppsala-Leipzig, sect. III, pp. 155ff.

Beings come to peace. Garuḍa is a link between heaven and earth; he is born of a divine mother (Vinatā, the sky) but an earthly father (Tārkṣa, Kaśyapa).

The Indradhvaja Festival

The occasion for enacting this play was most probably the festival of Indradhvaja which was celebrated in India with great enthusiasm and fanfare towards the concluding days of the rainy season, in the lunar month of Bhādrapada (from the twelfth day of the bright fortnight, now the Vāmana Dvādasī/Oṇam, onwards) for about a week and during which several events of cultural importance used to take place in honour of Indra, the king of heaven and the lord of rains, who is also responsible for bestowing bounties on earth, not solely in the form of rains. Our text also ends with Garuḍa — who has actually proved himself to be superior in might than all the gods taken together and has even defied the thunderbolt of Indra — becoming a close friend and ally of Indra and uttering a *laudatio* in Indra's praise, thus recognizing his ultimate supremacy.

Indradhvaja is perhaps the oldest festival not only of India, but of the whole Indo-European stock of people. In the form of Maypole, it is still celebrated in many parts of Europe, especially in the south of Germany, southern part of France and also in England of which I myself have been a witness many a time during my stay in these countries. The timings have changed according to the local cycle of seasons and the nature also a little bit; but a decorated "pole" is still an indispensable part of it. It is now celebrated on 1 May and has the purpose of welcoming the first month of summer which is known as the month of "all round bliss" (*Wonnemonat* in German). The pole is usually decorated with colourful ribbons and at the top is fixed a wreath made of soft twigs of a particular fir tree (*Tannen-baum*) looking similar to our *devadāru*. Music, dances and merrymaking are the usual parts of celebrations during which formerly the most accomplished girl of the village used to be crowned as "Mayqueen". It goes without saying that the festival is pre-Christian in nature (much like Christmas which was originally a festival celebrating the start of the northern course of the Sun, similar to our Makara Saṁkrānti/Bihu/Poṅgaḷ which marks the beginning of spring) although in some places the Church has tried to Christianize it a little bit by placing a wreath at the top, singing corals in honour of Mary and the like, wih a view to get it integrated into the current religious system.

The oldest Indian texts which refer to this festival are the *Kauśika-Gṛhyasūtra* 140 and the *Atharvapariśiṣṭa* 19. It also finds mention in the Ādiparvan of *Mahābhārata* 57.23-24 in which Vasu Uparicara, the king of Chedi (roughly today's Bundelkhanda), is said to have performed it for the first time whereupon Indra promises him that his royal authority would henceforth be inviolable, he will attain wealth and glory and that his subjects would also live happily (*muditāś ca janapadāḥ*), peacefully and without natural calamities. Vālmīki also refers to the banner of Indra many times and in the Yuddhakāṇḍa 90.73, he compares a fallen commander of Rāvaṇa's army lying flat in the battlefield with the pole of Indradhvaja when it is uprooted after the festival and is let lying on ground for a few days.[2]

That the Indramahaḥ or Indrotsava was highly popular in the south India as well, is evident from a detailed poetic description of this festival in sect. V of the Tamil classical work *Cilappatikāram* composed in the fifth century. One may

---

[2] *hataḥ sa nipapātātha dharaṇyāṁ rākṣasātmajaḥ* ।
śakradhvaja ivotkhātaḥ kampayan vasudhātalam ॥
— [N.S. ed. of] *Rām*. Yudha. 90.73

also recall in this context the famous episode of the Govardhana-dhāraṇa by Kṛṣṇa narrated so vividly in the *Śrīmadbhāgavatam* (X.25) in which the people of Gokula have to bear the wrath of Indra because Kṛṣṇa has advised them against celebrating the Indrotsava. Varāhamihira (sixth century) in his *Bṛhat Saṁhitā* (chap. 43) describes the festival in great detail which includes its unique importance, the preliminary preparations, the way of decorating the pole with symbols signifying various divine powers, religious rites involved and the manner in which they are to be carried out. He strongly recommends its regular performance as a mandatory annual rite by a king for his own, as well as for his subjects' safety and welfare. For its integration in the Vaiṣṇavite temple cult of Odisha, its regional variant and for other details one may refer to my paper "Das Indradhvaja-Fest in Orissa: Üeberreste der Indra-verehrung in Ostindien" published in *ZDMG* (1977).[3]

Indra may have lost most of his importance for the present-day Hindus, but the festival of Indradhvaja, celebrated in his honour has survived to this day. It was pompously celebrated till recent times by the Rājā of Mysore,[4] by the people of Nepal and in the Jagannātha Temple of Odisha, because Lord Jagannātha is considered to be the "real" ruler of Odisha. A number of cultural events, including

[3] G.C. Tripathi, 1977, "Das Indradhvaja-Fest in Orissa: Die Üeberreste der Indra verehrung in Ostindien", in *ZDMG*, Supplement III.2, pp. 1002-14, Wiesbaden.

[4] I am thankful to Shri Nandakumara of Mysore for this information who, together with his wife and under the direction of his father, also made an excellent dance presentation of the theme of the "Origin of Indian drama on the occasion of Indradhvaja festival" as described in the *Nāṭyaśāstra* at the Indira Gandhi National Centre of Arts, New Delhi twice in 2009 and 2012, where I previously worked as head of its Kalākośa division.

dance, drama and musical concerts, are to take place everyday near the Pole of Indra, as per the recommendations of Varāhamihira. It is also noteworthy that according to the statement of the author of the *Nāṭyaśāstra* (chap. I) the enactment of the first Indian play took place at the time of Indradhvaja.

With the emergence of important temples for Hindu deities the Indradhvaja festival slowly receded into background, although it never got totally wiped out. Most of the temples, in imitation of the much older Royal custom of the king regularly visiting his subjects annually and living in the *skandhāvāras* (canvas tents) with his retinue, adopted the custom of taking out with great fanfare the main images of their deities to a park in the city every year for a few days for a public view of their deities and for making them accessible even for those who were usually not allowed to enter into the temple. The deities were placed under a permanent or a temporarily built *maṇḍapam*. The whole function came to be known as *yātrā* or *jātrā* [as in Bengali and Oriya]. Already in the *Kathāsaritsāgara* (eleventh century) of Somadeva, an abridged Sanskrit version of the much older *Bṛhatkathā* (first century) we find mention of the *devayātrās* of the temple deities. As on the occasion of Indradhvaja festival, so also during about a weeklong stay of the deity in the open, a number of items of music, dance and drama were presented in front of the common people. The wonderfully erudite play of the poet Murāri (CE 900) had its debut performance at such a *yātrā* of Puruṣottama-Jagannātha in Purī, as the *sūtradhāra* in the *prastāvanā* (prologue) section of the work informs us.[5] Short plays with themes varying from Purāṇic

---

[5] *bho bho lavaṇoda-velā-vanālī-tamāla-taru-kandalasya tribhuvana-mauli-maṇḍana-mahā-nīla-maṇeḥ . . . puruṣottamasya yātrāyām upasthāniyaḥ sabhāsasadaḥ . . .* ।

stories to the contemporary problems are presented these days in the proximity of the deity and these performances themselves have now acquired the nomenclature of *jātrās* in the common parlance of Bengal and Odisha.

Origin of India's Dramatic Tradition

There are only three ancient cultures in the world which have developed the genre of drama, namely the Greek, the Indian and the Chinese. Of these the drama in Chinese literature is comparatively of late origin and can convincingly be shown to have been influenced by the Buddhist dramas of Indian origin (e.g. the *Śāradvatīputra-prakaraṇa* of Aśvaghoṣa). Now remains the question to be answered: which between these two is the birthplace of drama, India or Greece, and more importantly, what is the original source and inspiration of Indian drama?

European Indologist, who mostly came to Sanskrit after having a thorough training in Greek and Latin, very often tended in favour of assigning greater antiquity to drama in Greece and were of the opinion that drama became known in India with the settlement of Greeks in the north-west of this country after the invasion of Alexander. Sanskrit word *yavanikā* (curtain) which can yield the sense of "something belonging to the *yavanas*" was cited by Albrecht Weber as a sure proof for establishing the indebtedness of Indian drama to the Greek one. Although it was pointed out by some that the Greek drama, enacted in an amphitheatre did not have a curtain at all, the argument held good for a long time. The best explanation of this word according to me is to trace its origin to the Vedic root *yu* meaning "to separate" (cf. *divānaktam śarum asmad yuyotam* — *ṚV* VII.71.1); *yāvanam* (separation), *yavanikā* (a device which separates the spectators from the stage), an etymology which deserves serious consideration by the scholars. In any case, the theory of the Greek origin of Indian drama seems now to have been finally rejected, to quote F.B.J. Kuiper (1979) from *Varuṇa and Vidūṣaka*: "The old idea of a Greek origin and that of the Greek-Roman pantomime being the source of the (north) Indian drama have definitely been refuted." Same is the case with the theories seeking its origin in shadow plays or puppet theatre.

Because of a sizeable number of inherent dramatic and emotional elements, postures, facial and hand gestures, etc. the Indian classical dance has a better claim to be considered as the precursor of drama, a theory which gets support by the etymology of the root *nṛt/naṭ* which is the base for a number of words connected with the art of drama (e.g. *nāṭya* (drama), *nāṭaka* (a play), *naṭa* (an actor), etc.) and which seems to be a direct and regularly built Prākṛta descendant of the Sanskrit root *nṛt* (to dance). It is also true that both dance and drama are regarded as inseparable from each other and are treated together in such works of dramaturgy as the *Nāṭyaśāstra* of Bharata. The word *bharata* has even come to denote *an actor* in later times as is clear from the technical term *bharatavākyam* which is a benedictory verse uttered in chorus by the whole team of a drama at the end of a performance.

In spite of this legitimate claim of the dance being a possible or one of the major sources of Indian drama, the role of the ritual of the Vedic sacrifices with a number of mimic and pantomimic elements in its several rites has also to be considered seriously in giving rise to drama and towards determining its nature and structure. Sacrificial activities are closely associated with the Vedic notion of the universe. Sacrifice is not only a ritual reproduction of the cosmic events, but at the same time, has also the power and the purpose of influencing the cosmic events. A number of rites in every sacrificial undertaking are related to the myths connected with the deities whom the offerings are made, or are justified through reference to their character.

F.B.J. Kuiper has done an intensive study[6] on the origin of Sanskrit drama and comes to the conclusion that the origin of Indian drama must be sought in Vedic ritual. According to him, further, the character of *vidūṣaka* in Sanskrit drama is a replacement of the bald and disfigured brāhmaṇa (*jumbaka*) who served as a scapegoat in the rite of *avabhṛta* for making good the shortcomings of the performed sacrifice, or for expunging the sins of the sacrificer (pp. 217-22).

There is no doubt as to the fact that the first dramatic works of Sanskrit were based on the myths related to our deities or legends connected with the heroes of ancient times. Patañjali makes a mention in his *Mahābhāṣya* of the plays *Kaṁsavadha* and *Balibandhana,* both of which appear to have such type of character. If we give credence to the *Nāṭyaśāstra* of Bharata pertaining to the origin of the drama it becomes clear that the first enactment of a drama in India was done at the time of the great folk festival of Indradhvaja, as already mentioned. During this the most colourful event of ancient India lasting for many days the whole community participated with music and dances, and probably also with enactments of some earlier forms of drama presenting the mythological events connected with Indra such as killing of Vṛtra by him, or like the present one which is based on the story of robbing the Soma by Suparṇa-Garutmān from the heaven of Indra.

---

6 F.B.J. Kuiper, 1979, *Varuṇa and Vidūṣaka: On the Origin of Sanskrit Drama,* Amsterdam, Oxford, New York: North-Holland Publishing Co.

I feel that we have here at least one surviving specimen of such a dramatic work out of many which once existed, in the form of our present work, the *Suparṇādhyāya,* alternatively also known as *Suparṇākhyānam* or *Sauparṇam.* It is a late Vedic text of probably the age of the Upaniṣads, fully accented, though about 10 per cent of the 800 words used show a different accent when compared with the same words occurring in the *Ṛgveda*.

In this context let me also mention that the Vedic tradition of classical age produced one more work on the myth of bringing of *soma/amṛta* from heaven by Garuḍa after having a tough fight with gods. The work, called the *Amṛtāharaṇam*, is anonymous, as expected, and belongs to the tradition of *Sāmaveda*. It does not have the character of drama like our *Suparṇādhyāya*, but of a narrative. It is composed in a very melodious prose which is broken into paragraphs, each one describing the progression of the story, event by event.

After each prose segment a part of some relevant verse from the *Sāmaveda Saṁhitā* which is appropriate to the context, is quoted with proper indication of musical notes on each syllable. These notes are according to the *sāmagāna* system of the Kauthumīyas in the north Indian manuscripts and according to the Jaiminīyas in the only available south Indian manuscripts of the work. The prose of the work has the beauty of classical Sanskrit poetry and some of the sections actually read like the prose version of versified compositions.

The anonymous author of the *Amṛtāharaṇam* work was familiar with our *Suparṇādhyāya*. He seems to have been influenced by its structure and content, but, on the contrary, does not particularly use the version of the *Mahābhārata* as its source. The work has been critically edited and published by me (for the first time) on the basis of certain paper and palm-leaf manuscripts in 2005 with an introduction in Hindi.[7]

The Suparṇādhyāya

The text of the *Suparṇādhyāya* was first published in Roman script by Elimar Grube, a pupil of A. Weber, in 1875 with a small introduction in the Latin language. Because of its unique structure, nature and character which are very akin to a *khaṇḍa-kāvya* with a complete and closed episode and which is composed in Vedic metres in an accented language, it drew attention of the scholars immediately. The motif of bringing the drink of immortality from heaven had already been treated in detail by this time in the work of A. Kuhn titled *Die Herabkunft des Feuers und des Göttertranks* ("Descent of the Fire and the Drink of Gods", Berlin 1859, 2nd edn, Gütersloh, 1886) who compared it with the Greek myth of bringing fire from the heaven by Prometheus defying the thunderbolt of Zeus, and tried to prove its Indo-European origin. Swedish scholar K.F. Johansson in his work *Solfa°geln i India* ("Sunbirds in India", Uppsala, 1910) expressed the opinion that Suparṇa and Viṣṇu were originally identical and that they both represented the "Sun-bird" (cf. *atho divyaḥ sa suparṇo garutmān* — *ṚV* I.164.46). *Suparṇādhyāya* was translated into German by J. Hertel in 1909 and published in volume XXIII of the *WZKM* (pp. 273ff., a revised and improved translation appeared as an appendix to his *Indische Märchen*, Jena 1919) together with an analysis of the character of the text, and in 1920 appeared an extensive study of 398 pages on it by a Swedish scholar named J. Charpentier under the title *Die Suparṇasāge* which contains inter alia many suggestions for the amendment of the text. The study was critically reviewed by J.Von. Negelein in *Göttingische gelehrte*

---

[7] Published by Nag Publishers, Delhi, 2005.

Anzeigen, vol. 186 (Berlin, 1924), parts 1-2, pp. 65-72, 87-119 who also did a kind of critical study of the text and suggested a number of "corrections" and "improvements" of the readings. A few amendments were suggested by Caland (*Archiv fuer Religionswissenschaft*, Leipzig-Berlin, vol. 25 [1927], pp. 287-90) and Oldenberg (*Nachr. zu königl. Gesell. zu Göttingen*, Berlin, 1919, pp. 61-94) too and later by W. Rau in *ZDMG*, vol. 117 (1967), pp. 353-62, all of which we have taken note of in the present edition.

The publication of the *Suparṇādhyāya* which is considered as a *khila* ("non-genuine" supplement) to the *Ṛgveda* kindled a lot of interest among the Indologists as to its nature and the purpose of its composition. The first to comment on its nature was H. Oldenberg who contributed a paper on its nature to the 37th vol. (1883) of the *ZDMG*, pp. 54-86, titled "Das altindische Ākhyāna, mit besonderer Rücksicht auf das Suparṇākhyāna". In this paper he termed the *Suparṇādhyāya* as an *ākhyāna.* An *ākhyāna,* according to him, is basically an oral text mixed with prose and verses meant for narration in public in which the prose is improvised every time ad hoc by the narrator whereas the verses are fixed and are handed down traditionally. The metrical portion of the text has come down to us whereas the prose portion connecting the *sūktas*, and sometimes also appearing between the verses, which was invented afresh each time, is naturally not available. J. Hertel, an expert on Indian fables and story literature, did not agree with him. For him, it has the character of a folk drama comparable to the north Indian *swāṅg* performances of today. This view he propagated in his article "Der Suparṇādhyāya, ein Vedisches Mysterium" published in *WZKM*, vol. 23, parts 3-4 (1909). He designates the work as a "mystery play" similar in nature to the medieval pantomimic performances based on events or characters of Christian scriptures, especially the last days of Jesus Christ. He did not mention the purpose or occasion of the performance of this our text.

Hertel seems to have picked up this idea from the work of L. von Schroeder whose classic work *Mysterium und Mimus im Ṛigveda* had appeared only an year earlier (Leipzig, 1908) and which interprets many of the *saṁvāda-sūktas* of the *Ṛgveda* as dialogues of ritual dramas.[8] The theory of Hertel did not find support with J. von Negelein who in his review of Charpentier's work (*Goett. Gel. Anzeigen*, vol. 186, 1924) totally rejected it, so also did Oldenberg in his paper "Zur Geschichte des altindischen Erzählstils" published in 1919 in the *Nachrichten zu koenigl. Gesell. zu Berlin* (pp. 61-94). Charpentier in his *Die Suparṇasāge* discussed the theories of Oldenberg and Hertel in detail and rejected them both. He expressed himself more in favour of considering the text as an *itihāsa* in the ancient Indian sense of the term, "an epic poem" (*ein episches Gedicht*, p. 396). Further, according to his view, the "older and genuine portion" (i.e. the Triṣṭubh verses) of the *Suparṇādhyāya* are co-eval with the Brāhmaṇas or the early Upaniṣads in their origin.

Two more contributions which partly deal with the *Suparṇādhyāya* deserve mention here; the first by Georg von Simson in the *Indologica Taurinensia* (XV-XVI, 1989-90, pp. 353-60) titled "Remarks on the Suparṇa/Garuḍa Myth" who tries to show that the Suparṇa myth is an allegory and "it is closely associated with the general idea of Soma sacrifice and

---

[8] It was in fact Sylvain Lévi who first strongly expressed the opinion that the "dialogue hymns" of the *Ṛgveda* are mutilated pieces or remnants of some "ritual dramas" in his work: *Le théâtre indien,* Paris 1890 (cf. p. 370 "Il est impossible de lire la plupart de ces hymnes sans s'imaginer une sorte de spectacle dramatique . . ."). L. v. Schröder got the idea from him and worked it up extensively taking each *saṁvāda-sūkta* individually and adding anthropological material to it.

the Vedic fire altar, and the source of inspiration . . . for these concepts has been the experience of the new-moon period." Garuḍa-Suparṇa is the "driving force" which pushes the black moon (alias Soma) on the last day of dark fortnight — when it disappears and enters into plants and waters — across the Sun (fire) into the bright fortnight making for it possible to swell and achieve its full form on the *pūrṇimā* day when offers are given to Agni and Soma.

The second work is by Sadashiva A. Dange titled *Myths from the Mahabharata*, vol. I [*Quest for Immortality*] (1997) in which he deals with the "Legend of Garuḍa" (pp. 3-150), occasionally referring to the *Suparṇādhyāya*. He deals with the legend mainly from the sociological point of view and thinks that the Garuḍa and the Nāgas stand here for two groups of human beings who originally belonged to the same clan (i.e. had the same progenitor) but who turned antagonists to each other. One adopted Nāga as their totem and the other Eagle. The Nāgas were many, the Eagles relatively less and being hostile to the serpents, they were supposed to possess the *gāruḍī vidyā* whose promulgator and great master is said to have been one "Kaśyapa" in the *Mahābhārata* and elsewhere.

I think, we can ignore both these contributions since they are quite off the mark, suffer from over-interpretation of the text and are little helpful in understanding the text.

Barring these two, all other works and discussions on the *Suparṇādhyāya* being in German, they never actually became properly known in India and not even the Sanskrit text is available in the Nāgarī script till this date. No wonder, therefore, that its full importance for the history of Indian drama is yet to be assessed. I am happy to present here not only the Sanskrit text of *Suparṇādhyāya* with *padapāṭha* but also a hitherto unknown and unreported *bhāṣya* of

Jayasvāmin on it, along with a logically emended text with critical notes, as well as the English and Hindi translations of this emended version. These are not strictly literal, or word to word translations. In the Hindi translation I have taken some liberty in order to adapt it to Hindi idioms and usages, so that it has become more of a *bhāvānuvāda*. Speakers of the different verses, and sometimes also the situations under which they are spoken, have been identified and inserted at the beginning of each verse or group of verses.

The *Suparṇādhyāya* is mostly a metrical composition containing some 160 verses which are grouped under fifteen *sūktas* and thirty-one *vargas*. Of these the first two *sūktas* seem to be added later. They are composed in Anuṣṭubh metre and have a purely narrative character whereas almost the entire body of the remaining verses is in Triṣṭubh in a dialogue form. Though the *Suparṇādhyāya* is primarily a metrical work, occasionally some short pieces of prose which refer to some event, or a sudden turn in the event, occur among the verses and seem to have been uttered either by a narrator from or behind the stage, or by the *sūtradhāra*, i.e. the stage director, or the leader of the orchestra (*kutapa*) for the sake of joining two events or for cutting short the narration. Some such sentences are: *sā kadrū suparṇīm ajayat, sā 'bravit* (*varga* 5), *tārkṣyaputra tvam brūhi manasêpsitaṁ varam, vainateya* (*varga* 30).

As already stated, the *Suparṇādhyāya* is based on the story of fetching the *soma* (the *amṛta* of the later period) violently from Indra's heaven by Suparṇa-Garutmān (an Eagle) for the sake of the Nāgas (serpents) whom his mother Vinatā (the Sky) has to serve as a slave because she has lost a bet to their mother Kadrū (the Earth). It represents an older version of the story than the one that we meet in the *Mahābhārata* (cf. Āstīkaparvan of the Ādiparva 14-32). The text has been very cleverly and clearly structured. There is a narrator who starts telling the story and introduces his characters, let us say: the dramatis personae. These characters then appear on the stage, take over the narration in the form of dialogues (two at a time, on the lines of the *saṁvāda-sūktas* of the *Ṛgveda* which they presumably deliver accompanied with proper dramatic actions. The story continues to unfold itself slowly in this manner event by event. Any new character appearing in the text on the stage for the first time, first introduces himself to the spectators. For instance, Garuḍa when he appears on the scene, utters the words: "I am Garuḍa, sent by my elder brother Aruṇa" (*ahaṁ suparṇah prahito 'ruṇena* . . . 8.2). Vinatā, while carrying the snakes on her back, says about herself: "I am Vinatā and I am flying through the air over the ocean with snakes on my back, as if I were a slave to them" (7.5). In the beginning of the *sūkta* 11 (*varga* 21) Indra appears on the scene and introduces himself with the words *ahaṁ svid indraḥ* and continues with a question addressed to Bṛhaspati:

> *. . . vainateyaḥ kataraḥ śuśrāva bhuvanāni icchan* ।
> *induṁ parāñcam nihitaṁ vicaksaṇaṁ mamêt tu*
> *somam sahasā hared yat* ॥

> But who is this son of Vinatā about whom I have heard that he wants to rob me of my cleverly protected Soma.

The fifteen *sūktas* of the *Suparṇādhyāya* are not seamless poetic narration of the story in the manner and the style of an epic. On the contrary, they may be considered as fifteen independent acts of a drama with twice as many *scenes* represented by each *varga*. With every new *sūkta*, there is a slight change in the *situation* of the story and with every *varga*, the *scene* changes. The first *varga*, of the *sūkta* 3 shows Kadrū and Suparṇī talking about a white horse standing on the yonder shore of an ocean. In the next *varga* they are already there looking at the horse and Vinatā losing the bet. In the next *varga* Vinatā is shown as carrying serpents on her back to an island and in the next Garuḍa is carrying them towards the sun. In the following the serpents are lying scorched on the ground while the mother Kadrū (or, the Sage Kaśyapa) invokes God Parjanya to shower rains. In the next *varga* Garuḍa is seen wailing upon his fate as a born-slave (*garbhadāsatva*) and shedding tears. *Vargas* 17 and 18 describe Suparṇa as devouring the Niṣādas and the 19th shows him as talking to Bṛhaspati before finally flying to the heaven. Suddenly the scene changes. There is a loud noise in the sky and Indra is shown as asking Bṛhaspati, his *guru*, as to the source and the reason of this tumultuous sound.

Bharata and other dramaturgists have given instructions in their works that a few specific scenes should not be presented on the stage. These include also the scenes of war. The proceedings of war can only be referred to indirectly and their details may only be described through a dialogue between two or more persons. The *Suparṇādhyāya* has thoroughly followed this injunction. The fight between Suparṇa and the protectors of the Soma has been depicted very vividly *through the dialogues* between Indra and Bṛhaspati in the *sūktas* 13 and 14 (*vargas* 22-26). In the same way, the act of consuming the water-monster (or alligator, *grāha*) and elephant by Garuḍa is simply hinted at in *sūkta* 7.6 (*varga* 14.1) as well as in *sūkta* 8.5 (*varga* 15.5) and, further, the act of devouring the Niṣādas (*sūkta* 9.6-11, *varga* 18) does not form part of the action on the stage but simply *described* by the narrator.

After the war, three persons appear on the scene: Garuḍa, Indra and Bṛhaspati. Indra is angry with Garuḍa and expresses his intention to hurl his thunderbolt at him which he actually also does, but which bounces back, upon which he requests

Garuḍa to pay at least some minimum respect to this "ultimate" weapon of the gods. Garuḍa drops a small feather from the front part of his body. Indra further requests Garuḍa not to let the poisonous snakes drink the *soma* (ambrosia), lest they should become immortal and finish the creation. Garuḍa indicates that he has no such intentions.

The next scene shows Garuḍa in the habitat of snakes asking them to personally witness that the *soma* has been brought from the heaven and with that the condition of the liberation of Vinatā and her progeny from bondage has thus been fulfilled. Since the condition as spelt out by the snakes was that of "*bringing* of *soma*" and not that of "letting the snakes *drink* the *soma*", Garuḍa flies away with the *soma* after having shown it to them and the next scene shows him in the heaven returning the *soma* to Indra and striking a bond of fast friendship with him.

The narrator is switched in again and again in the work. It is he who joins the disjoint elements in the story with each other with his descriptions and who introduces new scenes. What has taken place between two scenes which has not been shown on the stage, is put in the form of narration in the mouth of the narrator. I feel that there was perhaps a group of persons as narrators sitting with musical instruments either on some part of the stage (much like the standing chorus boys of the Greek plays) or that they were reciting verses and giving musical effects to the scenes from behind the stage (i.e. from *nepathya*). Music must have been there, because in many cases the characters refer to sounds. Indra, for example, asks Bṛhaspati in *sūkta* 11 (*varga* 22), *śl*. 4

kinnu ghoṣaḥ śrūyate yatra somo
bṛhaspate hanta vedāvagatvā ।
jyā ha śiṅkte yadâvasṛṣṭā
rorūyate vadhiraḥ somapālaḥ ॥

> What kind of sound is this which is taking place at the spot where *soma* is kept? Bṛhaspati, go and find it out. I also hear the tinkling sound of the bowstring of my *soma*-protector while he is shooting arrows and also his intensive cries.

Except portions of the story which a narrator is supposed to utter from time to time, the whole of the *Suparṇādhyāya* is composed as a dialogue between two characters at a time and hence the verb forms usually appear in the 1st or 2nd person of conjugation, whereas only the narrative portion makes use of the 3rd person. Had the *Suparṇādhyāya* been simply an *ākhyāna*, to be narrated (by a *sūta*) to a gathering of public, it must have been composed in an indirect speech in the 3rd person on the lines of *Mahābhārata* or the Purāṇas, and not as a dialogue. This textual character of the *Suparṇādhyāya* is a very strong indicator of the fact that the text was originally conceived as a play to be presented on a stage before the public as a folk-drama. The metrical character of the text in no way hampers the possibility of its being so since it belongs to a period which is known as *chandas* and in which metrical form was much preferred over the prose. Metrical delivery of a dialogue is much more effective in a play. However, it is possible that the text was supported in between with a couple of prose dialogues which were either improvised ad hoc by the actors, as it often happens in the *nauṭaṅkīs* of these days, or which were left out when the verses were collected, "edited" and enlarged by *four* additional *sūktas* (making fifteen out of the original eleven) to serve some ritual purpose, the exact character of which we do not know. Our Parsi theatre companies have utilized this metrical form extensively in their plays and all the dramas of Shakespeare are composed in metrical blank verses. Same is the case with the majority of the Greek dramas.

Apart from its purpose of folk entertainment, the piece might also have served the purpose of a magical rite meant for subduing the enemies of the king who let it performed or in whose kingdom it was performed, as is attested by one of the concluding stanzas in which "Vainateya" is requested to kill the enemies:

śubhaṁ su sīmañ ca sukhaṁ ca dhehi,
vainateya jahi enaḥ sapatnān । — *varga* 31.2

The commentators Medhātithi, Kullūka and Rāghavānanda on *Manusmṛti* 3.2.32 also make a reference to *Sauparṇam* and recommend its use for conquering the enemies which seems to have been inspired by the scenes of the victory of undaunted Suparṇa singlehandedly over a host of enemies (*sūktas* 11-14). This ritual importance is perhaps also the reason why it has survived till now but at the same time explains also why its original character as a dramatic work of great literary merit has been pushed into background and forgotten.

The *viniyoga* passage in the beginning of the text lists *parvaṇi adhyayanam* and *brāhmaṇābhiśrāvaṇam* as its two main purposes. These have been explained in the commentary as *pāpa-kṣayārtham* or *puṇyārtham* (for destroying sins or for gaining merit) and *śrāddhabhujāṁ śrāvaṇam pitṝṇām tṛptaye* (reciting before the brāhmaṇas when they dine at the time of *śrāddha* ceremony) [for the sake of converting the food into nectar for the ancestors], respectively. The opening verse of the text has, however, a longer list and promises progeny (to childless), cattle, wealth, longevity, good eyesight and heaven to its regular reciters. Sharp eyesight like that of Suparṇa (eagle) is again promised in the last verse of the text, along with heaven, etc. It is also possible that the composite form of the metrical text was believed to serve as an effective charm against the venom upon a serpent bite.

The language and the contents of the *Suparṇādhyāya* leave no doubt as to the fact that it is a work of later Vedic period and definitely pre-dates the *Mahābhārata* which also has the story of Garuḍa bringing *amṛta* from Indra's heaven.[9] But the version of the legend contained in the *Suparṇādhyāya* is decidedly older than the version of *Mahābhārata*. Viṣṇu, whose *vāhana* (mount) later Garuḍa becomes, does not come here into picture at all (even in the Āstīkaparvan it is a later patchwork!) and the Suparṇa-Garutmān in our text is said to be a physical embodiment of the totality of the metres of the *Ṛgveda*, as well as the *yajus* (sacrificial formulae) and *sāmans* (melodies), as already mentioned above.

eṣa chandāṁsi sahitāni śakra, yajurmayaḥ sāmatanuḥ suparṇah । — *Sūkta* 14.3 (*varga* 27)

This idea is a further development of some references found in the traditions of both *Black* and *White Yajurveda*. Whereas in the *Maitrāyaṇī Saṁhitā* 4.1.1, *Kāṭhaka Saṁhitā* 44.3, *Taittirīya Saṁhitā* 3.5.7.1 and *Taittirīya Brāhmaṇa* 1.11.3.10, it is the metre Gāyatrī which assumes the form of a falcon (*śyena*) to bring *soma* from the heaven cf.,

tṛtīyasyām vai divi somam āsīt ।
taṁ gāyatrī śyeno bhūtvā āharat ।
tasya parṇam acchidyat । — *MS* 4.1.1

gāyatrī vai somam āharat śyeno bhūtvā — *KS*

---

[9] For the notion of Suparṇa-Garutmān as a combined form of Vedic metres and its further development as an avian-semi-divine mount of Viṣṇu, identified with Sacrifice, and Suparṇa's role in bringing ambrosia from heaven, see also my book, *Vaidika Devatā: Udbhava aur Vikāsa,* 2nd edn, Delhi, 2011, pp. 347-50 and 546-52.

taṃ gāyatrī śyeno bhūtvā āharat — *TS*

In the *Vājasaneyī Saṁhitā* 12.4 the sacrificial fire burning in the sacrificial pit *(vedī),* which has a brick fundament laid out in the form of a falcon (*śyena-citi*), is addressed as Suparṇa (being a carrier of oblations to gods), different parts of whose body consist of various *chandas* and *sāmans*:

suparṇo 'si garutmān, trivṛt te śiraḥ, gāyatraṁ cakṣuḥ, bṛhadrathantare pakṣau, stoma ātmā, chandāṁsi parṇāni (v.l. nāmāni), divaṁ gaccha, svaḥ pata, svāhā ।

On the other hand, the development stage of the Suparṇa story in the *Suparṇādhyāya* proves conclusively that it belongs to a period later than that of the *Ṛgveda* since in the hymns *ṚV* IV 26-27 it is a *śyena*, i.e. a falcon, and not a Suparṇa (an eagle) which is sent out by Manu to bring *soma for Indra* robbing the *enemies* of Indra (*anti gods* are hinted at). *Soma* is hidden behind the fortification of one hundred iron walls. The falcon flies over the walls, dives down, picks up a stalk (*aṁśu*) of *soma* in its beak and tries to fly out with trepidation in his heart (*vevijānaḥ*) but is detected in the meanwhile by the guard Kṛśānu who shoots an arrow at it which severs a feather from its body. Energized by the drops of *soma* oozing from the stalk of *soma* in his mouth, Garuḍa completes his perilous journey without getting hurt. He brings the *soma* to Manu, the progenitor of human race, who sacrifices with it to gods, especially to Indra to enhance his divine powers.

ṛjīpī śyeno dadamāno aṁśuṁ
parāvataḥ śakuno mandraṁ madam ।
somaṁ bharad dādṛhāṇo devāvān
divo amuṣmād uttarād ādāya ॥ — *ṚV* IV.26.6

Our *Suparṇādhyāya* concludes with a laudation of Suparṇa, along with that of Indra, although he is not the victor. Suparṇa also pays his respect to him and recognizes him as the overload of the earth and the heaven:

> *. . . bhūto 'si bhavyaś ca bhavaṁśca śakra* ।
> *tvaṁ goptā 'si śaraṇam tvaṁ samudras*
> *tavedaṁ vīśvaṁ bhuvanam saṁ suśādhi* ॥ — *varga* 30.2

This points towards the antiquity of the work placing it in a period when Indra was still a very important god and his importance was not yet eclipsed by Viṣṇu or Śiva. This also seems to support our assumption that the text was originally meant to be played or enacted annually during the Indradhvaja festival, since, in spite of the heroic deeds of Suparṇa, after all, it was Indra who was to be glorified during this festival.

The Character of the Text

As already mentioned, the credit of bringing the *Suparṇādhyāya* to light and saving it from oblivion goes to Elimar Grube (b. 1852) who prepared an edition of the text within two years (1873-74) for the Doctorate degree of the University of Berlin under his teacher Albrecht Weber. In Germany the candidate has to submit a certain number of copies in print of his thesis to the university after the viva voce is over (unless it is published within a year as a book). The universities use these additional copies for circulation to other universities in the country and elsewhere in Europe. Grube got the work printed personally for submission.[10] It is a relatively small work consisting of 87 pages in fine print, comprising an Introduction in Latin (35 pages), the text (31 pages) with sporadic text-critical remarks in Latin as footnotes and index verborum (21 pages).

---

10 "*Suparṇādhyāyaḥ*: Superni fabula". Dissertatio inauguralis ad summos in philosophia honores in alma litterarum universitate Friderica Guilelma, Berolini 1875.

Grube used altogether six manuscripts for restoring the text which he designates as ABCDE and F. Of these the first four (A-D) contain the text and the last two (E-F) the *padapāṭha*. I reproduce very briefly their details:

A. Paper, 15 folia, accents marked with red ink, writing good but not without mistakes, many corrections made later with red colour, vs (Vikrama Saṁvat) 1691.

B. Paper, 12 folia, accents marked, fairly well written, vs 1590.

C. Paper, 13 folia, accents marked with red ink, damaged at many places, but most diligently written (*diligentissime conscriptus* — Grube), vs 1755.

D. Paper, 19 folia, with accents, very well preserved, but not without mistakes, vs 1718.

E. Paper, 16 folia, *padapāṭha*, accurately written, vs 1691.

F. Paper, 23 folia, *padapāṭha*, accents marked with red, damaged at many places, vs 1692.

Among the manuscripts containing the text, the readings of A and C mostly tally with each other. B and D have not much in common; they seem to belong to two separate groups. Of these two, B has fewer scribal mistakes but D abounds in them. Neither the provenance nor the script of any of these copies is mentioned by Grube, but it is presumed that all of them are in the Nāgarī characters.

Grube has reproduced the basic text of the *Suparṇādhyāya* with great care and in marking the accents he has adhered to the same system as found in the Indian manuscripts. He marks the *anudātta* and the *svarita* with a horizontal and a vertical stroke respectively and leaves the *udātta* unmarked. At a few places (at least four) the accents marked in his edition are not correct; either they are wrongly placed (e.g. *ādi̱tyā́n* in 26.2 is printed wrongly as *ā́dìtyān;* it is not the initial *a* which carries the acute but the final one) or totally absent (e.g. *maruto* in 22.3 which ought to be *márùto̱*). This latter feature could be a technical defect also, due to the accent in the hand-composed matter being fallen off or broken under pressure while in print.

Grube has divided his text of each *varga* into three sections: *saṁhitā, pada* and *variants.* He does not reproduce the *padapāṭha* of the verses *in toto* but restores the original accents of only those words which have changed their accents in the *saṁhitā* under the influence of the preceding or the following words, or have remained unmarked therein.

The *Suparṇādhyāya* consists of fifteen *sūktas*, distributed over thirty-one *vargas* which contain altogether 161 verses out of which the first five verses of the prologue (*varga* 1) and the last six verses of the epilogue (4-9 of the *varga* 31) are, inter alia, evidently later additions. Further, the *vargas* 2-4 also have a different form and a different linguistic style. They, strictly speaking, do not form part of the play, have a narrative character and are composed in a language which is akin to the archaic classical language of the epics. It is possible that they were added later with a view to provide a sort of introduction to the actual play and were meant to be recited by the narrator, or sung in a chorus, for furnishing a kind of background for the forthcoming events of the play. It is also significant that the opening verse of the text referring to the extent of the text, mentions it as consisting of eleven *sūktas* whereas in the form as we have it today, it consists of fifteen hymns. Further, the 15th verse of the 15th *sūkta* (*varga* 31, verse 2) mentions that the *ṛṣi* has lauded Suparṇa in the foregoing text in the Triṣṭubh metre (*sa me stutas chandasā traiṣṭṭubhena . . .*). If we discard the first and the last *vargas* of the text, we notice that out of these 150 verses, 107 are in Triṣṭubh and the rest forty-three are set in Anuṣṭubh which admits strong possibility of later accretions. Many verses of the *vargas* 16-18 (especially the whole of 18th), for example, which vividly describe the act of devouring the Niṣādas by Garuḍa, are totally irrelevant to the story and appear to be such later additions. The secondary character of *varga* 18 is also evident from the absence of the Ṛgvedic *kampa-svara* on certain words (e.g. *vīryàm* instead of *vīryai̱m* in 18.3) which otherwise appear with *kampa* in the text (cf. 12.5). Since, on an average, a *sūkta* contains ten-eleven verses, the material added later (mainly in Anuṣṭubh) is to the extent of about four *sūktas* subtracting which we get the original figure of eleven *sūktas*. The matter added, however, is not in the form of complete *sūktas*, but mostly in the form of stray verses which are interspersed in the text.

The condition of the text as it has come down to us is far from being satisfactory. Altogether eight manuscripts of the work are known to exist in India and abroad but they all seem to go back to one single source and except for the individual scribal mistakes, all have the same misreadings and show the same disturbance in the text. These misreadings are also attested by the manuscripts of the *padapāṭha*, and the *bhāṣyakāra* also does not seem to have had recourse to any better text, although he had definitely consulted more than one manuscript before setting out on his work, as is evident from his quoting a few variants here and there. However, since he takes every word of the text as *śruti,* hence sacrosanct and genuine, very often his helplessness in explaining wrong readings becomes evident. I have tried to give a slightly reconstructed version of the text separately with extensive notes giving my reasons for choosing or altering a particular reading or changing the place or the order of a verse. However, I am far from believing that my version is the ultimate version of the text, or that it is a "critical" edition of the text which is supposed to be nearest to the original one. In fact, it is questionable whether we shall ever be able to restore the text to its original and pristine form with the help of those few manuscripts which are now left at our disposal and all of which seem to go back to one single corrupt source.

The *Suparṇādhyāya* is composed in a kind of later Vedic Sanskrit which is akin to the language of the Brāhmaṇas and the Upaniṣads. As already pointed out, it is anterior to the *Mahābhārata*. Among the 800 or so words that it uses, there are many expressions, verbs and verb forms which are Vedic. However around 10 per cent words, as already mentioned, carry different accents as compared to their counterparts in the Vedic Saṁhitās and many of the accents are totally contrary to the rules of grammar, for example, an acute (*udātta*) on a vocative within a sentence or the accentuation of the verbal syllable in a past-perfect participle. *Ánanta* (31.5), *áyuta* (23.1, 26.4) and *dákṣiṇā* (26.2) in our text are accented on the first syllable, in the *Ṛgveda*, however, the first word on the last syllable (I.113.3), the second on the second syllable (IV.26.7) and the third on the last syllable (II.27.11). *Anénas* (11.4) and *apátyam* (16.2, 24.2, 30.3, etc.) carry the *udātta* in our text on the second syllable; in the *Ṛgveda*, however, the former on the last syllable (VI.66.7) and the latter on the first syllable (I.174.6), and so on. Whether this variation of accent is due to phonetic changes of the later age, a dialectical difference, ignorance of the author or due to continued scribal errors, it is difficult to say. All the variations in the accents of the text are borne out and supported by the *padapāṭha* which shows that this corruption of accent has a long and steady tradition. Not much positive can be said about the scholar who prepared the *padapāṭha*. Many a time the splitting up of a particular compound or a conjunct word appears questionable from the point of view of the accent. The *bhāṣyakāra* Jaya also does not seem to have taken any special note of the word- or the sentence-accent with the result that he sometimes goes astray in his explanations, for example, in the verse XIV.10 (*varga* 28.4) he does not take note of the acute accent in the word *té* (they) and understands it as meaning *tava* (your), as if it were the unaccented enclitic pronoun *te*. All the *mantras* and their *vigraha* appear in the *bhāṣya* without accent.

The language of the *Suparṇādhyāya* is generally simple and lucid except for the fact that it is corrupt at many places, mostly due to a faulty text tradition. It appears to be later than that of the older Upaniṣads but still abounds in the expressions occurring in the Saṁhitās; *sadhastham, śarman, voḷhā, āśaṁsaḥ, samparāyas, tarasā, rajaso-vimānaḥ, viṣahyam, bhakṣaḥ, saṃvatsaraḥ* (*vatsalaḥ*), *mumuhuḥ, atūrtam, bilintha, abhimātisāham, abhiyat-pratīkam, samat, varīyam-vāram, aṁhomucam, sambādhaḥ, jihīriṣuḥ, praśiṣam, andhaḥ, jāgṛviḥ, asthirāḥ, bahulam, īḍyaḥ* and *asahya-sāham* are some of such nouns and adjectives, besides verbs, participles and verb-forms like *mṛḷa, prajighāti, ārchat, vīyate, rorūyate, śiṅkte, pravṛṅgdhi, pathāmi* (also *patheyam*), *dhrajiṣyan* (?), *dhinoti, prorṇuvīmi-ūrṇavema, āhartave, abhikranda-stanaya* and so on.

The general tenor of the language has a pronounced Vedic character and while going through it one gets the feeling that one is reading a Vedic text. Some *sandhi* rules, which are valid only in the Vedic language, have also been followed (like the insertion of a *t* between the final *n* of a word and the initial *s* of the following word (e.g. *dvīpān-t-samudrasya* in 4.5, *udayodadhīn-t-samāḥ* in 5.3 and *garutman-t-sa* in 6.2, etc.). Many of the *pādas* of Triṣṭubh have apparently only ten syllables and one needs to break the artificial [*yaṇ*-]

sandhi in order to achieve the metrical length. On the other hand, *pādas* exceeding the prescribed length, i.e. with twelve or thirteen syllables, are also not uncommon. The *padapāṭha* of the *Suparṇādhyāya* treats the work as a pure Vedic text and splits it according to the very same rules which are commonly applied to the text of the *Ṛgveda*, including the feature of *kampa*. In fact, the manuscript bearing the *sigillum* E of Grube ends with a post-colophon *ity ṛgvedīyānāṁ suparṇādhyāyaḥ samāptaḥ*.

The manuscript of the *padapāṭha* which I have used is deposited in the Ranbir Sanskrit Manuscripts Library of Jammu and bears the Catalogue No. 5077. It consists of seventeen folia. Previous owner's name as given on the cover page is "Anantadeva". The condition of the manuscripts is good, writing excellent and it is devoid of any grave mistakes. The manuscript was prepared in the Vikrama Era 1738 or CE 1681. After its initial preparation, some corrections are made by the second hand (*secundā manū*, L.) and also a few variants noted. The person noting these variants seems to have been a scholar who was conversant with the *bhāṣya* as well, since in all those cases where the *bhāṣyakāra* entertains a different reading, he makes a note of it and writes it down on the lower or the upper margin. The colophon originally contained the name of the owner of the manuscript which was obliterated later so that what is left now, reads:

> *ṛgvedīyanāṁ suparṇādhyāyaḥ samāptaḥ* । *svasti saṁvat 1738 varṣe mārgaśīrṣa-kṣayamāse kṛṣṇapakṣe caturthyām ravau rātryantayāme . . . suta . . . svātma-paṭhanārthaṁ pareṣām ca* । *sūbhaṁ bhavatu . . . paṭṭhanārtham* । *śivo jayatu* ॥ . . . . ।

Only one *bhāṣya* of the present text is known to exist till date which is available in one single paper manuscript, also deposited in the Ranbir Sanskrit Library of Jammu and bears the accession No. 5075. The name of the owner of the manuscript as it appears on the cover page is "Bālakrishna" (*di/bālakṛṣṇsya pustakam suparṇādhyāyasya*). The closeness of its accession number with that of the manuscript of the *padapāṭha* (5077) indicates that it was procured perhaps at the same time and probably from the same source. The scribe of the manuscript mentions on the cover page that it consists of seventy-four folia and the extent of the written matter is that of 2,000 *ślokas* (a unit of thirty-two syllables) which is approximately correct since each page contains eleven lines of thirty-eight to forty syllables each.

At present, however, the manuscript is in very bad shape. The thin paper on which it is written is very brittle and is falling apart. At several places it is heavily worm-eaten, so that only left-half or the right-half of some folia is available; of a few, only one-third. These bits are kept haphazardly, sometimes also joined with other pages so that the text at places is totally incoherent. There is a big gap in the middle. Major part of the commentary starting from the 7th verse of the 11th *sūkta* (*kiṁ nu ghoṣaḥ śrūyate . . .*) up to the 6th verse of the 13th *sūkta* (ending in *mahad vaiśasam akarot suparṇaḥ*) which originally stood on folio nos. 44-61 is missing and only broken sentences here and there on torn folios, or pieces thereof, are available. I have mostly tried to fill up the lacunae with my own short explanatory notes for this portion. There is no colophon. It simply ends with the sentence: *iti suparṇādhyāya-bhāṣyam samāptam* । *srīr astu* ॥. It is, therefore, not possible to determine its exact date but on the basis of the writing and the condition of the manuscript, it seems to belong to the seventeenth century.

The *bhāṣya* of the text is ascribed to one Jayasvāmin. The *Catalogus Catalogorum* of Bühler corroborates it. This name appears in the 8th verse in the group of the preliminary verses, appended to the text with which the author begins his commentary and which are meant to furnish some information about himself and his preceptors. Jaya seems to have been a *saṁnyāsin* (recluse) living in some [Śaiva?] *maṭha*. He does not mention the proper name of his *guru* (as per tradition which forbids disciples *to utter* the name of ones *guru*) and refers to him only as "Ācārya Bhaṭṭa". This monastery appears to have been headed by an Abbot called "Devendra" whom Jaya refers to as *yatīndra* (great *saṁnyāsin*) and *siddha* (an accomplished one). The latter word refers to a particular branch of the Śaivaite mendicants, but may also mean someone who has attained spiritual perfection. This "Devendra Yatīndra" was the first *guru* of Jaya when he entered into the *saṁnyāsa-āśrama* (*āśramasya ādyaguruḥ*) which means that he was initiated into the order, or received his formal *dīkṣā*, originally from him. Only a vague surmise is possible in case of his actual *guru* "Ācārya Bhaṭṭa". Since the surname *bhaṭṭa* is found normally in Gujarat, Maharashtra and Karnataka area (also in Kashmir, which I exclude as unlikely), I would think that both our *bhāṣyakāra* Jaya as well as his *guru* belonged probably to Gujarat.

Jaya seems to have been a very modest person. He does not boast about his scholarship. On the contrary, he remarks that he is not a good scholar of Grammar, nor of the discipline of Mīmāṁsā, but he is still committing the audacity of writing a *bhāṣya* on Sauparṇa, on the basis of those few grains of scholarship which he has picked up from the treasure of knowledge of his *vidyā-guru* who is as great a scholar [of Veda] as God Brahmā himself. In this endeavour he also hopes to receive the blessings of his spiritual *guru* Yatīndra Devendra.

The last of these introductory verses poses great difficulty as to its reference and to its context. It simply says:

> He who was famous in all the ten directions for long under the name "Dhanadatta" and who salvaged the *pada-mañjarī* from the mango-tree of grammar . . .

The verse seems to refer to the famous sub-commentary *Nyāsa* on the *Kāśikā-vṛtti* by Haradatta belonging to the southern country, but how is he associated with Jaya is not known. It seems that the owner of the manuscript noted it some time on the margin of the first folio for some reason which then was incorporated in the cluster of the *maṅgala*-verses by a later scribe for whom this previous copy served as an examplar.

The original owners of all the three manuscripts of the text, the *padapāṭha* and the *bhāṣya*, were Gujaratis as is evident from the sentences indicating their names and ownership in Gujarati language (and Nāgarī script) on the cover page of each manuscript. The manuscripts were prepared in southern part of Rajasthan which has a good presence of Gujarati Vedic brāhmaṇas of the Kauṣītaki *śakhā* of the *Ṛgveda*, especially in its Banswara district. The script typically belongs to the Rajasthan/Gujarat area and certainly not to the Nāgarī of Maharashtra which has different forms for certain letters (e.g. a, jha, śa).

The text rendered by the scribe is by and large satisfactory, but not absolutely correct. The strokes for vowels (*mātrās*) are often missing, so also certain letters in quite a few words. There is duplication and at times also disappearance of letters due to haplology (e.g. *lavaṇāvaṇatīre* for *lavaṇāvatītīre* in the commentary on the VIII.7, *varga* 16.2).

The language of our *bhāṣyakāra* is lucid and his explanations are direct and simple. In spite of his humble "confession" in the opening verses that he has not properly studied Pāṇini, his knowledge of grammar is perfectly well. He analyses the words correctly, very often under quotation of the relevant *sūtras*; further, he seems to have been well versed in the *Nirukta* as well, since he quotes Yāska also on many occasions. Occasionally he is laid astray, of course, in his explanations assigning fanciful meanings to certain words and expressions but this happens mainly due to the problem that he did not get a totally clean and correct text to write his commentary on. And although he sporadically makes mention of variant readings at a few places in the text, which shows that he had seen more than one manuscript of the *Suparṇādhyāya*, yet he passes over many an obviously wrong reading, accepts them as genuine and is forced to perform linguistic acrobatics explaining them. There was no concept of a "critical edition" during his times and one could not meddle with the readings of a "Vedic" text unless strongly supported by parallel manuscripts.

The plot of this our *kāvyarūpaka Suparṇādhyāya* is ingeniously woven together with the help of the following four elements:

1. Ubiquitously observed fact that an eagle (Garuḍa) is a natural enemy of the snakes and preys upon them. Added to this, symbolic representation of the Sky as the mother of birds and of the Earth as the mother of snakes.
2. The ritualistic belief prevailing since the Ṛgvedic times that the plant of *soma* was originally in the heaven from where it was brought to the earth by a falcon (*śyena*) sent by Manu, the primeval ancestor of human beings (cf. *ṚV* IV.26-27 for details of the incident) who intended to sacrifice with it to gods.[11] In later development, the *plant* becomes *juice*, is the drink of heavenly gods, hence the drink of immortality.

---

[11] For details see Ulrich Schneider, 1971, *Der Somaranb des Manu, Mythus und Ritual*; Freibruger Beitrage zur Indologiē, vol. 4, Wiesbaden.

3. The identification of the [Vedic] *metres* which are recited while extracting the juice of *soma* with Suparṇa-Garutmān in the Brāhmaṇas and in the Saṁhitās of [especially] the *Black Yajurveda*.
4. The fact that the bottom of a sacrificial pit (*vedī,* altar) is laid out with the bricks of different shapes and sizes in order to work out the form of a falcon which is identified with Suparṇa or eagle. This eagle "carries" sacrifice to gods in heaven. Since the sacrifice is identified with Viṣṇu in the Brāhmaṇas (*viṣṇur vai yajñaḥ* is a frequently occurring sentence in the *Śatapatha Brāhmaṇa* and elsewhere; in the Purāṇas he is the *yajña-puruṣa*), this eagle (Garuḍa) becomes the "carrier" or mount of God Viṣṇu in the later (from the *Mahābhārata* onwards) mythology, although in the story of fetching *soma/amṛta* by Garuḍa from heaven in the *Mahābhārata*, this fact still looks like a later addition. In the *Suparṇādhyāya* it is missing anyway.

This plot of the story of the *Suparṇādhyāya* becomes very popular in the later age and in the *Mahābhārata* (Ādiparvan, Adh. 14-32), it develops in the form of a long *upākhyāna* of considerable poetic merit. There are even some verbatim borrowings in the *Mahābhārata* from our text.

The association of an eagle-like bird with *haoma* (Iranian counterpart of *soma*) is also firmly rooted in the Iranian belief and is frequently mentioned in the Avesta and the ancillary literature. According to Zoroastrian belief there are two types of *haoma,* one is the earthly *haoma* of golden colour, which is the king of healing plants (Bundahish 58.10; cf. *oṣadhīnāṁ rājā* used for Soma in the *Ṛgveda*, e.g. *oṣadhayaḥ saṁ vadante somena saha rājñā. . . .* X.97.22) and is prepared for offerings to gods (esp. to Ahura Mazda); the other is the heavenly white *haoma* called *gaokerena* (cf. Sanskrit *gokarṇa=soma*[12]) which is the drink of immortality. The latter grows up in the middle of the sea *vouru-kasha* surrounded by ten thousand healing plants (Fargard 20.4). It is by drinking of *gaokerena* that departed souls on the day of resurrection shall become immortal (Bundahish 42.12, 59.4). Adjacent to the tree of *gaokerena* stands the huge "tree of all seeds" which is the source of all plants growing on earth. On this tree is the nest of *saeno-meregho* (*śyeno mṛgaḥ* of Sanskrit, i.e. the "falcon bird"; *meregho* equivalent of Sanskrit *mṛga,* means "bird" in Iranian; [cf. the mod. Per. word *murgha, murghi* for fowl]; later Per. *si-murgh,* Eng. *simurg* = the mythic eternal bird), which is a giant avian endowed with certain animal features since it suckles its young (cf. *Suparṇādhyāya* 15.14, *varga* 31.1 in which Garuḍa is said to live in a nest set up on a śālmali tree:

> *su ṣū-parvaṇy avasānam mahādrau kṛtvā nīḍaṁ śālmalau taṁ mahāntam* । *garutmantaṁ garuḍam* . . . ॥

This bird *saeno* (Vedic *śyena*) is mighty, powerful and heavy. It almost entirely covers the tree. When it rises aloft, hundreds of twigs shoot up and when it alights hundreds of them break off. It also bites off the seeds of the tree which come down to the earth with rain drops and grow forth as plants.

The idea of large and mighty Avians capable of lifting even big animals has always dominated the imagination of Indians. Though certain species of eagles inhabiting the area around Mediterranean are reported to be so strong that they can carry away not only big hare but also young gazelles and are especially fond of turtles whom they lift and then drop on rocks in order to get their shell broken, the

---

[12] "Gokarṇa: A Borrowed Word from Avesta?" by G.C. Tripathi in *Kalākalpa* (Journal of the Indira Gandhi National Centre for Arts), vol. I.1 (January 2004), pp. 127-31.

description of huge *bheruṇḍa* birds in the *Vāsudevahiṇḍī* and *Kathāsaritsāgara,* etc. is unique in this respect. In the story of "Sindbad, the sailor", which has an Indian origin (*sindhupati*), the sailor lets himself be carried out of an island by such a bird holding on to its feet. It is quite possible that in ancient times bigger varieties of eagles than what are available today in India were seen hovering in the sky which have now become extinct. Even today some of our neighbouring countries in the West (highlands of Iran and Turan) and in the East have bigger and grandeur varieties of eagles. Thailand, for example, is rightly proud of its beautiful "golden eagle" with a span of more than 100 cm for each wing. The white eagle of the United States inhabiting the mountainous regions of its west is also famous for its strength and beauty and finds its well deserved place on many US coins as well as elsewhere.

The motif of enmity between eagles and snakes is also quite common in Indian writings and it extends right up to Indonesia. It has stirred the imagination of many a poet and writer. A very important Sanskrit dramatic work called *Nāgānanda* by Harṣadeva is based on it in which the self-sacrificing Jīmūtavāhana of the Vidyādhara race, a *bodhisattva*, practising the Buddhist values of *karuṇā* and *maitrī*, willingly offers himself as food to Garuḍa in order to save a Nāga boy Śaṅkhacūḍa who is chosen to become the meal of Garuḍa for that day. The distinction between a reptile and a human is lost here and the Nāga Śaṅkhacūḍa is more of a human than a serpent, though still a *bhakṣya* (food) of Garuḍa. The original home of the serpents is said to be the ocean in this drama (cf. *nāgānām ālayaṁ pūrvam* of our text, cf. IV.2). Garuḍa mutilates the body of Jīmūtavāhana while plucking flesh from it, causing ultimately his death, but when he comes to know of the self-sacrifice of the kind-hearted Jīmūtavāhana he is so touched by it that he repents his addiction of having one Nāga each day for his food. He promises to practise non-violence henceforward, flies to heaven and picking up a fight with the guards of the drink of immortality, snatches it from them and rains its drops on the dead body of Jīmūtavāhana, as well as on the skeletons of the previously devoured Nāgas, bringing all of them back to life. The story is also found in the *Kathāsaritsāgara* of Somadeva which testifies its antiquity and proves that it goes back to at least first century, i.e. to the time of Guṇāḍhya. In fact, the Buddhists (especially of the Mahāyāna school) have avidly appropriated this motive in order to propagate their doctrine of *karuṇā.* The *Garbhasūtra* of Mahāyāna (Indic version lost) which was translated into Chinese in *c.* CE 400 under the title *Pu su chu tai jing* contains this story while describing the eight rules whose observation is mandatory for the laity. Five Chinese translations of a *Nāga-and-Garuḍa-Sūtra* done between CE 300 and 700 and probably belonging to the Mahāyānic *Dīrgha-Āgama* (now lost) are available and the Hīnayānic Pāli sources too do not lag behind with the existence of a "Nāga-saṁyutta", and "Supaṇṇa-saṁyutta" belonging to *Saṁyutta Nikāya* as well as two Jātaka stories, the *Pandara-Jātaka* and the *Campeyya-Jātaka* in which this very motif is worked out.[13]

Garuḍa/eagle is also a symbol of royal power and authority in a number of countries, especially in Germany,

[13] Elsa Legittimo, "Der älteste bisher bekannte Vorläufer des buddhistischen Dramas Nāgānanda", paper presented at the XXX German Oriental Conference in Freiburg, September 2007 and Monika Zinn, "Das Drama Nāgānanda und der Ursprung der Jimutavahana-Legende", in *Studien zur Indologie und Iranistic,* vol. 23, 2002, pp. 143-63. See also: Roland Steiner, 1997, *Untersuchungen zu Harṣadevas Nāgānanda und zum indischen Schauspiel,* Swisstal-Odendorf (Indica et Tibetica, 31).

Austria and the United States where it finds an honourable place on their national insignia and on their coins. Germany had a fierce-looking eagle (Adler) with open beak and the head turned towards right on its coins till the introduction of Euro. A number of the states of Germany before its unification had eagle as their state symbol in their royal insignia, or on the "coat of arms". Saxony, for example, had an eagle holding a bunch of arrows in one claw and the royal sceptre in the other. Austria's regal symbol was a double-headed eagle looking towards right and left, and the United States have chosen their magnificent white eagle as their state symbol. Indonesia as well has eagle as the state symbol of their country, their airline is named "Garuḍa" and as soon as one enters their embassy in Delhi, a most wonderful and grand, multicoloured, image of Garuḍa greets him. In Asia the symbol of royal power was mostly a lion, in countries without lion population, an eagle. One is here also reminded of the important part that Eagle plays in the Greek mythology where he serves as a mount to Zeus (Vedic Dyaus), the supreme ruler of Olympus and the overlord of Greek Pantheon. Like Indra, Zeus too wields a thunderbolt as his weapon. The Eagle of Zeus however is occasionally also assigned the task of punishing those who make themselves guilty of offence against gods like that of bringing fire from heaven for human beings by Prometheus.

Present Edition

The present edition of the *Suparṇādhyāya* is divided into four sections. The first and the main section contains the traditionally handed down accented text with its *padapāṭha* and the *bhāṣya* of Jayasvāmin. I have not disturbed the text, nor the accents and also not the order of the verses and the *vargas*. The text is mostly akin to the text as reconstructed by Elimar Grube and closely follows the *padapāṭha* with a few exceptions where the *bhāṣyakāra* has a different reading. In fact, the different manuscripts of the text of *Suparṇādhyāya* do not deliver variant readings, but only scribal mistakes which can be set right by comparing the manuscripts with each other. At places, however, where the traditionally handed down common reading of the text seems to be problematic, or the accent is obviously not in order, I have mentioned and discussed it with my suggestion for emendment in the footnotes which are in Sanskrit. In this section wherever the manuscript of the *bhāṣya* was deficient due to lacunae, or where certain folios were missing, I have tried to fill up the gaps with my own short notes (in Sanskrit) and have given such an indication at the end in brackets.

A short note on the excessive use of *anusvāra*, especially in the *padapāṭha* and in the commentary, which in the purer form of Sanskrit orthography demand the fifth nasal letter of each *varga*, is perhaps called for. The manuscripts of both the *padapāṭha* as well as the *bhāṣya* shun the *vargīya* nasal and have a predilection for the simpler *anusvāra* sign. I have mostly retained the *anusvāra* in order to give the reader an idea of the text as found in the manuscripts. However for the *saṁhitā-pāṭha* I have strictly followed the grammatical rule.

The second section contains a critically evaluated version of the text with emendations. In a few verses it has slightly emended readings which I think were the original ones before they got corrupted due to an inadvertent scribal tradition. Many previous scholars have tried to "correct" the text according to their views, especially Hertel, Negelein, Charpentier and Rau. I have quoted their emendations and critically evaluated them in my notes appended at the end of each *sūkta*. Some are acceptable to me, some are not. I have given my reasons and at several places suggested my own preferences.

I have also the impression that a few verses got dislocated and shunted to wrong places very early due to disarrangement of certain folios in the "mother" manuscript which seems to have been the single archetype existent at a particular point of time and which served as a source for all further exemplars/ copies. I have tried to put such verses at places which I think should or could have been their original ones. This rearranged text printed in smaller characters does not contain accents. It would have been surely possible to put [Ṛgvedic] accents on the emended readings but I have refrained from putting accents on this emended text because it is now no more a text belonging to a genuine *śruti-paramparā*. Further, we do not yet know to which period the *Suparṇādhyāya* belongs and what was the position of accents during the times of its origin. As I have said earlier, in the cases where the *Suparṇādhyāya* exhibits accents different from identical words in the *Ṛgveda*, it is difficult to say whether it was a scribal error or whether the accent on those particular words got changed over the time or the variation is due to their being spoken in a region or in a dialect different from that of the original home of the *Ṛgveda*.

The third and the fourth sections are devoted to the English and Hindi translations of this revised text which is to say that the translations do not follow the text of the first section, but are according to the emended readings and emended positions of the verses. I have also added before each verse the name of the person who is supposed to utter it. In a few cases small additional remarks are also added in order to clarify the situation under which they are uttered. Going through these translations, the dramatic character of the *Suparṇādhyāya* becomes transparent to the reader.

It is an ardent desire of mine that somebody some time may present our *Suparṇādhyāya* on stage. Who knows? *Kālo hyayam niravadhir vipulā ca pṛthivī!*

पदपाठोपेतः सभाष्यः

॥ श्री सुपर्णाध्यायः ॥

अथ

॥ श्री सुपर्णाध्यायः ॥

(वैदिकं काव्यरूपकम्)

पदपाठसंवलितः, श्रीजयस्वामिकृतभाष्योपेतश्च

ॐ नमः श्रीगणेशाय।

यस्य निःश्वसितं वेदा यो वेदेभ्योऽखिलं जगत्।
निर्ममे तमहं वन्दे विद्यातीर्थमहेश्वरम्॥१॥

वागीशाद्याः सुमनसः सर्वार्थानामुपक्रमे।
यं नत्वा कृतकृत्याः स्युस्तं नमामि गजाननम्॥२॥

वेदार्थस्य प्रकाशेन तमो हार्दं निवारयन्।
पुमर्थांश्चतुरो देयाद् विद्यातीर्थमहेश्वरः॥३॥[1]

क्रीडापुष्करिणीकर्तुम् ऋग्भाष्याब्धिं यदीक्षणात्।
धार्ष्ट्यं समवलम्बे तं वन्दे विद्यामहेश्वरम्॥४॥

कृतश्रमाः स्मो न हि पाणिनीये
न जैमिनीये च वयं कदाचित्।
आचार्यभट्टाख्यगुरोः पदाब्ज-
संसृष्टरेणूञ्छमिहैकमेव॥५॥

सामर्थ्यमाश्रित्य सुचापलोत्थ-
धार्ष्ट्येन संचोदितचित्तवेगाः।

---

[1] एतदाद्यं पद्यत्रयं सकलवेदभाष्यकृन्मूर्द्धन्येन श्रीसायणाचार्येण विरचितस्य ऋग्भाष्यस्य मङ्गलश्लोकाः। प्रथमं श्लोकद्वयं तावत्तत्र प्रत्येकमष्टकस्यादौ, तृतीयश्च श्लोकः पर्यन्ते विराजते। मातृकायां त्वेतेषां केवलमाद्यश्चरण उद्धृतः।

औचित्यमात्रे कृतबु[द्धय]श्च
सौपर्णभाष्यं तनितुं प्रवृत्ताः॥६॥

औचित्यसामर्थ्यमिहैकमेव
लब्ध्वा गुरोः पङ्कजभूसमस्य।

आचार्यभट्टाभिधयाप्तकीर्त्तिः(र्त्तेः)
पादारविन्दोत्थरजःप्रसादात्॥७॥

सौपर्णभाष्ये (यं?) प्रयते विधातुं
सुदुष्करे (रं?) मन्दमतिर्जयाख्यः।

औत्सुक्यनुन्नः समुपेतधार्ष्ट्या-
ददृष्टशास्त्रोऽप्युपहासपात्रम्॥८॥

तथापि देवेन्द्रयतीन्द्रसिद्ध-
मदाश्रमस्याद्यगुरोः प्रभावात्।

अमोघसंकल्पवरार्यनेत्र-
कृपावलोकात्तु निजेष्टसिद्धिम्॥९॥

संभावयन्नस्य कृतौ प्रवृत्ते (प्रवर्ते)
किं किं भवेन्नो महतां महिम्ना।

तस्मान् ममैषाऽनधिकारिणोऽपि
भूयादवन्ध्याऽर्थे (०र्थ?) इह प्रवृत्तिः॥१०॥

यश्चिराय धनदत्त(हरदत्त?)संज्ञया
विश्रुतो दशसु दिक्षु दक्षिणः(णे?)

उज्जहार पदमञ्जरीमसौ
शब्दशास्त्रसहकारपादपात्॥११॥[२]

[२] एष अन्तिमः श्लोको नैव भाष्यकृता विरचितस्य मंगलाचरणस्यांशः अपितु काशिकावृत्ते'न्यास' इत्युपरि हरदत्तकृतपदमञ्जर्याख्योपटीकायास्तृतीयो मंगलश्लोको यः कस्माच्चिदन्यस्मात् स्थानादत्र लेखकस्य प्रमादेनापतितः।

॥ अथ प्रथमं सूक्तम् ॥

॥ अथ प्रथमो वर्गः ॥

सौपर्णानि पवित्राणि सूक्तान्येकादशाभ्यसेत्।
वाञ्छन् पुत्रान् पशून् वित्तं स्वर्गमायुरनन्धताम्॥१॥

॥ *पदपाठः* ॥

सौपर्णानि। पवित्राणि। सु० उक्तानि। एकादश। अभ्यसेत्।
वाञ्छन्। पुत्रान्। पशून्। वित्तं। स्वः ऽगं। आयुः। अनन्धताम्।

॥ *भाष्यम्* ॥

"एता ते अग्न उचथानि वेधो जुष्टानी"त्येतस्याः (ऋ. १.७३.१०) परमेकादश खिलानि सौपर्णानि सूक्तानि सन्ति। तेषां वामदेव ऋषिः। सामान्यतः क्वचिद्विशेषं तत्र तत्र वक्ष्यामः। गरुडेन्द्रतार्क्ष्यविनताकद्रूसर्पदेवा यथायथमृक्षुदेवताः। छन्दस्त्रिष्टुप्। एषां च श्राद्धं भुञ्जानानां ब्राह्मणानामभिश्रावणे पित[तृ]य[श]स्कामस्य, पर्वसु चाध्ययने कल्मषक्षयकामस्य, पुत्रपशुवित्तायुश्चक्षुष्मत्तास्वर्गेप्सोश्च काम्यजपे विनियोगः। अर्थज्ञानमन्तरेण समीचीनफलस्य दुर्लभत्वात्तावत्तेषामर्थो यथामति प्रकाश्यते। तेषां सूक्तानां वामदेवदृष्टस्य त्रिवर्गस्य (एकत्रिंशद्वर्गस्य०?) आदिमस्य पञ्चदशर्चस्य सूक्तस्यैषा प्रथमा। तस्याश्चायमर्थः। वामदेव आह। सुपर्णो गरुडो देवता येषां तानि सौपर्णानि एकादश एकादशसंख्याकानि सूक्तान्यभ्यसेत् जपेत्। किं कुर्वन् पुत्रादीन् षट्पदार्थान् वाञ्छन् इच्छन् सन्। अनन्धताम्, अन्धोनाम चक्षुरिन्द्रिये विकलः। न अन्धः अनन्धः, तस्य भावः अनन्धता, ताम्। पवित्राणि पापक्षयकारीणि।

सौवर्णपर्णममितद्युतिमप्रमेयम्
छन्दोमयं विविधयज्ञतनुं वरेण्यम्।
पक्षौ बृहच्च भवतो रथवच्च यस्य
तं वैनतेयमजरं प्र नमामि नित्यम्॥२॥

॥ *पदपाठः* ॥

सौवर्ण०पर्णं। अमित०द्युतिं। अप्र०मेयं। छंदः ऽमयं।
विविधयज्ञऽतनुं। वरेण्यं। पक्षौ। बृहत्। च। भवतः। रथ०वंत्।
च यस्य। तं। वैनतेयं। अजरं। प्र। नमामि। नित्यम्॥

॥ *भाष्यम्* ॥

अथ द्वितीया। ग्रन्थादौ इष्टदेवतां नमस्कुरुते। अहं, तं वैनतेयं नित्यं सर्वदा प्रणमामि (!) नमस्करोमि विनतायाः अपत्यं वैनतेयस्तं। तं कं। यस्य पक्षाविमे सामनी भवतः। इमे के। बृहच्च, बृहत्साम्ना '*त्वामिद्धि हवामहे*' इति। रथवत् रथन्तरं साम। '*अभि त्वा शूर नो नुम*' इति। अजरो जरामरणादिदोषवर्जितः। छंदोमयो वेदचतुष्टयात्मकदेहः। अत एव बृहद्रथन्तरयोः पक्षत्वं। छान्दसं स्वरूपम् अभिवर्ण्य साकारशरीरं वर्णयति। कीदृशं तं वैनतेयं, सौवर्णपर्णं, सुवर्णं हिरण्यं सुवर्णस्येमानि सौवर्णानि। हिरणमयानि तादृशानि पर्णानि पत्राणि पिच्छानि यस्यासौ सौवर्णपर्णः तं। अमितद्युतिं। न मिता द्युतिः कान्तिर्यस्यासौ अमितद्युतिः तं। अप्रमेयं, प्रमातुं ज्ञातुं शक्यः प्रमेयः। न प्रमेयः अप्रमेयः। ज्ञातुं अशक्यः। तं विविधयज्ञतनुं। विविधास्त्रिप्रकाराः पाकसंस्थाहविःसंस्थासोमसंस्थाख्यैर्भेदैर्भिन्नाः। विविधाश्च ते यज्ञाश्च विविध यज्ञाः विविधयज्ञा एव तनवो मूर्तयो यस्यासौ विविधयज्ञतनुः। सर्वयज्ञमयशरीरः। तं। वरेण्यं, वरेण्यो वरणीयः वरीतुमुपासितुमाराधयितुमर्हः वरणीयः। अविद्यापाकरणकामैः॥

ये बालखिल्या मुनयः प्रसिद्धास्
तेषां तपोऽर्द्धेन विवृद्धतेजाः।
जातो गरुत्मान्परमेश्वरांशः
स नोऽनिशं रक्षतु पक्षिराजः॥३॥

॥ *पदपाठः* ॥

ये। बाल०खिल्याः। मुनयः। प्र० सिद्धाः। तेषां। तपःऽअर्द्धेन।
विवृद्ध० तेजाः। जातः। गरुत्मान्। परमेश्वर० अंशः। सः।
नः। अनिशं। रक्षतु। पक्षि० राजः॥

॥ *भाष्यम्* ॥

तेषां ऋषीणां तपसः अर्द्धेन ताक्ष्यशरीरे प्रविष्टेन तपोमयतेजसा विवृद्धतेजाः सन् गरुत्मान् गरुडो जातः। विनतायामण्डरूपेणोत्पन्नः। अत एव परमेश्वरस्य

सर्वकर्तुरंशावतारः। तेषां केषां। ये मुनयः बालखिल्या इति संज्ञया प्रसिद्धाः बभूवुः। स पक्षिराजः नो अस्मान् अनिशं निरंतरं रक्षतु पातु, इत्येवं वामदेव आशास्ते।

यन्मंङ्गलं सुंपर्णस्य विनंताऽकल्पयत्पुरा।
अमृतार्थं प्रंयातस्य तन्मे भवंतु मङ्गलंम्॥४॥

॥ *पदपाठः* ॥

यत्। मङ्गलम्। सु० पर्णस्यं। वि० नंता। अकल्पयत्।
पुरा। अमृत० अर्थं। प्र० यातस्य। तत्। मे। भवंतु। मङ्गलंम्॥

॥ *भाष्यम्* ॥

एषा अनुष्टुप्। मङ्गलं प्रास्थानिकं स्वस्त्ययनं अन्यच्च आचारप्राप्तम्। अकल्पयत्, प्रायुङ्क्त। शेषं निगदव्याख्यातम्।

सुपर्णाऽख्यानमेंकत्रिंशद्वर्गंसूक्तं वामदेंव ऋषिंर्गरुडेंन्द्रताक्ष्यं-विनंता- कद्रूसर्पादेवा देवतास्त्रैष्टुंभं छन्दंः पर्वंण्यध्ययने ब्राह्मणाभिश्रावणे चं विनियोगः॥५॥

॥ *पदपाठः* ॥

सुपर्ण० आख्यानं। एकत्रिंशद्वर्गं० सूक्तं। वाम० देंवः। ऋषिंः। गरुडेंन्द्र० ताक्ष्योंः। विनंताकद्रूसर्पाः। देवाः। देवतांः। त्रैस्तुंभं। छन्दंः। पर्वंणि। अध्ययने। ब्राह्मण० अभि० श्रावणे। च। विनि० योगः॥

॥ *भाष्यम्* ॥

एतया सकलग्रन्थस्य ऋषिदैवच्छन्दो विनियोगान् प्रदर्शयितुमुपक्रमते।

एकेन अधिका त्रिंशत् एकत्रिंशत् तावन्तोः वर्गाः। येषु सूक्तेषु तानि एकत्रिंशद्वर्गाणि। एकत्रिंशद्वर्गाणि सूक्तानि यस्मिन् आख्याने तत् एकत्रिंशद्वर्गसूक्तं। अत्रासमाप्ति सूक्तानां समुदायो विवक्षितः। सर्वाणि सूक्तानि सम्भूय एकत्रिंशद्वर्गाः सन्ति एतादृशं सुपर्णाख्यानम्। अस्याख्यानस्य सामान्यतो वामदेव ऋषिर्द्रष्टा। विशेषतस्तु या ऋक् यस्य वाक्यं स तस्याः ऋषिः। गरुडादयः सप्त यथायथमृक्षु देवताः। तत्तद्व्याख्यानसमये विशदं वक्ष्यामः। अनादेशे त्रिष्टुप् छन्दः। यत्र तु छन्दोऽन्तरं तत्र वक्ष्यते। विनियोगस्तु पर्वणि पुण्यकाले दर्शपूर्णमासं

संक्रमणव्यतीपातादौ पापक्षयार्थे पुण्यार्थे वाऽध्ययने। तथा श्राद्धभुजां श्रावणे च पितॄणां तृप्तये। इति प्रथमो वर्गः॥

॥ अथ द्वितीयो वर्गः ॥

द्यावापृथिव्यौ भवतो भगिन्यौ
ते मूर्तिमत्यौ चरतस्तु लोकान्।
द्यौरासीत्तत्र विनता सुपर्णी
भूमिस्तु नाग्यभवत् कद्रुनामा॥६॥

॥ पदपाठः ॥

द्यावापृथिव्यौ। भवतः। भगिन्यौ। ते इति। मूर्ति०मत्यौ। चरतः। तु। लोकान्। द्यौः। आसीत्। तत्र। विनता। सु०पर्णी। भूमिः। तु। नागी। अभवत्। कद्रु० नामा।

॥ भाष्यम् ॥

द्यौश्च पृथिवी च। द्यावापृथिव्यौ। द्वन्द्वः। द्यौरन्तरिक्षं व्योम। एते उभे क्वचित्कल्पे केनापि शापादिना कारणेन अंगनावतारधारिण्यौ भगिन्यौ स्वसारौ दक्षदुहितरौ भवतो बभूवतुः। ते उभे मूर्तिमत्यौ जङ्गममूर्ती सत्यौ लोकान् ब्रह्माण्डान्तर्गतान् चरतः चेरतुः। तत्र तयोर्द्यावापृथिव्योर्मध्ये या द्यौः सा विनता आसीत्। कीदृशी विनता? सुपर्णी। सुष्ठु पर्णानि पिच्छानि, पक्षाः यस्याः सा सुपर्णी शोभनपिच्छा पक्षिणी आकाशगामिन्यासीत्। या भूमिः सा कद्रुनामा कद्रूनाम्नी नागी सर्पिणी अभवत्। ह्रस्वत्वं छान्दसम्।

ते देवसत्रे अपराध्नुवन्त्यौ
ततो देवैर्जपहोमैः प्रबाधिते।
प्र पद्येतां तार्क्ष्यमृषिं भयार्ते
दृष्ट्वाक्षि कद्र्वा हुतिभिर्विनाशितम्॥७।

॥ पदपाठः ॥

ते इति। देव० सत्रे। अपराध्नुवन्त्यौ। ततः। देवैः। जप० होमैः। प्रबाधिते इति प्र०बाधिते। प्र० पद्येतां। तार्क्ष्यं। ऋषिं। भयार्ते इति भय० आर्ते। दृष्ट्वा। अक्षि। कद्र्वाः। हुति०भिः। वि०नाशितम्।

॥ *भाष्यम्* ॥

अत्रापराध्नुवन्त्यावितीदं क्रियापदं, ते विनताकद्र्वौ देवसत्रे देवानां सत्रे यज्ञे अपराध्नुवन्त्यौ। अपराधं कृतवत्यौ। यद्यप्येकया कद्रवैव अपराद्धं, तथापि द्वयोः साहचर्यातिशयात् द्विवचनमनपराद्धायामिति विनतायाः निरर्थकं व्यवहारमात्रं द्वित्वस्य। कद्रूः कंचिदपराधं कृतवती। हविःफूत्करणलेहनगरलोद्वमनादि। ततस्तस्मादपराधात्प्रकुपितैर्देवैस्ते उभे विनताकद्र्वौ प्रबाधिते प्रपीडिते। कैरुपायैरित्यत आह। जपहोमैरिति। अभिचारार्थे प्रयुक्तैः। तेनाभिचारेण कद्रुनाम्न्याः सर्पिण्याः अक्षिगोलकः स्फुटितः। चक्षुःस्थाने छिद्रं जातं। ते उभे एवं शंकिते। नैतावतैव दण्डेनालं, किन्तु अन्यदपि भूयिष्ठमनिष्टं सुरैः पातयिष्यते। एवं भयातुरे सत्यौ ताक्ष्यं कश्यपऋषिं प्रापद्येताम्। शरणं प्रपन्ने। किं कृत्वा। कद्र्वाः अक्षि लोचनं हुतिभिर्होमैः आभिचारिकैर्हवनैर्विनाशितं स्फुटितं दृष्ट्वा। हवनं हुतिः भावे स्त्रियां क्तिन्। भगवन् महर्षे त्वमावयोः शरणार्थिन्योः पतिर्भव। पाणिग्रहणेनानुगृहाणेति शरणं गते।

पला॑श॒पर्ण॑वृन्त॒स्य स॒मिद॑र्थे गृ॒हान॑नौ।
तर॑न्तौ॒ गोष्प॑दे॒ कौचि॑त् प॒ङ्कम॑ग्नावु॒भावृषी॑॥८॥

॥ *पदपाठः* ॥

पला॑श॒पर्ण॑वृन्त॒स्य। स॒मित्० अर्थे॑। गृ॒ह० आन॑नौ। तर॑न्तौ।
गोः ऽपदे॑। कौ। चि॒त्। प॒ङ्क० म॑ग्नौ। उ॒भौ। ऋ॒षी इति॑।

॥ *भाष्यम्* ॥

अत्रेयमाख्यायिका। बालखिल्यसंज्ञकाः शतश ऋषयो व्यङ्गुलप्रमाणदेहाः बभूवुः। तेषां वृन्दं समिदाहरणार्थं कदाचिद्वने गतं, तैश्च लघीयोदेहत्वात्समित्काष्ठस्थानीयानि वृन्तानि गृहीतानि। द्वौ द्वौ मिलित्वा एकैकस्य पर्णवृन्तस्योद्वहनमतिप्रयासेन चक्रतुः। एवं द्वन्द्वशो द्वन्द्वशो बहूनि वृन्तान्युदूहुः। तत्र कौचिदेकं वनं (वृन्तं) वहन्तौ गोष्पदे वृष्टिजलपूर्णे महानद्यामिव तरन्तौ पिच्छिले पङ्के आकण्ठमग्नौ। पङ्कान्निःसरितुं तावक्षमाविव प्रेक्ष्य शक्रो जहास। शक्रोपहासेन तौ मुनी प्रकुपिताविन्द्रस्य गर्वपरिहारार्थं ताक्ष्र्यापरनामधेयं कश्यपं प्रार्थयामासतुः। तयोः सहायतयान्येऽपि सर्वे सजातीयाश्च तत्र गत्वा कश्यपं प्रार्थयामासुः, अयमर्थोऽत्र वर्ण्यते। बालखिल्यवृन्दमध्यात् कौचित् पालाशीनां समिधां भारस्याहरणार्थं गत्वैकं वृन्तं द्वावपि सम्भूयोद्वहन्तौ गृहाननौ गृहाभिमुखौ बभूवतुः। गृहं प्रति आननं मुखं ययोस्तौ गृहाननौ। तयोर्मध्येमार्गं वारिपूर्णं गोष्पदगर्तं स्थलमासीत्। तन्मध्ये प्रविश्य तत्तेरतुः। तरन्तौ सन्तौ पङ्के मग्नौ। अथैतौ द्वौ मग्नौ। तथेतरेऽपि भूयांसो द्वन्द्वशः पर्णवृन्तान्युद्वहन्तः पङ्के ममज्जुः। तांस्तदवस्थानालोक्य मघोना

तदोपहसितं। तेन ते क्रुद्धाः। तदनन्तरं ताक्ष्यं कश्यपमृषिं प्रति गताः। अयमर्थ उत्तरस्याम्।

पङ्के स॒न्नानृषीन् दृ॒ष्ट्वा बा॒लखिल्या॒ंस्तु गोष्पदे।
इन्द्रेण॒ हसिंते क्रु॒द्धास्तत॒स्ताक्ष्य॒मृषिं गताः॥९॥

॥ *पदपाठः* ॥

पङ्के० स॒न्नान्। ऋषीन्। दृ॒ष्ट्वा। बा॒ल०खिल्यान्। तु। गोःऽपदे।
इन्द्रेण। हसिंते। क्रु॒द्धाः। ततः। ताक्ष्यं। ऋषिं। ग॒ता॒ः॥

॥ *भाष्यम्* ॥

ऋषीन् बालखिल्यान् कर्दमे सन्नान् मग्नान् पीडितान् दृष्ट्वा इन्द्रेण हसिते सति ते क्रुद्धाः कुपिताः। तदनन्तरं ताक्ष्यं कश्यपं प्रति गताः। तं गत्वा किं चक्रुरित्यत आहु(र)परामृचम्।

तपोऽर्द्धं तवं दास्या॒मः सु॒तमुत्पाद॒याण्डंजम्।
इन्द्रस्य॒ वि नयेद्द॒र्पमा॒त्मसंम्भावितस्य॒ यः॥१०॥

॥ *पदपाठः* ॥

तपःऽअर्द्धं। तवं। दा॒स्या॒मः। सु॒तं। उत्पादय। अण्डजं। इन्द्रस्य।
वि। न॒ये॒त्। द॒र्पं। आ॒त्म० सम्भावितस्य। यः॥

॥ *भाष्यम्* ॥

अस्यां बालखिल्या ऋषयः, ताक्ष्यो देवता अनुष्टुप्, छन्दः। हे ताक्ष्य कश्यप। वयं स्वतपसः अर्द्धं तवेति तुभ्यं दास्यामः। तेन अस्मत्तपोऽर्द्धेन त्वं तं अण्डजं विहंगं सुतमुत्पादय। तं कं? यः इन्द्रस्य दर्पं गर्वं विनयेत् अपहरेत् परिहरेत्। कीदृशस्य इन्द्रस्य? आत्मसम्भावितस्य। कश्यपेन आत्मना स्वयमेव सम्भावितः अदित्यामुत्पादितः। तस्य स्वज्येष्ठसुतस्य। इत उत्तरयेन्द्रो (read ताक्ष्यः!) बालखिल्यप्रार्थनामङ्गीकृत्य तथैव कृतवानित्याह वामदेवः।

तपोऽर्द्धं बालंखिल्यान॒ां ताक्ष्यः पी॒त्वा म॒हायंशाः।
विनंतायां दधौ॒ गर्भंमा॒ण्डजांनाम॒नुत्तंमम्॥११॥

॥ *पदपाठः* ॥

तपःऽअर्द्धं। बालं० खिल्यानां। ताक्ष्यः। पी॒त्वा। म॒हा० यंशाः।
वि० नंतायां। द॒धौ॒। गर्भं। आ॒ण्डजांनां। अ॒नुत्तंमम्॥

॥ *भाष्यम्* ॥

ताक्ष्यर्ः कश्यपो बालखिल्यानां तपसोऽर्धं पीत्वा स्वदेहे सङ्क्रमय्य तत्तपःप्रभावेणेन्द्रगर्वपरिहरणक्षमं गर्भं विनतायां पक्षिण्यां स्वयं पक्षिरूपो भूत्वा दधौ। आहितवान् आरोपितवान्। कीदृशं गर्भं? आण्डजानां मध्ये अनुत्तमम्। निर्धारणे षष्ठी। अण्डेषु भवा अण्डजाः पक्षिणः। तेषां इमे आण्डजाः, पक्षिसम्बन्धिनो गर्भाः। तेषां आण्डजानां गर्भाणां मध्ये अनुत्तमः। न विद्यते उत्तमो यस्मादन्यः कश्चित्सोऽनुत्तमः। तं। कीदृक् ताक्ष्यर्ः? महायशाः महाकीर्तिः। सुप्रजास्त्वात्। यस्य पुत्रा आदित्याः सर्वे देवाश्च गरुडश्च। इति द्वितीयो वर्गः।

॥ अथ तृतीयो वर्गः ॥

अत्र वर्गे वामदेव ऋषिः। इतिहासो देवता। चतस्त्रोऽनुष्टुभः। अन्त्या त्रिष्टुप्।

लब्ध्वा बीजवरं पुण्यं शौनकी तु गुरूदरी।
शुद्धंक्षेत्रे च, सम्पूर्णे कालेऽमुक्त त्रिरण्डजम्॥१२॥

॥ *पदपाठः* ॥

लब्ध्वा। बीज०वरं। पुण्यं। शौनकी। तु। गुरु० उदरी। शुद्धं० क्षेत्रे। च। सं० पूर्णे। काले। अमुक्त। त्रिः। अण्डजम्॥

॥ *भाष्यम्* ॥

शुनकदक्षौ पर्यायौ। शुनकस्यापत्यं स्त्री शौनकी दक्षसुता। विनता। सा ताक्ष्यार्त् बीजवरं लब्ध्वा गर्भाधानं प्राप्य गुरूदरी गर्भिणी भूत्वा काले प्रसवकाले सम्पूर्णे सति शुद्धक्षेत्रे कुरुक्षेत्रादिदेशे त्रिरण्डजं अमुक्त, मुच्लृ-मोक्षणे। अमुक्त मुमोच। अमुञ्चदिति वा पाठः। अण्डजं अण्डोद्भवं गर्भम् अमुक्त सुषुवे। कथं? त्रिवारं। अनुक्रमेण त्रीण्यण्डान्यमुञ्चदित्यर्थः।

आतुरा सा तु सुंश्रोणी क्षतं कृत्वाऽग्रजाण्डंजे।
भिद्यमानोर्ध्वनिष्क्रान्ता विद्युन्मेघसखाऽम्बरे॥१३॥

॥ *पदपाठः* ॥

आतुरा। सा। तु। सु० श्रोणी। क्षतं। कृत्वा। अग्रज० अण्डंजे। भिद्यमाना। ऊर्ध्व० निःऽक्रान्ता। वि० द्युत्। मेघ० संखा। अम्बरे॥

॥ *भाष्यम्* ॥

सा सुश्रोणी विनता अग्रजाण्डजे क्षतं नखप्रहारं कृत्वा आतुरा दु:खार्ताऽभूत्। अग्रजाण्डजे प्रथमापत्यगर्भे। अग्रे आदौ जायत इति अग्रजं, अग्रजं च तत् अण्डं च अग्रजाण्डं। अग्रजाण्डे जात उत्पन्नः अग्रजाण्डजः प्रथमापत्यकारणं गर्भः। तस्मिन्। आतुरत्वे हेतुमुत्तरार्द्धेनाह। अण्डमध्ये गर्भरूपेण विद्यमाना अण्डे भिन्ने भिद्यमाना सती विद्युत् तडित् सौदामिनी ऊर्ध्वं निःक्रान्ता। ऊर्ध्वमन्तरिक्षे निःसृता निर्गता सा। कीदृशी विद्युत् ? अम्बरे अन्तरिक्षे मेघसखा मेघस्य घनस्य सखेव सहाय इव दिवि स्थिता। समासस्तु बहुव्रीहिः। मेघः सखा यस्याः सा मेघसखा। टच् प्रत्ययो माभूदित्येतदर्थं बहुव्रीहिः। अपक्वे अण्डे अकाले चापलाद्भिन्ने तत्रत्यगर्भस्य व्यर्थत्वं मत्वाहुः आतुरा। पश्चात्तापदग्धमनस्का विनताभूत् –

ह्रिया सा परमापन्ना चिन्तयन्ती मुहुर्मुहुः।
मध्यमं निर्बिभेदाण्डं जातोऽर्कस्य सखाऽरुणः॥१४॥

॥ *पदपाठः* ॥

ह्रिया। सा। परं। आपन्ना। चिन्तयन्ती। मुहुःऽमुहुः। मध्यमं।
निः। बिभेद। अण्डं। जातः। अर्कस्य। सखा। अरुणः॥

॥ *भाष्यम्* ॥

अकालकृतेनाण्डभेदेन तस्मिन् व्यर्थीकृते स्वकृतापराधाल्लज्जया सा परमं खेदं कुर्वाणा सती मध्यममण्डं निर्बिभेद। व्यदारयत्। पाटयामास। तस्मादण्डादरुणो जातः। स चार्कस्य सखा सहायः सारथिर्बभूव॥

अरुणेन जातमात्रेण शप्ता माता तपोधना।
दुष्कृतं किं महापुण्ये पादहीनोऽस्मि चण्डि हे॥१५॥

॥ *पदपाठः* ॥

अरुणेन। जात० मात्रेण। शप्ता। माता। तपःऽधना। दुःऽकृतं।
किं। महा० पुण्ये। पाद० हीनः। अस्मि। चण्डि। हे॥

॥ *भाष्यम्* ॥

जातमात्रेण अर्द्धदेहेन अरुणेन माता शप्ता। धिक्कृता। निहिता (निन्दिता, गर्हिता ?)। कथं? हे महापुण्ये, पुण्यवति। हे चण्डि, क्रूरे। त्वया इदं किं दुःकृतं। दुष्टं कर्म कृतं। यदिदमण्डमपक्वमकाले चापलात् स्फोटितं। अहं पादहीनोऽस्मि॥

तस्मिन्प्रसूते रविराजगाम
ब्रुवन् वाक्यं देवि देहीति मह्यम्॥
तवं सुतोऽयं मम वाजिवेगान्
धर्तुं शक्तो भवं च मोदमाना॥१६॥

॥ *पदपाठः* ॥

तस्मिंन्। प्र० सूंते। रविंः। आ०जगामं। ब्रुवंन्। वाक्यं। देवि। देहि। इतिं। मह्यं। तवं। सुतः। अयं ममं। वाजिं०वेगान्। धर्तुं। शक्तः। भवं। च। मोदमाना॥

॥ *भाष्यम्* ॥

तस्मिन् अरुणे प्रसूते प्रादुर्भूते सति रविः सूर्यः समीपे आजगाम। किं कुर्वन्? इति वाक्यं ब्रुवन् सन्। इतीति किं? हे देवि। विनते इमं अपादं त्वत्सुतं मह्यं देहि। न ह्ययं पङ्गुत्वान्निरर्थकः। किं तु तवायं सुतः पङ्गुरपि सन् मम वाजिनामश्वानां वेगान् रश्मिग्रहणेन धर्तुं रोद्धुं शक्तो दृश्यते, अत एव मम कार्यकृत्। त्वं च एतेन पुत्रेण मह्यं दत्तेन सती मोदमाना हर्षिता भव। सन्तुष्टा भव॥ इति तृतीयो वर्गः।

॥ अथ द्वितीयं सूक्तम् ॥

॥ अथ चतुर्थो वर्गः ॥

वामदेव ऋषिः। गरुडो देवता। अनुष्टुप् छन्दः। तत्रैषा प्रथमा॥

गरुडस्य जातमात्रस्य त्रयो लोकाः प्रकम्पिताः।
प्रकम्पिता मही सर्वा सशैलवनकानना॥१॥

॥ *पदपाठः* ॥

गरुडस्य। जात० मात्रस्य। त्रयः। लोकाः। प्र०कम्पिताः।
प्र०कम्पिता। मही सर्वा। स० शैलवनकानना॥

॥ *भाष्यम्* ॥

जातमात्रस्य गरुडस्य तेजसा त्रैलोक्यमभिभूतमित्ययमर्थोऽत्र। वनानि फलपुष्पसमृद्धलताद्रुमवंति। काननान्यतिगहनानि उद्वसानि[?] निरर्थवृक्षादिव्याप्तानीति विवेकः।

गगनं नष्टचन्द्रार्कं न ज्योतींषि चकासति।
देवता भयवित्रस्ता नष्टचेष्टश्च मारुतः॥२॥

॥ *पदपाठः* ॥

गगनं। नष्टचन्द्र० अर्कं। न ज्योतींषि। चकासति। देवताः।
भय०वित्रस्ताः। नष्ट०चेष्टः। च। मारुतः॥

॥ *भाष्यम्* ॥

ज्योतींषि नक्षत्रताराग्रहादीनि न चकासति, न भान्ति। नष्टा चेष्टा गतिर्यस्य। न ववावित्यर्थः॥

नार्यो गर्भं न गृह्णन्ति समुद्राः शोषमागताः।
गावः क्षीरविवर्जिता विद्रवन्ति भयातुराः॥३॥

॥ पदपाठः ॥

नार्यः गर्भं। न। गृह्णन्ति। समुद्राः। शोषं। आ। गताः।
गावः। क्षीर० विवर्जिताः। वि०द्रवन्ति। भय० आतुराः॥

॥ भाष्यम् ॥

गावः इतस्ततः विद्रवन्ति स्म। धावन्ति स्म। पलायन्ते स्म।

ब्राह्मणा वेदविभ्रष्टाः सर्वत्रासुरुरोगमाः।
सर्वतो गरुडं ज्ञात्वा तमेव शरणं गताः॥४॥

॥ पदपाठः ॥

ब्राह्मणाः। वेद० विभ्रष्टाः। सर्वत्र। आसुः। उरःऽ गमाः।
सर्वतः। गरुडं। ज्ञात्वा। तं। एव। शरणं। गताः॥

॥ भाष्यम् ॥

वेदात् भ्रष्टाः च्युताः विस्मृतवेदाः सर्वत्रोर्व्यामुरोगमाः आसुः। सर्वत्र भूतले उरोगमाः सर्पाः बभूवुः। सर्वैर्भूतलं व्याप्तमित्यर्थः। गरुडतेजसा आकुलत्वात् ते सर्पाः सर्वतः दशभ्यो विदिग्भ्यः गरुडं आप्तं ततं ज्ञात्वा आशंक्य गरुडात् त्रस्ताः सन्तो गरुडस्य आप्ततां शंकमानाः त्राणार्थमन्यं कमप्यलमभानास्तमेव गरुडं शरणं गताः। हे प्रभो भगवन् अपराजिता वयं त्वामेव शरण्यं शरणं प्राप्ताः स्म। अस्मान् वराकान् दीनान् त्वत्तेजसा दह्यमानान् त्वत्तो भीतांस्त्रायस्व त्रायस्वेति।

ततः सर्वे यथास्थानं तत्क्षणेनोरुगाः[३] गताः।
गरुत्मत्सम्भवे नष्टाः पुनः सृष्टाः स्वयम्भुवा॥५॥

॥ पदपाठः ॥

ततः। सर्वे। यथा० स्थानं। तत्० क्षणेन। उरुगाः। गताः।
गरुत्मत्० सम्भवे। नष्टाः। पुनरिति। सृष्टाः। स्वयं० भुवा॥

॥ भाष्यम् ॥

ये पूर्वे सन्त्रासादेकत्रावस्थातुमशक्नुवन्त इतस्ततो विचेरुस्ते गरुडादभयं प्राप्य सद्यस्कालं उरगाः यथास्थानं स्वे स्वे स्थाने गताः। तथापि गरुत्मतः सम्भवे प्रादुर्भावे जन्मकाले उत्पन्नस्वहृद्गतसन्तापबलादेव नष्टाः मृताः। स्वयम्भुवा पुनः सृष्टाः। न केवलं सर्पा एव। अन्येऽपि चन्द्रार्कसमुद्रादयः पुनः सृष्टाः॥

---

[३] 'उरुगाः' इत्यस्य स्थाने एका पदपाठमातृका 'उर्व्याम्' इति पाठान्तरं स्वीकरोति।

म॒घान॑क्षत्रजाताना॑ं, स॒र्ववे॑॑दश॒रीरि॑णाम्।
स॒हस्त्रं॑वर्षग॒र्भाणां अ॒ग्निस्तं॑म्भः स्म॒ जायंते॥६॥

॥ *पदपाठः* ॥

म॒घान॑क्षत्र०जाताना॑ं। स॒र्ववें॑द०श॒रीरि॑णां। स॒हस्त्रं॑०वर्षग॒र्भाणां। अ॒ग्नि० स्तं॑म्भः। स्म॒। जायंते॥

॥ *भाष्यम्* ॥

एवंविधो दुर्जयो महाप्रतापतेजोमयोऽतिदुःसहो गरुड एवासीत्तत्र किं कारणमित्याशङ्कायामुत्तरत्वेन सूक्तस्यान्त्यामृचमाह। सा षष्ठी। मघानक्षत्रेत्यादि। सहस्त्रवर्षाणि यस्यासौ स सहस्त्रवर्षः। सहस्त्रवर्षो गर्भो गर्भवासः। अण्डमध्ये वासो येषां तैजसशरीरावयवानां ते अवयवाः सहस्त्रवर्षगर्भास्तेषामवयवी अग्निस्तम्भ इव जगद्दाहको जायते स्म। स च गरुडः। किंलक्षणानामवयवानां? सर्ववेदशरीरिणां। सर्वे च ते वेदाश्च सर्ववेदाः। शरीरमेषामस्तीति शरीरिणस्तैजसदेहावयवाः। एषां शरीरं कार्यमस्तीत्यर्थः। अवयवाः कारणं। सर्ववेदैः कारणभूतैः शरीरिणः शरीरारम्भकाः। सर्ववेदशरीरिणः। तेषां सर्ववेदशरीरिणां अवयवविशेषणानि। त्रीण्यपि षष्ठीबहुवचनानि। पुनः किंलक्षणानां शरीरावयवानां? मघानक्षत्रजातानां। यद्यपि अवयवाः मघायां न जातास्तथापि अवयवानामशेषाणां देहो मघायां प्रसूतः। अण्डं निर्भिद्य बहिर्निःसृतः। अवयविनो जन्म तदीयेष्ववयवेषूपचर्यते। अथवा प्रकारान्तरेणार्थः। तदैवं योजना। एकस्यैव गरुडस्य दुर्निरीक्ष्यप्रकाशतया अनन्तैरिव शरीरैर्भासमानत्वाद्बहुत्वनिर्देशः। सहस्त्रवर्षगर्भाणां गरुडानां मयूखराशिरेकत्र मिलितः सन् अग्निमयः स्तम्भ इव जायते स्म। अण्डं गरुडे निःसृते सति। सहस्त्रं वर्षाणि गतानि यस्यासौ सहस्त्रवर्षः। सहस्त्रवर्षं गतो गर्भवासो येषां ते सहस्त्रवर्षगर्भाः तेषां॥ यद्वा सहस्त्रवर्षो गर्भो गर्भावस्था येषां ते सहस्त्रवर्षगर्भाः तेषां। पुनः किंलक्षणानां? खगेश्वराणां। मघायां जातानां अण्डे स्फुटिते बहिःप्रादुर्भूतानां। एकस्यैव गरुडस्य बहुत्वेन व्यवहारोऽत्रानन्तरूपभ्रमजनकत्वात्। किं लक्षणानां गरुत्मतां? सर्ववेदशरीरिणां। शरीरमेषामस्तीति शरीरिणः। सर्ववेदैः शरीरिणः। सर्ववेदशरीरिणः। तेषां वेदशरीरिणां। एवंविधानां वैनतेयानां रश्मिसमूहः। अग्निमयस्तम्भ इव दृश्यते स्म॥ इति चतुर्थो वर्गः।

॥ अथ तृतीयं सूक्तम् ॥

॥ अथ पञ्चमो वर्गः ॥

ओजस्विनं वीरमसह्यसाहं
स्तोष्याम्यहं गरुडं वैनतेयम्।
मातरं यो निरक्रीणात्कद्रवा दास्ये पराजिताम्॥१॥

॥ पदपाठः ॥

ओजस्विनं। वीरं। असह्य० सहं। स्तोष्यामि। अहं। गरुडं। वैनतेयं। मातरं। यः। निःऽअक्रीणात्। कद्रवा। दास्ये। परा० जिताम्॥

॥ भाष्यम् ॥

प्रस्तारपंक्तिः। वामदेव आह। अहं तं गरुडं स्तोष्यामि। परस्मैपदं अन्येषामुपकारार्थत्वात्। किंलक्षणं ओजस्विनं वीरं? ओजः आन्तरं बलं तद्वान् ओजस्वी। एवंविधो वीरः [वि-ईरः] शत्रूणामीरयिता प्रेरयिता अपनोदकः। शारीरबलवान् अत एव असह्यसाहं। न सोढुं शक्या असह्याः योद्धारः, तान् सहते इत्यसह्यसाट्। तं। ईदृक् प्रतापी कस्मात्? यतो वैनतेयः। विनता पतिव्रता व्रतवती महातपाः, ईदृश्याः [पुत्रः] एवंविध एव स्तुतो भवति। तं कं? यः उभाभ्यां सपत्नीभ्यां पराजयनिमित्ते पणे दास्ये दासीत्वेन पणीकृते सति कद्रवा सर्पिण्या पराजितां मातरं निरक्रीणात्। निःक्रयं दत्तवान्। दासत्वात् निःकृतिं चकार मातुः। अमृतकुम्भार्पणेन दासीभावात् मोचितवान्। यः मातरं मोचयितुं सुधाघटं निःक्रीणाति स्म। पणस्य निःक्रयत्वेनार्पितवान्॥

तदस्य कर्म वक्ष्यामि वैनतेयस्य श्रीमतः।
पृथिव्यां प्रथितयशसः सोमाहरणजं महत्॥२॥

॥ पदपाठः ॥

तत्। अस्य। कर्म। वक्ष्यामि। वैनतेयस्य। श्रीमतः। पृथिव्यां। प्रथित० यशसः। सोमाहरण०जं। महत्॥

॥ *भाष्यम्* ॥

निगदव्याख्याता।

अस्यैतादृशस्य वीरस्यौजस्विनोऽसह्य-
साहस्य, असह्यमपि शत्रुं प्रतिकर्तुं
क्षमस्य विनतापत्यस्य प्रशस्यं कर्म,
सोमरक्षकान् विजित्येन्द्रं च
परिभाव्य दिवः सोमानयनरूपमहं
प्रकाशयिष्यामि यस्य विश्वस्मिन्नपि
जगति अनेनान्यजनाशक्येन कर्मणा
कीर्तिः सर्वत्र प्रसृता वर्तते।। सं०

कद्रूश्च वै सुपर्णी चं पस्पृधांते सरूपयोः।
सा कद्रूः सुपर्णीमंजयत्,
साब्रंवीत्॥३॥

॥ *पदपाठः* ॥

कद्रूः। च। वै। सु०पर्णी। च। पस्पृधांते इति। स० रूपयोः।
सा। कद्रूः। सु०पर्णी। अजयत्। सा। अब्रंवीत्॥

॥ *भाष्यम्* ॥

सोमाहरणे प्रसंगमुत्पादयितुमाहोत्तरं। या पूर्वं 'भूमिस्तुनार्य [ग्य] भवत्कद्रुनामे'त्युक्ता सह्या [सा हि] कद्रूः। सुपर्णी पक्षिणी विनता च। सुष्ठु पर्णानि पिच्छानि पक्षौ वा यस्याः सा सुपर्णी। यद्वा सुष्ठु पतनं खमार्गे शीघ्रगमनं यस्याः सा। एते उभे सरूपयोः सदृशयोः समानयोर्भर्तुर्गृहे सर्वकार्यकरणे अधिकारयोर्विषये पस्पृधाते। '*स्पर्द्ध*' संघर्षे। अस्यात्मनेपदिनो लिटि प्रथमद्विवचनान्तं। अहं मुख्या स्यामिति। सापत्न्याद् द्वेषमूलमित्यर्थः। हृद्गतस्याधिकारयोरिति पदस्य सप्तम्यन्तं तस्य विशेषणं सरूपयोरिति। एवं स्पर्द्धामूले अन्तर्वैर उत्पन्ने दास्यरूपपणपूर्वके परस्परविवादेऽङ्गीकृते भिन्नयोर्मतयोर्निष्कर्षतः संशोधनार्थमुपाये कृते सा जिह्मा कद्रूः सर्पिणी सुपर्णीं विनतां कपटकृते[त्ये]नासत्योपायेनाजयत। यथा सुयोधनोऽजातशत्रुम्। तद्विवादोपक्रमे वादप्रसंजनकामया कद्रूवा पूर्वं ना(चा?)न्यप्रकारे अनुपपन्ने वाक्यसंदर्भे प्रागुक्ते सति पश्चात् सा विनतामब्रवीत्[४]। किमब्रवीदित्यत आह।

---

[४] 'सत्यं किलैतद्' इति परर्चा तु विनताया वाक्यं कद्रूं प्रतिं, उपालम्भस्वरूपम्।

सत्यं किलैतदपरे वदन्ति
दूरात्मकं दीर्घजात्याः सदैव।
अप्रज्ञाना कलहे या सुतं मे
काणा घोराणि वचनानि[5] कृन्तति॥४॥

॥ *पदपाठः*॥

सत्यं। किल। एतत्। अपरे। वदन्ति। दूर०आत्मकं। दीर्घ० जात्याः। सदा। एव। अप्रज्ञाना। कलहे। या। सुतं। मे। काणा। घोराणि। वचनानि[5]। कृन्तति॥

॥ *भाष्यम्* ॥

अस्याः पदान्येवं। सत्यं। किल। एतत्। अपरे। वदन्ति। दूरात्मकं। दीर्घ० जात्याः। सदा। एव। अप्रज्ञाना। कलहे। या। सुतं। मे। काणा। घोराणि। वचनानि। कृन्तति॥ पूर्वे आद्याः परे त्वाधुनिकाः। न परे अपरे। आद्याः पुरातनाः इत्यर्थः। दीर्घा मुख्या। आद्या जातिर्ब्राह्मणजातिः। दीर्घजातौ भवाः दीर्घजात्याः। अपरे आद्याः पुरातनाः। दीर्घजात्याः विप्राः। किलेति सर्वशास्त्रप्रसिद्धमेतद् वाक्यं सत्यमेव सदा वदन्ति। किं कृत्वा? ते वेदविदो वदन्ति। दूरात्मकमुद्दिश्येति शेषः। दूरेति विप्रकृष्टे गगने आत्मा शारीरं यस्यासौ दूरात्मक आदित्याश्वः। तमुद्दिश्यैतत्सत्यं वदन्ति। तमुद्दिश्येति कोऽर्थः? तस्य स्वरूपवर्णनार्थमित्यर्थः। एतत्किं? सूर्याश्वः श्वेत इति इदं हृद्गतं। सा तु विपरीतवादिनी कद्रूः कलहे निमित्तभूते सति, कलहे क्लेशे उत्पाद्ये सति अन्यथा वदतीति शेषः। अन्यथा किं? सूर्याश्वः कृष्ण इति कलहमुत्पादयितुमसत्यं वदतीत्यर्थः। सा का? या असत्यमप्रियं गर्हणात्मकं चेत्येवं दोषत्रयवद् घोरं। तादृशानि घोराणि दुःसहानि रौद्राणि वचनान्युक्त्वेति शेषः। मे सुतमरुणं दैव्या शक्त्या अणिमाद्यष्टविधैश्वर्यबलेन रात्रौ रात्रौ रूपान्तरेणास्मद्गृहे[हमे]त्यार्काश्वरूपं कथयन्तं सूर्यसारथिं सत्यज्ञं सत्यवादिनं घोराणि वचनानि श्रावयति[न्ती] कृन्तति। तं मत्पुत्रं छिनत्तीव। व्यथयतीत्यर्थः। सत्यज्ञानां सत्यशीलानां दुष्टैर्मूर्खैः प्रयुक्तमनृतं वचो वज्रप्रहारायत इत्याशयः। 'रवेरश्वोऽसितः। यानि शास्त्राणि सितमाहुस्तान्यलीकानि। आगमात् प्रत्यक्षं प्रमाणं बलीयः। अयं पंगुर्मूर्खोऽरुणः किं वेत्ति, मृषैव वदती'त्येवं विधानि वचनानि। कीदृशी कद्रूः। अप्रज्ञाना। नास्ति प्रकृष्टं सत्यं ज्ञानं यस्याः सा। काणा चैकनेत्रविकला। काणो हि प्रायेण दुःष्टान्तःकरणो भवति।

---

[5] 'वचनानि' इति पदं मूले शुद्धतया तृतीये 'ना' पदे उदात्तं किन्तु पदपाठमातृकायां भ्रान्तिवशाद् एतदाद्योदात्तरूपेण (वचनानि) अंकितम्।

अथाष्टम्या[६] कद्रूः वादे पराजयनिमित्तं पणमाविःकुर्वती तां प्रत्युवाच -

यावत्त्वं द्वाभ्यां विनते सुपर्णि
चक्षुंभ्यां पश्यंस्यरुणस्यं मातः।
तावंच्चेन्नाहमेकेंन पश्ये
तद्दासी तवं स्यां त्वमुं वा ममं स्याः[६]॥५॥

॥ *पदपाठः* ॥

यावंत्। त्वं। द्वाभ्यां। वि० नते। सु० पर्णि। चक्षुंः ऽभ्यां पश्यंसि। अरुणस्यं। मातरितिं। तावंत्। चेत्। न। अहं। एकेंन। पश्ये। तत्। दासीं। तवं। स्यां। त्वं। ॐ इतिं। वा। ममं। स्याः॥

॥ *भाष्यम्* ॥

हे विनते। हे सुपर्णि। हे अरुणस्य मातः। त्वं। द्वाभ्यां। चक्षुभ्यां यावदिति यावन्मात्रं पश्यसि अहं तु एकेनैव चक्षुषा चेत् तावदिति। तावन्मात्रं न पश्ये। पश्येयं। तत्तर्हि तव दासी अहं स्यां भवेयं। त्वमु वा मम स्याः। अथवा विवादे पराजयं प्राप्य त्वं मम दासी स्याः भवेः।

प्रेक्ष्यंः सुपारं विंनते सुपर्णि
सौपंर्णं चक्षुरिति वै श्रुतं में।
अश्वंः श्वेतोऽनगंसिष्ट स्थाणौ
तस्याऽसौ कृष्णस्तिर्यङ्ङवंवाति बालंः॥६॥

॥ *पदपाठः*॥

प्रेक्ष्यंः। सु०पारं वि० नते। सु० पर्णि। सौपंर्णं। चक्षुंः। इतिं। वै। श्रुतं। मे। अश्वंः। श्वेतः। अनक्। असिष्ट। स्थाणौ। तस्यं। असौ कृष्णः। तिर्यङ्। अवं। वाति। बालंः॥

॥ *भाष्यम्* ॥

हे विनते। हे सुपर्णे। आदित्यस्याश्वः आवाभ्यां प्रेक्ष्यः अवलोकनीयः। अर्थादुरित

---

[६] भाष्ये त्वेषा पञ्चमी ऋक् अस्य सूक्तस्य अष्टमी-ऋग्रूपेण 'अनृतं वै त्वं वदसि' इत्यस्याः ऋचः पश्चात् प्रतिष्ठापिता वर्तते।

[? अर्थादादित्य-]मात्रस्याध्याहारः। कथं? सुपारं यथा स्यात्तथा। क्रियाविशेषणं, सुतरां पारः। पर्यन्तो यत्र प्रेक्षणे तत् सुपारं। यावदन्तं। शक्तेरूर्ध्वमपि प्रेक्ष्यः। चक्षुः खलु सौपर्णमेव नान्यदीयं। यथा पक्षिणां चक्षुः प्रबलं तथा नान्येषां, तत्रापि सुपर्ण्याः बलवत्तमम्। अतस्त्वया विशेषेण सूर्याश्वः अवलोकनीयः। त्वं हि द्रष्टुं क्षमा। सूर्यस्याश्वः श्वेत इति यद्वाक्यं केचिद्वदन्ति। तदनक् अप्रमाणं। प्रतिश्रोणः(०श्रवणः?) स्थाप्यः। नगसिष्टेति श्रुतिर्नियामिनी। ननु अश्वः श्वेत इति वाक्ये वेदप्रमाणं तर्हि त्वन्मते सत्यं किं? वद। इत्यपेक्षायामिदमाह। तस्याश्वस्य असौ दूरदेशस्थः बालः पुच्छबालः स्थाणौ स्तम्भे वृक्षशंकौ अति प्रांशुतरे शुष्कद्रुमाग्रे असिष्ट। आशिश्लेष। असावित्यदसो रूपेण विप्रकृष्टत्वं बोधितं। किंभूतोऽश्वलांगूलबालः। कृष्णः। अमुं बालं प्रेक्षस्व। तस्य कार्ष्ण्यादश्वस्यापि कार्ष्ण्यमवधेहि।

ननु ऊर्ध्वतरस्वर्लोकवर्तिनोऽश्वस्य पुच्छबालो नीचैर्वर्त्तिभूतलस्थे स्थाणौ कथमागत्य लग्न इत्यपेक्षायामाह। तिर्यङ् अववातीति। तिरः अञ्चतीति तिर्यङ् तिर्यग्गतिर्वक्रसंचारीवायुः। एनं बालमाकृष्य अवेति अवकृष्टः नीचैः वाति। अवाञ्चं यथास्यात्तथा गच्छति। अतो वाय्वाकृष्टो बालः स्वर्लोकादमुष्मिन् वृक्षाग्रे लग्नः। 'अश्वमिव त्वा बालवन्तं' ('अश्वं न त्वा वारवन्तं', ऋ० १.२७.१), "बाला (='वाराः', सं०) दंशवारणार्था भवन्ति" इति निरुक्तम्। इति पञ्चमो वर्गः।

॥ अथ षष्ठो वर्गः ॥

आऽनुं दीदिहीष उन्न मर्देन माद्यसि?
न बालं पश्यामि, किमापंश्यसि?
यद्यश्वः श्वेतो यदि वाऽपि कृष्णः?
किन्नु केन नु कुथं नु[७] पंश्यसि॥७॥

॥ पदपाठः ॥

आ। अनुं। दीदिहीषे। उत्। न। मर्देन। माद्यसि। न। बालं। पश्यामि। किं। आ। पश्यसि। यदिं। अश्वंः। श्वेतः। यदिं। वा। अपिं। कृष्णंः। किं। नु। केनं। नु। कुथं। नु। पश्यसि॥

[७] काश्चिन्मातृका अत्र 'नु' इत्यस्य स्थाने 'न' इति पठन्ति यत्त्वर्थदृष्ट्या समीचीनतरम्। किन्तु पदपाठो भाष्यकारश्च अत्रापि पाठे 'नु' इत्येव स्वीकुरुतः।

॥ *भाष्यम्* ॥

अनया विनता वदति। कद्रूवा 'तस्यासौ कृष्णो बालः पुच्छोद्भवः स्थाणौ लग्नस्तिष्ठति, वायुना समाकृष्टस्ततोऽश्वमपि कृष्णं जानीहि' इति पूर्वयर्चा प्रतिज्ञाते विनता तस्या उक्तं दूषयितुं षष्ठ्योत्तरमाह। नु इति कोमलामन्त्रणे। हे कद्रूः। त्वं आसमन्ततः दीदिहीषे। दीप्यसे। स्वस्य दीप्तिं दर्शयसि। दीप्तेव भवसि। ज्ञानेन प्रकाशसहव(? सदृशीव?) अप्रमाणमपि स्वमतं मिथ्यादर्पेण प्रमाणमिव मन्यसे, किं च अनेन मदेन निःकारणगर्वेण उन्माद्यसि न? अयं 'न'-कारः काकूक्त्या। उन्मत्ता न भवसि किम् ? एवमलीकं स्थापयन्ती उन्मत्ता किं न भवसि? अहं तु सम्यक् चक्षुष्मत्यपि पक्षिजातित्वाच्च दृग्बलाधिक्यं धारयन्त्यपि स्थाणवग्रे लग्नं बालं न पश्यामि। त्वं नु आसमन्तात् बालं पश्यसि। अपि च अश्वः यदि श्वेतो यदि वा कृष्णोऽस्ति। तथापि नु इति कोमलामन्त्रणे त्वं किं पश्यसि। नु च। केन हेतुना विशिष्टेन कारणेन न पश्यसि। कथं नु वा किं रूपाद्यैः पश्यसि। अत्र त्रयाणामपि समानार्थानां पदानां प्रयोगो निर्भर्त्सनातिशयद्योतनार्थः।

अथ अष्टम्यर्चा विनता स्वप्रतिज्ञामाविष्करोति -

अनृतं वै त्वं वदसि कद्रु काणे प्रतिघृष्टदर्शने।
सर्वश्वेतं ह्य१हं मन्ये नाऽस्य कृष्णोऽस्ति कश्चन॥८॥

॥ *पदपाठः* ॥

अनृतं। वै। त्वं। वदसि। कद्रु। काणे। प्रतिघृष्ट० दर्शने।
सर्व० श्वेतं। हि। अहं। मन्ये। न। अस्य। कृष्णः। अस्ति।
कः। चन॥

॥ *भाष्यम्* ॥

कद्रु शब्दोऽत्र ग्रन्थे द्विविधोऽस्ति। उकारान्तो नद्यन्तश्च। '*यूस्त्र्याख्यौ नदीति*' (पा. १.४.३)। इह तु नद्यन्तस्य सम्बोधनम्। हे कद्रु। हे काणे। एकनेत्रे। हे प्रतिघृष्टदर्शने। काणत्वं तु प्रागेव '*द्यावापृथिव्यौ भवतो भगिन्यौ, ते देव सत्रे अपराध्नुवन्त्यौ।*' इत्यत्र कद्रूवा अक्षि आहुतिभिर्विनाशितमिति स्पष्टमुक्तं। हे प्रतिघृष्टदर्शने। घृष्टमिति घर्षः संघर्षः स्पर्द्धातिशयः द्वेषः। घृष्टं संघृष्टं संघर्षाक्रान्तं द्वेषाक्रान्तं। प्रतीतिप्रातिमुख्येन घृष्टं संघृष्टं घर्षान्वितं स्पर्द्धाबहुलं द्वेषाक्रान्तं दर्शनं अन्तःकरणं यस्याः सा प्रतिघृष्टदर्शना। तत्सम्बोधनमिदं। त्वमनृतं वदसि। वै निश्चये। काणत्वादर्द्धदृष्टेः सर्वसामान्यमपि द्रष्टुं सामर्थ्यं न विद्यते। तर्हि विश्वेभ्योऽप्यधिकं किमुत। हीति निश्चये। अहममुमश्वं सर्वश्वेतं मन्ये। सर्वत्र

सर्वाङ्गप्रत्यङ्गेषु अवयवरोमपुच्छबालबालैकदेशेषु श्वेतः। तं। अस्याश्व[स्य] कश्चन कोऽप्यंशः बालो बालैकदेशो वा कृष्णो नास्ति।

अथ विनता पराजये दास्यमेव पणत्वेनाङ्गी कुरुते। सा च नवमीमृचमाह -

दासी॑ ते स्यामि॒ह स॑र्पमा॒तर्
यद्ध्ये॒३॒॑तदे॒वं न मृ॒षा ब्र॑वीषि।
मम॑ वा॒ त्वम॑दिते दा॒स्यम॒द्य
क॑रि॒ष्यसि॒ हन्त॑ चे॒दाऽव॑गत्वा॥९॥

॥ *पदपाठः* ॥

दासी॑। ते॒। स्या॒ं। इ॒ह। स॒र्प॒० मा॒तः। यत्। हि। ए॒तत्। ए॒वं। न। मृ॒षा। ब्र॒वी॒षि॒। मम॑। वा॒। त्वं। अ॒दि॒ते॒। दा॒स्यं। अ॒द्य। क॒रि॒ष्यसि॑। हन्त॑। चे॒त्। आ। अ॒व॒० ग॒त्वा॥

॥ *भाष्यम्* ॥

विनतोवाच। हे सर्पमातः। हे कद्रूः। तर्हि अहं ते दासी स्यां भवेयं। इह संसारे। हि निश्चये। यत् यदि। त्वं। एतद्वाक्यं। पूर्वोक्तं अश्वः कृष्णो, बालश्च कृष्णः स्थाणौ लग्नो दृश्यत इत्येवं मृषा न ब्रवीषि। हे अदिते। अखण्डिते। सौभाग्यवति। हे कद्रूः। हन्तेति खेदे। पणे पराजयं प्राप्य त्वं मम वा अद्य दास्यं करिष्यसि। यद्वा हन्तेदानीं चेदश्वः श्वेतो भविष्यति। ततस्तं श्वेतमवगत्वा। अवगत्वा अवगत्य ज्ञात्वा। *'समासे क्त्वोल्यपि'* नियमेन प्राप्तेऽपि *'क्त्वाऽपि छन्दसी'*ति (पा. ७.१.३८) न ल्यप्।

अथ विनता दशम्यर्च्चाऽश्वस्य शौक्ल्यकार्ष्ण्यविवेकज्ञानाय दूतप्रेरणं स्वयं वोभाभ्यामर्कबिम्बसन्निधौ गमनमुपायत्वेनाचष्टे -

दू॒तं प्रहि॑ण्वो मा॒तरिश्व॑न-
आ॒शासा॑वो॒ वक्ष्य॑ति तद्य॑था॒तथम्।
उ॒भे वा॑ स्व॒यमे॒व ग॑च्छाव कद्रु॒
वहा॑मि त्वा वा॒जी[८] च॑रति॒ यत्रासौ॥१०॥

---

[८] मातृकायामत्र 'वाजी' इत्यस्य स्थाने 'दासी'-पदं प्राप्यते यत्तु तत्पठता अपरेण केनचिद् अनन्तरं शोधितम्।

॥ *पदपाठः* ॥

दूतं। प्र। हिन्वः। मातरिश्वने। आशासाव:। वक्ष्यति। तत्। यथा० तथं। उभे इति। वा। स्वयं। एव। गच्छाव। कद्रु। वहामि। त्वा। वाजी। चरति। यत्रं। असौ॥

॥ *भाष्यम्* ॥

हे कद्रु, मातरिश्वन इति द्वितीयार्थे चतुर्थी। मातरिश्वानं वायुं। तत्र (?तं) दूतं प्रहिण्वः प्रेरयावः। अमुना वायुना दूतेनोच्यमानं तथ्यत्वेन आवामाशासावः। आशास्वहे वाञ्छावः। असौ पवनो दूतो वक्ष्यति कथयिष्यति श्वैत्यं वा काष्र्ण्यं वा। तत् यथातथमेव (यथातथं) सत्यमेव मन्तव्यं। यद्वा आवामुभे अपि स्वयमेव गच्छाव। लडर्थे लोट्।

'ननु पक्षिणी गगने प्रयातुं क्षमा। अहमपात् काणा च निःपक्षा च, कथं वा गन्तुं शक्नोमि' इत्याशङ्क्य आह। हे कद्रु त्वा त्वां मत्पृष्ठेन वहामि तत्र प्रापयामि। '*वह*' प्रापणे। यत्रासौ वाजी यस्यां वीथ्यां चरति॥

एवं पूर्वयच्चर्या विनतया कद्रूं स्वपृष्ठ आरोप्याश्ववर्णपरीक्षार्थमर्करथनिकटे गन्तुमुपक्रान्ते सति कुटिलया कद्र्वा स्वात्मजान् सर्पान्प्रेष्यादित्याश्ववेष्टने कारितमौपाधिकं काष्र्ण्यमुत्पाद्य प्रांशुशुष्कद्रुमाग्रे कंचन तनयं केशवत् कृतातिसूक्ष्मं कृष्णशरीरं कपटेन लग्नं लम्बमानं च प्रागेव विधाय विनतामूर्ध्वगमनार्थे प्रेर्य चाचिरादेव वृक्षाग्रावलम्बी तुरगलाङ्गूलबालसदृशो नागो विनतायै प्रदर्शितः। तत 'एष बालो लम्बते' इत्यनया विनतां [विनते] त्वया विवादे हारितं, पराजयं प्राप्तासि इत्युक्तं च॥ इति षष्ठो वर्गः।

॥ चतुर्थं सूक्तम् ॥

॥ अथ सप्तमो वर्गः ॥

एष बालो लंम्बते वृक्षशङ्कौ
कच्चिदेनं पश्यंसि लम्बंमानम्।
जिता मेंऽसि समुद्रसाक्ष्याच्-
छूद्रा मे भव त्वमांश्रमात्॥१॥

॥ पदपाठः ॥

एषः। बालः। लंबते। वृक्ष० शंकौ। कत्। चित्। एनं। पश्यंसि। लंबंमानं। जिता। मे। असि समुद्र० साक्ष्यात्। शूद्रा। मे। भव। त्वं। आश्रमात्[१]॥

॥ भाष्यम् ॥

कद्रूराह। हे विनते पश्य। वृक्ष एव शंकुः, वृक्षशंकुः। तस्मिन् वृक्षशङ्कौ शुष्कवृक्षाग्रे लग्नः एषः बालः पुच्छोद्भवः लम्बते लम्बमानो दृश्यते। एष चार्काश्वस्य पुच्छात् त्रुटितो वातोद्धूतो वायुवशादागत्य वृक्षाग्रे लग्नः। कच्चिदिति प्रश्ने एनं लम्बमानमश्वस्य पुच्छजं बालं पश्यसि? काकूक्त्या क्रियापदं अर्थात् 'पश्यामी'ति विनतया प्रत्युक्ते कद्रूः परुषवाक्यमेव दुष्टचित्तोवाच। किं? हे विनते। त्वं मे मया जितासि। ततश्च पणनिमित्तं त्वं मे दासी भव। अत्र '*युष्मदस्मदोः षष्ठीचतुर्थीद्वितीयास्थयो*'रित्यनुवर्तमाने (पा० ८.१.२०) '*ते मयावेकवचनस्ये*'ति (पा० ८.१.२२) षष्ठीचतुर्थ्योरेकवचनयोगे अस्मदः प्राप्तो मे इत्यादेशो 'युष्मदस्मदोरिति सूत्रे विभक्तीनां व्युत्क्रमेणोपादानादिस्थं (-त्वं?) सूचितं। क्वचिदनुक्तविभक्तियोगेऽपि युष्मदस्मदोरेते आदेशा स्युः। तेनेह तृतीयैकवचन-टा-संयोगेऽस्मदो मे इत्ययमादेशः। 'जिता मेऽसि समुद्रसाक्ष्यादि'ति।

---

[१] आश्रमात् (आ०श्रमात्, श्रान्तिपर्यन्तम्) इत्यत्र पदपाठे पदच्छेदाभावः, उपसर्गस्य चानुदात्तत्वम्। एतदसामान्यम्।

हे विनते त्वं मे मया जितासि। 'पृथिवि ते धृता लोका' इत्यादिवत्। कथं जितासि समुद्रसाक्ष्यात्। साक्षिणो भावः साक्ष्यं समुद्रस्य साक्ष्यं समुद्रसाक्ष्यं तस्मात्। एतस्मिन् पणकरणे पराजये च सागरः साक्षी। अतः पराजितत्वात् त्वं मे मम शूद्रा भव। शूद्राशब्दो दासीत्वं लक्षयति। एवंलक्षणया दासी भवेत्यर्थः। न हि त्रैवर्णिकानां दासत्वेऽधिकारः। अतः शूद्राशब्देन दासी [व्यज्यते]। कथं भव। आ श्रमात्। श्रमादा। श्रमं खेदं गात्रावसादमभिव्याप्य। यावच्छरीरस्यावसादो जायते तावत्पर्यंतं प्रत्यहमहोरात्रं मम दासत्वं कुरु। उद्वहनादीनि अधमकर्माण्यविश्रान्तं कुरु। तदानी[म]सत्यवादित्वात्। ऋजुमनसा विनतया दासीत्वमङ्गीकृतं। अहं ते दास्यस्मीति। ततो विनतायां दासीभावापन्नायां हर्षिताऽनृतकारिणी दुष्टचित्ता कद्रूः परुषाणि वचांसि प्रायुङ्क्तोत्तरयर्च्चा -

कद्रूरुवाच -

स॒मु॒द्रे र॑म॒णीय॑कं॒ द्वीपं॑ शुश्रु॒म शाश्वं॑तम्।
नागा॑नामाल॒यं पूर्वं॒ तत्रं॑ नो विनते वह॥२॥

॥ *पदपाठः* ॥

स॒मु॒द्रे। र॒म॒णीय॑कं। द्वीपं॑। शु॒श्रु॒म। शाश्वं॑तं। नागा॑नां।
आ॒ल॒यं पूर्वं॑। तत्रं॑। न॒ः। वि॒ऽन॒ते॒। व॒ह॒॥

॥ *भाष्यम्* ॥

पदान्यस्याः सुगमानि। हे विनते। वयं समुद्रमध्ये रमणीयकं नाम द्वीपं कंचिच्छुश्रुम। शृणुमः। शाश्वतं नित्यं अकालभंगभयहीनम्। तं च द्वीपं नागानामुरगाणां पूर्वं मुख्यं परमप्रियमालयं निवासम्। त्वं दासी असि। अतः नोऽस्मान् पृष्ठे समारोप्य वह। तं द्वीपं प्रापय। तत्र मुंच। एवं प्रेरितया सत्याद् भ्रष्टया विनतया दास्यं प्राप्तया यद्यत् कद्र्वा समादिष्टं तत्तत्तथाकृतम्। चिरकालमुद्वहनं कृतम्। तदिदं मातुर्महद्दुःखं नित्यं पश्यन् गरुडः कदाचिदश्रूणि दुःखितो मुमोच। ततस्तं माताश्रुपातं निवारयन्त्युत्तरया प्राह -

व॒र्षस्य॒श्रूंणि॒ कि॒मि॒दं ग॑रुत्म॒ंस्
ता॒र्क्ष्यस्य पु॒त्रस्त्वमरिं॑ष्टनेमे[१०]।

---

[१०] 'अरिं॑ष्टनेमे' इत्यस्मिन् संबुद्धिपदे आद्युदात्तत्वस्य कारणमन्वेषणीयम्। गरुत्मन्, विहग, द्विजेन्द्र इत्यन्यानि त्रीणि पदानि सर्वानुदात्तानि। वाक्यारम्भे, प्रथम-तृतीयपादारम्भ एवं संबुद्धिपदस्याद्योदात्तत्वम्। कदाचिच्छुद्धं पदं षष्ठ्यन्तं ०'नेमेः' इति ('स्व॒स्ति न॒स्तार्क्ष्यो॒ अरिं॑ष्टनेमिः', ऋ० १.८९.६) तार्क्ष्यस्यैव नामान्तरमरिष्टनेमिरिति।

न तादृशानां विहग द्विजेन्द्र
शोचंत्यपत्यमिति वै श्रुतं मे॥३॥

॥ *पदपाठः* ॥

वर्षसि। अश्रूणि। किं। इदं। गरुत्मन्। ताक्ष्यस्य। पुत्रः। त्वं। अरिष्ट० नेमे। न। तादृशानां। विहग। द्विज० इन्द्र[११]। शोचंति। अपत्यं। इति। वै। श्रुतं। मे॥

॥ *भाष्यम्* ॥

हे गरुत्मन्! हे अरिष्टनेमे! इदं किमद्भुतं। अघटमानं। यत् त्वमश्रूणि वर्षसि। पर्जन्यो बिन्दूनिवाश्रान्तं मुञ्चसि। गरुत् पिच्छं, गरुंति पिच्छानि यस्यासौ गरुत्मान्। तत्सम्बोधनं। न रिष्टा नष्टा नाशं प्राप्ता नेमिर्मर्यादा धर्ममर्यादा यस्यासावरिष्टनेमिः। *रुष-रिष* हिंसायां। रिष्टा हिंसिता नाशिता। नेमिस्तु रथचक्रस्य धारा। '*रेखामात्रमपि क्षुण्णादि*ति' श्लोके कालिदासेन (रघु० १.१७) स्पष्टमुक्तम्। तव दुःखाश्रुमोचनमनुचितं। कुतः। यतस्त्वं ताक्ष्यस्य महर्षेः कश्यपस्य पुत्रः। हे विहग खेचर पक्षिन्, हे द्विजेन्द्र पक्षिराज, तादृशानां ताक्ष्यसदृशानां ब्रह्मवर्चसिनामपत्यं न शोचति। महत्यपि दुःखे शोकं न दर्शयति। धैर्यं न जहाति। इति मे मम श्रुतं। '*कृत्यानां कर्त्तरि वे*'ति (पा० २.३.७१) सूत्रेण मे इत्यत्र षष्ठी, मया श्रुतमित्यर्थः।

अथोत्तरया गरुडः कर्मविपाकरूपं दुःखमिति मन्वानो मातरं प्रत्युत्तरं वक्तुमात्मनः प्राग्जन्मकृतगुरुभक्तित्यागलक्षणं पापं निदानत्वेनानुमिमीते –

आर्तिं वै ते विंनते नयन्त्-
यपनतह्रिया त्वरुणस्यं मातः।
य आचार्यान्युवतो[१२] न चंक्रु-
रित्थं वै तेऽश्रुमुखाः[१३] पतन्ति॥४॥

---

[११] कस्याञ्चिद् अन्यस्यां मातृकायां पदच्छेदमकृत्वा द्विजेन्द्र इत्यपि पाठो वर्तते इत्यस्मन्मातृकायाम् एतत्पृष्ठस्य प्रान्तभागेऽङ्कितम्।

[१२] 'यान् आचारान् युवत्यः'?

[१३] 'अश्रुमुक्ताः'?

॥ *पदपाठः* ॥

आर्तिं। वै। ते। वि॰ नते। नयन्ति। अपनत॰ ह्रिया। तु।
अरुणस्यं। मातरिर्ति। ये। आचार्यान्। युवतः। न। चक्रुः।
इत्थं। वै। ते। अश्रुं॰ मुखाः। पतन्ति॥

॥ *भाष्यम्* ॥

हे अरुणस्य मातः। साभिप्रायं। अहं त्वकिञ्चित्करः पुरुषार्थहीनो मातुर्दुःखापाकरणाशक्तो गणितुमनर्हः। अतः अरुणस्यैव सत्पुत्रस्य त्वं मातासि। ते पुमांसः आर्तिं व्यथां नयंति गृह्णंति। *नी* प्रापणे। व्यथामात्मानं प्रापयन्ति। कया कृत्वा अपनतह्रिया कृत्वा। अपनता गता चासौ ह्रीश्च अपनतह्रीः तया अपनतह्रिया। गतया लज्जया कृत्वा निर्लज्जतया। लज्जानाशेन। आचार्यं प्रति निर्लज्जत्वेन। दाक्षिण्याभावेन। आचार्यस्य दाक्षिण्यं यस्य शिष्यस्यान्तःकरणाद् गतं स व्यथामात्मनि आनयति। पीडां लभते। ते के? अस्मिन् जन्मनि आर्तिं नयन्ति स्वस्मिन्। ये शिष्याः आचार्यान् गुरून् भक्त्या शुश्रूषया सेवया प्रसन्नान् न चक्रुः गतजन्मनि। पूर्वजन्मनि गुरुभक्त्यकरणस्यायं कर्मविपाक इहजन्मनि यत् शत्रुकृतेन पराभवेन दासत्वादि दुःखोपभोगदर्शनं मात्रादीनाम्। किं च ते। गतजन्मनि गुरुभक्तिहीनाः। तेन पापेन अस्मिन् जन्मनि अश्रुमुखाः पतन्ति। पतनं प्राप्नुवन्ति। नीचत्वं लभन्ते दासत्वादिपराभवम्। इत्यनुमानं गरुडः करोति। किंलक्षणान् आचार्यान्। युवतः। मिश्रकान्। मिश्रीकुर्वतः। मिश्रयतः। यु मिश्रणे इति धातोः शिष्यहृदयेष्वात्मनः स्वरूपं मिश्रयतः मेलयतः। स्वस्य ज्ञानं तपो ब्रह्मवर्चसमित्यादीन् गुणान् शिष्यान्तःकरणेषु प्रवेशयतः प्रक्षिपतः। एवं मिश्रणं मिश्रीकरणं। किंच इत्थं वै तेऽश्रुमुखाः पतन्ति। इत्थमुपकारिणां गुरूणां भक्तिसु(शु)श्रूषाहीनाः जन्मान्तरे इत्थमनेन प्रकारेण अहमिव दासत्वादिप्रयुक्तं दुःखं प्राप्य तेन दुःखेन दुःखिताः अश्रुमुखाः रुदन्तो भवन्ति। रुदन्तीत्यर्थः। पतन्ति च। पतनं नीचैस्तरत्वं नीचभावं अधमदासत्वादिकं प्राप्नुवन्ति च। एतावता पूर्वजन्मनि गुरुभक्तिर्न कृता। तेन पापेन मातृद्वारा दासत्वं प्राप्तोऽस्मीत्यनुमानेन दास्यनिदानं गुर्वभक्तित्वं निरूपयति।

एवं गरुडेन विषादे प्रदर्शिते विनता स्वदुःखं पापकर्मविपाक इति वदन्ती पश्चात्तापेन स्वदुःखं वर्णयति, इतः परयच्चर्चा –

अहं वंहामि परि तान्वंहामि
सर्पान्वहामि यथां दुष्कृतकारिणीं।

द्वीपांन्त्समु॒द्रस्य॑ वहा॑मि दु॒ष्कृत् (–)
कु॒द्रून्त्सपु॒त्रामु॑दु॒कं स्पृ॒शन्तीम्॥५॥

॥ *पदपाठः* ॥

अ॒हं। व॒हा॒मि॒। परि॑। तान्। व॒हा॒मि॒। सर्पा॑न्। व॒हा॒मि॒। यथा॑। दु॒ःकृ॒त॒०का॒रिणी॑। द्वीपा॑न्। स॒मु॒द्रस्य॑। वहा॑मि। दु॒ःऽकृत्। क॒द्रूं। स॒० पु॒त्रां। उ॒दु॒कं। स्पृ॒श॒न्तीम्॥ *अथवा स्पृ॒श॒न्ती इति पाठः*।

॥ *भाष्यम्* ॥

गरुडं प्रति विनतोवाच। अहं वहामि। अत्र वहामीति क्रियापदस्य सामान्यतो निर्देशेन सर्वं वहामीत्यर्थसम्पत्तौ अहं दासीत्वाद्भारवाहिका जातास्मीत्युक्तम्।

अथ विशेषतो निर्देशार्थमाह। परितान्वाहमि। *'ते प्राग्धातोः'* (पा० १.४.८०) *'छन्दसि परेऽपी'ति* (पा० १.४.८१) सूत्रद्वयेऽनुवर्तमाने *'व्यवहिताश्चेति'* (१.४.८२) सूत्रेण परीत्युपसर्गस्य व्यवहितस्यापि धातुना साकं संयोगः। परिवहामीति। हे पुत्र। अहं वहामि भारवाहिका जातास्मि। बलीवर्दमहिषखरादिवत्। विशेषेण निर्दिशति। हे सुत। तान् प्रसिद्धान् नानाविधान् भारवतः पदार्थान् परि समन्तात् वहामि। निरन्तरं दूरदेशं नयामि। प्रापयामि इति परिशब्दार्थः। किंच सर्पान् नागान् तेषां इच्छया वहामि यथा तेषामिच्छा तथा वहामि। किंलक्षणा अहं? दुष्कृतकारिणी। पापकारिणी। अथोत्तरोऽर्द्धर्च्चः। अहं कद्रूं समुद्रस्य द्वीपान् प्रति वहामि। कीदृशीं कद्रूं? सपुत्रां। नागैः सहितां। पुनः कीदृशीं? उदकं समुद्रं स्पृशन्तीम्। यद्वा अहं समुद्रोदकं स्पृशन्ती। कीदृश्यहं? दुष्कृत्। दुष्टानि पापकर्माणि करोति इति दुःकृत्। गतजन्मनि। अन्यथा एवं कथं स्यात्। इति सप्तमो वर्गः॥

॥ अथ अष्टमो वर्गः ॥

अथ काद्रवेयाः सर्वे सम्भूय विनताया अबलाया वृद्धाया असामर्थ्यमालोक्य तत्सुतं युवानं बलिष्ठं जानन्तस्तमेवोद्वहनादीनि दासकर्माणि कारयितुं विनतां प्रत्याहुः परयर्चा –

यस्ते॑ कु॒मा॒रस्त॒रु॑णः सुपर्णि॒
यस्य॒ शाखा॒ः पत॑त॒ः खे नु॑दन्ति।
तं प्रे॑षयस्व ब॒लि॒नं॒ स ए॑तु
सर्वा॑न॒स्मान्त्रं॑यतु॒ यत्र॒ सूर्यः॑॥६॥

॥ *पदपाठः* ॥

यः। ते। कुमारः। तरुणः। सु०पर्णि। यस्य। शाखाः। पततः। खे। नुदन्ति। तं। प्रेषयस्व। बलिनं। सः। एतु। सर्वान्। अस्मान्। नयतु। यत्र। सूर्यः॥

॥ *भाष्यम्* ॥

अत्र 'पक्षवायवः' इति नुदतेः क्रियायाः कर्तुरध्याहारः। पक्षवायवः कर्ता। सर्पा ऊचुः। हे विनते। त्वं जराजीर्णा दुर्बला वासि। अतः अस्माकं दासकर्मकरणार्थं तव स्थाने तं त्वत्पुत्रं प्रेषयस्व। व्यत्ययेनात्मनेपदं, '*सुप्तिङुपग्रहलिंगनराणां कालहलत्स्वरकर्तृयणां च। व्यत्ययमिच्छति शास्त्रकृदेषां, सोऽपि च सिद्ध्यति बाहुलकेन*॥' इत्यनेन। प्रेषय। बलिनं शक्तिमन्तं। तं कं ते तव यः कुमारः पुत्रोऽस्ति। कुमारो लघुः, तरुणो यौवनं प्राप्तः। न त्वरुणमित्याशयः। स त्वया प्रेरितो दासत्वकरणार्थमेतु आगच्छतु। आगत्य च अस्मान् तं गगनभागं प्रति नयतु। तं कं? यत्र गगनांशे गगनमार्गे वीथ्यां सूर्यः प्रचरति।

सर्पाणां वाक्याद्विनतया प्रेषितेन गरुडेन नागानां निकटे गत्वा दास्यमित उत्तरया स्वीकृतं, सेयमृक्॥

अहं सुपर्णः प्रहितो ऽरुणेन
सर्पाः करिष्यामि यदाह शुंगी।
आ रोहत क्लिश्यंत मे शरीरं
वोळ्हाऽस्मि सर्वानचिरेण सूर्यम्॥७॥

॥ *पदपाठः* ॥

अहं। सु० पर्णः। प्र० हितः। अरुणेन। सर्पाः। करिष्यामि। यत्। आह। शुंगी। आ। रोहत। क्लिश्यंत। मे। शरीरं। वोळ्हा। अस्मि। सर्वान्। अचिरेण। सूर्यम्॥

॥ *भाष्यम्* ॥

गरुडः सर्पान् प्रति वदति। हे सर्पाः। अहं सुपर्णो नाम। अरुणेन अग्रजेन प्रहितः प्रेषितोऽस्मि। यद्यप्यरुणः सूर्यरथेऽस्ति तथापि कदाचिद् गरुडो मातुर्दास्यस्य दुःखवार्त्तां कथयितुं तत्र गतः। अरुणाग्रे सर्वमुक्तवान्। ततोऽरुणेन 'त्वं तत्र गत्वा मातुर्दासत्वनिर्वाहं स्वयं कुरु' इत्यादिष्टः। सर्पाणामग्रे अरुणेन प्रहित इत्याह। हे सर्पाः। शुंगी नाम विनता। मम माता यत् प्रागाह 'दासी ते स्यामिह

सर्पमातरि'त्यादि दासकर्म स्वीकारमाह। तदेतन्मात्रांगीकृतं दासकर्म समस्तमहं करिष्यामि। यूयमारोहत। मे शरीरं यूयं क्लिश्यत पीडयत यथेष्टम्। अहं तु अचिरेण वः सर्वान् सूर्यं यावत् वोढाऽस्मि। '*वह*' प्रापण इति धातोरनद्यतने लुटि परस्मैपदमुत्तमपुरुषैकवचनं। वहनं करिष्यामीत्यर्थः। ततः सर्पान् पृष्ठे आरूढानूढ्वा सूर्यमण्डलसमीपं निनाय। तदा तेऽर्कसमीपं नीयमाना मयूखैर्दह्यमाना अधोनयनमिच्छन्तः पृथ्वीतलं गन्तुकामाः अपरमृग्द्वयमाहुर्गरुडं प्रति –

सर्पा ऊचुः –

तीक्ष्णाः सुपर्णा[१४] बहुधा मरीच्यः
सूर्यस्य ता नः प्र दहन्ति भोगान्।
नमः पतङ्गाय नि वर्त्त साधु
यत्र माताऽदितिस्तत्र गच्छ॥८॥

॥ *पदपाठः* ॥

तीक्ष्णाः। सु० पर्णाः। बहुधा। मरीच्यः। सूर्यस्य। ताः। नः। प्र। दहन्ति। भोगान्। नमः। पतंगाय। नि। वर्त्त। साधु। यत्र। माता। अदितिः। तत्र। गच्छ॥

॥ *भाष्यम्* ॥

हे गरुड। सूर्यस्य मरीच्यः। मरीचयः। मयूखाः तीक्ष्णाः दुःसहाः। यद्यपि मरीचिशब्दः पुंसि, तथाप्यत्र स्त्रीलिङ्गरूपेण गृहीतः। छान्दसत्वाल्लिङ्गव्यत्ययो न दुष्टः। ता इमाः मरीच्यः नः भोगान् शरीराणि बहुधा प्रदहन्ति। हे गरुड। पतंगाय। आदित्याय नमः। अथवा पतंगः पक्षी। पतंगाय तुभ्यं नमः, त्वं साधु यथा स्यात्तथा यत्नेन निवर्त्त। आत्मनेपदस्थाने व्यत्ययेन परस्मैपदं निवर्तस्वेत्यर्थः। यत्र अस्माकं माता कद्रूस्तिष्ठति भूतले। तत्र गच्छ। किंभूता माता अदितिः? पृथिवीनामैतत्। पृथिव्यवतारः।

---

[१४] सर्वास्वपि मातृकासु 'सुपर्णा[:]' इत्येव पाठो यस्तु पदपाठेनापि सम्पुष्य द्रढीक्रियते। तथाप्यनाविलः पाठः 'सुपर्ण' (संबुद्धौ) एव भवितुमर्हति। भाष्यकारोऽपि एतदेवांगीकरोति यतः स स्वकीया व्याख्या 'हे गरुड' इत्यनेन सुपर्णपर्यायवाचिना प्रारभते।

परा –

अलं सूर्यस्य सदनं गतेनं
दुग्धा नंस्तन्वंः सवितुः शिखाभिंः।
विहायं वा त्वा प्र पंताम भूमौ
नि वंर्त्त वा शकुने नोद्यमांनः॥९॥

॥ *पदपाठः* ॥

अलं। सूर्यस्य। सदंनं। गतेनं। दुग्धाः। नः। तन्वंः। सवितुः। शिखाभिंः। वि० हायं। वा। त्वा। प्र। पताम। भूमौ। नि। वर्त्त। वा। शकुने। नोद्यमांनः॥

॥ *भाष्यम्* ॥

सर्पा आहुः। हे गरुड। सूर्यस्य सदनं गृहं रथं प्रति गतेन गमनेन अलं, पूर्यतां। नः। तन्वः। देहलताः सवितुः शिखाभिः किरणाग्रैर्दग्धाः। हे शकुने विहंग। त्वं निवर्त्त वा न निवर्त्तस्व वा। चेत् त्वं नोद्यमानः न निवर्त्तसे। तर्हि। वयं त्वां विहाय भूमौ प्रपताम।

ततः तस्मिन्नवसरे कद्रूर्विनतापृष्ठमारुह्य तामर्कमण्डलं प्रति प्रैरयत्। सा च पृष्ठारूढां कद्रूं सूर्यसमीपं निनाय। तत्र सर्वेऽन्योन्यसमीपस्था बभूवुः। तत्र कद्रूर्दह्यमानानां नागानां क्रन्दितं श्रुत्वा विनतां प्रत्युत्तरयोवाच। कद्रूवाक्यम् –

इदं न साधु यदिदं सुंपर्णि[१५]
सुतान् ममैनानवंहत्सधस्थैं।
विचेष्टंमानानुरगांनसक्ताञ्[१६]–
जवेन सूर्यं प्रतिं दह्यमांनान्॥१०॥

---

[१५] 'यदयं सुपर्णः' यदि वा 'यदयं सुपर्णि' इति साधुतरः पाठः।

[१६] 'असक्तान्' इत्यस्य स्थाने 'अशक्तान्' इत्येव पाठः साधीयान् प्रतिभाति किन्तु भाष्यकारोऽपि एतदेव स्वीकरोति।

॥ *पदपाठः* ॥

इदं। न। साधु। यत्। इदं। सु॰पर्णि। सुतान्। मम॑। एनान्। अव॑हत्। सध॰ स्थे॑। वि॰ चेष्ट॑मानान्। उर॰गा॑न्। अस॒क्तान्। जवेन॑। सूर्यं॑। प्रति॑। दह्यमा॑नान्॥

॥ *भाष्यम्* ॥

हे सुपर्णि इदं कर्म साधु न। धर्म्यं न। इदं किं यत् तव सुतोऽसौ गरुडः इदं मेघाडंबरमुल्लंघ्य मम एतान् सुतान् सधस्थे सूर्यस्य सहस्थाने रथमार्गसमीपे। सूर्यं प्रति जवेन अवहत् अनयत्। किंभूतान्? दह्यमानान्। अत एव विचेष्टमानान्। सन्तापाकुलतया विविधाः चेष्टाः कुर्वाणान्। कान् सुतान्? उरगान् नागान्। कथं भूतान्? असक्तान्। सक्तिरासक्तिः सूर्यदिदृक्षा। रविं द्रष्टुमौत्सुक्यं, तद्रहितान्। यद्वा सक्ताः गरुडपृष्ठे लग्नाः। श्लिष्टाः। न सक्ताः असक्ता अश्लिष्टाः। गरुडस्कंधात् वियुक्तान् पृथग्भूतान् 'भाविनि भूतवदुपचार' इति न्यायात् गरुडपृष्ठं विहातुमिच्छन्तो वियुक्ता एवेत्युक्तं। यद्वा सन्तापव्याकुलत्वादुद्वेगातिशयादेकत्रा-वस्थातुमशक्नुवन्तः पार्श्वपरिवर्तनादिकं भूयोभूयः कुर्वन्तोऽन्योऽन्यसंश्लिष्टा इत्याकूतम्॥ इत्यष्टमो वर्गः॥

॥ अथ पञ्चमं सूक्तम् ॥

॥ अथ नवमो वर्गः ॥

तत्रैवार्कविमाननिकटस्था कद्रूररुणं प्रति गरुडस्यौद्धत्यदोषं स्पष्टं वदति परया।
कद्रूरुवाच -

एते सूर्यस्य तपसाऽभितप्ताः
क्षितौ वर्तन्तेऽरुण भोगवन्तः।
अहं न विन्दामि हतिं सुतानां
न चेऽह तार्क्ष्यः स हि शर्म विद्यात्॥१॥

॥ *पदपाठः* ॥

एते। सूर्यस्य। तपसा। अभि० तप्ताः। क्षितौ। वर्तन्ते। अरुण। भोग० वन्तः। अहं। न। विन्दामि। हतिं[१७]। सुतानां। न। च। इह। तार्क्ष्यः। सः। हि। शर्म। विद्यात्॥

॥ *भाष्यम्* ॥

हे अरुण। एते भोगवन्तो भोगिनः सर्पाः। सूर्यस्य तपसा तापेन अभितप्ताः। अभिमुखं तप्ताः सन्तापं प्राप्ताः सन्तः क्षितौ क्षये नाशे वर्तन्ते। नाशं प्राप्स्यन्ति। अथवा भूम्यां पतिष्यन्ति। अहं तेजसा अन्धीकृतानां सर्पाणां हतिं हननं तापेन क्रियमाणं मारणं गरुडकृतं न विन्दामि न लभेयं। '*विद्लृ*' लाभे। सुतान् म्रियमाणान् ज्ञात्वापि न म्रियेयं। हननं हतिः। 'स्त्रियां क्तिन्' (पा० ३.३.९४)। यद्वा हतमित्येव भावान्तं, हतं मारितं। किञ्च। इहास्मिन् विश्वासघाते नेक्षते स तार्क्ष्यो गरुडः। स प्रसिद्धः, शर्म सुखं सांसारिकमैहिकमामुष्मिकं वा कदाचिन्न विद्यात् न लप्स्यते।

---

[१७] 'हतम्' इत्यप्यन्यत्र पाठः इत्यस्माकं पाण्डुलिपिपत्रस्य प्रान्तभागेऽङ्कितम्। किन्तु वस्तुतः अत्र 'गतिम्' इति पदं साधु स्यात्।

अथ पृष्ठारूढार्कमण्डलसन्निधिं नि(नी)यमानोत्तरयच्चर्वा कद्रूर्विनतामब्रवीत् –

एतत्ते कर्म परुषं सुपर्णि
यत् सौरसेयानवहो बलात्त्वम्।
आर्ता कद्रूर्वदति दुग्धपुत्रा
नीचैर्वर्तेथाः प्रभवत्सु नित्यम्॥२॥

॥ *पदपाठः* ॥

एतत्। ते। कर्म। परुषं। सु० पर्णि। यत्। सौरसेयान्। अवहः। बलात्। त्वं। आर्ता। कद्रूः। वदति। दुग्ध० पुत्रा। नीचैः। वर्तेथाः। प्रभवत्०सु। नित्यम्॥

॥ *भाष्यम्* ॥

हे सुपर्णि, एतत् तव कर्म त्वया क्रियमाणं आचरणं परुषं निष्ठुरं कठोरं निर्दयं महादुष्टं। एतत् किं? यत् त्वं सौरसेयान् भूमेः पुत्रान् सर्पान् ऊर्ध्वनयनमनिच्छतो बलात् बलेन रविसमीपं ज्वालामालाव्याप्तं अवहः अनयः प्रापयसि। सुतेन क्रियमाणोऽपराधो मातर्यारोप्यते। उपचारात्। वस्तुतस्त्वयैवादिष्टो गरुड एतान् बलादर्कसन्निधिं नयति, अतितरां तापेन दह्यमानान्। रसा पृथ्वी। सु उपसर्गः। सुष्ठुरसा सुरसा भूमिरेव। यथा मेरुः सुमेरुः। सुरसायाः अपत्यानि सौरसेयाः नागाः तान् सौरसेयान्। 'भूमिस्तु नाग्यभवत् कद्रूनाम्नी'ति (०नामा, १.६) प्राग्गतं। भूः स्वयमहमेव कद्रूः तस्याः मे सुताः सौरसेयाः। तान्। आर्ता दुःखातुरा पुत्राणां सन्तापं ज्ञात्वा स्वयं सन्तप्ता कद्रूर्विनतां प्रति वदति–दग्धेत्यादि, निवर्तमानं पर्यालोच्य। किं वदति? हे विनते त्वं दास्यसि। नागाश्च प्रभवन्तः। प्रभवन्ति प्रभवो भवन्ति इति प्रभवन्तः स्वामिनः। तेषु प्रभवत्सु स्वामिषु। तेषां प्रभवतां प्रभूणां नागानामाज्ञां किं लुम्पसि वार्यमाणाप्येतानूर्ध्वं कथं नयसि। अयं तु दास्याः धर्मो न भवति यदप्रियाचरणं प्रभूणां। तर्हि मया किं विधेयमित्याशङ्क्याह। त्वं नितं(त्यं) नियमेन। नित्यं सर्वदा ममसुतानामग्रे नीचैर्यथास्यात्तथा वर्तेथाः। नीचवृत्या तिष्ठ। नीचवृत्तिमाचर। प्रभुषु विषये दासानां नीचत्वेन अधमत्वेन तच्चित्तानुवृत्त्या वर्त्तनस्योचितत्वात्। सेवका ह्यादेशकारिणो भवन्ति। यद्वा नीचैरतिनीचप्रदेशगामित्वेन वर्तेथाः वर्त्तस्व। नीचनीचतरप्रदेशगामिनी भव। भूतलं गच्छेत्यर्थः। सुपर्णकृतस्यापराधस्य तन्मातर्यारोपः क्रियते। 'त्वमेवं एवं कुरुष्वे'त्यादेशोऽपि मातृद्वारा तत्पुत्रस्यैव दीयते। त्वं स्वतना(तनया)नेवं शिक्षय। इत्थं कारयेत्याकूतेन।

अथोत्तराभ्यामृग्भ्यां कद्रूः पर्जन्यं वर्षणाय प्रार्थयते वृष्टिकामा। कद्रूरुवाच मेघं समीपस्थमभ्ररूपं प्रति –

अभि क्रन्द स्तनयोदयोदधीन्
समास्तैं(ताः)[१८] पर्जन्य गिरिभिः सन्त्वापः।
आ हन्तु शेषः शिखरं गिरीणां
गच्छन्तु सर्पाः सलिलस्य मध्यम्॥३॥

॥ *पदपाठः* ॥

अभि। क्रन्द। स्तनय। उत्० अय। उद० धीन्। समाः। ते। पर्जन्य। गिरि०भिः। सन्तु। आपः। आ। हन्तु। शेषः। शिखरं। गिरीणां। गच्छन्तु। सर्पाः। सलिलस्य। मध्यम्॥

॥ *भाष्यम्* ॥

हे पर्जन्य। मेघ। त्वं अभि अभितः आभिमुख्येन क्रन्द क्रन्दनं परुषशब्दोच्चारणं कुरु। अपि च। स्तनय गर्ज। उदधीन्। चतुःसंख्याकान् सागरान् अभि इति समुद्रचतुष्टयाभिमुखं क्रन्दनं दुःसहशब्दमोक्षणं। स्तनयेति गर्ज। गर्जनं च गभीरश्रवणसुखशब्दमोचनं च कुरु। महतीं वृष्टिं कर्तुमिदं पूर्वचिह्नं कुरु। अभिवर्ष। वृष्टिं मुञ्च। तया वृष्ट्या ताः आपो गिरिभिः पर्वतैः समाः उच्चैस्तराः सन्तु। यथा गिरयोऽप्यप्सु निमज्जन्ति तथातिवृष्टिं कुर्वित्यर्थः। तव शेषः त्वदीयजलराशेः शेषः उर्वरित (?) एकोंऽशः गिरीणां शिखरं शिखराणि। आहन्तु आस्फालयतु। तत्समः प्रांशुर्भूत्वोर्मिभिस्ताडयतु। त्वया एवं कृते सति मत्सुताः निषिद्ध्यमानेनापि सुपर्णेनोर्ध्वं नीताः रवितापेन दग्धाः, प्रार्थ्यमानेऽपि वैनतेये क्रूरे अप्रत्यावर्त्तमाने तस्य पृष्ठात् अवरुह्य देहानधः पातयन्तः सर्पाः सलिलस्य गिरिसमस्य वृष्टिजलस्य मध्यं गच्छन्तु। एवं मध्येजलं निपततां देहभेदो न भवति, परितापश्च शाम्यति। सैव पुनरुत्तरयर्च्चा वृष्टेर्बाहुल्यं याचते –

एकोदकं पारमंपारमंस्तु
मण्डूकिकां वदतु सर्वरात्रम्।

---

[१८] समास्ताः (समाः ताः) इति भाष्ये पाठः। ग्रूबेमहाशयधृतपाठस्तु 'समास्तास्तैं' अस्ति (त्रयोदशाक्षरमयः पादः)।

उप॑ दु॒ग्धप॑दीं॒ गां दु॑हन्तु
मृळ[११] ए॑तु स्थल॑मि॒च्छमा॑नः॥४॥

॥ *पदपाठः* ॥

एक॒० उ॒द॒कं। पा॒रं। अ॒पा॒रं अ॒स्तु। म॒ण्डूकिका॑। व॒द॒तु। स॒र्व॒०
रा॒त्रं। उप॑। दु॒ग्ध०प॑दीं। गां। दु॒ह॒न्तु। मृळः। ए॒तु। स्थल॑।
इ॒च्छमा॑नः॥

॥ *भाष्यम्* ॥

कद्रूराह। इदं भूतलं एकोदकमस्तु। हे पर्जन्य त्वत्प्रभावात्। एकं उदकमेव यस्मिन् तत् एकोदकं। यज्जलमधुना पारं गाधमस्ति नद्यादौ, तदप्यपारमगाधमस्तु। यस्योदकस्य पारस्तलभूमिस्पर्शो लभ्यते तज्जलमपि पारमित्युच्यते। मण्डूकिका मण्डूकी दर्दुरी मण्डूकस्त्री। इदं जात्यभिप्रायमेकवचनम्। समस्ताः मण्डूक्यः। यद्वा मण्डूकिका मण्डूकजातिः मण्डूकश्रेणिः सर्वरात्रं वदतु क्रन्दतु शब्दायतां। किं च। गां पृथ्वीं त्वज्जलराशयः दुहन्तु प्रपूरयन्तु। दुह प्रपूरणे। किं कृत्वा? उपेत्य। उपसर्गबलाद्धातोरध्याहारः। यद्वा त्वयि वृष्टे, नागेषु जलराशौ पतितेषु, जलराशौ च कालेन वेगबलेनोदधौ लीने, भूतले प्रकटीभूते, नागव्रतिनो नागोपासका जनाः जलार्द्रायामुर्व्यां हरिततृणैर्व्याप्तायां नानासस्योत्पत्तौ च गवामाहारेण सौहित्ये जाते बहुक्षीराः [याः] गाः, ते नागोपासकाः नागान् पयः पाययितुं [ताः] गाः दुहन्तु। मत्सुतान् उपेत्य तत् क्षीरं निवेदयन्तु जनाः। यतो मत्सुतास्तापसन्तप्तास्तृष्णार्ताः क्षुत्पीडिताः। अतः क्षीरं भक्ताः पाययन्तु। मृडयति सुखयति पयोदानादिना इति मृडः नागव्रती मनुष्यजनः, प्राग्जलभयेन गिरिशिखराण्यारूढः ततोऽवरुह्य गतजलं स्थलं महीतलमेतु। इच्छमानः भूमेर्निर्जलत्वमिच्छन्। पदव्यत्ययः। यद्वा मृडयति सुखयति मां इति मृडः सर्पसमूहः गगनात्स्थलमेतु। तापशान्तिमिच्छन्।

इदानीं प्राग्बुद्धमपि विषादातिशयान्मातुर्दास्यनिदानमंहः पृच्छति वैनतेयः। वैनतेय आह जननीं प्रति –

स्वर्गा॑न्लो॒कांश्चक्षु॒षान्वे॑मि मात॒रहमोज॑सा तर॑सा॒ बले॑न।
अथ॑ कु॒थं दा॒सो॑ऽस्मि जा॒तः,
किं स्वि॑त् पा॒पं च॒कर्थ॑?
अथो॑ पि॒ता मे॒ दुश्च॑रितं च॒चार॑?॥५॥

[११] अत्र 'मृग' इति मूलपाठोऽनुमातुं शक्यते।

॥ *पदपाठः* ॥

स्वः॒ऽगान्। लो॒कान्। चक्षु॑षा। अनु॑। ए॒मि॒। मा॒तः॒। अ॒हं। ओज॑सा। तर॑सा। बलेन। अथ॑। कु॒थं। दा॒सः॒। अ॒स्मि॒। जा॒तः॒। किं। स्वि॒त्। पा॒पं। च॒कर्थ॑। अथो॒ इति॑। पि॒ता। मे॒। दुः॒ऽच॑रितं। च॒चार॑।

॥ *भाष्यम्* ॥

हे मातः अहं चक्षुषा स्वर्गान् लोकानत्र स्थितान् (स्थितः) एमि पश्यामि। ईदृक् मे दृग्बलं। अनु च। ओजसा धैर्येण हार्दसामर्थ्येन तानेमि। शारीरेण बलेन च। तरसा वेगेन। ईदृक्शक्त्युपेतोऽपि दासः केन कर्मणा पापेन मातृकेण पैतृकेण वा जातोऽस्मि, तद्वद, चेद्वेत्सि। मातस्त्वं किं पापं चकर्थ कृतवत्यसि, अथवा मे पिता किं दुश्चरितं चचार आचीर्णवान्? ॥ इति समाप्तो नवमो वर्गः ॥

॥ अथ दशमो वर्गः ॥

एवं पृष्टे इहैव जन्मनि यन्मयापराद्धं तदेव तवापि दास्यकारणमिति मातोत्तरयावदत्। विनतोवाच सुतं प्रति –

अ॒हं त॒या स्पर्द्ध॑माना क॒द्र्वाऽऽशंस॒ उपाद॑दे।
अ॒जा॒न॒ती भयं॑ क्रो॒धात् सा मांऽजयत्सम्प॒रा॒ये॥६॥

॥ *पदपाठः* ॥

अ॒हं। तया॑। स्पर्द्ध॑माना। क॒द्र्वा। आ। शं॒से॒।[२०] उप॑। आ। द॒दे॒। अ॒जा॒न॒ती। भयं॑। क्रो॒धात्। सा। मा॒। अ॒ज॒य॒त्। सं॒ प॒रा॒ये॥

॥ *भाष्यम्* ॥

अहं तया ज्ञातस्वभावया कद्र्वा स्पर्द्धमाना स्पर्द्धामसूयां कुर्वती सती जयं आशंसे। पणे जयाशां अकार्षम्। आशंसां कृतवत्यस्मि। उपाददे च। दासत्वरूपं पणं पणस्य अंगीकारमकार्षं च। 'दासी ते स्यामिह सर्पमातरि'त्यादिना। कस्मात्

---

[२०] 'आशंसे उपाददे' इत्येवंप्रकारकः पदच्छेदश्चिन्त्यः। 'आशंस उपाददे' इति मूलपाठः समीचीनश्चेत्तदा एकमात्रमत्रैव प्रयुक्तः (*hapax legomenon*) पयस्-तमसादिवत् क्लीबलिंगः 'आशंसस्(:)' शब्दः 'ग्लहः', 'पणः', 'आह्वानं' वा (bet, wager, challenge) इत्यस्य वाची प्रतिभाति। 'आशंस (कर्म) उपाददे'=पणं स्वीकृतवती। भाष्यकारोऽपि 'आशंसे(सः)' संज्ञारूपेण व्याख्याति (आशाम्, आशंसाम्)।

क्रोधाद्धेतोः। किं कुर्वती। भयमजानती। दासत्वे यद्दुःखं तस्य दुःखस्य भयमजानती दास्यदुःखमजानती अनुभवाभावात्। ततः संपराये संग्रामे विवादे सा कद्रूः मा मां अजयत्। मया सूर्याश्वः श्वेतोऽस्तीत्यंगीकृतं कद्र्वा तु कृष्ण इति। तत्त्वतो निःकर्षे कृतेऽश्वः कृष्ण इति सिद्धान्तितं। दैवबलात् केनापि कपटेन तेनाहं पराजयं प्राप्य दासी जाता। अयमर्थः प्रागेव 'एष बालो लंबते' (४.१) इत्यत्र स्पष्टीकृतः।

अथोत्तरया सुपर्णः जननीं दासत्वान्मोचयितुमुपायं विचारयन्नाह। वैनतेय उवाच मातरं प्रति –

कथं दास्यान्मोचयितुं विषह्या
मया दासेन यदिं वा पृथिव्या[२१]।
आ चंक्ष्व शुंगे दृळ्हमंस्म्यार्त्तो-
ऽन्नेन[२२] वाप्युत वा धनेन॥७॥

॥ *पदपाठः*॥

कथं। दास्यात्। मोचयितुं। वि० सह्यां। मयां। दासेनं। यदिं। वा। पृथिव्या (*पृथिव्याः*) आ। चक्ष्व। शुंगे। दृल्हं। अस्मि। आर्तः। अन्नेन। वा। अपिं। उत। वा। धनेन॥

॥ *भाष्यम्* ॥

'*अन्येन वे*'ति पाठान्तरम्। हे शुंगे मया दासेन मातृद्वारा दासत्वं प्राप्तेन त्वं दास्यात् मोचयितुं कथं केनोपायेन विसह्यासि। सोढव्याऽसि। शक्या भवसि। केनोपायेन त्वं मोचयितुं शक्यासि तमुपायमाचक्ष्व। वद। पृथिव्या आसमुद्रान्तया किं शक्यासि मोचयितुं? यदि सकलक्षितिमण्डलेनार्पितेन कद्रूस्त्वां दास्यान्मुञ्चति, तर्हि अहं तद्ददामि इति भावः। अपीति प्रश्ने। अपि स्वित् धनेन लंकास्थली स्यमंतकमणिमेर्वद्रिप्रमुखेण चेत् मोचयितुं विसह्या शक्या भवसि तर्हि तद्वद। अहं तद्ददामि। उत अथवा अन्येन केनाप्यतिदुर्लभेन पदार्थेन यदि मोचयितुं शक्यासि तमपि पदार्थं दातुं क्षमोऽस्मि। 'अन्नेन वा' इति पाठे अन्नं सोमलक्षणं पेयं प्राणरक्षणसाधनं अमृतमित्यर्थः। तेन चेत् त्वं दास्यात् मोचयितुं शक्यासि तर्हि तदप्यहर्तुंमहमुत्सहे। कथंभूतमुपायं वद। दृढं कार्यक्षमं। 'पृथिव्या' इति षष्ठ्यन्तत्वे

---

[२१] 'पृथिव्याः' इति वैकल्प्येन भाष्यकारधृतपाठान्तरम्।

[२२] 'अन्येन' 'अन्नेन' चेति पाठद्वयं परम्पराप्राप्तम्।

अयमर्थः। पृथिवीनाम कद्रूः। तस्याः सम्बन्धिनः दास्यात्। हे शुंगे, दृढं अत्यन्तमार्तो दुःखि(तो)स्मि। यद्वा दृढं यथास्यात्तथार्तोऽस्मि। अतीवेत्यर्थः। गरुडो मातुर्दासत्वनिष्कृतये यत् परमदुर्लभं सर्पैः समातृकैर्याच्यते तदहं दास्यामि। हे विनते गत्वा तान् पृच्छेत्याहोत्तरया। गरुड उवाच मातरं प्रति –

गच्छांऽनुयुक्ष्वं[२३] सुर्पान् यदि मोक्षोऽस्ति केनंचित्।
मयां वा यदिं वाऽरुणेनं पशुभिर्धनेंन वा॥८॥

॥ *पदपाठः* ॥

गच्छं। अनु० युक्ष्वं। सुर्पान्। यदिं। मोक्षः। अस्ति। केनं। चित्। मयां। वा। यदिं। वा। अरुणेनं। पशु०भिः। धनेंन। वा॥

॥ *भाष्यम्* ॥

हे मातः। त्वं सर्पान् कद्रूसहितान् प्रति गच्छ। तान् अनुयुङ्क्ष्व। पृच्छ। अनुपूर्वको *यु[जि]र्योगे* इत्ययं धातुः प्रश्ने वर्तते। मद्वचनेन पृच्छ। किं पृच्छामि इत्याशङ्क्य आह। एवं पृच्छ। 'हे सर्पाः मात्रा साकं विमृशत। यदि केनापि परमदुर्लभेनापि पदार्थेन मम मातुः दास्यात् मोक्षः अस्ति भवति तर्हि तमुपायं वदत, केन केन पदार्थेन। 'मया वा' अहं गरुड एव भवतां दासो भवामि। एवं मया कृत्वा चेत् दासत्वात् मोक्षः स्यात्तर्हि वदत। यदि वा अरुणेन दासेन मातुर्मोक्षोऽस्ति तर्हि वदत। अरुणः पंगुरपि यथाशक्ति करिष्यति। पशुभिर्गवादिभिः। यदि नन्दाद्याः कामधेनव उच्चैःश्रवःप्रमुखा दिव्याश्वाः ऐरावणादयो दिग्गजा वा अपेक्ष्यन्ते तर्हि तदर्पणेऽपि समर्थोऽस्मि। धनेन कुबेरादिकोशस्थेन तव निद्ध्र्यादिना मोक्षो भवति [चेत्, तदप्यानेष्यामि। एतेषां] मध्ये यत्रापेक्षा भवति तद्वस्तु ब्रूत। तदर्पयित्वा दास्यनिःकृतिं करिष्यामि'।

अथ पुत्रेण प्रेरिता विनता सर्पान् प्रति गत्वैवमुवाचोत्तरया –

न पुत्रान् वेद न पतिं तथाऽहं
युष्मान् वंहन्त्यबलां कृशास्मिं।

[२३] 'अनुयुक्ष्व' इत्यस्य स्थाने "अनुयुङ्क्ष्व" इति लौकिकव्याकरणदृष्ट्या साधुतरः, किन्तु पदपाठोऽपि "अनुयुक्ष्व" इत्येव स्वीकरोति। भाष्यकारस्तु उभयत्र "अनुयुङ्क्ष्व" इत्येवांगीकुरुते।

क्षीणो धातु[२४]र्न जवो ममाऽस्ति
कथं दास्यात्परि मुच्येय वृद्धा॥९॥

॥ *पदपाठः* ॥

न। पुत्रान्। वेद। न। पतिं। तथा। अहं। युष्मान्। वहन्ती। अबला। कृशा। अस्मि। क्षीणः। धातुः। न। जवः। मम। अस्ति। कथं। दास्यात्। परि। मुच्येय। वृद्धा॥

॥ *भाष्यम्* ॥

उत्तरार्धर्चारम्भे पाठान्तरम्। *'यकृत् क्षीणो न जवो ममास्ति'*[२५]। विनतोवाच। हे सर्पाः अहं युष्मान् वहन्ती सती [न] पुत्रान् वेद। मम पुत्राः कति सन्ति, क्व वा तिष्ठन्ति, किं वा विदधति इत्येतन्न वेद। न जाने। ननु द्वावेव पुत्रौ विद्येते, पुत्रानिति बहुवचनं किम्? आकुलत्वादित्याशयः। पतिं प्राणेश्वरं वा न वेद्मि। युष्माद् वहन्ती सती कृशा क्षीणावयवा निर्मांसा जातास्मि। किंच। मम धातुः शारीरो *'रसरक्तपिशितमेदःस्नाय्वस्थिमज्जाशुक्राख्यो'* धातुगणः क्षीणः क्षयं प्राप्तः। धातुरित्युकारान्तपुंलिंगस्य प्रथमैकवचनं जात्यभिप्रायम्। अथ पाठान्तरं। *यकृत् क्षीणः* इति। यकृत् हृदयान्तर्गतं कालिजम्[२६]। तत् क्षीणं। अत एव मम जवो वेगो नास्ति। हे सर्पाः। अहं दास्यात् दासी भावात् कथं केन प्रतिकोशेन निष्क्रयपदार्थेन प्रतिमुच्येय। मुक्ता भवेयं। कीदृश्यहं? वृद्धा। इति दशमो वर्गः ॥

---

[२४] धातवः सप्त '*त्वगसृङ्मांसमेदोऽस्थिमज्जाशुक्राणि धातवः।*' अत्र सर्वेषां समाहारतया एकवचनेनैव कथनम्।

[२५] भाष्यकारेणोल्लिखितं 'यकृत् क्षीणो . . .' इति पाठान्तरं चिन्त्यं विशेषणविशेष्ययोर्भिन्नलिङ्गत्वात्। वार्धक्ये न केवलं यक्नः क्षीणता अपितु सर्वेषामपि शरीरस्थानां अस्थिमज्जावसामांसरक्तादिसप्तधातूनामिति 'क्षीणो धातु'रित्येव पाठः साधीयान्।

[२६] 'कालिजम्' इति शब्दस्तु नैव संस्कृतम्। वैदेशिकोऽयं शब्दः पारसीकभाषाया आगतः हिन्दीभाषायां 'कलेजा' इति रूपेण परिणतः यकृद् द्योतयति। अनेकासु पाश्चात्यविचारसरणिषु चैतन्यस्य जीवस्य वा स्थितिः यकृति संभाव्यते। 'कालिजम्' इति शब्दस्य प्रयोगः भाष्यकारस्य स्थितिं मोहम्मदीयानामागमनादनन्तरं मध्यकाले (१३-१६ शताब्द्योर्मध्ये) संसूचयति।

॥ अथ षष्ठं सूक्तम् ॥

॥ अथ एकादशो वर्गः ॥

अथ नागाः परयर्चा स्वेष्टं याचमानां विनतां प्रत्युत्तरमाहुः। नागा ऊचुर्विनतां प्रति –

इन्द्रस्य सोमो निहितो गुहायां
तृतीये पृष्ठे रजसो विमाने।
तमाहृत्य तरसा शंतमेन
तेनात्मानं निष्क्रीय शं चर त्वम्॥१॥

॥ *पदपाठः* ॥

इन्द्रस्य। सोमः। नि०हितः। गुहायां। तृतीये। पृष्ठे। रजसः। वि०माने। तं। आ। हृत्य। तरसा। शं० तमेन। तेन। आत्मानं। निःऽक्रीय। शं। चर। त्वम्॥

॥ *भाष्यम्* ॥

इदं नागानां वाक्यं विनतां प्रति। हे विनते। त्वं इतो गरुडं प्रति गत्वा एवं अस्मद्वाक्यं तं प्रति कथय। कथं। तृतीयेपृष्ठे स्थाने स्वर्लोके गुहायां निगूढतमे क्वचित्प्रदेशे इन्द्रस्य सोमः निहितः स्थापितः संगोपितः। अमृतं निहितं। सोम इत्यमृतपर्यायः। संगोपितं किंलक्षणे? तृतीये पृष्ठे स्वर्लोकाख्ये। प्रथमं पृष्ठं भूतलं। द्वितीयं पृष्ठं भुवर्लोकः। तृतीयं स्वराख्यः। रजसः रजोगुणात् विमाने विगतमाने। विगताभिमाने। तत्रत्यानां हि राजसत्वाभिमानो विशेषेण गतः नष्टः। वयं राजसाः इत्यभिमानो गलितः, यतः असौ लोकः सत्त्वगुणनिधिः। हे गरुड, त्वं तं इन्द्रेण महाप्रयत्नतो गोप्यस्थाने संगोपितं हिरण्यकलशस्थं द्रवरसात्मकं सोममाहृत्य। तत आनीय। तमस्मभ्यं दत्त्वा तेन सोमेन आत्मानं समातृकं निष्क्रीय दासत्वन्निःकृतिं प्रापय। ततः शं सुखं यथास्यात्तथा त्वं विचर गच्छ। यथेष्टं विचर। दासभावात्समातृको मुक्तः सन्। आत्मानं निष्क्रीय आत्मनो निष्क्रयं

दत्त्वेत्यर्थः। इत्थं सर्पाणां वाक्यं श्रुत्वा विनता गरुडाग्र आगत्योत्तरयोवाच। विनतोवाच गरुडं प्रति –

सोमं सर्पाः पिपासन्त्यस्माभिर्दिव आ हृतम्।
दुराहरो दिवश्चेन्दुर्गरुत्मंत्स चं निष्क्रयः॥२॥

॥ *पदपाठः* ॥

सोमं। सर्पाः। पिपासन्ति। अस्माभिः। दिवः। आ०हृतं।
दुःऽआहरः। दिवः। च। इन्दुः। गरुत्मन्। सः। च। निःऽक्रयः॥

॥ *भाष्यम्* ॥

हे गरुत्मन्। सर्पाः सोमं अमृतं पिपासन्ति। पातुं इच्छन्ति। अमृतपानमिच्छन्ति। कीदृशं सोमं? अस्माभिः इति। मया त्वया वा दिवः द्युलोकादाहृतमानीतं संतं। च शब्दः पक्षव्यावृत्तौ। सोमश्च दिवः सकाशाद्दुराहरः। दुःखेन आह्रियते इति दुराहरः। आहर्तुमशक्यः। निष्क्रयः दास्याद्विमुक्त्यर्थं निःक्रयः स च। अयं चकारोऽवधारणे। निःक्रयः। स एव। सोम एव।

इत उत्तरया गरुडोऽमृतमाहर्तुमङ्गीकुरुते। गरुड उवाच विनतां प्रति –

आ ते शृणोमि विनते सुपर्णि
यदि ब्राह्मणं न जंघन्थ मातः।
पतिष्यामि तव कामाय दूराद्
दिवस्पृष्ठात्सोममाहर्त्तवा उं॥३॥

॥ *पदपाठः* ॥

आ। ते। शृणोमि। वि०नते। सु०पर्णि। यदि। ब्राह्मणं। न।
जघन्थ। मातरिति। पतिष्यामि। तव कामाय। दूरात्। दिवः।
पृष्ठात्। सोमं। आ० हर्त्तवै। ऊँ इति॥

॥ *भाष्यम्* ॥

हे विनते। हे सुपर्णि। ते तव वाक्यं। तवादेशं। अमृताहरणोपक्रममाशृणोमि। अंगीकुर्वे। आश्रवणमङ्गीकारः। तर्हि तव कामाय। अभिलाषाय। अभिलाषं पूरयितुं सर्पेभ्योऽमृतार्पणेन दासत्वनिष्कृतये दिवः ऊर्ध्वलोकस्य पृष्ठात्। उपरितनकटाहात् नाकलोकस्थलात्। सोममाहर्तवै इत्याहर्तुं। *'तुमर्थे सेसेनसे असन्०'* (पा० ३.४.९)। इतः ऊर्ध्वं पतिष्यामि उत्पतिष्यामि। उड्डीय गमिष्यामि। दूरात्

उत्पतिष्यामि। तर्हि कथं। हे मातः। त्वं यदि जन्मनः आरभ्य इदं दिनं यावत् कदाचित् कमपि ब्राह्मणं न जघन्थ अहनः। न हतवत्यसि। तर्हि अमृतार्थमुत्पतिष्यामि। ब्रह्महत्याग्रहणमितरेषां चतुर्णां महापातकानामुपलक्षणार्थं। यथा स्मृतौ – *जन्मप्रभृति पापानि बहूनि विविधान्यपि। कृत्वार्वाग्ब्रह्महत्यायाः षडब्दं कृच्छ्रमाचरेत्*॥ इत्यत्र। ननु किमर्थमिदमुक्तं यदि ब्राह्मणं न जघन्थेति। अधर्मकृतैरुपसर्गैर्मनोरथाः न सिद्ध्यन्ति। तर्हि मातुः कल्मषे सति तवोपक्रान्तकार्यस्य कुतो विनाशः? मैवं। '*यदि नात्मनि, पुत्रेषु, न चेत् पुत्रेषु, नप्तृषु। न त्वेवं तु कृतोधर्मः कर्तुर्भवति निःफलः*' इति मनुस्मरणात् (४.१७३)। अत्र अकारस्य विश्लेष-प्रश्लेषाभ्यां पदविभागेन योजना। कृतः अधर्मः। कृतः धर्मः। इति।

विनतोवाच सुतं प्रति –

न ब्रा॑ह्म॒णं ज॑घ॒नाऽहं ग॑रुत्म॒न्
न स॑त्र॒घ्नाप्य॑भवद् द्वि॒तीया॑।
नाऽनेन॑समेन॑सा॒ प्रोऽऽर्णु॑वीमि॒
नाऽऽग॑ःस्पृशो॒ अप॑हरा॒म्येन॑ः॥४॥

॥ *पदपाठः* ॥

न। ब्रा॒ह्म॒णं। ज॒घ॒न। अ॒हं। ग॒रु॒त्म॒न्। न। स॒त्र॒०घ्ना। अपि॑। अ॒भ॒व॒त्। द्वि॒तीया॑। न। अ॒नेन॑सं। एन॑सा। प्र० ऊ॒र्णु॒वी॒मि॒। न। आग॑[स्]० स्पृशः। अप॑० ह॒रा॒मि॒। एन॑ः॥

॥ *भाष्यम्* ॥

हे गरुत्मन्। अहं ब्राह्मणं न जघन। अहनं। न हतवती। द्वितीया शब्देन सखी उच्यते। मम काचित्सख्यपि सत्रघ्ना न अभवत्। सत्रं यज्ञं हन्तीति सत्रघ्ना। सत्रशब्दोऽत्र यज्ञपर्यायो लक्षणया धर्ममेव वदति। सत्रघ्ना। धर्मघ्ना। धर्मनाशकरी। मम या सखी सापि धर्मं न नाशयति। तर्हि अहं स्वयं किमुत। अथवा प्रकारान्तरेण योजना। द्वितीया मम सपत्नी। कद्रूः सत्रघ्ना न अभवत्। सत्रं अवारितान्नं। इन्द्रलोकादाहरिष्यमाणममृतं। आनेष्यमाणं। तद्धन्तीति सत्रघ्ना। तादृशी नाभवत्। अयमभिप्रायः। अमृतस्य हन्त्री न अभूत्। किं तर्हि? आनयने हेतुरभूत्। यतः पूर्वं विषादपराजये दास्यपणं कृतवती। तन्निष्कृतौ अमृतमङ्गीकरोति। ततश्च अमृताहरणे हेतुभूता कद्रूरेव। एवं न सत्रघ्नाऽभवत्। तस्मादवश्यं त्वया सोम आहर्तव्य इत्याशयः। किं च। महापातकानां कथापि दूरे तिष्ठतु। अहं तु अन्यदपि पापं मिथ्याभिशंसनादिकं न करोमि। इत्याशयेनाह। न विद्यते एनः

पापं यस्यासावनेनाः। तमनेनसं निःपापं एनसा पापेन न प्रोर्णुवीमि। मिथ्याभिशस्तं न करोमि। *'ऊर्णुञ्'* आच्छादने। ऊर्णुवीमि आच्छादयामि। वेष्टयामि। कस्यापि निर्दोषस्य मिथ्यापवादं न वदामि। तथा साक्षात् कृतपापस्यापि निन्दां न करोमि। पापसंकीर्त्तनं न करोमि, इत्यमुमर्थं विवक्षुराह। नागस्पृश इत्यादि। अहं आगःस्पृशः जनस्य एनः अघं नापहरामि गृह्णामि। आगः पापं स्पृशति संचिनोतीत्यागःस्पृक् पापकर्त्ता। तस्य आगःस्पृशः पापकर्तुः जनस्य एनः कल्मषं न हरामि। यः परस्य पापं कीर्तयति स एव तद् गृह्णाति। *'मिथ्याभिशंसिनो दोषोऽहिसमोऽभूतवादिन'* इति स्मृतेः। एवं विनता गरुत्मन्तमुक्त्वा नागान् प्रति त्विदमपरयर्चाह।

विनतोवाच सर्पान् प्रति –

किमाहृत्वा किं विजित्वा किमुं कृत्वा तु पौरुंषम्।
दास्याद्वो वि प्रंमुच्येय तदु शंसंत लेलिहाः॥५॥

॥ *पदपाठः* ॥

किं। आ। हृत्वा। किं। वि। जित्वा। किं। ऊँ इतिं। कृत्वा। तु।
पौरुंषं। दास्यात्। वः। वि। प्र०मुच्येय। तत्। ऊँ इतिं। शंसंत।
लेलिहाः॥

॥ *भाष्यम्* ॥

हे लेलिहाः सर्पाः। लेलिहन्ति जिह्वया द्रवरसं आस्वादयन्ति इति लेलिहाः। *'लिह'* आस्वादने। किं वस्तु आसमन्तात् हृत्वा भवद्भ्यो निवेद्य च युष्माकं दास्यात् अहं मुच्येय। मुच्ये मुक्ता भवेयं। किं वस्तुविशेषेण किं वस्तु जित्वा। यद्वा किं विजित्वा। कं पुरुषं दुर्जयं जित्वा। किं पौरुषं कृत्वा कं पुरुषार्थं कृत्वा। तत् शंसत कथयत इत्येवं मत्पुत्रः पृच्छति। परया नागाः विनतां प्रत्यूचुः।

वारं वरीयं दिव्युंत्तमायां
रहंः शृणुमो बृहदिन्द्रंरक्षितम्।
तमा हृत्वाऽमृतपोऽऽर्णुवेम
दास्यान्मुंच्यस्व यदि शक्तिरस्तिं ते॥६॥

॥ *पदपाठः* ॥

वारं। वरीयं। दिवि। उत्० तमायां। रहंः। शृणुमः। बृहत्।
इन्द्रं० रक्षितं। तं। आ। हृत्वा। अमृत० पाः। ऊर्णवेम। दास्यात्।
मुच्यस्व। यदिं। शक्तिंः। अस्तिं। ते॥

॥ *भाष्यम्* ॥

हे विनते गच्छ। गरुडं प्रति एवं वद। सर्पाः इति कथयन्ति। वयं वरीयं वरणार्हं सोमं, दिवि स्वर्गे, रहः एकान्ते। बृहत् यथा स्यात्तथा। महता प्रयत्नेन इन्द्ररक्षितं शृणुमः। आकर्णयामः। बृहदिति क्रियाविशेषणं प्रयत्नातिशयद्योतनार्थे। रक्षणक्रियायाश्चेदं विशेषणं। रक्षणं संगोपनम्। इन्द्रेण संगोपितं गुप्तं कृतं। निगूढं कृत्वा निक्षिप्तं अथवा बृहदिति लुप्तविभक्तिकं सप्तम्येकवचनान्तं। बृहत् बृहति महति सद्वस्तुनः निक्षेपणस्थाने इन्द्रेण रक्षितं संगोपितं। किंलक्षणं सोमं?। वारं वाः इति रेफान्तशब्दः (वार्) स्त्रीलिंग उदकवाची। वारं उदकं उदकस्वरूपं। द्रवरसमित्यर्थः। यथा वा। उदकं जगज्जीवनं तथाऽयं सोमोऽपि जगज्जीवनः। हे गरुड। त्वं आ इति आपत्य, इतः उड्डीय, तं सोमं तस्मात् दिवि संगोपनस्थानात् आहृत्य आनीय अस्मभ्यं समर्प्य च दास्यात् मुच्यस्व मुक्तो भव। यदि तव शक्तिरस्ति। एतद्दुःकरं कर्तुं। एवं त्वया सोमे आनीते सति वयं अमृतपानकरणेन आत्मानं ऊर्णुवेम। आच्छादयाम। अमृतपेत्याकारान्तं पुंसि तृतीयैकवचनं। अमृतं पिबतीत्यमृतपाः। तेन अमृतपा अमृतपानशीलेन अस्मत्परिचारकनागवर्गेण आत्मानं ऊर्णुवेम। आच्छादयाम। 'ऊर्णुञ्' आच्छादने। अमृतं पिबता नागवृन्देन परितो वृताः भविष्यामः इति मनोरथं प्रकटयन्ति। इति एकादशो वर्गः॥

॥ अथ द्वादशो वर्गः ॥

इन्द्र॑स्य॒ सोमं॒ निहि॑तं गुहा॑यां
तृ॒तीया॑त् पृ॒ष्ठाद्रज॑सो विमाना॑त्।
नि॒हत्य॒ रक्ष॒स्तर॑सा प्रणु॒द्या-
ऽऽह॑रिष्यामि च व॒ इन्दुं॒ नु मै॒व॥७॥

॥ *पदपाठः* ॥

इन्द्र॑स्य। सोमं॑। नि॰हि॑तं। गुहा॑यां। तृ॒तीया॑त्। पृ॒ष्ठात्। रज॑सः। वि॒माना॑त्। नि॒॰ हत्यं॑। रक्षः॑। तर॑सा। प्र॒॰नु॒द्य॒[27]। आ॰ ह॒रि॒ष्या॒मि॒। च॒। व॒ः। इन्दुं॑। नु। मा॒। ए॒व॥

---

[27] 'प्र॒णु॒द्य॒' इत्यस्य पदपाठेऽङ्कितं सर्वानुदात्तत्वं चिन्त्यम्। ल्यब्योगे धातौ, क्त्वायोगे च प्रत्यये उदात्तस्वरः, इति नियमः। अतः प्र॒णु॒द्य॒ इत्यस्य स्थाने शुद्धं रूपं 'प्र॒णुद्य॑' इत्येव भाव्यम्। (संहितापाठेऽपि आ-उपसर्गस्य उदात्तत्वात् 'प्र॒णुद्याह॑रिष्यामि' इतिवत् अस्माभिः शोधितम्। मूले तु 'प्रणु॒द्याऽऽहरिष्यामि' इति पाठः)।

॥ *भाष्यम्* ॥

खगेन्द्रः सोमाहरणे स्वोत्साहशक्तिं विवृणोति। गरुड उवाच। विनतां प्रति –

हे मातः। गच्छ। सर्पान् इति मद्वाक्यं ज्ञापय। इतीति किं। नु इति कोमलामन्त्रणे। हे सर्पाः। अहं वः युष्मभ्यं युष्मदर्थे तृतीयात् पृष्ठात् इन्द्रस्य सोमं आहरिष्यामि आनेष्यामि। तृतीयं पृष्ठं स्वर्लोकः। किंभूतात् रजसः। रजोगुणस्य विमानात्। गताभिमानात्। मानो गर्वोऽहंकारः। स चाभिमानो रजसः सम्बन्धी। रजोगुणस्य कार्यं। अत्र '*षष्ठी शेषे*' (पा० २.३.५०) इति संबन्धे षष्ठी। कोऽत्र सम्बन्धः। कार्यकारणभावः सम्बन्धः। रजः कारणं। अभिमानः कार्यं। विगतो मानोऽहंकारो यस्मात् असौ विमानः तस्मात्। किंभूतं सोमं? गुहायां रहसि। अगोचरे क्वचित्प्रदेशे निहितं गोपायितं। पुनः कथंभूतं सोमं? इन्दुं। ईश्वरं। सर्वार्थसम्पादनसमर्थं। '*इन्दति*' ईष्टे इतीन्दुः। तं। इन्दतिरैश्वर्यकर्मा। 'इन्दतेरैश्वर्यकर्मण' इति यास्कः। यद्वा 'लोका रजांस्युच्यन्त' इति यास्कः। रजसो देवलोकस्य समूहस्य विमानात् लोकात् गणः समूहः तस्य विमानस्वरूपात्। '*देवयानं विमानोऽस्त्रीत्यमरः*'। तत्र हि सर्वे वैमानिका एव वसंति। किं कृत्वा हरिष्यामि। रक्षः यातुधानान्। निहत्य नितरां हत्वा। रक्ष इत्येकवचनं जातौ। रक्षांसीत्यर्थः। किं च तरसा। बलेन देवगणान् सर्वान् सोमपालान् प्रणुद्य प्रेर्य दूरे प्रक्षिप्य। निरस्य। हे सर्पाः, मा एव इत्यत्र *वद्*-क्रियापदस्याध्याहारः। मा वदिष्ट। एवं पूर्वोक्तं 'यदि शक्तिरस्ति ते' इति। यदि शब्दः संशयमुत्पादयति। तं मा वदत। निश्चयेन शक्तोऽस्मि इत्याशयः।

अथ जननी सुतं सोमस्याजिहीर्षया जिगमिषुं प्रेक्ष्य तस्य सुरकृतं निग्रहं शंकमाना विरहं चासहाना स्नेहात्तं निवारयन्त्युत्तरामृचमाह। विनतोवाच गरुडं प्रति –

सर्वे॑ दे॒वा दि॒वि र॑क्षन्ति॒ सोमं॑
भू॒तानि॑ चा॒न्यानि॑ म॒हान्ति॑ तात।
तस्य॒ जानी॑ष्व॒ यदि॑ ते वि॒षह्यं॑
श्रेयो॒ऽभौजि॑ष्यात्तवं॑ जीवि॒तम्मे॑॥८॥

॥ *पदपाठः* ॥

सर्वे॑। दे॒वाः। दि॒वि। र॒क्षन्ति॒। सोमं॑। भू॒तानि॑। च॒। अ॒न्यानि॑। म॒हान्ति॑। ता॒त॒। तस्यं॑। जानी॑ष्व। यदि॑। ते॒। वि॒०सह्यं॑। श्रेयः॑। अ॒भौजि॑ष्यात्। तवं॑। जी॒वि॒तं। मे॒॥

॥ *भाष्यम्* ॥

हे सुत, सोमाहरणं दुःशकं यतः दिविस्थितं सोमं सर्वे देवाः रक्षन्ति। च अपरं। अन्यानि देवव्यतिरिक्तानि अपि भूतानि यक्षरक्षःपिशाचगुह्यकादीनि। हे तात। तस्य सोमस्य आहरणं यदि ते विशेषेण सह्यं सोढुं शक्यं भवति, तर्हि तज्जानीष्व जानीहि। विचारय। शक्यमशक्यं वेति। यदि शक्यं स्यात्तर्हि प्रयतस्व नो चेन्मा प्रयतेथाः। येन तव हननमाशंक्यते तेन कार्येण अलं। मे मम अभौजिष्यात् दासत्वाभावादपि तव जीवितं श्रेयः वरं। भुजिष्या दासी। तस्या भावः भौजिष्यं। न भौजिष्यमभौजिष्यं। दास्याभावः। अमृतार्पणनिःक्रयेण दासत्वापाकरणं। दास्याद्विमोचनं। तस्मादपि तव जीवितं श्रेयः हितं। दासत्वमपि चिरं तिष्ठतु। परं तु इन्द्रादीनां प्रहारैस्तव नाशो मा भूत्।

परयर्चा स्वस्याभयं दर्शयन् गरुड उवाच मातरं प्रति –

छन्दांसि वै स्मो विनते सुपर्णि
यज्ञं यानि विततं धारयन्ति।
असंकृद्वै यज्ञमहे पुरस्तान्
मा नो दाता नि दमेऽव मंस्थाः॥९॥

॥ *पदपाठः* ॥

छन्दांसि। वै। स्मः। वि॰नते। सु॰पर्णि। यज्ञं। यानि। वि॰ततं। धारयन्ति। असंकृत्। वै। यज्ञ॰ महे। पुरः। तान्। मा। नः। दाता। नि। दमे। अव॰ मंस्थाः॥

॥ *भाष्यम्* ॥

हे विनते विशेषेण नते। नित्यं नम्रे। त्वं सर्वदा पूज्यान् प्रति नम्रा भवसि। अतो विनतेत्युच्यते। सर्वदा नम्रायां त्वयि सानुग्रहाः देवाः तवापत्यस्य निग्रहं न करिष्यन्ति इति साभिप्रायमिदं पदं। हे सुपर्णि सुपतने। '*पत्लृ*' गतौ। पतनं गमनं गतिः क्रमणमिति यावत्। सुष्ठु शोभनं। अनिषिद्धं सन्मार्गे गमनं यस्याः सा सुपर्णी। सन्मार्गवर्तिनी। हे सन्मार्गगामिनी। यतस्त्वं सन्मार्गे एव प्रवर्त्तसे धर्ममार्गे एव तिष्ठसि, अतस्त्वत्संततेः कोऽपि हन्ता न भविष्यति इत्याकूतवता प्रयुक्तं सुपर्णीत्यपि पदं साभिप्रायं। वयं तानि छन्दांसि स्मः। वेदा भवामः। वयं हि वेदात्मकाः स्मः। 'छन्दोमयं विविधयज्ञतनुं वरेण्यं' इत्युक्तं प्राक्। तानि कानि। यानि विततं विस्तीर्णं यज्ञं धारयन्ति प्रतिपादयन्ति। वै निश्चितं। पुरः पूर्वं। पूर्वकाले अहं तान् देवान् असकृत् अनेकशः। बहुवारं अतर्पयमिति शेषः। क्व।

यज्ञमहे। महः उत्सवः। यज्ञ एव महः यज्ञमहः तस्मिन् यज्ञमहे यज्ञोत्सवे। छन्दोमयत्वात्। यज्ञस्य वैदिकवेद्यत्वाच्च। किंलक्षणो वेदात्मकोऽहं? दाता। याज्यापुरोऽनुवाक्याभ्यां हविषां निदाता। नितरां दाता[२८]। अतः हे मातः दमे दण्डे सुरैः क्रियमाणे निग्रहे सम्भाव्यमाने शंक्यमाने सति नः अस्मान् त्वं माऽवमंस्थाः। देवैः क्रियमाणस्य पराभवस्य पात्रमिति मन्वानं च माऽवमन्येथाः। अशक्तं मा जानीथाः। असावशक्तः पराभूयिष्यत इति सम्भावनमेवावमाननं।

इदमेव प्रमेयं हृद्यवधार्योद्धृत्योत्तरामृचमाह स एव –

यानि छन्दांसि चतुरुत्तराणि
यज्ञं वहन्ति विततं सप्ततन्तुम्।
तान्यहमस्मि विनते सुपर्णि
मां देवताः प्राहिन्वन्त्सोममच्छ॥१०॥

॥ *पदपाठः* ॥

यानि। छन्दांसि। चतुःऽउत्तराणि। यज्ञं। वहन्ति। वि० ततं। सप्त० तन्तुं। तानि। अहं। अस्मि। वि०नते। सु० पर्णि। मां। देवताः। प्र। अहिन्वन्। सोमं। अच्छ॥

॥ *भाष्यम्* ॥

हे विनते, हे सुपर्णि। अहं तानि छंदांसि अस्मि। तद्रूपोऽस्मि। तानि कानि? यानि छन्दांसि। ये वेदाः। यज्ञं विततं विस्तृतं यथास्यात्तथा वहन्ति धारयन्ति। प्रतिपादयन्ति। कीदृशानि छन्दांसि। चतुरुत्तराणि। चत्वार्येवोत्तराणि मुख्यानि उत्कृष्टानि प्रधानानि येषु तानि चतुरुत्तराणि। एवं विधान्यायुर्वेदधनुर्वेदगान्धर्ववेदार्थशास्त्रप्रमुखाण्युपवेद-पुराणेतिहासादीनि छन्दांसि सन्ति। एतेषु सर्वेषु गौणं वेदाभिधानमस्त्येव। चत्वार एव ऋग्वेदादयः प्रधानरूपाः। ननु अस्तु नाम चतुर्भ्यो व्यतिरिक्तेषु वेदशब्दाभिधेयत्वं परं तु कथं तेषां यज्ञप्रतिपादकत्वं? शृणु। यैर्नियमैर्यज्ञाः फलवन्तो भवन्ति तेषां विस्तरो धर्मशास्त्रपुराणेषु। एवं यज्ञोपकारित्वाद्यज्ञं वहन्तीति युज्यसे।

---

[२८] ग्रन्थान्तर्गतात् 'निदमे' इत्यस्मात् सोपसर्गक्रियापदात् 'नि' इत्युपसर्गं निष्कास्य 'दाता' इत्यनेन तत्पूर्वगतस्वतन्त्रपदेन संयोज्य भाष्यकारेण या 'नितरां दाता' इति व्याख्या कृता सा सुधीभिश्चिन्तनीया। अस्माभिस्तु 'निदमे' इत्यत्र 'निदधे' इति मूलगतपदस्य पाठाविलत्वमूह्यते। 'दाता' इत्यत्रापि 'धाता' इत्येव मूलगतपाठः प्रतिभाति (धाता यज्ञमहे असकृत् नः पुरस्तात् निदधे)।

ननु तर्हि आयुर्वेदादीनां किमागतं? सत्यं। आयुर्वेदः शरीरस्य स्वास्थ्यसाधकतया ऋत्विग्यजमानानां प्रवर्तकः। धनुर्वेदो मखविघ्नकर्तृदुष्टनिग्राहकतया यागोपकारित्वेन। गान्धर्वस्य क्वचित्प्रयोगोऽस्तीति। अर्थशास्त्रस्यार्थसाधकत्वादर्थमन्तरेण यज्ञानुष्ठानस्यासाध्यत्वात्। चतुरुत्तराणीत्यत्रतद्गुणसंविज्ञानो बहुव्रीहिः। किं च। देवताः मामच्छ, मां अभिलक्ष्य, मदभिमुखं सोमममृतं प्राहिण्वन्। व्यत्ययेन लृडर्थे लङ्॥ प्रहिणुष्यन्तीत्यर्थः, प्रेरयिष्यन्ति। '*हिनु*' प्रेरणे। सपदि तत्कालमागतं मां ज्ञात्वा ते देवाः स्वयमेव सोमं नीत्वा मह्यं दास्यन्ति॥ ('अच्छा' इत्यत्र छान्दसं दीर्घत्वम्, सं०)

यावदहं बुभुक्षितस्तावत्किमपि कर्तुं न शक्नोमीत्यतो भक्षं मे ज्ञापयेति आहोत्तरया। गरुड उवाच –

नाऽनंशनतो वी१र्यं किञ्चनाऽस्त्-
यस्मिन्लोके चरंतः सुपर्णि।
पृच्छामिं त्वा विनतेऽहमेतत्
किं स्विंद् भुक्त्वाऽथ पथांमि देवलोकम्॥११॥

॥ *पदपाठः* ॥

न। अनंशनतः। वीर्यं। किं। चन। अस्तिं। अस्मिन्। लोके। चरंतः। सु०पर्णि। पृच्छामिं। त्वा। वि०नते। अहं। एतत्। किं। स्वित्। भुक्त्वा। अथं पथांमि। देव० लोकं॥

॥ *भाष्यम्* ॥

हे सुपर्णि। अनश्नतः अकृतभक्षणस्य मे किंचन वीर्यं सामर्थ्यं नास्ति। कीदृशस्य। अस्मिन् लोके मर्त्ये चरतः विचरतः सतः तर्हि लोकान्तरे दैविके गन्तुं कथं शक्यते। हे विनते, अहं त्वां एतत्पृच्छामि। स्विदिति वितर्के। किं भुक्त्वा देवलोकं पथामि गच्छामि॥ इति द्वादशो वर्गः ॥

॥ सप्तमं सूक्तम् ॥

॥ अथ त्रयोदशो वर्गः ॥

जननी सुतस्य भक्ष्यं ज्ञापयति –

एष म॒हान्पर्व॑त॒स्तस्य॒ कूटे॑
म॒हान्ह्र॒दस्तत्र॑ भू॒तं म॒हान्त॑म्।
तद्धस्तिन॒मव॑ ती॒र्णं ग्र॑हीष्यसि॒
स ते॑ भ॒क्षस्ता उ॒भौ प॑श्य गरुड॥१॥

॥ *पदपाठः* ॥

ए॒षः। म॒हान्। पर्व॑तः। तस्य॑। कूटे॑। म॒हान्। ह्र॒दः। तत्र॑। भू॒तं। म॒हान्त॑ं। तत्। ह॒स्तिन॑ं। अव॑। ती॒र्णं। ग्र॒ही॒ष्य॒सि॒। सः। ते॒। भ॒क्षः। तौ। उ॒भौ। प॒श्य॒। ग॒रु॒ड॒॥

॥ *भाष्यम्* ॥

हे सुत, एष प्रत्यक्षं दृश्यमानो महान् अमितप्रांशुः। चतुरशीतिर्लक्षाणि योजनानां प्रमाणतः उच्चैस्तरः पर्वतो मेरुः उत्तरतस्तिष्ठति कांचनमयः। तस्य मेरोः कूटे महान् अगाधो ह्रदो जलाशयोऽस्ति तडागः। तत्र ह्रदे अन्तर्गतं महान्तमतिप्रमाणभूतं जलचरं प्राणिनं ग्राहाख्यं स्थितं ग्रहीष्यसि। तत् तस्मिन् ह्रदे अवतीर्णं प्रविष्टं स्थलचरं हस्तिनं गजं (च) ग्रहीष्यसि। स ग्राहः, ते भक्षः। स च हस्ती ते भक्षः। तौ उभौ ग्राहहस्तिनौ पश्य। दृष्ट्वा गृहाण। गृहीत्वा च भक्षय।

इत्थं मातुरुपदेशं लब्ध्वा सुपर्णस्तस्मिन् ह्रदे गत्वा तस्माद् ह्रदाद् ग्राहगजावुद्धृत्यादाय मातुरग्रे गत्वेदमाह॥

गरुड उवाच मातरं प्रति –

महानागो घोषवान्नाम पत्मी
महादन्तो मेघ[२९] इवाऽवभासते।
तं तेऽददात्सह सख्येन धाता
तौ भक्षयित्वाऽथ पथामि[३०] देवलोकम्॥२॥

॥ *पदपाठः* ॥

महानागः। घोष०वान्। नाम। पत्मी। महा०दन्तः। मेघःऽइव। अव। भासते। तं। ते। अददात्। सह। सख्येन। धाता। तौ। भक्षयित्वा। अथ। पथामि। देव० लोकं॥

॥ *भाष्यम्* ॥

हे मातः। अयं महानागो महाहस्ती मया गृहीतः। स च मेघ इव अवभासते। शोभते। नाम्ना घोषवान्। किंलक्षणः? पत्मी। पत्म पतनं गमनं तदस्यास्तीति पत्मी गमनशीलः। '*पत्लृ*' गतौ। महादन्तः। तमेतं नागं धाता स्त्रष्टा परमेश्वरः। मह्यमदात्। केन कारणेन। ते तव सख्येन मैत्र्या। या हि सती सत्यवती सत्यवादिनी धर्मनिष्ठा भवति तस्याः परमेश्वरः सखा मित्रं भवति, पितृवत् स्निग्ध इष्टदश्च। कथमदात्? नक्रेण ग्राहेण सह सहितं। अहं ताविमौ ग्राहगजौ भक्षयित्वा अथ देवलोकं पथामि गच्छामि।

गरुड उवाच –

वयांसि वै स्मो विनते सुपर्णि
नाऽस्मान्भूमौ भक्ष्यमाणं धिनोति।
वृक्षं नो ब्रूहि यदि वेत्थ कञ्चिद्
यत्राधिरुह्याद्म[३१] रुच्याम्बं भक्ष्यम्॥३॥

---

[२९] संधिद्वयं विधाय मूले क्वचिद् 'मेघेवाव भासते' इत्यपि पाठः समुपलभ्यते (मेघः इव >मेघ इव >मेघेव)।

[३०] मध्यमपुरुषान्तं 'पथासि' पदमेवात्र संगच्छते। नागराक्षरेषु सकार–मकारयोराकृतिसाम्याद् व्यत्ययः। गमनार्थस्य वैदिकपथ्धातोर्लेटि रूपमेतत्। (पथासि=[त्वं] गच्छेः), विनतोक्तिश्च।

[३१] 'अधिरुह्याद्म' इत्येतत्पदद्वयस्य सन्धिं पदपाठः (भाष्यमपि) 'अधिरुह्य+अद्म' इतिवद् विच्छिनत्ति। अत्र 'अद्म' इतिक्रियापदं चिन्त्यम्। भाष्यकारस्तु 'भक्षयाम' →

॥ *पदपाठः* ॥

वयांसि। वै। स्मः। विनते। सु०पर्णि। न। अस्मान्। भूमौ। भक्ष्यमाणं। धिनोति। वृक्षं। नः। ब्रूहि। यदि। वेत्थ। कं। चित्। यत्र। अधि०रुह्य। अद्म। रुच्या। अम्ब। भक्ष्यं॥

॥ *भाष्यम्* ॥

हे विनते। हे सुपर्णि वयं वयांसि पक्षिणः स्मः भवामः। भूमौ निराधारायां भक्ष्यमाणं खाद्यं अदनीयं अस्मान् पक्षिजातिं न धिनोति प्रीणाति। '*धिनु*' प्रीणने। नोऽस्मभ्यं कंचित् वृक्षं ब्रूहि। यदि वेत्थ। जानासि। यत्र वृक्षे अधिरुह्य आरुह्य। हे अम्ब, अद्यास्मिन् दिने[32] भक्ष्यमदनीयं द्रव्यं रुच्या इच्छया रुचिपूर्वकं सास्वादं यथास्यात्तथा अद्म[32]। भक्षयाम।

मातोवाच –

यत्र ऋषयो बालखिल्याः सुपर्ण
वैखानसाश्च मुनयो वसन्ति।
यस्य शाखाः पतिता योजनानि
तमारोह शाखिनं भोजनाय॥४॥

॥ *पदपाठः* ॥

यत्र। ऋषयः। बाल० खिल्याः। सु०पर्ण। वैखानसाः। च। मुनयः। वसन्ति। यस्य। शाखाः। पतिताः। योजनानि। तं। आ। रोह। शाखिनं। भोजनाय॥

॥ *भाष्यम्* ॥

हे सुपर्ण, यत्र अस्मिन् वृक्षे, अत्र[यत्र-]शब्देन तदीया छाया लक्ष्यते। यस्य तरोः छायायां बालखिल्याः एतत्संज्ञकाः ऋषयो वसन्ति। तपश्चरणार्थं। च अपरं। अन्ये ऋषयो वैखानसाः वानप्रस्थाः तृतीयाश्रमाः वसन्ति। यस्य तरोः

← इति शब्दान्तरेणैतद् विवृण्वन् आज्ञार्थकमुत्तमपुरुषबहुवचनान्तं (लोट्) मन्यते। लौकिकसंस्कृते त्वेतद् रूपम् 'अदाम' इति, तदेव रूपं वैदिकस्य लेट्-लकारस्यापि (लेट् : उत्तमपुरुषरूपाणि लौकिकसंस्कृते लोटि गृह्यन्ते)। तथापि वैदिक्यां भाषायां कदाचिद् लेटि 'अद्म' इत्यपिरूपं प्रचलितमासीद् इत्यनुमीयते।

[32] 'अद्म' इत्यस्य स्थाने कुत्रचिद् 'अद्य' इत्यपि पाठ उपलभ्यते। भाष्यकारस्तु द्वावपि पाठौ साधु मत्वा, समेत्य व्याख्याति!

शाखाः चतसृषु दिक्षु शतं शतं योजनानि दैर्घ्येण पतिताः गताः प्रसृताः। तं शाखिनं तरुं भोजनाय अदनार्थं आरोह अधितिष्ठ॥

सैवोवाच –

नगश्रेष्ठं रौहिणं गच्छं शीघ्रं
बृहच्छांखं जनयितुः सखांयम्।
तमारुंह्य भक्षंयेथाः सुपर्ण
स चेंद् गरुत्मन्वृषंयेन्न चान्यः॥५॥

॥ *पदपाठः* ॥

नग० श्रेष्ठं। रौहिणं। गच्छं। शीघ्रं बृहत्० शांखं। जनयितुः। सखांयं। तं। आ०रुंह्य। भक्षंयेथाः। सुपर्ण। सः। चेत्। गरुत्मन्। वृषंयेत्। न। च। अन्यः॥

॥ *भाष्यम्* ॥

हे सुपर्ण, नगाः पर्वताः। तेषां श्रेष्ठो नगश्रेष्ठो मेरुः। तं आश्रित्य स्थितं रौहिणं एतन्नामानं वृक्षं प्रति शीघ्रं गच्छ। कीदृशं तरुं। बृहच्छाखं। बृहत्यो महत्यः शाखाः दीर्घतराः स्थूलतराश्च यस्यासौ बृहच्छाखः। तं। तव जनयितुः पितुः सखायं मित्रं। त्वत्पित्रा पूर्ववयसि चिरं स एव आश्रितः सेवितः। तस्यैव छायायामुषितं। अतः सखेत्युच्यते। हे सुपर्ण। तं रौहिणं तरुमारुह्य इमौ ग्राहगजौ भक्षयेथाः। व्यत्ययेन आत्मनेपदं। हे गरुत्मन्, चेत् त्वं वृषयेत् वृषीकुर्यात्। वृषसदृशं कुर्यात्। वृषः कामानां वर्षि(षयि)ता। इष्टकामप्रदः। तादृशं कुर्यात्। सर्पाणाममृतार्पणद्वारा कामपूरकं कुर्यात्। मम च दास्यापाकरणेन कामप्रदं कुर्यात्। तर्हि स एव रौहिणः वृक्षः कुर्यात्। अन्यः न च। एतावता अमुष्मिन् तरौ उपविष्टस्य ते भक्षणं समीचीनं भविष्यति। तेन तृप्तस्त्वं इन्द्रलोके गन्तुं शक्तो भविष्यसि। तत्र देवैः साकं योद्धुं च। ततोऽमृतमाहर्तुं च। एवं कार्यपरंपरायाः हेतुभूतत्वेन स एव तरुः वृषयेत्। वृषं कुर्यात्। कामानां वर्षयितारं कुर्यात्। कामान् वर्षितुं शक्तं कुर्यात्। अन्यो न च। इति त्रयोदशो वर्गः॥

॥ अथ चतुर्दशो वर्गः ॥

इदानीं खगेन्द्रो भक्ष्यमत्तुं मात्रोपदिष्टं तरुं जिगमिषुस्तामापृच्छते। मातुराज्ञां प्रार्थयते।

गरुड उवाच मातरं प्रति –

अहमिमौ वाशितायामिव शुद्धपद्मौ-
नागौ मतङ्गाऽनुचरौ प्रभिन्नौ[33]।
अग्रहैषं प्रमुदितो महान्ता-
वध्वानमेतं पतैतद्ध्रजिष्यन्॥६॥

॥ *पदपाठः* ॥

अहं। इमौ। वाशितायांऽइव। शुद्ध॰पद्मौ। नागौ। मतङ्ग॰ अनुचरौ। प्र॰ भिन्नौ। अग्रहैषं। प्र॰ मुदितः। महान्तौ। अध्वानं। एतं। पते। एतत्। ध्रजिष्यन्॥

॥ *भाष्यम्* ॥

हे मातः। पूर्वं त्वदुपदेशादहं। महाह्रदाद् ग्राहगजौ संयुक्तावेव इमौ नागौ हस्तिनौ अग्रहैषं। अग्रहिषं। गृहीतवानस्मि। जलचरस्यापि ग्राहस्य तावन्मात्रदेहत्वान्नागनाम्ना व्यपदेशः। यथाऽयं स्थलहस्ती तथासौ जलहस्तीत्याशयेन। गृहीत्वा च सद्यः प्रमुदितो हर्षितः। कस्यां सत्यां प्रमुदितः? अपत्य[श्रे]ण्यां अनुत्पन्नपक्षायां नीडमध्यस्थायां पितृभ्यामाहृतस्य भक्ष्यस्य भक्षणार्थमुत्सुकायां चिराय चुंकृतैर्वाशितायां कूजन्त्यामिव त्वरितमागंतुमिच्छुः प्रमुदितो हर्षितः। किं लक्षणाविमौ ग्राहगजौ। शुद्धपद्मौ। शुद्धं शुक्लवर्णं पद्मं पद्मलाञ्छनं ययोः शरीरे। तौ शुद्धपद्मौ। उभयोर्भाले पद्मसदृशं चिह्नमस्ति। सितोत्पलाकारं लांछनं। कीदृशौ तौ। मतंगानुचरौ। मतंगाः सिन्धुराः द्विरदाः, [अनुचराः ग्राहादयः] अप्सुचराः ययोः तौ मतंगानुचरौ इति बहुव्रीहिः। कीदृशौ। प्रभिन्नौ। मदस्रावेण प्रभिन्नललाटौ स्फुटितकुम्भस्थलौ स्रवन्मदोदकौ। महांतौ पर्वतप्रायौ। ताविमौ गृहीतावेव वर्तेते। हे मातः अहमधुना एतं अध्वानं रौहिणवृक्षगमनमार्गं पते पतामि। गच्छामि। किं करिष्यन्। सन्। एतत् नाकं स्वः। ध्रजिष्यन्। गमिष्यन् सन्। ध्रजति रजति लजति इत्येवमादीनि, वर्तते, अयते इत्यादिषु द्वाविंशत्युत्तरे गतिकर्मणां धातूनां नामसु पठितानि। तत्र ध्रजति इति पठित्वाद् गत्यर्थोऽयं धातुः। ध्रजति गतिकर्मेत्यर्थः। ततस्तौ गृह्णन्नेवोड्डीय

[33] त्रयोदशाक्षरात्मकस्य प्रथमपादस्य पाठाविलत्वं सुस्पष्टम्। 'वाशितायामिव शुद्धपद्मौ' इत्यादिकं दुर्व्याख्येयम्। भाष्यकारो निःसहायतया यदेव व्याचष्टे। तन्नैव विद्वज्जनमनोरञ्जकम्। कदाचिद् 'वाशिता' इत्यस्य स्थाने 'अशिता' (बुभुक्षा) अथ च 'शुद्धपद्मस्य' स्थाने महाभारते उल्लिखितं 'सुपद्म' इति पठनीयं स्यात्। 'ध(ध्र)जिष्यन्' इत्यपि चिन्तनीयम् (हनिष्यन्? जिघित्सन्?)। '*अहमिमावशितायां सुपद्म-*'। अपरञ्च द्वितीये पादे 'अनुचरौ' इत्यस्य स्थाने 'अप्सुचरौ' इत्यपि कुत्रापि पाठ इति भाष्ये संकेतितम्।

महातरुं रौहिणं प्रति प्रयातः। ततो दूरादागच्छतो गरुडस्य पक्षवातांशेनातिदूरा-दागतिना दोधूयमानो रौहिणतरुः स्वाधिष्ठातृदेवता मुखेनेदमुवाच।

रौहिण्यवृक्ष उवाच। स्वस्य सखीन् प्रति –

महावीर्यं हस्तिनं मेरुमात्रं
सहग्राहं धारयन्नन्तरिक्षे।
जवेन वायुं बलवन्तमीरयन्-
नुपैत्यसौ कम्पयन्मा सुपर्णः॥७॥

॥ *पदपाठः* ॥

महा॰वीर्यं। हस्तिनं। मेरु॰ मात्रं। सह॰ग्राहं। धारयन्। अन्तरिक्षे। जवेन। वायुं। बल॰वन्तं। ईरयन्। उप। एति। असौ। कंपयन्। मा। सु॰ पर्णः॥

॥ *भाष्यम्* ॥

असौ सुपर्णः मा मां उपैति समीपे आगच्छति। किं कुर्वन् सन्। हस्तिनं गजं अंतरिक्षे धारयन् सन्। कथंभूतं? मेरुमात्रं। महावीर्यं। सहग्राहं। ग्राहसहितं। जवेन वेगेन वायुं ईरयन् प्रणुदन् प्रेरयन् निराकुर्वन् अतिक्रामन्। उल्लंघयन् जयन्नित्यर्थः। यद्वा जवेन पक्षाभ्यां वायुं ईरयन्नुत्पादयन् पक्षद्वयान्दोलनजन्यं वातं नूतनं सृजन् सन्। किंभूतं। बलवंतं प्रबलं। पुनः किं कुर्वन्। मा इति मां कंपयन्। पक्षवातेन आंदोलयन् सन्।

निकटे गत्वा त्र्यवसानया षट्पदयर्चा सुपर्णो रौहिणवृक्षं प्रार्थयते –

गरुड उवाच वृक्षं प्रति –

अहं वै तें मघवन्त्संवत्सरः
पृष्ठे ऽधिमात्रा निहितोऽयमस्मि।[३४]

---

[३४] अस्यामष्टम्यामृचि भाष्यकारः प्रारम्भेऽष्टमसूक्तगताया तृतीयाया ऋचः (अहं वै मघवन् . . . संहरस्व) प्रथमं पादद्वयं संयोज्य षट्पादात्मिकामेनामृचं निर्मिमीते। उत्तरार्धं (तृतीयतुर्यपादौ) त्वस्या ऋच अग्रिमायाम् ('एषा प्राची . . .' इति) ऋचि पञ्चमषष्ठपादरूपेण संयुक्तं तिष्ठति। पदपाठेऽष्टमसूक्ते स्थिताया अपि एतस्या ऋचः पदपाठो भाष्यकृदनुरोधेनास्माभिः ततः संगृह्य विच्छिद्य च अत्र, तत्र च प्रदत्तः। अत्रैव चैतत् प्रसंगानुकूलम्। अष्टमसूक्ते त्वस्या ऋचोऽवस्थितिः तत्रत्यप्रसंगविरुद्धैव।

प्रतिं तिष्ठ रौहिणं धारयंस्व
श्रमेण वै मोंमुमुहुर्भवांनि।
छन्दोंभिर्मिश्रः सह देवतांभि-
रात्वां रोक्ष्यामि सहंसाऽहं गरुत्मांन्॥८॥

॥ पदपाठः ॥

अहं। वै। ते। मघ०वन्। संवत्सरः। पृष्ठे। अधिं। मात्रा। नि० हिंतः। अयं। अस्मि। प्रतिं। तिष्ठ। रौहिणं। धारयंस्व। श्रमेणं। वै। मोमुमुहुः[३५]। भवांनि। छन्दःऽभिः। मिश्रः। सह। देवतांभिः। आ। त्वा। रोक्ष्यामि। सहंसा। अहं। गरुत्मांन्॥

॥ भाष्यम् ॥

हे रौहिणवृक्ष। हे मघवन् धनवान्। प्रष्टव्यसर्वपदार्थसम्पन्न। रौहिणवृक्ष। अयं। अहं। वै प्रसिद्धौ। संवत्सरोऽस्मि। संवत्सरात्मकोऽस्मि। संवत्सरः। परमः कालः। कालरूपोऽस्मि। स चाहं। मात्रा मम जनन्या विनतया ते तव पृष्ठे शाखा मध्यभागे। अधिरोढुं निहितः। आरोपितोऽस्मि। तत्रोपवेशनं कर्तुं प्रेरितः उपदेशितोऽस्मि। मां प्रति। त्वं तिष्ठ। स्थिरो भव। मां च भक्षाभ्यां गजग्राहयोर्देहाभ्यां सहितं धारयस्व। पदव्यत्ययः। वै इति प्रसिद्धौ। पुरातनाः बहवः शरीरिणः भवानि, इति छांदसत्वाददुष्टं सप्तम्येकवचनान्तं। भवानि भवति त्वयि स्थिताः। आरूढाः सन्तो मोमुमुहुः। अध्वक्रमणश्रमेण खिन्नाः क्लान्ताः संतः त्वदनुज्ञां विनैव दूरदेशादागत्य त्वामारूढाः संतः तव अधिष्ठात्र्याः देवतायाः प्रकोपात् अतिशयेन मोमुमुहुः। मोहं वैचित्त्यं मूर्छां अचेतनत्वं प्रापुः। '*मुह*' वैचित्त्ये। अतोऽहं त्वां प्रार्थये। त्वदनुज्ञया त्वा त्वां अहं गरुत्मान्। गरुडः। आरोक्ष्यामि त्वदारोहणं करिष्यामि। मामनुचरन्त्यो बह्व्यो देवताः मामारूढं दृष्ट्वा तवारोहणं करिष्यंति।

ततो रौहिणवृक्षः स्वाधिष्ठात्र्याः देवतायाः सामर्थ्येन दिव्यवाचा गरुडं प्रति आह। त्र्यवसानयैव षट्चरणया परयर्चा –

एषा प्राचीं गरुड तां श्रंयस्व
यस्यां वैखानसा ऋषंयो बालंखिल्याः।

---

[३५] कच्चित् 'मा उं मुमुहुः (भवानि)' यदि वा 'नो मुंमुहुर्भवानि' इति पठनीयं स्यात्?

परस्यां नमति तावत्तिरश्ची
स चेद् गरुत्मन् वृजिनाद् बिभेषि॥
पदाऽनुशाखामधरां प्रवृन्धि[३६]
बिलिन्थे पक्षावपि संहरस्व॥९॥

॥ *पदपाठः* ॥

एषा। प्राचीं। गरुड। तां। श्रयस्व। यस्यां। वैखानसाः। ऋषयः। बाल० खिल्याः। परस्यां। नमति। तावत्। तिरश्ची। सः। चेत्। गरुत्मन्। वृजिनात्। बिभेषि। पदा। अनु। शाखां। अधरां। प्र० वृंधि। बिलिंथे। पक्षौ। अपि। सं। हरस्व॥

॥ *भाष्यम्* ॥

इति त्र्यवसाना षट्पादा ऋक्। अनयर्चा वृक्षो गरुडाय विश्रामस्थानं दिदिक्षुराह। रौहिण वृक्ष उवाच –

हे गरुड एषा मम प्राची प्राग्गामिनी पूर्वगामिनी शाखा। तां प्राचीं पूर्वगामिनीं पूर्वाग्रां शाखां आश्रयस्व आरुह। अधितिष्ठ। तां काम्? यस्यां बालखिल्याः ऋषयः वसंति। अत्र लक्षणयाऽस्यामिति अस्याः शाखायाः छायायां इत्यर्थो लभ्यते। तथा अन्येऽपि वैखानसाः वानप्रस्थाः। तावत् इति तावत्येव तन्मात्रैव अन्या मम शाखा। परस्यां पश्चिमायां दिशि नमति नता तिष्ठति। पश्चिमाग्रा प्रसरतीत्यर्थः। तथा तावदेव। तावत्यौ एव। तावत्प्रमाणे एव। द्वे अन्ये मम शाखे। तिरश्ची इति तिरश्च्यौ। तिर्यक्गामिन्यौ वर्तेते। एका दक्षिणाग्रा द्वितीयोत्तराग्रेति द्वे तिर्यग्गामिन्यौ। एवं चतुःशाखो [+वृक्षो?] गरुड मेऽस्ति। हे गरुत्मन्। सः प्रसिद्धः। त्वं चेत् वृजिनात् पापात् बिभेषि। भीतोऽसि। तर्हि त्वं इमां प्राचीं शाखां अधरां किंचिदधोनतां अवाङ्मुखीं पदा प्रपदेन धृत्वा प्रवृंधि। बृंहय। बृंधि। बृंहितां कुरु। बृंहणं दार्ढ्यं। बृंहय। दृढां कुरु। बलवत्तरां कुरु। पादेन धृत्वा उन्नतं कृत्वा तथैव चिरं धारय। यावत्ते कार्यं तावत् पादाग्रेणोर्ध्वं यत्नेन धारय। भंगो मा भूत्। चरणाधारेण तुलयन् रक्ष। अस्मिन् बिलिंथे बिलिंथवृक्षे रौहिणवृक्षे मयि त्वं स्वौ उभौ पक्षौ च संहरस्व। संवृतौ कुरु। संक्षिप्तौ कुरु। पक्षौ संकुचितौ कुरु। पक्षयोः संकोचं, संवरणं कुरु। बिलिंथो रौहिणः पर्यायौ। स एव वृक्षः शाखाधारणप्रयत्नाकरणे तीव्रं भयं दर्शयति दिव्यवाचा वदन् परयर्च्चा।

---

[३६] 'प्रवृंधि' इति मूले स्थितस्य पाठस्य स्थाने कदाचित् प्रवृङ्ग्धि (प्र-वृञ्ज्/वृज्= अपसारय) एव साधुः स्यात्।

वृक्ष उवाच –

अभांक्षीः शाखां वृजिनं करिष्यसि
हनिष्यसि ब्राह्मणान् ये पृथिव्याम्।
अतूर्त्तं तमो रजो विनंशिष्यसि
नाऽऽहरिष्यसि सोमंमेतं गरुत्मन्॥१०॥

॥ *पदपाठः* ॥

अभांक्षीः। शाखां। वृजिनं। करिष्यसिं। हनिष्यसि। ब्राह्मणान्। ये। पृथिव्यां। अतूर्त्तं। तमः। रजः। वि। नशिष्यसि। न। आ। हरिष्यसि। सोमं। एतं। गरुत्मन्॥

॥ *भाष्यम्* ॥

हे गरुड! अनयोर्गजग्राहयोस्तव भारभरेण इमां प्राचीं शाखां अभांक्षीः। लृडर्थे व्यत्ययेनायं [लुङ्-]लकारः। भंक्ष्यसि। भग्नां करिष्यसि। ततः शाखाभंगे सति महत् वृजिनं पातकं करिष्यसि। किमित्यत आह। ये पृथिव्यां उषिताः संति तपोऽर्थे। तान् ब्राह्मणान् शाखापातेन मर्दयित्वा हनिष्यसि। अतूर्त्तं। अत्वरं शनैः शनैः विनष्यसि। विनाशं क्षयं प्राप्स्यसि। तेन ब्रह्मवधपापेन। किं कृत्वा? रजः तमश्च वर्धयित्वा। रजोगुणं तमोगुणं च प्रवृद्धं कृत्वा तद्दोषेण ब्राह्मणान् हत्वा तत्पापेन नाशं प्राप्स्यसि। ततश्च एवं प्रसिद्धं देवलोके स्थितं सोमं न आहरिष्यसि। आनेष्यसि। एवं ते सर्वकार्यनाशः। तस्माच्छाखाधारणे प्रयत्नं कुर्वित्यर्थः। इति चतुर्दशो वर्गः ॥

॥ अष्टमं सूक्तम् ॥

॥ अथ पञ्चदशो वर्गः ॥

इत्थं शाखाभंगोपद्रवं भाविनं गरुडो मनसा विभाव्य प्रयत्नेन दृढतरमेकेन हस्तेन तां शाखां नमन्तीमुद्दधार। अपरेण करेण तयोर्देहौ।

अथ स्वगृहे पुत्रकार्यनिमित्तामनिवृत्तिं मनसि धारयन्तीं विनतां[तस्याः] सत्यतपोव्रतसत्त्वधर्मे(ण) सततं प्रसन्नः परमेश्वर आकाशे वर्तमानया दिव्यवाचा बोधयत्यपरामृचं पठित्वा। आकाशवाणी प्रोवाच विनतां प्रति –

सव्येन शाखां धारयति दक्षिणेनेतरा उभौ।
बलं पश्यं सुपर्णस्य न वाचा परिमाय्यम्॥१॥

॥ *पदपाठः* ॥

सव्येन। शाखां। धारयति। दक्षिणेन। इतरौ। उभौ। बलं।
पश्यं। सु०पर्णस्यं। न। वाचा। परि०माय्यं।

॥ *भाष्यम्* ॥

हे विनते। सुपर्णस्य बलं शक्तिं पश्य। किंलक्षणं बलं? वाचा वागिन्द्रियेण कृत्वा केनापि वक्त्रा न परिमाय्यं परिमातुं न शक्यं। इयत्तया वर्णितुमशक्यम्। किं तद्बलमित्यत आह। सव्येन करेण महतीं शाखां धारयति। दक्षिणेन इतरौ उभौ ग्राहगजौ। ततस्तां वाचं श्रुत्वाऽऽश्चर्य्याविष्टा सा एकैव श्रोतृजननी(नि)रपेक्ष-प्रह(व)णेदमुवाच।

विनतोवाच केवला –

को नु वाचमीरयत्यन्तरिक्षे महोदयाम्।
एकः स्वपिति मे सुतो द्वितीय उपजायते[३७]॥२॥

---

[३७] 'उपजायते' इति तु 'उपजीव्यति' (=भुङ्क्ते, अस्मिन् समये गजग्राहादिभक्षणे व्यापृतः) इत्यस्य वैकृतिकं रूपं प्रतिभाति।

॥ *पदपाठः* ॥

कः। अनु[३८]। वाचं। ईरयति। अन्तरिक्षे। महोदयां। एकः।
स्वपिति। मे। सुतः। द्वितीयः। उप। जायते।

॥ *भाष्यम्* ॥

अन्तरिक्षे इमां वाचं वाणीं, नु इति वितर्के, कः ईरयति। वदति। कीदृशीं। महोदयां। महान् उदयोऽभ्युदयः पुरुषार्थवर्णनं मत्सुतस्य यस्यां वाचि सा महोदया, तां। यदि मम द्वयोः सुतयोरन्यतरो वक्ता संभाव्यते। तर्हि तन्न संभवति। कुतः। एको मे सुतः अरुणः स्वपिति। पंगुत्वात्सूर्यरथे ध्रुव आस्ते। अतः खेदाच्छेत इत्युपचर्यते। द्वितीयः सुतो गरुडः। कदा उपजायते। उपेत्य जायते। जनिष्यते। प्रादुर्भविष्यति। *'जनि'* प्रादुर्भावे। भविष्यदर्थे वर्तमानार्थप्रयोगः। सोऽपि सन्निधौ नास्तीत्याशयः। अथ भक्षणीयं मांसं भक्षयित्वा कदाचिन्मातृ-समीपमागत्य तां प्रणम्य खगेन्द्रः तदग्रे पुराजातं वृत्तमावेदयति।

अहं वै तें मघवन्त्संवत्सरः
पृष्ठेऽधिमात्रा निहितोऽयमस्मि।
पदाऽनु शाखामधरां प्रवृन्धि
बिलिन्थे पक्षावपि संहरस्व॥३॥

[पदपाठः भाष्यं च पूर्वमेव (द्र० सप्तमे सूक्ते अष्टमी ऋक्) प्रदत्तम्। मूले त्वस्या ऋचोऽत्रावस्थितिरिति पुनरप्युद्धृता – सं०]

सुपर्ण उवाच मातरं प्रति –

नैनां वध्रः[३९] परि हरच्छतचर्माऽनुच्छिदः।
यामम्ब रौहिणस्याहं श्रान्तः शाखामधारयम्॥४॥

---

[३८] पदपाठे 'को नु' इत्यस्य 'कः अनु' इतिरूपे विच्छेदेऽपि भाष्ये 'कः नु' इत्येव स्वीकृतम्।

[३९] मूले पदपाठे च विद्यमानस्य 'वध्रः' इत्यस्य स्थाने भाष्यकारः 'बद्धः' इति पठति तथैव च विवृणोति। 'शुद्धं पदं तु' 'बध्-बन्ध्' धातोर्निष्पन्नं 'बद्ध्रः', 'बद्ध्रिः' ('बद्धी' इति हिन्दीभाष्याम् = leather strap, 'चमड़े की पट्टी') इति वा प्रतिभाति, यस्यार्थः 'बन्धनार्थे प्रयोजनीयः चर्मरज्जुः' इति॥ (अग्रे द्रष्टव्यम्)

॥ *पदपाठः* ॥

न। ए॒नां॑। वध्रः॑। परि॑। ह॒र॒त्। श॒त॒ऽचर्मा॑। अ॒नु॒ऽच्छिं॑दः यां।
अ॒म्ब॒। रौहिं॑णस्य। अ॒हं। श्रा॒न्तः॑। शाखां॑। अधा॑रयं॥

॥ *भाष्यम्* ॥

हे अंब, रौहिण्यस्य द्रुमस्य शाखां शतचर्मा, महिषाणां चर्मणां क्षुरेण पाटितानां सूक्ष्मसूत्रसदृशो बद्धः[३१] चर्ममयस्तन्तुः। इतरेतरेण खण्डेन सीवितः संततः एकगुण एव परिवेष्टनाय प्रयुक्तः सन् परिहरत्। पर्यहरत्। परिहरणं कृतवान्। परितः हरणं वेष्टनं परिहरणं। तन्नाकरोत्। एतेन शाखायाः स्थौल्यं सूचितं। किंलक्षणो बद्धः? अनुच्छिदः। न विद्यते उच्छिदा यस्यासौ अनुच्छिदः। छिदा छेदः। अविच्छिन्नः। एनां शाखां अहमधारयम्। करेण धृतवान्। श्रांतः खिन्नोऽपि सन्।

अथोत्तरया तावन्मात्रेण भक्षिते स्वस्यातृप्तिं ज्ञापयित्वा तृप्तये मातरं भक्ष्यांतरं बहुलं किमपि याचते। गरुड उवाच मातरं प्रति –

न ह॒स्तिनं॑ भ॒क्षयि॑त्वा बिलि॒न्थे
स॒हग्रा॑हं भुक्तवा॑नस्मि शुंगे।
दिश॒ भूयो॑ भ॒क्ष्यम॒न्यं म॒हान्तं॑
यथा॑ तृ॒प्तः स्व॒ः पथे॑यं क्ष॒णेनं॑॥५॥

॥ *पदपाठः* ॥

न। ह॒स्तिनं॑। भ॒क्षयि॑त्वा। बि॒लिं॒थे। स॒ह॒ऽग्रा॑हं। भु॒क्त॒ऽवा॑न्।
अ॒स्मि॒। शुं॒गे॒। दिशं॑। भूयः॑। भ॒क्ष्यं। अ॒न्यं। म॒हांतं॑। यथा॑।
तृ॒प्तः। स्वः॒॑इति॑ स्वः॑। पथे॑यं। क्ष॒णेनं॑॥

॥ *भाष्यम्* ॥

हे शुंगे। अहं सहग्राहं ग्राहसहितं हस्तिनं करिणं बिलिंथे। बिलिंथवृक्षे रौहिणद्रुमे। बिलिंथोपरि तस्य शाखायामुपविश्य भक्षयित्वापि तृप्तवान्नास्मि। किन्तु अतृप्त एवास्मि। भुक्तवानप्यभुक्तवानिव तृप्तेरभावात्। हे मातः भूयः पुनरपि अन्यं(त्) कंचित् (किञ्चित्) भक्ष्यं दिश देहि। अथवा दिश, आदिश, कथय। उपदिश, ज्ञापय। यथा येन भक्ष्येण भक्षितेन अहं तृप्तः सन् क्षणेन क्षणमात्रेण स्वः स्वर्गं पथेयं गच्छेयम्। इति पंचदशो वर्गः ॥

॥ अथ षोडशो वर्गः ॥

अथास्मै भक्ष्यान्तरमुपदेष्टुं विनता प्रथमया न्यायमुक्त्वा द्वितीयया भक्षणीयद्रव्यं तृप्तिपर्याप्तमुपदिशति। विनतोवाच गरुडं प्रति –

जङ्गमं स्थावराण्यत्त्येषा वृत्तिः संनातना।
वयांस्युभयंमश्नन्ति स्थावरं जंगमं च यत्॥६॥

॥ *पदपाठः* ॥

जंगमं। स्थावराणि। अत्ति। एषा। वृत्तिः। सनातना। वयांसि। उभयं। अश्नंति। स्थावरं। जंगमं। च। यत्॥

॥ *भाष्यम्* ॥

हे पुत्र, जङ्गमं प्राणिजातं स्थावराणि वनस्पत्यादीनि धान्यफलादीनि वस्तूनि अत्ति। भक्षयति। एषा सनातना आद्या कल्पादितः प्रवर्तमानाऽस्ति वृत्तिः। वयांसि पक्षिणस्तु उभयं द्वयमपि अश्नन्ति भक्षयन्ति। द्वयं किम्? यत् यत्स्थावरं यच्च जंगमं तदुभयमश्नन्ति। अथोत्तरया माता भक्ष्यांतरमुपदिशति पुत्राय।

विनतोवाचं सुतं प्रति –

निषादराष्ट्रं बह्वेकंभेदं
तदद्धि त्वं मम कामाय शूर।
नाऽऽश्रांवयन्ति[40] न यंजन्त्येते-
ऽन्नं शिवं शुंश्रुमैतद् गंरुत्मन्॥७॥

॥ *पदपाठः* ॥

निषाद०राष्ट्रं। बहु। एकं० भेदं। तत्। अद्धि। त्वं ममं। कामाय। शूर। न। आ० श्रवयंति[40]। न। यजंति। एते। अन्नं। शिवं। शुश्रुम। एतत्। गरुत्मन्॥

॥ *भाष्यम्* ॥

हे शूर। गरुत्मन्। लवणावती–तीरे[41] बहु इति बहुलं। अतिप्रमाणं। असंख्येयं निषादराष्ट्रमस्ति। निषादानां भिल्लानां राष्ट्रं देशः। देशशब्देन तेषां महद् वृन्दं

---

[40] पदपाठमनुसृत्य भाष्यकारेणापि 'नाश्रवयन्ति' इति पाठं स्वीकृत्य व्याख्यातम्।

[41] मातृकायामत्र 'लवणावणतीरे' इत्यपपाठः।

लक्ष्यते। किं भूतं एकभेदं। एक एव भेदः विविधत्वहीनः। नानाजातिरहितो यस्य तत् एकभेदं। तत् निषादवृन्दं हे शूर, त्वमद्धि अशान। भक्षय। किमर्थं। मम कामाय। मम कामं मनोरथं पूरयितुं। परंपरया। '*तुमर्थाच्च भाववचनादि*'ति (पा० २.३.१५)। एते निषादाः न आश्रवयंति। आश्रवणप्रत्याश्रवणे न कुर्वन्ति। अधिकाराभावात्। 'ॐ श्रावय, अस्तु श्रौषदि'त्यश्रावणप्रत्याश्रवणे। यज्ञेष्ट्यादिकर्तारो न भवन्ति। न यजंति, याज्यां पठन्ति। अतः एतेषु नाशितेषु का हानिः। अयज्ञियत्वात्। हे गरुत्मन्, अत एव एतत् इदं निषाद-स्वरूपमन्नमदनीयद्रव्यं शिवं कल्याणकरं वयं शुश्रुम। शृणुमः। प्रत्यवायाभावात्।

विनतोवाच –

ब्राह्मणं स्म तु मा हिंसीश्चरन्तं जनतामनु।
देवं क्षमापरं शूर स मृत्युर्न तव[ा]परः[४२]॥८॥

॥ *पदपाठः* ॥

ब्राह्मणं। स्म। तु। मा। हिंसीः। चरंतं। जनतां। अनु। देवं। क्षमा० परं। शूर। सः। मृत्युः। न। तव। परः॥

॥ *भाष्यम्* ॥

हे शूर। त्वं ब्राह्मणं मा स्म हिंसीः मा स्म वधीः। किंलक्षणं जनं? तेषां निषादादीनां समूहं अनु, लक्ष्यीकृत्य विचरंतं। निषादानां मध्ये विचरंतं। पुनः कीदृशं देवं, भूमिदेवं। क्षमायां परं, तत्परं, अक्रोधं। ते च। स ब्राह्मणः प्रकोपितः सन् मृत्युरेव। परः अन्यः ब्राह्मणः (जनः?) योऽपि कोऽपि मृत्युर्न च। इतरस्मात् मा भैषीः।

गरुड उवाच –

एकशीर्षा द्विपादा द्विहस्ता
अव गृहीता मम ते (चेत्?) सुपर्णि।

पृच्छामि त्वा विनतेऽहमेतत्
किं स्विद्रूपं भवति ब्राह्मणस्य॥९॥

---

[४२] 'परः' इत्यत्र अपपाठः, 'अपरः' इत्येव भवितव्यम्।

॥ *पदपाठः* ॥

एकं० शीर्षाः। द्वि० पादाः। द्वि० हस्ताः। अवं। गृहीताः। ममं। ते। सु०पर्णि। पृच्छामिं। त्वा। विनते। अहं। एतत्। किं। स्वित्। रूपं। भवति। ब्राह्मणस्यं॥

॥ *भाष्यम्* ॥

हे सुपर्णि। ते त्वया मम ये भक्ष्याः अवगृहीताः अनुज्ञाताः निषादाः तेऽपि, तथा ये अभक्ष्याः उपदिष्टाः ब्राह्मणाः तेऽपि च। उभये एते सदृशरूपाः। कथं? उभयेऽपि एकशीर्षाः एकशीर्षाणः, एकशिरसः। तथा उभये द्विपादाः द्विहस्ताश्च। हे विनते। अहं त्वा। त्वां प्रति। एतत् पृच्छामि। किं स्विदिति वितर्के। ब्राह्मणस्य रूपं किं भवति कीदृशं भवति। कंचिद्ब्राह्मणशरीरे विशेषं वद। असाधारणधर्मं वद। असाधारणं विप्रस्य लक्षणं वद। इत उत्तराभिर्विप्रचिह्नानि। विनतोवाच –

रजस्वलो जंटिलः पंङ्कदन्तोन्नींत-
शिखो[43] वदंति सत्यमेव।
अमित्रमध्ये न बिंभेति मृत्योः
स ब्रांह्मणस्तं स्म मा हंन् गरुत्मन्॥१०॥

॥ *पदपाठः* ॥

रजस्वलः। जटिलः। पंक०दंतः। उन्नींत० शिखः। वदंति। सत्यं। एव। अमित्र०मध्ये। न। बिभेति। मृत्योः। सः। ब्राह्मणः। तं। स्म। मा। हुन्। गरुत्मन्॥

॥ *भाष्यम्* ॥

हे गरुत्मन्। स ब्राह्मणो ज्ञेयः। तं च मा हन्। भवान् मा हिंसीत्, मा वधीत्। तं कं? यः रजस्वलः। धूलिधूसरगात्रः। भस्मोद्धूलितदेहः। '*रजः कृष्यासुतिपरिषदो वलच्*' (पा० ५.२.११२)। जटिलः जटाव्याप्तशिराः। पंकदंतः। पंको मलः। पंकयुक्ताः मलिनाः दंताः यस्यासौ पंकदंतः। यद्वा 'पंकिदंत' इति पाठः। पंकः एष्वस्तीति पंकिनः। पंकिनो दन्ताः यस्यासौ पंकिदन्तः। उन्नीतशिखः। उन्नीता ऊर्ध्वं नीता शिरसः उपरि स्पष्टीकृता शिखा यस्यासौ उन्नीतशिखः। ब्राह्मणानां

---

[43] पङ्कदन्तः+उन्नीतशिखः, पङ्कदन्त–उन्नीतशिखः, पङ्कदन्तोन्नीतशिखः। सन्धेरेतदार्षं द्वित्वं रामायणमहाभारतपुराणादिष्वपि दृष्टिपथमायाति (यथा – 'निशाचरः स ववृधे, व्याधयोपेक्षिता इव', इति युद्धकाण्डे)।

पर्युप्तशिरसामपि शिखारक्षणमावश्यकं। यद्वा शिखा नाम सा यः (यत्र?) ब्रह्मग्रंथिर्बद्धो भवति। यः सत्यमेव सर्वदा वदति स ब्राह्मणः। एतानि ब्राह्मणलक्षणानि। यश्च अमित्राणां शत्रूणां मध्ये स्थितोऽपि सन् मृत्योः सकाशात् न बिभेति। हननात् भयं न शंकते। यः मां जिघांसति क्रूरदृष्ट्याऽवेक्षते वा, स अवश्यं सद्यः नश्यति। भस्मीभवति। भस्मसाद्भवति, इत्यभिप्रायवान्। इति षोडशो वर्गः॥

॥ नवमं सूक्तम् ॥

॥ अथ सप्तदशो वर्गः ॥

षळग्नयो यं पुरुषं तपन्ति
जैह्वो हार्द्द औदरो रैतसश्च।
तप्तश्च घर्मः शिशिरश्च शीतः
स ब्राह्मणस्तं स्म मा हन् गरुत्मन्॥१॥

॥ *पदपाठः* ॥

षट्। अग्नयः। यं। पुरुषं। तपंति। जैह्वः। हार्द्दः। औदरः।
रैतसः। च। तप्तः। च। घर्मः। शिशिरः। च। शीतः।
(शेषं पूर्ववत्)

॥ *भाष्यम्* ॥

हे गरुत्मन्। स ब्राह्मणः ज्ञेयः। सः कः। यं पुरुषं षट् अग्नयः तपंति संतपंति। संतापयंति पीडयंति। अन्तर्नीतण्यर्थरूपं। '*तप*' संतापे। के ते षट् अग्नयः जैह्वः हार्द्दः औदरः रैतसः एते चत्वारः। पञ्चमो घर्मः घर्माग्निः। उष्णोऽग्निः। शीतः षष्ठः। शीताग्निः। एते षट्। जिह्वायां भवो जैह्वः अग्निः स तु वाक्संयमद्वारेण संतापयति, तथा अक्षारालवणाशाकवृत्त्यान्नाशनेन रसनेंद्रियविषयरोधद्वारेण। द्वितीयो हार्द्दः हृदि भवो हार्दः। मनः संयमनसाध्यो ध्यानाग्निर्ज्ञानाग्निर्वा निर्मर्यादानर्गल-संकल्पविकल्पनिरोधदुःखेन संतापयति। तृतीय औदरः। जठराग्निः स च उपवासादिना धातून् दहति। चतुर्थो रैतसः। रेतसि भवः रैतसः। स च रेतःसंनिरोधेन ब्रह्मचर्यचरणात् दुःखमुत्पाद्य संतापयति। पञ्चमो घर्माग्निः। घर्म उष्णः। अर्कातपकृतेन तापेन वैश्वानरकृतेन च देहं संतापयति। पंचाग्निसाधनव्रते। षष्ठः शीताग्निः। तुषाराग्निः। हिमकृतवेदनाद्वारा संतापयति। किंलक्षणो घर्मः? उष्णाग्निः। तप्तः। विशेषणमेतत्। चतुर्णां वैश्वानराणां स्थण्डिलेषु स्थापितानां खादिरेन्धनैः प्रदीपनात् प्रतप्तः। प्रदीप्तः। सूर्यस्य च अभ्रावरणराहित्येन गगनमध्यगतत्वेन च तप्तः प्रतप्तः। किंलक्षणः शीतः? शिशिरः। विशेषणमिदं। शिशिरः अतिहिमसंसृष्टो

हिमाग्निः संतापयति, हिमवेदनया त्वचं दहति। एवं षट् अग्नयः। प्रकारान्तरेण योजना। षट् अग्नयः यं पुरुषं आदित्ये तपंति प्रकाशंते देदीप्यन्ते। स ब्राह्मणः। शेषमभिन्नं। अपरयच्चर्चा विप्रलक्षणान्येव दर्शयति सा।

विनतोवाच –

मत्स्येंव[४४] बिलिशं जग्रसानो
गुरूदंरो भवंति ब्राह्मणेनं।
अङ्गांरेव[४४] विदहंन्नेति कुण्ठं
स ब्रांह्मणस्तं स्म मा हंन् गरुत्मन्॥२॥

॥ पदपाठः ॥

मत्स्यंःऽइव। बिलिशं। जग्रसानः। गुरु०उंदरः। भवंति। ब्राह्मणेनं।
अंगांरऽइव। वि०दहंन्। एति। कंठं।

॥ भाष्यम् ॥

हे गरुत्मन्। ब्राह्मणेन गिलितेन गलादधस्तादुत्तीर्णेनोदरमध्यस्थेन गुरूदरो महोदरो भवति। उदरवृद्धिरोगी भवति। उदरे प्रविष्टो विप्रो नैव जीर्यते। चिह्नान्तरमाह। विप्रः गले यदा प्रविशति तदा कंठस्य मध्ये विदहन् विशेषेण दहन् सन् कंठे एति। यः ईदृशः। स ब्राह्मणः। हे गरुड तं मा हन्। मास्म वधीत् भवान्। अथ गरुडः विप्रलक्षणानि श्रुत्वा हर्षितः प्रत्युत्तरमाह।

गरुड उवाच मातरं प्रति –

आ हंरिष्यामि ते सोमं ज्ञातो भक्षः संनातनः।
आऽन्ततो भक्षंयिष्याम्युभयं स्थाष्णुं जंगमंम्॥३॥

॥ पदपाठः ॥

आ। हरिष्यामि। ते। सोमं। ज्ञातः। भक्षः। सनातनः। आ।
अंततः। भक्षंयिष्यामि। उभयं। स्थाष्णुं। जंगमं॥

---

[४४] अनुष्ठितेऽपि सन्धिद्वित्वे छन्दोऽनुरोधेन क्वचित् संहितरूपेण (यथा 'अंगारेव' इति चतुरक्षरे पदे), क्वचिच्च विखण्डितरूपेण (यथा 'मत्स्य इव' एवं चतुरक्षराणि विधाय) गीयते प्रतिपादमेकादशाक्षरा त्रिष्टुभ्, इति प्रतीयते।

॥ *भाष्यम्* ॥

हे मातः। त्वदर्थं तव दास्यविमोचनार्थं सोममाहरिष्यामि आनेष्यामि। यतः मे भक्षः सर्वोऽपि तृप्तिपर्याप्तो ज्ञातः। सनातनः। शास्त्रविहितः। त्वदुपदेशात् उभयं भक्षयिष्यामि। कथं। अंततः आंतात्। आ। अंतमभिव्याप्य। अभिविधावाङ्। अंतपर्यंतं सर्वं भक्षयिष्यामि, निःशेषमित्यर्थः। उभयं किं? स्थाष्णु तत्रत्यं स्थावरं। जंगमं च, तत्रत्यं सर्वं चरिष्णु। एतदुभयं॥

अथ मेर्वद्रौ महारौहिणद्रुमशाखाच्छायेऽध्युषितस्य ताक्ष्र्यमहर्षेर्विनतापतेर्गरुडपितुः समीपस्थे वामदेव ऋषिर्देशकालव्यवहितानपि पदार्थान् अप्रतिहतगतिना चक्षुषा पश्यन्, गरुडस्य वेदराशिमयदेहत्वं परमेश्वरांशत्वं च जानन्, गरुडे परमभक्तिमान् गरुडस्योपक्रमं विदित्वा परया त्रिष्टुभा सुपर्णं नमस्कुरुते।

वामदेव उवाच –

वयं॒सां राजा॑नमभिमाति॒षाहं॑
दि॒व्यं सु॑प॒र्णं वयं॑सा बृ॒हन्तं॑म्।
शू॒रं सु॑प॒र्णम॒भि यत् प्रती॑कं॒[४५]
ताक्ष्यं॑ शौङ्गे॒यं नम॒सोऽपं॑तिष्ठे॥४॥

॥ *पदपाठः* ॥

वयं॑सां। राजा॑नं। अ॒भि॒मा॒ति॒० सहं॑। दि॒व्यं। सु॒०प॒र्णं। वयं॑सा।
बृ॒हंतं॑। शू॒रं। सु॒०प॒र्णं। अ॒भि। यत्। प्रती॑कं। ताक्ष्यं॑। शौ॒ङ्गे॒यं।
नमं॑सा। उपं॑ति॒ष्ठे॒॥

॥ *भाष्यम्* ॥

अहं वामदेवः ताक्ष्र्यं ताक्ष्र्यनामानं शौंगेयं शुंगायाः सुतं नमसा प्रणत्य उपतिष्ठे। उपस्थितोऽस्मि। शरणं गतोऽस्मि। किंलक्षणं ताक्ष्र्यं? वयसां पक्षिणां राजानं। अभिमातिसहं। अभिमातयः शत्रवः तान् सहते। योद्धुं हंतुं च शक्नोतीत्यभिमातिसहः तं, अभिमातिसहं। शत्रूणामभिभवितारं। दिवः द्युलोकस्यार्हः दिव्यः। भूमौ जातोऽपि अनेनैव देहेन द्युलोके उषितुमर्हः। तं। सुपर्णं। शोभने साममये पर्णे द्वौ पक्षौ यस्य असौ सुपर्णः। तं बृहद्रथंतरसामात्मकपक्षं। वयसा आयुषा बृहंतं महांतं। अतिदीर्घायुष्यं। जरामरणवर्जितं शूरं। अजय्यं। किं च। सुपर्णं गरुडं

[४५] कदाचित् "अभियत्प्रतीपम्" (अभियाति जनान् प्रति गच्छतीति अभियत्, शत्रुः, तं प्रतीपं वर्तयति, परास्यतीति) पठनीयं स्यात्?

अभि। अभिलक्ष्य यदन्यत्प्रतीकं रूपं तदुपजीविपरिचारकादिकं तदप्यहं नमस्कारेणोपतिष्ठे। उपस्थितोऽस्मि।

अथ विनतायाः पतिर्ऋषिर्जिगमिषया मेघवत् सिंहवत् च गर्जन्तं गरुडं श्रुत्वा प्रहर्षित उल्लासबलात्तत्रस्थः वामदेवादिषु समीपस्थेषु शृण्वत्सु इदमाहापरयर्च्चा। कश्यपपर्यायः तार्क्ष्य ऋषिरुवाच –

शब्देनाऽसौ पृथिवीं दिवं च
संनादयन्नेति नभो दिशश्च।
मन्ये शौंगेयो गरुडोऽरुणो वा
प्रियः पुत्रो भवति मे क्षयेऽद्य॥५॥

॥ *पदपाठः* ॥

शब्देन। असौ। पृथिवीं। दिवं। च। सं॰नादयन्। एति। नभः। दिशः। च। मन्ये। शौंगेयः। गरुडः। अरुणः। वा। प्रियः। पुत्रः। भवति। मे। क्षये। अद्य॥

॥ *भाष्यम्* ॥

असौ विप्रकृष्टप्रदेशवर्ती कोऽपि पुमान् शब्देन स्वगर्जितघोषेण पृथिवीं दिवं स्वर्गलोकं च संनादयन् प्रतिशब्दोत्पादनेन मुखरीकुर्वन् सन्नेति आगच्छति। नभः अंतरिक्षं मध्यलोकं दिशश्च संनादयन् एति। अहं इति मन्ये। संभावयामि। असौ मम पुत्रो भवति। आंतरानंदातिशयोद्गमादनुमिमीते। ननु पुत्रास्ते विविधाः, सन्त्यनेके शतशः कोऽसाविति। तत्राह। शौंगेयः। शुंगायाः सुतः। तस्याश्च द्वौ। तयोरन्यतर इत्यनुमानं कुरुते पक्षवातमाकर्ण्य। अरुणो वा। गरुडो वा। पंगोऽरुणस्य गतेरसंभवेऽप्यभिधानग्रहणं प्रेम्णा व्याकुलतया वैचित्त्यात्। प्रियो वल्लभः। स चाद्य मे मम क्षये निवासे अत्रत्ये आश्रमे एष्यति। इति सप्तदशो वर्गः॥

॥ अथ अष्टादशो वर्गः ॥

वामदेवर्षिः सुपर्णचरित्रं वर्णयति।

वामदेव उवाच –

ततः॑ सु॒पर्णः॑ सम॑याद् बु॒भु॒क्षि॒तो
मा॒त्राऽऽज्ञा॒तो भ॑क्ष॒यान्वै[46] निं॑षा॒दान्॥

आ॒कृष्यं॑ प॒क्षाव॑नु॒गम्यं॑मानान्त्-
सं॑प्रा॒प्यांस्तु मु॒खं प्र॒यच्छं॑ते॥६॥

॥ पदपाठः ॥

ततः॑। सु॒पर्णः॑। सं। अ॒यात्। बु॒भु॒क्षि॒त०। मा॒त्रा। आ॒०ज्ञातः॑। भ॒क्ष। यान्[46]। वै। नि॒०सा॒दान्। आ॒० कृष्यं॑। प॒क्षौ। अ॒नु॒० गम्यं॑मानान्[47]। सं॒० प्रा॒प्यान्। तु। मु॒खं॑। प्र॒० यच्छं॑ते॥

॥ भाष्यम् ॥

पाठांतरे 'भक्षयानु वै निषादान्'। मात्रा। आ० ज्ञातः। भक्षया० अनु। वै। नि० षादान्। अन्यत्समानं। ततः सुपर्णः मात्रा इति आज्ञातः सन् समयात् सम्यक् विधिना अयात्। अयासीत् अगमत्। इतीति किं? हे पुत्र। त्वं यान् यान् निषादान् किरातान् निश्चिनोषि। निश्चयेन जानासि। तान् तान् भक्ष अशान। भक्षय, खाद। किंलक्षणान् निषादान्? स्वौ पक्षौ आकृष्य विस्तार्य अनुगम्यमानान्। अनु लक्ष्यीकृत्य गम्यमानान् प्राप्यमानान्। पुनः किंलक्षणान् भिल्लान्? [यान्] मुखं व्यादाय विस्तार्य प्रयच्छते निजं मुखविवरं, तेषां प्रवेशार्थे ददते अर्पयते। तुभ्यं संप्राप्यान् सुखेन लभ्यान्। अधरं मुखकटाहं चिबुकं भूमौ स्थापयित्वा उत्तरं मुखकटाहमुद्धृत्य मध्यविवरे बृहंतमवकाशं कृत्वोपविष्टायते। मुखं [व्या]ददते। [एवं] सम्यक् लभ्यान्। एवं ते स्वयमेव तव मुखविवरे प्रवेक्ष्यंति। पाठान्तरे 'आकृष्य पक्षौ ननु गम्यमानान्'। ननु इति कोमलामन्त्रणे। पक्षौ आकृष्य विस्तीर्य गम्यमानान्। गते प्राप्यंत इति गम्यमानाः, तान्। 'मात्राज्ञातो भक्षयानु वै निषादान्' इति वा पाठः। मात्रा इति आज्ञातः सन्। इतीति किं? हे सुपर्ण। वै निश्चये। निषादान् भिल्लान् अनु वारं-वारं भक्षय। अनुसृत्य अनुसृत्य भक्षय। शेषं तुल्यं।

वामदेव उवाच –

उत्प्लु॒त्योत्प्लुं॑त्य भ॒क्षाणां॑ (णों?) नि॒षा॒दा॒न्वै वि॒ह॒ङ्गं॑मः।
गतें॑ कु॒ण्ठे तु चैकं॑स्मिन्द॒ह्यतें॑ स्माऽग्नि॒राशिं॑वत्॥७॥

---

[46] पाठश्चिन्त्यः। 'भक्षयन् वै निषादान्' इति साधीयः प्रतीयते। भाष्यकारस्तु 'भक्षयानु वै . . .' (भक्षय अनु वै . . .) इत्यपि पाठान्तरं क्वचिदुपलभ्यत इति सूचयति।

[47] 'आकृष्य पक्षौ ननु गम्यमानान्' इत्यपि क्वचित् पाठ इति भाष्यकृत्।

॥ *पदपाठः* ॥

उत्ऽप्लुत्य। उत्ऽप्लुत्य। भक्षाणां। निऽसादान्। वै। विऽहंगमः[४८]। गते। कंठे। तु। च। एकस्मिन्। दह्यते। स्म। अग्निराशिऽवत्॥

॥ *भाष्यम्* ॥

वै निश्चये। विहंगमः खगेंद्रः। उत्प्लुत्य उत्प्लुत्य। उच्छल्य उच्छल्य। उड्डीयोड्डीय, भक्षाणां सर्वेषां मध्यात् केवलान् निषादानेव जग्राहेति शेषः। अजीगिलदिति वा। च। अपरं। एकस्मिन् पुरुषे कंठे गते सति स दह्यते स्म। केनेव। अग्निराशिवत्। अग्निराशिनेव। अंगारेणेव।

वामदेव आह।

निर्धूमेऽविष्फुलिंगे चार्तः शुंगावचः स्मरन्।
अहो वीर्यं द्विजातीनां जातिमात्रोपजीविनाम्॥८॥

॥ *पदपाठः* ॥

निःऽधूमे। अऽविऽस्फुलिंगे। च। आर्त्तः। शुंगाऽवचः। स्मरन्। अहो इति। वीर्यं। द्विऽजातीनां। जातिमात्रऽउपजीविनां॥

॥ *भाष्यम्* ॥

अत्र 'एकस्मिन् कंठे गते सति' इत्यनुवर्तते। किंलक्षणे एकस्मिन् पुरुषे? निर्धूमे। अविस्फुलिंगे। विस्फुलिंगाः अग्निकणाः। तद्रहिते। स खलु आर्त्तः कंठे दग्धः सन् मनसा इत्युवाच। किं कुर्वन् सन्? शुंगायाः विनतायाः वचः स्मरन् सन्। 'अंगार इव विदहन्नेति कंठ'मिति मातुर्वचः। इतीति किं उवाच – अहोवीर्यं द्विजातीनां जातिमात्रोपजीविनामिति। अहो इत्याश्चर्ये। द्विजातीनां वीर्यं ब्रह्मतेजो विलोक्यताम्। कीदृशानाम्? जातिमात्रोपजीविनां। जातिमात्रं उपजीवंति तच्छीलाः जातिमात्रोपजीविनः। तेषां।

अथोत्तरया सुपर्णः कंठात् द्विजं बहिर्निःकाशयितुं विप्रं प्रति आह। गरुड उवाच। गलमध्ये स्थितं विप्रं प्रति –

---

[४८] 'विहंगमः' इति मन्त्रे पठितस्य शब्दस्य पदपाठे 'विऽहंगमः' इतिरूपेण पदच्छेदः कुतूहलं जनयति। पदच्छेदे प्रादय उपसर्गा एव पृथक्क्रियन्ते। नात्र 'वि'-वर्णस्तादृशः। विहं, विहायसं, विहायसा वा गच्छतीति विहंगमः, विहगो विहंगो वा।

निष्क्रंमाऽस्माद्[४१] द्विंजश्रेष्ठ न भक्षस्त्वं हि में भवेः।
एते भक्षा मयाऽत्रोप्ता न त्वं शोंचितुमर्हंसि॥९॥

॥ *पदपाठः* ॥

निः। क्रम। अस्मात्। द्विज० श्रेष्ठ। न। भक्षः। त्वं। हि। मे। भवेः। एते। भक्षाः। मया। अत्र। उप्ताः। न। त्वं। शोचितुं। अर्हंसि॥

॥ *भाष्यम्* ॥

तेन ब्राह्मणेन इतरा गृहीता काचित् निषादस्त्री। तस्याः पूर्वभर्तुर्निषादादुत्पन्नाः पंचषाः पुत्राः। ते च मात्रा विप्रगेहे भार्यात्वं प्राप्तुं गच्छन्त्या सहैव तत्र नीताः। विप्रस्य दुराचारस्य तेषु परपुत्रेष्वपि स्व स्वपुत्रेष्विव स्नेह उत्पन्नः। तान् इमे मत्पुत्रा इत्यभिमानवान् मन्यते स्म। तस्य ते पुत्राः सा च निषादी भार्या एतत्सर्वं कुटुंबं सुपर्णेन प्रागेव गिलितं, पश्चात् स दुराचारो विप्रो गिलितः। तेन गलमध्ये दग्धं। ततो गलात् तं बहिर्निःकाशयितुं गरुडः प्रायतत। तथापि स द्विजः स्वकुटुंबं विना न निःसरति। तदा गरुडः अनयच्चर्या तं विप्रं बहिर्निःकाशयितुं प्रबोधयति।

हे द्विज। ते त्वत्कुटुंबमनुष्याः मया अत्र अस्मिन् उदरे उप्ताः प्रक्षिप्ताः। एतेषां वापनमुदरे कृतम्। '*टुवप्*' बीजसंताने। अस्य धातोः प्रयोगः उप्ताः इति। एतान् तव मनुष्यान् आमाशये प्रवेशितान् त्वं शोचितुं नार्हसि। हे द्विजश्रेष्ठ। त्वं अस्मात् गलमध्यात् निःक्रम। निःसर। हि। यस्मात् त्वं मे भक्ष्यः न भवेः। एते तु त्वन्मनुष्याः भक्ष्याः। अत एव मया अत्र स्वोदरे उप्ताः। त्वं तु एतान् स्वकुटुंबमनुष्यान् शोचितुं नार्हसि। अथ विप्रः प्रत्युत्तरमाह।

ब्राह्मण उवाच –

न मंन्ये जीवंदात्मानं भार्यापुंत्रैर्विंवर्जिंतः।
द्विजस्तु सनिंषादीकः ससुतंस्त्वन्मुखे विषम्॥१०॥

॥ *पदपाठः* ॥

न। मन्ये। जीवंत्० आत्मानं। भार्या० पुंत्रैः। वि०वर्जिंतः।
द्विजंः। तु। स०निंषादीकः। स०सुतंः। त्वत्०मुखे। विषं॥

---

[४१] 'अस्माद्' इत्यस्य स्थाने मूलपाठः कदाचित् 'अस्मत्' (अपादाने पञ्चमी) यदि वा 'आस्यांत्' (मुखात्) आसीदिति अनुमीयते।

॥ *भाष्यम्* ॥

अहं जीवदात्मानं शुभं न मन्ये। मह्यं हितं न मन्ये। जीवंतं आत्मानं शुभं शोभनं श्लाघ्यं न मन्ये। गुणकरं न मन्ये। त्वत्कंठमध्यात् न बहिर्निर्गमिष्यामि। किं भूतः। भार्यापुत्रैश्च वर्जितो रहितः। हीनः। तु पुनः। हे गरुड। सनिषादीकः निषादीसहितः। निषाद्या भार्यया संयुक्तः ससुतः सुतैः सहितश्च त्वन्मुखे तव मुखे स्थितोऽयं मदात्मकः मल्लक्षणः तव साक्षात् विषमेव। विषवद्भविष्यति। विषं यथा प्राणान् हरति तथा प्राणान् हरिष्यति॥

अपरयच्र्चा वामदेवः इतिवृत्तं वर्णयति। पुत्रभार्यासहितं तं उद्वास्य गरुडः कृतार्थोऽभूत्।

वामदेव उवाच –

सजं॑नं तं द्विजं॑ त्यक्त्वा ती॒र्त्वा चा॒ऽऽज्ञां वि॒ह॒ङ्गं॑मः॥
इतं॑रा॒न्भक्षं॑यित्वै॒व सि॒द्धिं या॒तस्त॒तो॑ ध्रु॒वम्॥११॥

॥ *पदपाठः* ॥

स० जं॑नं। तं। द्विजं॑। त्य॒क्त्वा। ती॒र्त्वा। च॒। आ॒ज्ञां। वि॒०
हं॒गं॑मः। इतं॑रान्। भक्षं॑यित्वा। ए॒व। सि॒द्धिं। या॒तः। ततः॑। ध्रु॒वं॥

॥ *भाष्यम्* ॥

सजनं सपरिवारं तं द्विजं कंठात् त्यक्त्वा उद्गीर्य, अपरं च मातुराज्ञाः सर्वास्तीर्त्वा निस्तीर्य। 'निषादानां मध्यगतं ब्राह्मणं कदाचित् मा खादीः' इतीमां मातुराज्ञां अन्याश्च तीर्त्वा। संपाद्य। ततः इतरान् निषादान् भक्षयित्वा। ततः कार्यं गतः। ध्रुवं निश्चितं।

अथोड्डीय स्वर्गलोकद्वारे दैवात् आगतं बृहस्पतिमृषिं दृष्ट्वा तं प्रणम्य कार्यसिद्धिं प्रार्थयामासापरयच्र्चा। इति अष्टादशो वर्गः ॥

॥ दशमं सूक्तम् ॥

॥ अथ एकोनविंशो वर्गः ॥

गरुड उवाच –

अहं सुपर्णः पततां वरिष्ठो
मात्राशिष्टः सोमहारश्चरामि।
भौजिष्यमृच्छत्यरुणस्य माता
तन्माऽशिवेनाभि भव द्विजेन्द्र॥१॥

॥ *पदपाठः* ॥

अहं। सु० पर्णः। पततां। वरिष्ठः। मात्रा० शिष्टः[५०]। सोम० हारः। चरामि। भौजिष्यं। ऋच्छति। अरुणस्य। माता। तत्। मा[५१]। अशिवेन। अभि। भव। द्विज०इन्द्र।

॥ *भाष्यम्* ॥

हे बृहस्पते अहं सुपर्णो नाम पततां पक्षिणां वरिष्ठः श्रेष्ठः मात्रा शिष्टः अनुशिष्टः शिक्षितः आज्ञातः सन् चरामि। सोमहारः सोमस्य हरणार्थी। कस्मादित्यत आह अरुणस्य माता विनता भौजिष्यं दासत्वं ऋच्छति प्राप्नोति। तत्तस्मात्कारणात् हे द्विजेन्द्र। ब्राह्मणेश्वर। अशिवेन अकल्याणेन अशुभेन शापाभिचारादिना मा अभिभव। मा पराभव। अर्थात् 'माम्' इत्यध्याह्रियते। मां मा अभिभव। मा पराभव। मम पराभवं मा कार्षीः। भौजिष्यं दासीत्वं। भुजिष्या दासी। भुजिष्यायाः भावः भौजिष्यं। उत्तरया बृहस्पतिः सुपर्णस्याशिषं प्रयुज्य कुशलं पृच्छति।

---

[५०] 'मात्राशिष्टः' इत्युत्तरपदप्रधानस्य तत्पुरुषस्य 'मातृ–आशिष्टः' इत्येवंरूपः पदच्छेदः साधुतरः स्यात्। 'मात्रा० शिष्टः' इत्येवंरूपेऽलुक्समासनिर्माणे किमौचित्यम्?

[५१] 'मा' इत्येतत्पदं 'माम्' इत्यस्मिन्नर्थे त्वनुदात्तम्, परं निषेधार्थे उदात्तम्। अतः 'मा' इत्यस्यानुदात्तत्वं चिन्त्यम्। 'माम् अशिवेन अभिभव' इति सर्वथा प्रसंगविरुद्धमर्थं जनयति। पदपाठमातृकालेखकस्य प्रमादः प्रतीयते। संहितापाठे तु 'मा' निषेधार्थमेव।

बृहस्पतिरुवाच गरुडं प्रति –

अभ्यायुंषा वर्चंसा त्वा वंदामि
कच्चिंद् वस्तात् कुशंलं गृहेषुं॥
कच्चिंद् गरुत्मत्यंरुणस्यं माता
न शोंचति स्पर्शंनं [स्पर्धंनम्[५२]] मानंसं वा॥२॥

॥ *पदपाठः* ॥

अभि। आयुंषा। वर्चंसा। त्वा। वदामि। कत्। चित्। वः।
तात। कुशंलं। गृहेषुं। कत्। चित्। गरुत्मती। अरुणस्यं।
माता। न। शोचति। स्पर्शंनं [स्पर्द्धंनं]। मानंसं। वा॥

॥ *भाष्यम्* ॥

बृहस्पतिराह। हे गरुड। अहं त्वा त्वां अभिवदामि। प्रत्यभिवादनवाक्यं प्रयुंजे। केन। आयुषा वर्चसा च। कोऽर्थः? 'आयुष्मान् भव सौम्य३'। 'वर्चस्वी च भव'। वर्चस्तेजः। हे तात। पुत्र। कच्चिदिति कोमलामन्त्रणे। भवद्गृहेषु कुशलमस्ति? कच्चित् प्रश्ने। अरुणस्य। माता गरुत्मती पक्षिणी विनता। स्पर्शनं स्पर्शनेन्द्रियं स्वकीयं। मानसं मनश्च न शोचति। तयोरुभयोः शोकं न करोति। स्पर्शनेन्द्रिये पृष्ठे उह्यमानानां सर्पाणां संयोगः दुःखदः। मानसे शत्रूणां चित्तानुवृत्त्या वर्तनं दुःखदम्। शत्रुचित्तानुकूलं आचरणं। अतः स्वस्य स्पर्शनं मानसं वा किं न शोचतीत्युक्तम्।

अथ परस्याः ऋचस्त्रिभिः पादैर्बृहस्पतिः प्रेम्णा वदति। तुरीयपादेन तु गरुडः स्वकार्यमावेदयति। बृहस्पतिरुवाच –

वेदाहमेतत्कुशंलं गृहेषुं
दास्याद् दुःखं वेंदयते सुपर्णी[५३]।

---

[५२] भाष्यकारेणात्र स्वीकृतः पाठः "स्पर्शनम्" किन्तु मूलपाठान्वितेषु हस्तलेखेषु पदपाठेऽपि च 'स्पर्द्धनम्' इत्येव प्राप्यते यत्तु साधीयः प्रतिभाति। वयमत्र भाष्यकारमनुसरामः।

[५३] वेदयते=विज्ञापयति। 'सुपर्णी' इति प्रथमान्तस्य पदस्य स्थाने द्वितीयान्तं 'सुपर्णीम्' इति पदं कदाचिन्मूलपाठे आसीदित्यस्माकमूहा। 'दुःखं सुपर्णी वेदयते'=वेदनाम् उत्पादयति।

आ मं॑न्त्रये त्वा पततां वरि॒ष्ठ
पतां॒म्य॒हं त्रिं॒दि॒वमि॒न्दु॒मच्छं॑॥३॥

॥ *पदपाठः* ॥

वेदं॑। अ॒हं। ए॒तत्। कु॒शलं॑। गृ॒हेषु॑। दा॒स्यात्। दुः॒ऽखं। वे॒द॒य॒ते। सु॒० प॒र्णी। आ। म॒ंत्र॒ये॒। त्वा॒। प॒त॒तां। व॒रि॒ष्ठ। पतां॑मि। अ॒हं। त्रि॒० दि॒वं। इ॒न्दुं॑। अच्छं॑॥

॥ *भाष्यम्* ॥

बृहस्पतिराह। हे गरुड। अहं एतद्वेद। जानामि। एतत् किं? सुपर्णी दुःखं वेदयति लभते। ज्ञापयति वा। कस्मात्? दास्यात्। अहं तु स्वर्गे स्वस्थाने सुधर्मायां गंतुकामोऽस्मि। त्वां आमंत्रये। आपृच्छे। अथ चतुर्थपादेन गरुडस्तं प्रत्युवाच –

हे गुरो, अहं त्रिदिवं स्वर्गं प्रति पतामि उत्पतामि। किमर्थं। इन्दुं सोमं अमृतं अच्छ। अभिलक्ष्य। उद्दिश्य। पुनर्बृहस्पतिर्गरुडाय आशिषमाशास्ते।

य॒ज्ञस्यं॑ त्वा॒ रक्षं॑तु॒ दक्षि॑णाश्च॒
वारं॑ व॒रीय॒ं पतं॑त॒ः पूर्वं॑मस्तु ते[५४]।

ऋ॒चो यजूं॑षि॒ परिं॑तः[५५] सुप॒र्ण॒
सर्वा॑स्त्वा॒ऽहोत्रा॑[५६] अ॒भि चं॑ श्रयन्ताम्॥४॥

॥ *पदपाठः* ॥

य॒ज्ञस्यं॑। त्वा॒। रक्षं॑तु। दक्षिं॑णाः। च॒। वारं॑। व॒रीयं॑। पतं॑तः। पूर्वं॑। अ॒स्तु॒। ते॒। ऋचं॑ः। यजूं॑षि। परिं॑तः। सु॒०प॒र्ण॒। सर्वाः॑। त्वा॒। अ॒होत्रा॑। अ॒भि। च॒। श्र॒य॒न्ता॒म्।

---

[५४] भाष्यकारेणात्र मूले 'अश्नुते' इति पाठो धृतः किन्तु 'अस्तु ते' इतिरूपेणैव व्याख्यातम्। ग्रूबेमहाशयेन उपयुक्तानां षण्णां मातृकाणां मध्ये मातृकाद्वयमिममपपाठं धारयति।

[५५] एलिमार् ग्रूबे महाशयः 'परितः' इत्यस्य स्थाने पदपाठेन संपुष्टं 'पततः' इति पाठं स्वीकरोति (द्वितीयपादात् पुनरावृत्तम्)। भाष्यकारेणादृतः 'परितः' पाठोऽपि परम्पराप्राप्तः।

[५६] ग्रूबेमहोदयेनात्रोररीकृतः पाठः 'सर्वास्त्वा अहोरात्रा' इति। भाष्यकारः 'अहोत्राः' इति पठति अस्माकं मतुं तु 'हौत्रा' (हौत्रम् इत्यस्य बहुवचनं)=होमयागाः इत्यस्य पक्षेऽस्ति।

॥ *भाष्यम्* ॥

वरीयं वर्यं वरणीयं वरिष्ठं वरणार्हं सोमं। वारं उदकरूपं द्रवरसं प्रति पतन्तं गच्छन्तं त्वा त्वां। यज्ञस्य यज्ञानां समूहः। [तस्य] याः दक्षिणाः, समृद्धिहेतवः, ताः दक्षिणाः त्वा त्वां रक्षंतु। पूर्वमस्तु ते। ते तव कार्यसिद्धिः पूर्वं प्रागेव आदावेव शीघ्रमेवास्तु। हे सुपर्ण, गरुड। ऋचः यजूंषि च त्वां परितः समन्तात् पान्तु। [अथ] च अपरं सर्वाः अहोत्राः (०त्राणि) कर्मविशेषाः त्वा त्वां अभि अभ्येत्य श्रयंतां सेवंताम्।

अथोपक्रमकाले सुपर्णः स्वपितरमिष्टदेवतां स्मरति।

गरुड उवाच –

स्वस्त्ययनं ताक्ष्यमरिष्टनेमिं
महद्भूतं वायसं देवतानाम्।
असुरघ्नमिन्द्रसखं समत्सु
बृहद्यशो नावमिवारुहेम॥५॥

॥ *पदपाठः* ॥

स्वस्ति० अयनं। ताक्ष्यं। अरिष्ट० नेमिं। महत्० भूतं। वायसं। देवतानां। असुर० घ्नं। इन्द्र० सखं। समत्०सु। बृहत्। यशः। नावंऽइव। आ। रुहेम॥

॥ *भाष्यम्* ॥

स्वस्त्ययनं ताक्ष्यं। वयं ताक्ष्यमृषिं कश्यपमस्मत्पितरं स्मृत्वा मनसा प्रणम्य च समत्सु संग्रामेषु बृहत् यशः आरुहेम। किमिव? नावमिव तरणसाधनं। किंलक्षणं ताक्ष्यं? स्वस्तेः अविनाशस्य अयनं स्थानं प्रापकं अरिष्टनेमिं। न रिष्टः नेमिः मर्यादा शास्त्रमर्यादा यस्य। '*रिष्*' हिंसायां। रिष्टः हिंसितः महद्भूतं महानुभावं देवतानां सुराणां वायसं वयःप्रमाणज्ञं। असुरघ्नं। असुराः कामक्रोधलोभगर्वशोकमोहाः। इन्द्रस्य सखा इन्द्रसखः। यज्ञप्रवर्तकत्वात्।

सुपर्णः अमृतार्थी कार्यसिद्धये इष्टदेवताः स्मरति –

अंहोमुचमांगिरसं गयं च
स्वस्त्यात्रेयं मनसा च ताक्ष्यम्।

प्रयंतपाणिः शरणं प्रपंद्ये
स्वस्ति संबाधेष्वभंयं नो अस्तु॥६॥

॥ *पदपाठः* ॥

अंहःऽमुचं। आंगिरंसं। गयं। च। स्वस्त्यांत्रेयं। मनंसा। च। ताक्ष्यैं। प्रयंतऽपाणिः। शरणं। प्र। पद्ये। स्वस्ति। सं० बाधेषु। अभंयं। नः। अस्तु।

॥ *भाष्यम्* ॥

अहं आंगिरसं अंगिरसो वंशे उत्पन्नं गयं ऋषिं प्लुतेः सूनुं शरणं प्रपद्ये। कीदृशं गयं। अंहोमुचं। अंहांसि पापानि मोचयतीत्यंहोमुक् तं च। अपरं स्वस्त्यात्रेयं नाम अत्रिसूनुं शरणं प्रपद्ये। मनसा चेतसा। ताक्ष्यैं पितरं च। प्रयतौ संपुटीकृतौ पाणी यस्य मे। नः संबाधेषु कालेषु नः अभयमस्तु। संपूर्णा बाधा पीडा येषु ते संबाधाः। इति एकोनविंशो वर्गः ॥

॥ अथ विंशो वर्गः ॥

अथ गरुडे अमृतकोशगृहद्वारे आगते सति इन्द्रश्चिन्ताविष्टः गुरुं पृच्छति –

अपिं स्वित्किञ्चिंदिह भूतमस्तिं
भविष्यद्वाऽपिं बृहस्पते।
यन्में रक्षां निहिंतामतींत्य
वीर्येंण सोमं सहंसा हरेंदितः॥७॥

॥ *पदपाठः* ॥

अपिं। स्वित्। किं। चित्। इह। भूतं। अस्तिं। भविष्यत्। वा। अपिं। बृहस्पते। यत्। मे। रक्षां। नि० हिंतां। अतिं० इत्य। वीर्येणं (वीर्येंण)। सोमं। सहंसा। हरेंत्। इतः॥

॥ *भाष्यम्* ॥

हे गुरो। अपि संभावनायां। स्विदिति प्रश्ने। इत्थं मया संभाव्यते। इह त्रिलोक्यां एतादृशं भूतं प्राणिस्वरूपं किंचिदपि अस्ति। भूतं पुरा जातं न वा? त्वं तु त्रिकालदर्शी। यद्वा। ईदृशं प्राणिवस्तु किमपि भविष्यत्। भविष्यति न वा? यत् प्राणि वीर्येण शक्त्या मे मम सोमं इतः सुरलोकात् हरेत्। हृत्वा प्रयातीति। किं कृत्वा? मे मम रक्षां रक्षणं नानाविधं आवरणं अतीत्य उल्लंघ्य सहसा बलेन।

कीदृशीं रक्षां। मया परितः निहितां स्थापितां प्रयुक्तां। एवमद्भुतं पूर्वं कदापि भूतं जातं, अथवा भविष्यत् कालान्तरे भविष्यति? तद्वद॥

उत्तरया बृहस्पतिरिन्द्रं प्रत्युवाच –

षष्टिं सहस्त्राणि रजस आचितानां
नवनवतीर्वेद्याः शतानि।

आ हरिष्यसि गरुडो वैनतेयः
प्रसह्य[57] सोमं निहितो[58] जिहीरिषुः॥८॥

॥ *पदपाठः*॥

षष्टिं। सहस्त्राणि। रजसः। आ० चितानां। नव। नवतीः। वेद्याः। शतानि। आ। हरिष्यसि। गरुडः। वैनतेयः। प्र० सह्य। सोमं। नि०हितः। जिहीरिषुः॥

॥ *भाष्यम्* ॥

हे इन्द्र। जिहीर्षुः। हर्तुमिच्छुर्गरुडः विनतासुतः त्वया आचितानां आसमंतात् रोपितानां परितः स्थापितानां, सोमस्य रक्षणार्थं परितः नियुक्तानां रजसः इति, रजसां लोकानां सुरगन्धर्वयक्षरक्षःप्रभृतीनां सोमपालानां षष्टिं सहस्त्राणि। तथा ९ नव संख्याकाः ९० नवतीश्च, जित्वेतिशेषः। जित्वा गरुडः प्रसह्य बलात्कारेण सोमं आहरिष्यति ग्रहीष्यति। रजस इति व्यत्ययेन बहुवचनार्थे एकवचनं। रजसामिति ज्ञेयम्। *"लोका रजांस्युच्यंत"* इति यास्कः (४.१९)। रजसां लोकानां वेद्याः परितः। आचितानां नियुक्तानां व्यापारितानां। वेदिः अमृतकुंभनिक्षेपणभूमिः। निक्षेपणप्रदेशः। सुधासंगोपनप्रदेशः। तस्याः परितो रक्षणार्थे व्यापारितानां। किंलक्षणं सोमं? निहितं। तत्र आरोपितं। गुप्तं। स्थापितं। जिहीर्षुः इति पदस्य छंदसि रेफे इकारं प्रवेश्य सुखोच्चारणार्थं पृथग्वर्णप्रयोगः। अर्थकाले जिहीर्षुरित्येव। अपरयेंद्रो गुरुं गरुत्मतः संभवं सर्वं पृच्छति। इंद्र उवाच। गुरुं प्रति –

---

[57] 'प्रसह्य' इत्यस्य पदपाठे भाष्ये च सम्मानितस्य पदस्य स्थाने ग्रूबे 'प्रासहा' पठति। द्वयोरपि पदयोरर्थः प्रायः एक एव (बलात्)। किन्तु 'प्रासहा' प्राचीनतरम्, ऋग्वेदादिषु समादृतम् पदम्। अन्यच्च, अस्माकं पदपाठमातृका 'प्रसह्य'-पदे यदुदात्तद्वयं प्रदर्शयति (प्र०सह्य) तदशुद्धम्। अस्माभिस्तच्छोधितम्।

[58] ग्रूबेमहाशयेनात्र स्वीकृतः, पदपाठेनापि समर्थितः, पाठः 'निहितः' इति, यस्तु भाष्यकारेण संशोध्य 'निहितम्' इतिवत् पठितः।

कुतः स्विज्जातः कस्माल्लोकात्कतरस्याः पृथिव्याः।
भौवनं यो युयुत्सति धनुर्ग्राहमनुत्तमम्॥९॥

॥ *पदपाठः* ॥

कुतः। स्वित्। जातः। कस्मात्। लोकात्। कतरस्याः। पृथिव्याः।
भौवनं। यः। युयुत्सति धनुःऽग्राहं। अनुत्तमम्।

॥ *भाष्यम्* ॥

हे बृहस्पते। कुतः कस्मात् जनकाज्जातः। कस्यां वा मातरि। स्विदिति प्रश्ने। कस्मात् लोकात् आगतोऽत्र? किं भूर्लोकाद्वा, उत भुवर्लोकात्। आहोस्वित् स्वर्लोकात्? यद्वा महर्लोकादिभ्य इत ऊर्ध्वं लोकेभ्यः प्रकारान्तरेणार्थः। किं मनुष्याणां लोकात् ज्ञातिमध्यात्। उत यक्षाणां किं वा गन्धर्वाणाम्, आहोस्वित् सिद्धानां यद्वा नागानां अथवा उत रक्षसां असुराणां वा। तथा पृथिव्यां बहुविधाः संति पृथिव्यो भूमयः। मेरुपृष्ठभूमिः। हिमभूमिः। दृषद्भूमिः। मृद्भूमिः। ज्योतिर्भूमिः। अंधकारभूमिः। हेमभूमिः। रत्नभूमिः। सिकतामयी भूमिः। आदर्शतलसंनिभा भूमिः। जन्तुमती भूमिः। निर्जन्तुर्भूमिः। इत्येवमादयो बह्व्यो भूमयः नानारूपाः संति, तासां मध्ये कतरस्याः भूमेः सकाशादसाविहागतः। असौ कः। यः पुरुषः भौवनं मदीयतया सुधारक्षणे नियुक्तं विश्वकर्माणं युयुत्सति योद्धुमिच्छति। किंलक्षणं भौवनं विश्वकर्माणं। धनुर्ग्राहं। धनुर्धरं। कीदृशं। अनुत्तमम्। न विद्यते उत्तम उत्कृष्टतमोऽन्यः कोऽपि यस्मात् असौ अनुत्तमं तम्।

उत्तरया मघवानं प्रति गुरुरुत्तरमाह।

गुरुरुवाचेन्द्रं प्रति –

सुपर्णी विनता नाम तपोऽतप्यत दुष्टरम्।
तस्यां जातो गरुडो वैनतेयो
यश्च सोमं हर्त्ता शकुनिस्तस्यं विद्धि॥१०॥

॥ *पदपाठः* ॥

सु०पर्णी। वि०नता। नाम। तपः। अतप्यत। दुःऽतरं। तस्यां। जातः। गरुडः। वैनतेयः। यः। च। सोमं। हर्त्ता। शकुनिः। तस्यं। विद्धि॥

॥ *भाष्यम्* ॥

[दुष्टरमित्यस्य स्थाने] दुस्तपमिति वा पाठः[५९]। हे इन्द्र तस्य स्वरूपं विद्धि जानीहि। यः सोमं हर्त्ता। सा विनता नाम सुपर्णी पक्षिणी। शोभनानि पर्णानि पिच्छानि यस्याः सा सुपर्णी। सा दुस्तरं तपः अतप्यत। तप्यते स्म। तेपे। [अथवा] दुःखेन तप्यते इति दुस्तपं। सा का? यस्यां गरुडो जातः। स च वैनतेय इति ख्यातः। इति विंशतितमो वर्गः॥

---

[५९] 'दुश्चरम्' इति साधुतरं स्यात् (सं०)।

॥ एकादशं सूक्तम् ॥

॥ अथ एकविंशो वर्गः ॥

इन्द्र उवाच –

अहं स्विदिन्द्रं उत वैनतेयः
कंतरः शुंश्राव भुवंनानीच्छन्।
इन्दुं परांञ्चं निहिंतं विचक्षणं
ममेत्तु सोमं सहंसा हरेद्यत्॥१॥

॥ *पदपाठः* ॥

अहं। स्वित्। इन्द्रंः। उत। वैनतेयः। कतरः। शुश्राव। भुवंनानि। इच्छन्। इंदुं। परांञ्चं। नि० हिंतं। वि०चक्षणं। ममं। इत्। तु। सोमं। सहंसा। हरेत्। यत्।

॥ *भाष्यम्* ॥

हे बृहस्पते। स्विदिति वितर्के प्रश्ने। किं अहं वा इन्द्रः ऐन्द्रपदस्य स्वामी। अधिष्ठाता परमेश्वरः। '*इदि*' परमैश्वर्ये। सर्वेषां देवानां राजा। हे गुरो, उत अथवा। वैनतेयः इन्द्रः, ऐन्द्रपदस्य स्वामी, अधिष्ठाता, स्वर्गस्य राज्यस्य भोक्ता? ऐन्द्रपदाधिष्ठाता सुराणां प्रभुः। अनयोरुभयोर्मद्वैनतेययोर्मध्ये कः इन्द्रः। इन्द्रत्वं कः प्राप्तः। अहं वा इन्द्रः। उत वैनतयो गरुडो वा इन्द्रः। यः इन्द्रो भवति तं कथय। किं कुर्वन् सन् इन्द्रो भवति। किं कुर्वन् सन् अहमिन्द्रो भवामि। उत किं कुर्वन् सन् वैनतेयो गरुडः इन्द्रो भवति। भुवनानि त्रीणि स्वर्गमर्त्यलोकपातालाख्यानि इच्छन्। तेषां त्रयाणां भुवनानामाधिपत्यं इच्छन् सन् इन्द्रो भवति। अनयोर्मद्गरुडयोर्मध्ये कतरः इति कः इन्दुं सोमं शुश्राव। अमृतं अज्ञासीत्। अत्र श्रवणं नाम ज्ञानं, सोमं ज्ञातवान्। सोमस्य संगोपितस्य स्थानं निक्षेपप्रदेशं कः ज्ञातवान्। अहं वा वैनतेयो वा तद्ब्रूहि। किं लक्षणं इन्दुं सोमं? परांचं निहितं। पराङ्मुखं निक्षिप्तं। संगोपितं। पराङ्मुखमिति कोऽर्थः। अतीव

अप्रसिद्धे स्थले दुर्विज्ञाने निहितमित्यर्थः। किंलक्षणं इंदुं? विचक्षणं प्रवीणं। जरामरणनिवारणदक्षं। तत् कुतः इत्थं अभूतकल्पना। एवमसंभाव्यसंभावना किमिति विधीयते। अयुक्तं कथमुद्भाव्यते। तत्राह। यत् यस्मात् कारणात्। मम इत् ममैव सोमं, मदीयां सुधां, असौ सहसा प्रसह्य बलेन हरेत्। अतो दुःसहनिर्वेदबलाद्यत्किंचिद्ब्रवीमि। इत्याशयः। सुपुरोधाः शचीपतिं प्रत्युत्तरयति।

गुरुरुवाच इन्द्रं प्रति –

तवेन्द्र जातमुत यज्जनिष्यत्
तवेन्द्र भूतमुत यद् भविष्यत्।
तव दिशः प्रदिश उद्दिशो बृहत्
तवाऽशिषा प्रशिषा सर्वमुच्यते॥२॥

॥ *पदपाठः* ॥

तव। इन्द्र। जातं। उत। यत्। जनिष्यत्। तव। इंद्र। भूतं। उत। यत्। भविष्यत्। तव। दिशः। प्र० दिशः। उत्० दिशः। बृहत्। तव। आ० शिषा। प्र० शिषा। सर्वं। उच्यते।

॥ *भाष्यम्* ॥

हे इन्द्र। यत् जगत् जातं इतोऽर्वागुत्पन्नं उत अपि च यद्वर्तमानं प्राणिजातं यच्च भविष्यत्। कालान्तरे जनिष्यते। उत्पत्स्यते। तत् सर्वं त्रैकालिकं प्राणिजातं देवतिर्यङ्नरादिकं तवैव उपजीवकं। त्वमेवोपजीवति त्वामेव श्रयते। सेवते। त्वं हि तस्य सर्वस्य प्रभुरधिपः। तथा यत् प्राणहीनं वस्तु। सौधविमानगृहनदीवृक्ष-पर्वतपंचमहाभूतादिकं तदपि तवैव त्वदीयमेव। तस्यापि त्वमेवेशः। किंलक्षणं प्राणं? क्षित्यादिकं। भूतं प्राचीनकाले निष्पन्नं। तथा उत, भवत् अधुनापि निःपाद्यमानं। यत् भविष्यत् आयत्यां भविष्यति। तदेव विस्तारयति। दिशः प्राच्यादयः चतस्रः तव। प्रदिशः। आग्नेयीप्रमुख्यः ईशानांताः चतस्रः तवैव। तथा प्रदिशः। पातालप्रभृतयः तथा दिग्विदिशोरंतरा वर्तमानाः। तव। उद्दिशः। ऊर्ध्वस्थाः लोकाः ताः उद्दिशोऽपि तव। तासां त्वं स्वामी। यत्किंचित् बृहत् महाप्रमाणं व्यापकं तदपि च। तवैव या आशीः शुभचिन्तनं। तया सर्वं जगत् कृतार्थं उच्यते। तथा तव या प्रशीः। तया प्रशिषा त्वदीयया सर्वं कृतार्थं उच्यते। प्रार्थ्यमानात् प्राप्तं वरदानवाक्यमाशीः। अप्रार्थ्यमानाल्लब्धं वरदानवचः प्रशीः, इति इयान् भेदः। तया प्रशिषा सर्वं वस्तु इष्टं मनोरथगोचरं लभ्यते। कृतार्थं चोच्यते॥

अथापरया विनतोड्डीय सूर्यमण्डलपर्यन्तं गत्वा तत्रार्करथस्थं स्वज्येष्ठपुत्रमरुणं प्रति व्याकुलांतःकरणत्वाद्युक्तायुक्तविवेकशून्या सत्येवमाह। विनतोवाचारुणं प्रति –

म॒हान्घोष॑ उ॒परि॑ श्रूयते॒ऽसौ
क॒थं पु॑त्र॒ भ्रात॑र॒ं नाऽभिधा॑वसि॥
एक॑ः सुप॒र्णो॑ ब॒हव॑श्च॒ देवा॑
न॒ह्यै॑न॒मेक॒ः प्र स॑हेत श॒क्रः॥३॥

॥ *पदपाठः* ॥

म॒हान्। घोष॑ः। उ॒परि॑। श्रू॒य॒ते॒। अ॒सौ। क॒थं। पु॒त्र। भ्रात॑रं। न। अ॒भि। धा॒व॒सि॒। एक॑ः। सु॒॰प॒र्णः। ब॒हव॑ः। च॒। देवा॑ः। न॒हि। ए॒नं। एक॑ः। प्र। स॒हे॒त॒। श॒क्रः।

॥ *भाष्यम्* ॥

विनतोवाचारुणं प्रति –

हे पुत्र अरुण उपर्युपरि अन्तरिक्षे अत्यूर्ध्वं स्थिते। स्वर्लोकेऽसौ महान् प्रबलो घोषः कोलाहलः श्रूयते। युद्ध्यमानानां वीराणां परुषो ध्वनिः। तथापि हे पुत्र अरुण त्वं भ्रातरं गरुडं परैरनेकैरेकमेवाभिभूयमानं जानन्नपि कथं नाभिधावसि। अभिलक्ष्य किं न धावसि साहायिकं विधातुं। सुपर्णः खल्वेक एव। सुधारक्षकाः देवास्तु बहवः, [अ]परिसंख्येयाः मिलिताः। यदि शक्र एक एव भवेत् असहायः। तर्हि एनं सुपर्णं न सहेत। अस्य पराक्रमं सोढुं न शक्नुयात्। परंतु तथा नास्ति। अतो गरुडः पराभूयते। तं गरुडं पराभूतं जानन् त्वं, हे अरुण, कथं अभिलक्ष्य न धावसि॥

इत्थमत्याकुलमनस्का पंगोर्गतौ सामर्थ्यं नास्तीति विवेकशून्यत्वादरुणमुपालम्भनेन धिक्करोति। अपरया सूर्यसारथिर्योद्धुमशक्नुवान आत्मानं गर्हयन् परितप्तहृदयो मातरं बोधयन्नाह।

अरुण उवाच मातरं प्रति –

अ॒भ्रा॒ता भ्रात्रा॑ गरु॒डौ॑ऽरु॒णेना॑-
पु॒त्रा शु॒ंगा विन॑ता सुप॒र्णी।

नहि मातररुणो याति नूनं
गच्छं स्वयं त्रिदिवं सोमहारः॥४॥

॥ *पदपाठः* ॥

अभ्राता। भ्रात्रा। गरुडः अरुणेन। अपुत्रा। शुंगा। वि०नता। सु०पर्णी। नहि। मातः। अरुणः। याति। नूनं। गच्छं। स्वयं। त्रि०दिवं। सोम० हारः॥

॥ *भाष्यम्* ॥

अरुणः कथयति। हे मातः विनते। गरुडः अरुणेन मया भ्रात्रा अभ्रातैव। नास्ति भ्राता अस्येति अभ्राता। अरुणेन पुत्रेण मया भवती शुंगाख्या विनतापरपर्याया खल्वपुत्रैव। नूनं निश्चितं। हे मातः अरुणः अयं मल्लक्षणः कदाचिन्नहि याति। हे विनते, सुपर्णं इति उपदिश 'हे सुपर्ण, त्वं स्वयं गच्छ स्वर्लोकं सुधामाहर्तुं। अरुणविषयामाशां मा कृथाः'। किं भूतस्त्वं। सोमहारः। सोमस्य हर्ता। इत्येकविंशोवर्गः ॥

॥ अथ द्वाविंशो वर्गः ॥

अपाद् भौवनो न हि शं बट् करो-
त्यतिहा त्वासौ नहंसः प्र माद्यते।
अन्धो जागृविर्नहंसः प्र माद्यते
कथं सुपर्णो गरुडोऽतिमोक्षते॥५॥

॥ *पदपाठः* ॥

अपात्। भौवनः। न। हि। शं। बट्। करोति। अति० हा। त्वा। असौ। नहंसः। प्र। माद्यते। अंधः। जागृविः। नहंसः। प्र। माद्यते। कथं। सु० पर्णः। गरुडः। अति० मोक्षते॥

॥ *भाष्यम्* ॥

अरुण उवाच मातरं प्रति –

हे मातः। इन्द्रेण सुधारक्षणे नियुक्तो भौवनो विश्वकर्माख्यो देवः गरुडे गते सति, बट् इति सत्ये, शं सुखं न करोति। भविष्यदर्थे वर्तमानार्थलकारः। करिष्यति। अर्थात् स्वस्य आत्मनः सुखकृत् न भविष्यति। संग्रामे न विजेष्यतीत्याकूतं। संग्राममेव न करिष्यति। किंलक्षणो भौवनः। अपात् पादहीनः पंगुः। स तु

शिबिकारुढः उह्यते। तथाऽपरो नहसनामादेवोपीन्द्रेण सुधायां नियुक्तोस्ति। असौ नहसः। एतत्संज्ञो देवः। अति इति अतीत्य संग्रामांगणं अतिक्रम्य उल्लंघ्य हात्वा त्यक्त्वा च युद्धं हात्वा परित्यज्य च। अथवा सत्त्वं त्यक्त्वा यद्वा धैर्यं विहाय अपि वा लज्जां हात्वा हित्वा। युद्धप्रदेशात् पलायनं कृत्वा। प्रभुणा आज्ञाते कार्ये सुधात्राणे प्रमाद्यत एव प्रमादमेव करिष्यति। तत्कार्यं न साधयिष्यति। किंच असौ नहससंज्ञको देवः गरुडस्य तेजसा दग्धचक्षुः सन् अन्धो भविष्यति। तथा अजागृविर्भविष्यति। जागृविर्जागरूकः गतनिद्रः। न जागृविः। अजागृविः एवंविधः कार्यसाधने निद्रालुः। अलसः। नहसः। एतन्नामा देवः प्रकर्षेण माद्यत एव। कार्यं कर्तुं प्रमत्त इव भविष्यति। इत्थमेतदादयः सर्वेऽपि योद्धारः युद्धं त्यक्त्वा पलायिष्यंते परंतु गरुडः संग्रामं कथं मोक्षते। कथं मोक्ष्यति। '*मुच्लृ*' मोक्षणे। कथं त्यक्ष्यति। न त्यक्ष्यति। संग्रामविमोचनं न करिष्यति। कीदृशः गरुडः सुपर्णः शोभनपतनः। पतनं गमनं। शोभनगमनः। सुपक्षो वा। अति युद्धप्रदेशमतिक्रम्य कथं धैर्यं मोक्ष्यति॥ अरुण उवाच मातरं प्रति –

ओजे॑व॒ सहे॑व॒ नभे॑व॒[60]
बल॑मिवा॒भ्रमि॑व॒ भीरि॑व।
म॒हद् बल॑मप्रतिधृ॒ष्यमे॒तद्
ग॒रुत्म॑त्युप॒मा नास्ति॑ शुं॒गे॥६॥

॥ *पदपाठः* ॥

ओज॑ःऽइव। सह॑ःऽइव। नभ॑ःऽइव। बल॑ऽइव। अ॒भ्रंऽइ॑व। भीःऽइ॑व। म॒हत्। बल॑। अ॒प्र॒ति॒० धृ॒ष्यं। ए॒तत्। ग॒रुत्म॑ति। उ॒प॒० मा। न। अस्ति॑। शु॒ंगे॒।

॥ *भाष्यम्* ॥

हे शुंगे, गरुत्मति सुपर्णे एतत्प्रत्यक्षं बलं शौर्यं महत् वर्तते। अप्रमेयं। कीदृशं बलं। अप्रतिधृष्यं। न वर्तते प्रतिधर्षको यस्य तत् अप्रतिधृष्यं। धर्षणं पराभवः। धर्षकः अभिभविता। पराभवकर्ता। यद्वा एवं व्युत्पत्तिः। न प्रतिधर्षितुं अभिभवितुं शक्यं अप्रतिधृष्यं। किमिव अप्रतिधृष्यं अनाधृष्यं बलम्? ओज इव ओजस्तेजः। पुनः किमिव। सहो धैर्यं हृदयबलं, तदिव अप्रतिधृष्यं। पुनः किमिव। नभः आकाशं(:) तदिव। पुनः किमिव। बलमिव। बलं सैन्यं। यथा

---

[60] आर्षं सन्धेर्द्विस्त्वम् (नभस् इव, नभः इव, नभ इव, नभेव)। 'ओज इव' इत्यस्य स्थाने पदपाठमातृका 'रुजःऽइव' इति पठति।

गजाश्वरथपदातिव्याप्तं चतुरंगसैन्यमप्रतिधृष्यं भवति। तद्वदेकस्यापि गरुडस्य बलं सामर्थ्यं अप्रतिधृष्यं। दु:सहं। किं बहुनोक्तेन। हे शुंगे विनते अस्य गरुडस्य काचिदप्युपमानास्ति। एतादृशः कोऽपि नास्त्येव।

अरुण उवाच जननीं प्रति –

वातोऽस्य प्राणान्मरुतोऽस्य पक्षा-
वग्निः शिरो रक्षतु जातवेदाः।
अहं पुरस्तादहमस्मि पश्चाच्-
चन्द्रो ललामं गरुडस्यं पृष्ठे॥७॥

॥ *पदपाठः* ॥

वातः। अस्य। प्राणान्। मरुतः। अस्य। पक्षौ। अग्निः। शिरः। रक्षतु। जात० वेदाः। अहं। पुरस्तात्। अहं। अस्मि। पश्चात्। चन्द्रः। ललामं। गरुडस्यं। पृष्ठे।

॥ *भाष्यम्* ॥

हे मातः। मया पूर्वं "अभ्राता भ्रात्रा गरुडोऽरुणेने"त्येतस्यामृचि तुर्यपादे त्वां प्रति एवमुक्तम्। हे विनते। त्वं तत्र गत्वा गरुडं इत्थमादिश। हे गरुड। अरुणः खलु पंगुत्वादागन्तुं न शक्नोति साहायिकं ते कर्तुं, ततस्त्वमेव स्वयमेकाकी त्रिदिवं स्वर्गं गच्छ, कीदृशस्त्वं? सोमहारः सोमाहरणकर्ता सोममाहर्तुमित्यर्थः। इत्येवं मया अरुणेन हे मातः चतुर्थपादे त्वन्मुखेन गरुडं प्रति ख्यापितं। चतुर्थः पादः "गच्छ स्वयं त्रिदिवं सोमहार" इति। तस्मादहं गमनाशक्तोप्यस्मै अरुणाय (गरुडाय?) इत्थमाशिषमाशास्ते (आशासे)। आशीर्वादं प्रयुंजे। वातोऽस्य प्राणान्मरुतोस्य पक्षावित्यृचा॥ अस्याश्चायमर्थः। वातो वायुः अस्य गरुडस्य प्राणान् रक्षतु त्रायतां। मरुतः एकोनपंचाशत् साकं जनित्वात् समा(न)वयसो ज्यैष्ठ्यकानिष्ठ्यवर्जिताः इतरेतरं भ्रातरो देवविशेषाः इन्द्रानुचराः अस्य पक्षौ द्वावपि रक्षंतु त्रायन्ताम्। अग्निः शिरः। अहं तु पुरस्तादस्मि। सूर्यरथस्य गत्या कदाचित् पूर्वभागे वर्तमानः सुदृष्ट्या अस्य कुशलचिंतकोऽस्मि। तथा पश्चादस्मि। कदाचिदादित्यरथगत्या पश्चिमभागे वर्तमानः सन् कुशलं वांछिष्यामि। किंच। गरुडस्य पृष्ठे चन्द्रो ललाम। ऊर्ध्वं खे गतो [गतस्य] गरुडस्य पृष्ठोपरि चन्द्रमंडलं पृष्ठवंशे ललामवद्रत्नमिव लांछनं भविष्यति। लोकैर्लांछनमिव द्रक्ष्यते। इदमत्राकूतम्। चन्द्रमाः पृष्ठोपरि स्थितोऽस्य त्राणं करिष्यति। तर्हि एकाकिनोऽपि किं भयम्। इतः परं 'इदं देवानामभिघाति वज्र'मित्येतस्याः प्राक् इन्द्रबृहस्पतिसंवादः।

अपरयेन्द्रः खे गरुडेन सार्द्धममृतपालकानां युद्धे प्रारब्धे तत्कोलाहलं शृण्वन् गुरुं पृच्छति।

(*इतस्ततो निहितेषु विखण्डितेषु त्रिषु पत्रार्धेषु विकीर्णः संपादकेन यथाकथञ्चित् संस्कारितः पाठः*)।

इन्द्र उवाच गुरुं प्रति –

किन्नु घोषः॑ श्रूयते॒ यत्र॒ सोमो॒
बृह॑स्पते॒ हन्त॑ वे॒दाव॑ ग॒त्वा।

ज्या ह॑ शिङ्क्ते॑[६१] य॒दाऽव॑सृष्टा
रोरू॒यते व॑धि॒रः॑[६२] सौम॒पालः॥८॥

॥ *पदपाठः* ॥

किं। नु। घोषः॑। श्रू॒यते॒। यत्र॑। सोमः॑। बृह॑स्पते। हंत॑। वे॒द॒। अव॑। ग॒त्वा। ज्या। ह॒। शि॒ङ्क्ते॑। य॒दा। अव॑०सृष्टा। रो॒रू॒य॒ते। व॒धि॒रः[६२]। सो॒म॒०पा॒लः॥

॥ *भाष्यम्* ॥

नु इति प्रश्ने वितर्के वा। हे बृहस्पते। हन्तेदानीं तत्र प्रदेशे उत्पन्नो घोषो युद्धप्रयुक्तः कोलाहलः श्रूयते। तत् किं कारणं। तत्र कुत्र? यत्र सोमः सुधास्ति। एतत्कारणं भवान् किं वेद जानाति नो वा? हेति प्रसिद्धौ। यदा ज्या मौर्वी अवसृष्टा विसृष्टा सती आकर्णान्तमाकृष्य सहसा विमुक्ता सती कस्यापि शिङ्क्ते शब्दायते। टंकाररवं जनयति। तदा सोमपालः वधिरः कलकलस्वनेनातिपरुषेणाभिभूतश्रोत्रः सन् रोरूयते। रोरवणं कुरुते। प्रबलं ध्वनिं मुंचति। एतत्कारणं सम्यक् नावबुद्ध्यते। अ[व] अवेहि जानीहि। उपसर्गबलाद् धातोरध्याहारः। यद्वा अवेत्ययं नोपसर्गः। किन्तु अवरं अधस्तात् सूचयति। अवगत्वा इन्द्रस्य सर्वोच्चस्वर्गाद् अधो गत्वा। (*संस्कारितम्*)।

[बृहस्पतिरु]वाचेन्द्र प्रति –

---

[६१] सर्वत्रैव मातृकासु 'शिङ्ते' इत्येव पाठः। एतदेव ग्रूबेमहोदयेनापि स्वीकृतम्। किन्तु 'शिञ्ज्'-धातोर्निष्पन्नस्यैतस्य क्रियापदस्य 'शिङ्क्ते' इत्येव रूपं भवितव्यम्।

[६२] उभयत्र (मूले पदपाठे च) 'बधिरः' इति पाठः किन्तु 'वध्' धातोर्निष्पन्नस्यैतत्पदस्य वकारादित्वमेव शस्तम्।

अहमेतं मघवन् वेद घोषं
सुपर्णस्यैष पततः शचीपते।
वैनतेयो हरति यस्य सोमं
निहत्य तवं सोमपालान् गरुत्मांन्॥९॥

॥ *पदपाठः* ॥

अहं। एतं। मघ०वन्। वेद। घोषं। सु०पर्णस्यं। एषः। पततः।
शची०पते॥ वैनतेयः। हरति। यस्यं। सोमं। नि०हत्यं। तवं।
सोम०पालान्। गरुत्मांन्॥

(*पाठभ्रंशः*) मघवन्। एषः अहं सुपर्णस्य एतद्घोषं वे[द] वेद्मि। किंलक्षणस्य सुपर्णस्य? पततः। पततीति पततः। दूरादागच्छतः। तस्य कस्य, तव। यस्य तव सोमं [हर]ति। लोकपालान् अग्न्यादीन् निहत्य नितरां हत्वा।

"[हे मघवन् इन्द्र] अहम् एतं घोषं [शब्दं] वे[द] वेद्मि। एष घोषः पततः सुधाकलशं प्रत्याकाशादधो निपततः सुपर्णस्य शोभनपर्णस्य गरुडस्यास्ति, शच्या एतन्नाम्न्याः इन्द्रपत्न्याः पतिर्भर्ता, तत्संबुद्धौ। यस्य तव सोमं, विनतापुत्रो वैनतेयो गरुत्मान् इदानीम् त्वया नियुक्तान् अग्न्यादीन् लोकपालान् निहत्य नितरां हत्वा हरति अपनयति। सोमः सपद्येव ह्रियमाण अस्तीत्याशयः॥" (*संपादकः*) इति द्वाविंशो वर्गः॥

॥ द्वादशं सूक्तम् ॥

॥ अथ त्रयोविंशः वर्गः ॥

अपांद्भौवनः क्षिप्रधंन्वा क्वांसी-
द्यस्याग्निं बाणंमुखं तिरश्चतां।
यस्यं बाहुभ्यां वीयंते सायंको वृषां[६३]
त्रिंशत्स्तंबन्यान्ययुंतानि षष्टिम्॥१॥

॥ *पदपाठः* ॥

अपांत्। भौवनः। क्षिप्र० धंन्वा। क्वं। आसीत्। यस्यं। अग्निं। बाणं०मुखं। तिरश्चतां। यस्यं। बाहुभ्यां। वि० ईयंते। सायंकः। वृषां। त्रिंशत्। स्तबन्यांनि[६४]। अयुंतानि। षष्टिम्॥

॥ *भाष्यम्* ॥

इन्द्रो गुरुं प्रति वद[ति] . . . [असौ] भौवनः विश्वकर्मा तस्मिन् काले अमृतहरणकाले। (*पाठभ्रंशः*)

कीदृक् भौवनः अपात् पंगुः। पुनः कीदृक्। क्षिप्रं वेगवत्तरं धनुषा बाणान् मुञ्चतीति क्षिप्रधन्वा। एतेन बाणानां लघुगतित्वं सूच्यते। अ . . . न प्रवर्त्तमानं। तिरश्चता पार्श्वान्निर्गमा . . .मकौ। तिर्यग्गत्या प्रवर्तमानं कोऽपि . . . अग्निमयं। अग्निस्वरूपं। प्रज्व[लता] अग्निना व्याप्तं। पुनरसौ कः। यस्य भौवन[: षष्टिं]त्रिंशच्च शत्रूणामयुतानि वीयते। . . . विविधं ९० नवति [त्रिंशत्+ षष्टिं] रिपूणामयुतानि व्याप्नोति। वि . . . बाणोऽपि तावत्संख्याको भूत्वा इत्यर्थः। यद्वा जात्यभि . . .॥ (*खण्डितम्*)

---

[६३] 'सायकोऽवृथा' इति साधीयान् पाठः। प्राचीनेषु नागराक्षरेषु थकारषकारयोः साम्यत्वाद् भ्रमः।

[६४] मूले पदपाठे च 'स्तवन्यानि' इति पाठः।

“[मया सोमरक्षणे नियुक्तः पादहीनः (अतः सर्वदा तत्रैवावस्थितः) स वृषा, बाणानां वर्षयिता, भौवनः कुत्रासीत्, क्षिप्रधन्वनस्तीव्रगत्या बाणान् क्षेप्तुं समर्थस्य यस्य, तिरश्चीनतया वामदक्षिणपार्श्वयोर्निमुक्ताः (‘अवृथा’ इति पाठे अमोघाः) अग्निमुखा अग्निमुद्गिरन्तः सायकाः रिपूणां षष्टि-त्रिंशच्च अयुतानि स्तबन्यानि स्तबकानि(न्) संकुलकानि समूहान् वा, एकपद एव, समकालमेव विद्ध्यन्ति व्याप्नुवन्ति वा? इत्याशयो मन्त्रस्य।]” (*सम्पादकः*)

अपादं वै भीषयंमाणः सुपर्णः
क्षिप्रधंन्वा चरति क्षिप्रेण शूरः।
नैनं चरंन्तं परिं बाण आंस
आ यत्सोमं यदार्चद्[६५] दिव्युंत्तमायाम्॥२॥

॥ *पदपाठः* ॥

अपादं। वै। भीषयंमाणः। सु० पर्णः। क्षिप्र० धंन्वा। चरति।
क्षिप्रेणं। शूरंः। न। एनं। चरंतं। परिं। बाणः। आस। आ।
यत्। सोमं। यत्। आर्चत्। दिवि। उत्० तमायां॥

॥ *भाष्यम्* ॥

“[सुपर्णः अपादं भौवननामानं सोमपालं भीषयमाणं भयाक्रान्तं कुर्वन् सोममर्चयन् तं प्रदक्षिणीकृत्य परिभ्राम्यति। यदा क्षिप्रधन्वा शूरश्च स भौवनः तमभिलक्ष्य क्षिप्रं बाणममुञ्चत् तदा नैरन्तर्येण भ्रमणकारणात् तं सुपर्णं बाणो नैवाविध्यत्। एवम् उत्तमायां दिवि, दिवः सर्वोच्चे स्थाने स्थितं सोमं स आर्चत् पूजयामास यदि वा आर्च्छत् अपजहार॥]” (*सं०*)

क्वांऽर्बुदो नंहुषः कांद्रवेय
उलूको बंल्बूलः श्वसंनः क्वांसीत्।
सपन्निमिषः[६६] प्रलिंशः क्वांसी-
द्यन्म इन्दुं हरंति वैनतेयः॥३॥

---

[६५] अत्र ‘आर्छत्’ (आर्च्छत्)=अपजहार, इति मूलपाठस्य विकृतिः संभाव्यते।

[६६] ‘स्वपन्ननिमिषः’ इति साधीयान् पाठः।

॥ *पदपाठः* ॥

क्वं। अर्बुदः। नहुषः। काद्रवेयः। उलूकः। बल्बूलः। श्वसंनः।
क्वं। आसीत्। सपत्० निमिषः। प्र० लिंशः। क्वं। आसीत्।
यत्। मे। इन्दुं हरंति। वैनेतेयः।

॥ *भाष्यम्* ॥

“[इन्द्रो बृहस्पतिं पृच्छति यत् तेन सोमरक्षणार्थं बहवः सर्पाः नियुक्ताः, तेषां नामानि परिगणयन् स जिज्ञासते यत् अर्बुद-नहुष-काद्रवेय-उलूक-बल्बूल-श्वसननामानः सर्पाः, अथ च अनिमिषं स्वपन्, चक्षुषी उन्मील्य निर्णिमेषं स्वपन् प्रलिशो नामाजगर एते सर्वे तस्मिन् समये कुत्रासन्, कथं च स्वं नियोगं नैवापालयन् यत् मया रक्षितं तदमृतभूतं सोममेष पक्षिराट् सुपर्णो बलाद् हरति।]” (*सं०*)

ककुब्भण्डश्चक्रतुंण्डः क्वांसी-
दश्वमुखः कुण्डकंर्णः क्वांसीत्॥
विक्रोशंनः खरकंण्ठः क्वांसीद्
यन्म इन्दुं हरंति वैनतेयः॥४॥

॥ *पदपाठः* ॥

ककुप्० भण्डः। चक्र० तुंण्डः। क्वं। आसीत्। अश्व०मुखः।
कुण्ड०कंर्णः। क्वं। आसीत्। वि० क्रोशंनः। खर० कंण्ठः।
क्वं। आसीत्॥

॥ *भाष्यम्* ॥

“[अन्येऽस्मिन् पद्ये नामोल्लेखपूर्वकं वर्णिताः ते रक्षकाः क्व, अथ च किं कुर्वाणाः आसन् यत् सुपर्णो गरुत्मान् मदीयं सोमं हरति?]” (*सं०*)

कशम्बूको वेंणुको अश्वंक्रन्दो-
ऽलगर्द्धः परुंषः क्वांसीत्।
नभोरूपसंरूपौ क्वांस्तां
यन्म इन्दुं हरंति वैनतेयः॥५॥

॥ *पदपाठः* ॥

कशंबूकः। वेणुकः। अश्वं०क्रन्दः। अल०गर्द्दः। परुषः। क्वं।
आसीत्। नभोरूप० संरूपौ। क्वं। आस्तां॥

॥ *भाष्यम्* ॥

"[कशम्बूकादयोऽनुचराः सप्त इन्द्रेण सोमरक्षणे नियुक्ताः कथं स्वं नियोगं सम्यक्तया नानुतिष्ठितवन्तः येन वैनतेयः सोममिदानीं मे अपहरन्नास्ते इति इन्द्रस्य प्रश्नो बृहस्पतिं प्रति।]" (*सं०*)

उपतीरं वर्तमानः शशाक्षः
क्रोधेनं मर्तो[६७] अजंनस्य कर्ता।
व्यादाय-स्वापी विभिंदुः क्वांसीद्
यन्म इन्दुं हरंति वैनतेयः॥६॥

॥ *पदपाठः* ॥

उप०तीरं। वर्त्तमानः। शश०अक्षः। क्रोधेनं। मर्तः। अजंनस्य।
कर्ता। व्यादाय०स्वापी। विभिंदः। क्वं। आसीत्॥

(*खण्डितभाष्यस्यावशिष्टोंऽशः*)

एवमजनस्य कर्ता। तथा विभिदो नाम किं . . . शत्रूणां भेत्ता। विशिष्टा भिदा भेदनं यस्य, सै (?) . . . मुखं [व्या] दाय स्वपितीति व्यादायस्वापी। व्यादाय प्रस् . . . [इ]न्दुं हरति स्म . . .॥ (*अग्रतोऽनुपलब्धम्*)

"[उपतीरं, तीरस्य समीपे उपतीरं, प्रवेशद्वारनिकटं, सोमस्य रक्षणे नियुक्तत्वात्तत्रैव सातत्येन वर्तमानः शशाक्षो नाम व्यालो यः क्रुद्धः सन् मृत्युरिव, काल इव, सर्वान् परितः संस्थितान्, सोमाहरणेच्छया समेत्यागतान् तस्करान्, निर्मथ्य तत्र सर्वमजनं जनरहितं प्राणिविरहितं करोत्यथ च स विभिदो नामापरो व्यालो यः सर्वदैव तत्र मुखं व्यादायोद्घाट्य स्वापी स्वपनशीलः, शयानो वर्तते, सोमजिहीर्षया समागतांश्च सर्वान् निगिरति, स वैनतेयेन सोमापहरणकाले कुत्रासीदितीन्द्रस्य गुरुं बृहस्पतिं प्रति प्रश्नः। अत्र '*स्वप्*' इति धातोरक्षिणी निमील्य निद्रातीत्येवंप्रकारकोऽर्थो नैव ग्राह्यः, यतस्तेन नैवाभीष्टसिद्धिः। भूमौ शयानस्तिष्ठति मुखं व्यादायेत्येव कवेराशयः। "क्रोधेन मर्त्तः" इति पाठे

---

[६७] कदाचिल्लेखकभ्रान्त्या समुत्थितः "मृत्युः" इत्यस्यापपाठः।

'मर्त्त'-शब्दश्चिन्त्यः। मन्यामहे यदयं 'मृत्युः' इत्यस्यैवापपाठः।]" (*सम्पादकः*)।
इति त्रयोविंशो वर्गः॥

॥ अथ चतुर्विंशो वर्गः ॥

गतिं विज्ञायं शकुनस्यं सुर्पास्
तैजोबलेनं गरुडस्यं शक्र।
ते पंन्नगा विहगैन्द्रस्य स्पर्शाद्
भीताः शिरांस्यप्यंदधुस्तनूभिः॥७॥

॥ *पदपाठः* ॥

गतिं। विऽज्ञायं। शकुनस्यं। सुर्पाः। तेजःऽ बलेनं। गरुडस्यं। शक्र। ते। पन्नगाः। विहगऽइन्द्रस्य। स्पर्शात्। भीताः। शिरांसि। अपिं अदधुः। तनूभिः॥

[इदा] नीम् उत्तरं गुरुराह। बृहस्पतिरुवाच - हे शक्र। ते सर्पाः [विहगेन्द्रस्य] गरुडस्य [स्पर्शात् चञ्चुप्रहाराद् भीताः भयाकुलाः सन्तः स्वानि शिरांसि] उत्तमांगानि अप्यदधुः अपिहितवन्तः। [केन प्रकारेण?] [तनूभिः] शरीरैः [स्वकीयानि शिरांसि शिरोऽतिरिक्तशरीरभागेनाच्छादितवन्तः]। यद्वा तनूभिर्गुहाभिः। गुहासु [पलाय्य निलीनाः] किंलक्षणाः स[र्पाः] . . . तेजोबलेन तापेन। कीदृशाः सर्पाः प[न्नं?] नीचैर्यथा स्यात्तथा गच्छन्तीति पन्न[गाः] . . . अद्यः[?] इत्युद्भावनामात्रं। कीद(दृ?)शस्य [शकुनस्य? विहगेन्द्रस्य। विहायसा गच्छन्तीति विहगाः पक्षिणः, तेषामिन्द्रो राजा, तेषु श्रेष्ठः, तस्य गरुडस्य गतिं वेगेन पतनं विज्ञाय ज्ञात्वा, दृष्ट्वा वा, तस्य तेजोबलेन ओजसा शरीरसामर्थ्येन भीताः सन्तः ते सर्पाःचञ्चुप्रहारमुत्प्रेक्षमाणाः स्वकीयानि शिरांसि पिहितवन्तः।]
(*पत्रस्यार्धभाग एवावशिष्टः। कोष्ठगतं संपादकेन पूरितम्*)

ये विद्युतौ चरंतः सुर्वतों घ्नती
अन्नं रक्षंन्ती अभंया भया चं।
चक्षुर्मुखावस्वंपन्नीक्षंमाणाः
कुथं स्विंदेवातिं पिपाति गृध्रंः॥८॥

॥ *पदपाठः* ॥

ये इतिं। विद्युतौं। चरंतः। सुर्वतः। घ्नती इतिं। अन्नं। रक्षन्ती

इति॑। अभ॑या। भ॒या। च॒। चक्षुः॑ऽमुखौ। अस्व॑पन्। ईक्ष॑माणाः।
क॒थं। स्वि॒त्। ए॒व। अति॑। पि॒पा॒ति॒। गृध्रः॑॥

[ये विद्यु]तौ सौदामिन्यौ [अभया-भया नाम्न्यौ] सर्वतः सर्वाभ्यो दि[ग्भ्यः] समागतान् दस्यून् घ्नती विनाशयन्त्यौ स्थिते। अथ च सर्वतः सर्वासु दिक्षु चरतः [सोमं परिवृत्य चक्ररूपेण भ्राम्यतः]। किं [कुर्वत्यौ]? अन्नम् अदनीयं पेयं सोमं रक्षन्त्यौ। पुनः किंल[क्षणे] . . . [चक्षुर्मुखौ, लिंगव्यत्य] यश्छान्दसः। स्त्रीलिंगार्थे पुंल्लिंगम्। चक्षुर्मुख्यौ। ययोर्मुखस्थाने चक्षुरेव। उ . . . मस्ति। विश्वतोमुखे। विश्वतो लोचने इ . . . स्फुरणरूपं तदेव चक्षुः। मुखचक्षुषोर्भेदस्या . . . (*पत्रं विखण्डितम्*)

“[ये त्वभयाभयानाम्न्यौ विद्युतौ सोमं रक्षन्त्यौ सततं तत्परितो भ्राम्यतः, चक्षुःस्फुरणमेव च ययोर्मुखं, स्वकीयेन वीक्षणेनैव तेजसा वा ये कमपि भस्मसात् कर्तुं समर्थे स्तः, ते अतिक्रम्य, अभिभूय, निर्जित्य वा कथमेष गृध्रः (गरुडः) सोममपहृत्य गच्छति। गरुडस्य कृते शक्रेण प्रयुक्तं ‘गृद्ध’ इत्यभिधानम् अवमाननार्थम्, अथ च सोमं प्रति तस्य गृध्नुतामपि संसूचयति। ‘अति पिपाती’ति अस्फुटार्थम् (कदाचित् आर्षम् ‘अतियियाति=अतिक्रम्य याति। यियाति=अतिशयेन, सत्वरं गच्छति?]”। (*सं०*)

ये वि॒द्यु॒तौ चर॑तः स॒र्वतो॑ घ्न॒ती
अन्न॒ं रक्ष॑न्ती अभ॑या भ॒या च॑।
ताभ्या॒ं सम॑ख्यद् गरु॒डो वैन॑ते॒यो
विषू॑च्यौ ते अया॒ट् स्वश्शु॒रभ॑यां भ॒यां च॑॥९॥

॥ *पदपाठः* ॥

ताभ्या॑ं। सं। अ॒ख्य॒त्। ग॒रु॒डः। वै॒न॒ते॒यः। विषू॑च्यौ। ते इति॑।
अया॑ट्। स्वः॑। अभ॑यां। भयां। च॒॥

“[बृहस्पतेरुत्तरमिन्द्रं प्रति। भवता नियुक्ते अभया-भया-नाम्न्यौ ते विद्युतौ येऽन्नं सोमं रक्षन्त्यौ सोमं परितः सर्वासु दिक्षु भ्रमन्ति, सोमं मोष्टुकामं जनं च घातयन्ति, ताभ्यां सह गरुडः प्रथमोद्भवाया आदिविद्युतः कनिष्ठभ्रातृत्वात् समख्यत् सख्यं साधितवान्। सख्या गरुडेन प्रार्थिते सत्यौ ते विषूच्यौ, सूक्ष्मत्वात् सर्वतः प्रसरणशीले, सोमं विहाय स्वं नियोगं च परित्यज्य स्वर् दिवं गतवत्यौ पलायित इत्यर्थः प्रतीयते। अथवा, ‘अयाट्’ इत्यस्पष्टार्थं क्रियापदम् एकवचनत्वाद् वाक्ये कर्तृपदेन ‘गरुडः’ इत्यनेन संगच्छतेतराम्। द्वितीयान्ते च अभया-भया-पदे।

अतः 'अयाट्' इत्यस्य 'यापयामास', 'प्रेषयामास' इत्यपि अर्थः ऊहितुं शक्यते। एवं सति 'गरुडः अभयां भयां च स्वः प्रति यापयामास' इति प्रकारान्तरेण व्याख्यानम्।]" (*संपादकः*) इति चतुर्विंशो वर्गः॥

॥ त्रयोदशं सूक्तम् ॥

॥ अथ पञ्चविंशो वर्गः ॥

या मे मायाऽनिमिषतो जवीयसी
सङ्कल्पज्योतिरनिवर्तमाना।
क्षुरपवि[६८]र्ब्रह्मन् क्व१ नु सा बभूव
यन्म इन्दुं हरति वैनतेयः॥१॥

॥ *पदपाठः* ॥

या। मे। माया। अनि०मिषतः। जवीयसी। सं०कल्पज्योतिः[६९]। अनि०वर्तमाना। क्षुर०पविः। ब्रह्मन्। क्व। नु। सा। बभूव। यत्। मे०॥

"[पुनरयमिन्द्रस्य प्रश्नो बृहस्पतिं प्रति। हे बृहस्पते, या मे मम मायानाम्नी शक्तिः सोमरक्षणार्थं नियुक्ता, या च निमिषतोऽप्यधिकं[७०] जवीयसी वेगवती, मदीयेन हृद्गतेन संकल्पैनैव जाज्वल्यमाना सती सोमतस्करं भस्मसात्कर्तुं क्षमा, अनिवर्तमाना न कदापि प्रतिनिवर्तमाना पलायमाना वा, सा कुत्रासीत् यत् सा सोमचौरं वैनतेयं नैव नाशितवती येन स मदिन्दुं हरति।]" (*सं०*)

या ते मायाऽनिमिषतो जवीयसी
संकल्पज्योतिरनिवर्तमाना।

---

[६८] एतद्विशेषणपदं मायया सह नैव संगच्छते। चक्रस्यैवैतत् स्वरूपं संभाव्यते। तस्य प्रसंगे पुनरपि चोद्धृतम्। पाठाविलत्वात् तत एव कदाचिदागत्य अस्यामृचि प्रविष्टम् इति प्रतीयते।

[६९] 'संकल्पज्योति'रिति समस्ते पदे उदात्तस्य द्वित्वं बुधैश्चिन्तनीयम्। पूर्वपदप्रधानो बहुव्रीहिरतः 'संकल्पज्योतिः' इतिवद् भाव्यम्।

[७०] मूले पदपाठे च स्थितस्य 'अनिमिषतः' इत्यस्य स्थानेऽस्माकं 'निमिषतः' (निमिषादपि जवीयसी) एवाभीष्टम् यत्तु तृतीयचतुर्थपद्ययोरपि विद्यते।

तामा॑त्मसा॒ची ग॑रु॒डो वै॑नते॒यो
जवा॒ज्जवी॑या॒न्यज॑हा॒द् बले॑न॥२॥

॥ पदपाठः ॥

या। ते॒। ०॥ तां। आ॒त्म॒० सा॒ची। ग॒रु॒डः। वै॒न॒ते॒यः। ज॒वात्।
जवी॑यान्। नि। अज॑हात्। बले॑न॥

॥ भाष्यम् ॥

"[या ते शक्र 'निमिषतो जवीयसी'त्यादिगुणविशिष्टा माया तां स्वात्मनिष्ठबलेन जवादपि जवीयान्, वेगादपि वेगवत्तरो गरुडो वैनतेयः पराजित्य गतः। तव माया केवलं निमिषतो जवीयसी, किन्तु वैनतेयो जवादपि जवीयोऽतस्तामतिशेते इत्याशयः।]" (सं०)

यन्मे॑ च॒क्रं नि॑मि॒षतो ज॒वी॑यः
संकु॒ल्पज्योति॒रनि॑वर्तमानम्।
क्षु॒रप॑वि ब्रह्म॒न् क्व१॒॑ नु तद् ब॑भू॒व
यन्म॒ इन्दुं॒ हर॑ति वैन॒ते॒यः॥३॥

॥ पदपाठः ॥

यत्। मे॒। च॒क्रं। नि॒०मि॒षतः। जवी॑यः। सं॒०कु॒ल्पज्योतिः॑।
अनि॑०वर्तमानं। क्षु॒र०प॑वि। ब्र॒ह्म॒न्। क्व॑। नु। तत्। ब॒भू॒व॥
यत्। मे॒। ०॥

॥ भाष्यम् ॥

"[पुनरपि गुरुं पृच्छति शक्रः। यन्मदीयं चक्रं तत्र सोमस्य रक्षायै नियुक्तं वर्तते, यच्च निमिषपतनादपि वेगवत्। निमेषपतने यः कालांशोऽपेक्ष्यते ततोऽप्यल्पीयसा कालेन शत्रोः शिरश्छिनत्ति। संकल्पमात्रेण ज्वालामालाभिरावृतं सत् अग्निमुद्गिरति। स्वकीयप्रान्तभागे परिधौ च क्षुरैर्युक्तं वर्तते। शत्रून् अनिहत्य न कदापि निवर्तते। तादृशं मच्चक्रं कुत्रासीत् यदेष वैनतेयो मम सोममपहरति।]" (सं०)

यत्ते॑ च॒क्रं नि॑मि॒षतो ज॒वी॑यः
संकु॒ल्पज्योति॒रनि॑वर्तमानम्।

तदात्मसाची[७१] गरुडो वैनतेयो
जवाज्जवीयान्यजहाद् बलेन॥४॥

॥ *पदपाठः*॥

यत्। ते।०। तत्।०॥

॥ *भाष्यम्* ॥

"[एतत्सर्वगुणविशिष्टं तव यच्चक्रं तद् आत्मसाची स्वकीयेन स्वात्मनिष्ठबलेन साची पतन् वैनतेयो वेगादपि वेगतरमुड्डीयमानस्तन्यक्कृत्य, तत् चक्रमतिक्रम्य, तत् पृष्ठतः त्यक्त्वा, पलायितः।]" (*सं०*)

पर्वताऽष्ठीराः क्षुरपव्यः सुबुध्न्यो
मोदा ह्रदा ह्रदिनीः सूर्यवर्चसः।
चन्द्र इव भान्तीर्बहुधा विश्वरूपाः
कथं स्विद्देवाऽतिं पिपाति गृध्रः॥५॥

॥ *पदपाठः* ॥

पर्वत० अष्ठीराः। क्षुर० पव्यः। सु०बुध्न्यः। मोदाः। ह्रदाः। ह्रदिनीः। सूर्य० वर्चसः। चन्द्रः ऽ इव। भांतीः। बहुधा। विश्व० रूपाः। ०।

॥ *भाष्यम्* ॥

"[पर्वताष्ठीराः सोमं परिवृत्य संस्थितानां पर्वतानाम् अष्ठीराः (लाः) महन्ति शिलाखण्डानि, वर्तुलाः पाषाणशिलाः वा; क्षुरैर्युक्ताः सोमं परितः भ्रमन्त्यः पव्यः चक्राकाराणि यन्त्राणि; बुध्नमधस्तलं गर्तो वा। सुबुध्न्यः अतीवगभीराः ह्रदाः जलपूर्णाः ('मोदाः' इत्यस्य स्थाने 'सोदाः' इत्येव साधु) परिखाः . . .]" (*सं०*)

. . . प्रमोदभरसम्पन्नाः। आनंदघनाः। किंलक्षणाः ताः मोदाः? एतन्नाम्न्यः शक्तयः। सूर्यवर्चसः। वर्चस्तेजः। सप्रतापतेजोबहुलाः। पुनः के सुधाध . . . मुक्ता [?]। [सुबुध्न्यः अतीवगभीराः] ह्रदाः अगाधजलाः महागर्ताः नदा इत्यर्थः। कीदृशाः ते नदाः। चन्द्रवत् भांतः भ्राजमानाः [भास्व]रवर्णाः शीतलाश्च।

---

[७१] अत्र 'आत्मसाची' इत्यत्र उभयोः पदयोरुदात्तत्वं परं, द्वितीये मन्त्रे उत्तरपदस्यैव (आत्मसाची) इति बुधैर्निभालनीयम्।

भांत इति विशेषणमर्थवशाल्लिंगविपरिणामतः। पुनः काः अमृतस्य [र]क्षणाय [का]रणत्वे[न] कल्पिताः। ह्रदिन्यः। नद्यः। ऋङ्मध्येन ह्रदिनीरिति द्वितीयाकर्मणि। . . . ति . . . कर्मत्वं। कीदृशो ह्रदिन्यः। चन्द्र इव भांत्यः। शोभमानाः। धवलोदका इत्यर्थः। पु . . . [सो]म संगोपनाय प्रयुक्ताः। विश्वरूपाः। नानाविधरूपाः शक्तयः योगिन्यः विश्वानि स[र्वा]णि अनेकप्रकाराणि रूपाणि यासां ताः विश्वरूपाः। कीदृश्यो विश्वरूपाः? बहुधा वि[विध]प्रकारं प्रवर्तमानाः। नानाविधाभिर्मायाभिर्युद्ध्यमाना इत्यर्थः। पुनः कीदृश्यः विश्वरूपाः शक्तयः? सूर्यवर्चसः उग्रतेजसः। इह पंचानामन्तर्द्धानानां क्षुरपविमोदह्रदह्रदिनीविश्वरूपाख्यानां व्यस्तान्वितत्वदोषमथाश्रित्य औचित्यमात्रबलाद्यथायोग्यं विशेषणानि प्रयुक्तानि। असौ गृध्रः सोमे लुब्धः पक्षी गरुडः एताः पंच अन्तर्द्धानत्वे प्रयुक्ताः स्थापिताः सर्वा अपि कथं अति पिपाति अतिक्रम्य गच्छति। अंतः प्रविशति स्म।

चतुर्थपादे पाठान्तरं। *'कथं स्विदेवाप्यति याति गृध्रः'*। पदानि तु। कथं। स्वित्। एव। अपि। अति। याति। गृध्रः। एताः कथमतियाति। अतिक्रामति। स्विदिति प्रश्ने। (*भाष्यमादौ क्वचिन्मध्ये च खण्डितम्*) (*सं०*)

बृहस्पतिः प्रत्युत्तरमुवाच –

ता ग्रीवच्छिन्ना[७२] अपि च मूर्द्धभिन्ना:[७२]
कृत्ताः संचन्ते बहुलानि शक्र।
अपाद् भौवनो निहंतस्तदासीन्-
महद् वैशसमकरोत्सुपर्णः॥६॥

॥ *पदपाठः* ॥

ताः। ग्रीव०छिन्नाः। अपि। च। मूर्द्ध०भिन्नाः। कृत्ताः। सचंते बहुलानि। शक्र। अपात्। भौवनः। नि० हंतः। तत्। आसीत्। महत्। वैशसं। अकरोत्। सुपर्णः॥

॥ *भाष्यम्* ॥

इह केचित् कुसांप्रदायिकाः जडाः चतुर्थपादे वैकारशकारयोरंतरा यकारं प्रवेशयंति। *'महद्वै यशसमिति'*। तद् वृथा। महद्वैशसमित्येव शुद्धं सत्सम्प्रदायागतं बोद्धव्यम्। गुरुः 'पर्वताष्ठीरा' इत्येतस्यामृचि निर्दिष्टानां पंचानां सोमांतर्द्धानानां

---

[७२] 'ग्रीवच्छिन्नाः' इत्यत्र उत्तरपदस्य, अथ च 'मूर्द्धभिन्नाः' इत्यत्र पूर्वपदस्य उदात्तत्वं कथमित्यन्वेष्टव्यम्। 'वैशस'मित्यत्र सर्वानुदात्तत्वमपि चिन्त्यम्।

गतिमिन्द्रेण पृष्टोऽनया 'ता ग्रीवच्छिन्नाः' इति यथास्वमुत्तराण्याह। हे इन्द्र। त्वया मोदा इति नाम्न्यः शक्तयः कुत्रेति पृच्छ्यते। ताः मोदानाम्न्यः योगिन्यः गरुडेन ग्रीवच्छिन्नाः कृताः। ग्रीवासु छिन्नाः ग्रीवच्छिन्नाः। ह्रस्वत्वं छांदसं। छिन्नग्रीवा इत्यर्थः। याश्च त्वं विश्वरूपा इति नाम्न्यः शक्तयः कुत्र गता इति पृच्छसि। ताः विश्वरूपाः योगिन्यः गरुडेन मूर्द्धभिन्नाः कृताः। मूर्द्धसु भिन्नाः विदारिताः मूर्द्धभिन्नाः। ता ग्रीवच्छिन्नाः मूर्द्धभिन्नाः इति स्त्रीलिंगानि सर्वाणि द्वितीयांतानि कर्मकत्वात्। बहुलानीति नपुंसकं प्रथमाबहुवचनं कर्तृत्वात्। अयमन्वयः। बहुलानि तानि प्राणिजातानि श्वशृगालकाकगृद्धादीन्यामिषभक्षकानि(णि), ताः सर्वाः उभय . . . मोदाख्याः विश्वरूपाख्याश्च कर्मभूताः सर्वं ते [सचन्ते] सेवंते खादन्ति भक्षयन्ति। अनु . . . आसन्। गरुडेन ताः शस्त्र्यः(?) कृताः, छिन्नाः खण्डशः कृताः। ताः गरुडः अपि [आ] हारेण योजन . . .। गरुडः ताः अदहत् भस्मसात् अकरोत्। याश्च ह्रदिन्यः आ . . . शब्दात् गरुडः ताः ह्रदिनीः अशोषयत्। शोषितवान्। शुष्कोदका अकार्षीत्। तथा ये ह्रदाः नदाः आसन्, च-शब्दात् गरुडः तान् ह्रदान् नदान् अशोषयत्। शोषितवान्। शुष्कोदकान् अकरोत्। च-शब्दात् क्रियापदाऽध्याहारः। तथा यः भौवनो विश्वकर्मा आसीत्। स तेन नितरां हतः। तदा। एवं सुपर्णः वैशसं हननं अकरोत्। वैशसं वधं अकरोत्। *'ताश्छिन्नग्रीवा अपि च मूर्द्धभिन्नाः'* इति पाठान्तरम्। (*पत्रं स्थाने स्थाने कीटभक्षितम्, सं०*)। इति पंचविंशतितमो वर्गः॥

॥ अथ षड्विंशो वर्गः ॥

'उदश्रयंतु सर्पा हर्षमाणाः' इत्यस्याः स्थानमन्यत्र (*फलश्रुतिप्रसंगे, सं०*)। इन्द्रः पृच्छति गुरुम् –

> आदि॑त्या रु॒द्रा व॒सवो॑ऽथ॒ सा॒ध्याः
> सोम॒ं रक्षं॑न्तो बहु॒धा निवि॑ष्टाः।
> मरु॑तो ब्र॒ह्म॒न् क्व१॒॑ नु ते ब॑भू॒व(वु॒ः)[७३]
> यन्म॒ इन्दु॒ं हर॑ति वैनते॒यः॥७॥

---

[७३] मातृकाणामालोचनेन ज्ञायते यद् "बभूवुः" इत्येव पाठः पारम्परिकः शुद्धश्च। १७३८तमे वैक्रमे वर्षे लिखिताऽस्माकं पदपाठमातृकापि 'ब॒भू॒वु॒ः' इत्येव पाठं स्वीकरोति। ग्रूबे महाशयोऽपि सुपर्णाध्यायस्य चिकित्सिते संस्करणे 'बभूवु'रित्येव स्वीचकार। तथाप्यस्माकं भाष्यकारस्य सविधे या मातृकाऽऽसीत्तत्र 'बभूव' इत्यशुद्धः पाठः समतिष्ठत, अतः एषा भ्रान्तिः। (अग्रेऽपि द्रष्टव्यम्)

॥ *पदपाठः* ॥

आदि॑त्या। रु॒द्राः। वस॑वः। अथ॑। सा॒ध्याः। सोमं॑। रक्ष॑तः।
ब॒हु॒धा। नि०वि॑ष्टाः। मरु॑तः। ब्र॒ह्म॒न्। क्व॑। नु। ते। ब॒भू॒वुः[७३]।०॥

॥ *भाष्यम्* ॥

हे गुरो एते मरुत्पर्यंताः देवाः सोमं रक्षंतः संतः बहुधा[बहु]भिः। प्रकारैः नानारूपवेशैः परितः परिवेष(श)रूपेण निविष्टाः व्यवस्थिताः। हे ब्रह्मन् ते सर्वे [क्व नु खलु] बभूव[७३] इति बभूवुः। व्यत्ययेन बहुत्वस्थाने एकवचनं। 'पुत्रं तु ब्रह्मणस्पति'रित्यादौ यथा व्यत्ययेनैकवचनस्थाने बहुवचनं। शेषं गतार्थम्॥

गुरुरुवाच –

प्राञ्च॑ आय॒न् वस॑वः प्रेक्ष॑माणा॒[७४]
उद॑ञ्चो॒ विश्वे॒ म॒रु॒तोऽथ॑ सा॒ध्याः।
दक्षि॑णा रु॒द्राः स॒ह ग॑न्धर्वसे॒नयां
प्र॒तीच॑ आदि॒त्यान॑नयद् वैन॒तेयः॥८॥

॥ *पदपाठः* ॥

प्राञ्च॑ः। आ॒य॒न्। वस॑वः। प्र॒० ईक्ष॑माणाः। उत्० अ॒ञ्चः।
विश्वे॑। मरु॑तः। अथ॑। सा॒ध्याः। दक्षि॑णा। रु॒द्राः। स॒ह। ग॒न्ध॒र्व॒०
से॒नया॑। प्र॒तीच॑ः। आ॒दि॒त्यान्। अ॒न॒य॒त्। वै॒न॒तेयः॥

॥ *भाष्यम्* ॥

हे इन्द्र। वसवः ८, प्रांचः पूर्वदिशि आयन् [अग]मन् गरुडत्रासात्। '*अय*' गतौ। विश्वे इति विश्वेदेवाः, तथा मरुतः ४९, अथ साध्याः एते उदंचः उदीच्यां आयन् आगच्छन्। रुद्राः ११, दक्षिणा इति दक्षिणस्यां आयन्। गताः। कथं। गंधर्वाणां सेनया सह। वैनतेयः आदित्यान् १२, प्रतीचः प्रत्यङ्मुखान् प्रतीच्यां अनयत् प्रापितवान्॥

इन्द्र उवाच –

वै॒श्वा॒न॒रो जा॒तवे॑दा॒ः क्वा॑सी॒द्
यो म॒ इन्दुं॑ परि॒गृह्याधि॑ तिष्ठति।

---

[७४] 'प्रेक्ष्य॑माणा' इति ग्रूबेमहाशयेन स्वीकृतः पाठः। अस्माकं मते तु 'प्रेर्य॑माणाः' इति साधीयः।

अर्चिर्ज्वलन्तमनिघृष्टतेजसं
कथं स्विद्देवाप्यति याति गृध्रः ॥९॥

॥ *पदपाठः* ॥

वैश्वानरः। जात०वेदाः। क्व। आसीत्। यः। मे। इंदुं। परि०
गृह्य। अधि। तिष्ठति। अर्चिःऽज्वलन्तं। अनिघृष्ट०तेजसं।
०। अपि। अति। याति। गृध्रः॥

॥ *भाष्यम्* ॥

हे ब्रह्मन् सः अग्निः क्व। स कः? यः मे इंदुं गृहीत्वा तिष्ठति। किं कृत्वा? अधि इति स्वस्थानं अधिरुह्य। गृध्रः गरुडस्तं वैश्वानरं कथं अति याति। अतिक्रामति। उल्लंघ्य गच्छति। स्विदिति प्रश्ने वितर्के वा। प्रकोपाद् गृध्र इति अवमानवचनं प्रयुङ्क्ते। कीदृशं जातवेदसं? अर्चिर्ज्वलन्तं। अर्चिर्भिः ज्वालाभिः ज्वलतीति अर्चिर्ज्वलन्। तं। कीदृशं वैश्वानरं? अनिघृष्टतेजसं। न निघृष्टं केनचित् प्रच्यावितं क्षरितं तेजो यस्य असौ अनिघृष्टतेजाः। तम् ॥

बृहस्पतिरुवाच –

घृतस्य सिन्धूननयद् वैनतेयो
बद्धं बद्धान्ययुतानि षष्टिम्।
तैस्तर्पयित्वा तवं जातवेदसं
हिरण्मयः स्त्रोत्यपतच्छकुन्तः॥१०॥

॥ *पदपाठः* ॥

घृतस्य। सिन्धून्। अनयत्। वैनतेयः। बद्धं। बद्धानि। अयुतानि।
षष्टिं। तैः। तर्पयित्वा। तवं। जात० वेदसं। हिरण्मयः।
स्त्रोति। अपतत्। शकुंतः॥

॥ *भाष्यम्* ॥

सिन्धवो ह्रदाः। मेर्वादिप्रमुखनानादिव्यभूमिषु वर्तमानाः। तान् घृतह्रदान् अनेकान् नानाप्रदेशेभ्यः अनयत् वैनतेयः आनिनाय। कतिसंख्याकान् घृतह्रदान्? ६० षष्टिं अयुतानि। एतावत्संख्याकान् षट्लक्ष्याणीत्यर्थः। तान् अमृतरक्षणे नियुक्तस्य वैश्वानरस्य समीपे गरुडः आनीतवान् पक्षाभ्यां कृत्वा। किंलक्षणानि षष्टिं अयुतानि? बद्धानि नियतानि। अन्यूनानि। अनतिरिक्तानि च। पूर्णान्येवेत्याशयः।

बद्धं सत्यं। तैः षड्लक्षसंख्यैः घृतस्य सिंधुभिः आज्यहृदैः हे इन्द्र तव जा[तवेदसं] वैश्वानरं तर्पयित्वा असौ हिरणमयः शकुंतः पक्षी सुपर्णः[७५]। स्त्रोति इति स्त्रो[तसि] . . . के सागरमध्ये अपतत्। उष्णेन तापेन संतप्तः सन्। स्त्रोतस्-शब्दस्य ङौ परे छांदसेन टिलोपेनैतद्रूपं सप्तम्येकवचनांतम्। स्त्रोति[७६] इति। अनेन तर्पणोपायेन वैश्वानरमाराध्य व[शम्]आनीय तस्मात् प्रदेशात् दूरतरं प्रेष्य, प्रवेशसौकर्यं कृतवान्। अपरया गुरुरेवो[वाच]–

वैश्वानरं तर्पयित्वा[७७] घृतेन
सर्वांनन्यान्त्सोमपालान् विजित्य।
महामेघेव निम्नानि समानि कुर्वन्
परांङ् गच्छद् गरुडो वैनतेयः॥११॥

॥ *पदपाठः* ॥

वैश्वानरं। तर्पयित्वा[७७]। घृतेन। सर्वान्। अन्यान्। सोम०पालान्। वि० जित्य। महामेघःऽइव। निम्नानि। समानि। कुर्वन्। परांङ्। गच्छत्। गरुडः। वैनतेयः।

॥ *भाष्यम्* ॥

वैनतेयो गरुडः वैश्वानरं षड्लक्षाणां घृतहृदानां घृतेन तर्पयित्वा, अन्यांश्च सर्वान् यमादी[न्] ईशानांतान् लोकपालान् दिक्पालान् विजित्य विविधप्रकारैर्जित्वा, तान् सर्वान् वैश्वा[न]रादीन् पराङ् इति पराङ्मुखान् सम्पाद्य पराङ्मुखीकृत्य

---

[७५] हिरण्यं नाम सुवर्णम्। सुवर्णं तु अग्नेः संभूतम् 'अग्नेरपत्यम्' इति प्राचीना धारणा, अतोऽत्यन्तानलसंयोगेऽपि नैव तस्य विनाशः। सुपर्णस्तु हिरण्मयः। अतोऽग्निस्तं दग्धुं नैव प्रभवति। अक्षतशरीरः स ज्वालाभ्यो निष्क्रामति। सुवर्णस्यादाह्यत्वे प्रमाणम् – "सुवर्णं तैजसम्। असति प्रतिबन्धकेऽत्यन्तानलसंयोगेऽपि अनुच्छिद्यमान-जन्यद्रव्यत्वात्" (सिद्धान्तमुक्तावली-तेजोनिरूपणम्)। "अग्नेरपत्यमेतद् वै सुवर्णमिति धारणा" (*महाभारते*, अनुशासनपर्वणि ८५.२४७॥)

[७६] दुर्व्याख्येयस्यासंगतस्य च 'स्त्रोति अपतत्' इति पदद्वयस्य शुद्धो मूलपाठः 'सोऽत्यपतत्' इत्येवं प्रतिभाति (=हिरण्मयः स शकुन्तः जातवेदसम् अत्यपतत्, अतिलंघ्य गतः)। 'स्त्रोति स्त्रोतसि अपतत्' इति सर्वथा विरुद्धमर्थं जनयति।

[७७] पूर्वस्मिन् मन्त्रे तर्पयित्वा इति पदमन्तोदात्तम्। परमस्मिन् मन्त्रे तदेव पकारस्योदात्तत्वात् (तर्पयित्वा) मध्योदात्तम् इति विसंगतिः। सामान्यतः क्त्वान्तानामन्तोदात्तत्वमेव, अतः पूर्वं शुद्धम्।

गच्छत्। अडागमाभावश्छांदसः। अगच्छत्। अमृतनिक्षेपणस्थानं सुगमं कृत्वा अगच्छत्। तत्र अगमत्। किं कुर्वन् सन् अगच्छत्? [निम्नानि स्थ]लानि समा[नि] कुर्वन् मृत्तिकया पूरयित्वा। अमृतस्थानात् परितः ये गर्ता . . . वा प्रमुखाः आसन्। तथा ये नदाः नदीश्च (!) आसन् ताः शोषयित्वा, तासां निर्जलान् मध्यगर्तान् मृद्भिः प्रपूर्य समा[नि]स्थलानि कुर्वन् अमृतबिले गतः। यथा महामेघः प्रबलपर्जन्यः विषमानि(णि) गर्तवंति स्थलानि उन्नतानि संपादयति। उन्नतस्थलानि खनित्वा परिखीकुर्वन्। इति षड्विंशतितमो वर्गः॥

॥ चतुर्दशं सूक्तम् ॥

॥ अथ सप्तविंशो वर्गः ॥

उत्तरस्या ऋच 'एक'माद्यमर्धर्चं बृहस्पतेर्वाक्यम् तदनन्तरमिन्द्रस्य। गुरुरुवाच –

एको बहून् भीमबलोऽध्यतिष्ठत्
तवैव[७८] शक्तः सदृशो[७९] बलेन।
यन्मे रक्षान्[८०] धर्षितवाञ्छकुन्तस्-
तेनाऽस्य क्रुद्धः प्र हरामि वज्रम्॥१॥

॥ *पदपाठः* ॥

एकः। बहून्। भीम०बलः। अधि। अतिष्ठत्। तव। एव[७८]। शक्तः। स०दृशः[७९]। बलेन। यत्। मे। रक्षान्[८०]। धर्षित०वान्। शकुन्तः। तेन। अस्य। क्रुद्धः। प्र। हरामि। वज्रम्॥

॥ *भाष्यम्* ॥

एकः गरुडः बहून् सोमपालकान् अधिरुह्य। आक्रम्य। अतिष्ठत्। आक्रम्य अभिभूय विजित्य। कीदृशः? हे इन्द्र। बलेन सामर्थ्येन तवैव सदृशः तुल्यः। अतएव भीमबलः। भयंकरशक्तिः। किंलक्षणो गरुडः? शक्तः। सर्वकार्यकरणसमर्थः। अथोत्तरार्धेनेन्द्रः स्वप्रकोपं विवृण्वन्नाह गुर्वादीन् प्रति।

इन्द्र उवाच –

यत् यस्मात् कारणात् शकुन्तोऽसौ पक्षी गरुडः मे रक्षां सोमरक्षां इति

---

[७८] 'तव एव' इत्यस्य स्थाने 'तव इव' (तवेव) पाठः साधीयान्।

[७९] 'सदशो' इति ग्रूबेमहाशयेन स्वीकृतः पाठः क्वचिदन्यत्रापि प्राप्यते।

[८०] भाष्यकारस्त्वत्र 'रक्षां' इति पठति तथैव च व्याकुरुते ('रक्षान्धर्षितवान्' इत्यनेनैष भ्रमः)।

सोमरक्षकान् सर्वान् चेतनाचेतनान् धर्षितवान् पराभू[तवा]न् तेन हेतुना अहं क्रुद्धोऽस्मि। अस्य गरुडस्यांगे वज्रं प्रहरामि। वज्रप्रहारं मुञ्चामि।

ए[वं प्र]तिज्ञाय गरुडसमीपे गत्वेन्द्रः सुपर्णपृष्ठे वज्रप्रहारं मुमोच। वज्रं तु वज्रोपरि आस्फालितं यथा निःफलं भवति तथैवासीत्। गरुडपृष्ठवज्रयोः परस्परास्फालनादग्निः पपात। न च गरुड[दे]हे व्रणमात्रमभवत्। ततो वितथप्रयत्न इन्द्रो गरुडं प्रति आगत्येदमवोचत्।

इन्द्र उवाच –

तपोमयं क्षुरपंवि स्ववीर्यं
येनं वृत्रस्य हृदंयं निकृंत्तम्[८१]।
तन्मे वज्रं प्रतिंहतं शकुन्ते[८२]
बृहंस्पते किन्नु भूतं सुंपर्णः॥२॥

॥ *पदपाठः* ॥

तपःऽमयं। क्षुर०पंविः। स्व०वीर्यं। येनं। वृत्रस्यं। हृदंयं। नि० कृंत्तं। तत्। मे। वज्रं। प्रतिं० हतं। शकुंते।[८२] बृहंस्पते। किं। नु। भूतं। सु०पर्णः।

॥ *भाष्यम्* ॥

हे बृहस्पते। नु इति वितर्के। तत् मे वज्रं शकुंते अमुष्मिन् पक्षिणि पातितं सत् प्रतिहतं। प्रत्युत भग्नधारमिवास। वंध्यमास। हे बृहस्पते। असौ सुपर्णः किं भूतं? एवंविधं आश्चर्यरूपं अपरिमेयबलं किं भूतं? किं प्राणि? तद् ब्रूहि। तत् किं वज्रं! येन वज्रेण वृत्रस्य वृत्रासुरस्य हृदयं नितरां कृत्तं विदारितं। '*कृती*' छेदने। कीदृशं वज्रं। तपोमयं। तपोबलेन व्याप्तं। दधीचऋषेः तपसा महाप्रभावं। तस्यास्थिमयत्वात्। पुनः कीदृशं? क्षुरपवि क्षुरधारं। स्ववीर्यं स्वस्यैव वीर्यं यस्मिन् तत् स्ववीर्यं सहायानपेक्षमित्यर्थः।

गुरुरुवाच –

एष छन्दांसि सहिंतानि शक्र
यजुर्मयः सामंतनूः सुंपर्णः।

---

[८१] ग्रूबेमहाशयः अत्र 'निकृन्तम्' इति पठति, तदशुद्धम्।

[८२] 'शकुन्ते' इत्यस्य सर्वानुदात्तत्वं चिन्त्यम्। नैतत् संबुद्धिपदम्।

इन्दुं पीत्वा वीर्यवांस्ताक्ष्र्यपुंत्रस्
तेन वज्रः[८३] प्रतिंहतस्तवात्रं ॥३॥

॥ *पदपाठः* ॥

एषः। छंदांसि। सहिंतानि। शक्रः। यजुःऽमयः। सामं०तनूः। सु०पर्णः। इन्दुं। पीत्वा। वीर्य०वांन्। ताक्ष्र्य० पुंत्रः। तेनं। वज्रः[८३]। प्रतिं०हतः। तवं। अत्रं॥

॥ *भाष्यम्* ॥

हे शक्र। एष गरुडः। सहितानि। एकत्र मिलितानि चत्वारि छंदांसि विद्धि। छंदोमयः। वेदमयशरीरत्वमेव प्रकटयन्नाह। यजुर्मयः सामतनूः। सामान्येव तनूर्यस्यासौ सामतनूः। उपलक्षणमेतत्। ऋङ्मयोऽथर्वमयश्च। कीदृक्। इंदुं पीत्वा वीर्यवान्। सोममदेनोत्कटबलः। तेन हेतुना अत्रास्मिन् सुपर्णे तव वज्रः प्रतिहतः। पफाल। वंध्यो जातः।

अथ प्रहारे निःफले सति इन्द्रः सामवाक्यैः सुपर्णमनुनयन् स्वार्थसिद्धिं प्रार्थयते। इंद्र उवाच। गरुडं प्रति –

इदं देवानामरिंघाति वज्रं-
मावृत्रंपूर्वमनिहत्य शत्रुंम्।
तदावृंत्तं[८४] तत् सुराणां न साधु
वज्रंस्य मानः क्रियंतां गरुत्मन्॥४॥

॥ *पदपाठः* ॥

इदं। देवानां। अरिं०घाति। वज्रं। आ०वृत्रंपूर्वं। अनि०हत्यं। शत्रुं। तत्। आ०वृंत्तं। तत्। सुराणां। न। साधु। वज्रंस्य। मानंः। क्रियंतां। गरुत्मन्।

---

[८३] 'वज्र'पदस्य पूर्वस्यामृचि नपुंसके, एतस्यां तु पुंल्लिंगे प्रयोग इति बुधैर्निभालनीयम्!

[८४] भाष्यकारस्तु 'तदावृत्तम्' इत्यस्य स्थाने कदाचिद् 'अनावृत्तम्' इति पाठं स्वीकरोति, किन्तु मूले पदपाठे च वर्तमानस्य 'तदावृत्तम्' इत्यस्यापि बोधस्तस्यास्ति। साधिष्ठः पाठस्तु 'यदावृत्त'मिति। (अग्रेऽपि द्रष्टव्यम्)

॥ *भाष्यम्* ॥

हे गरुत्मन्। तत् इदं वज्रं आवृत्रपूर्वं यथा स्यात्तथा सुराणां शत्रुं अनिहत्य अहत्वा न आवृत्तं।[८४] न आवर्त्तते स्म। न निवृत्तं। आवृत्रपूर्वमित्यस्य कोऽर्थः? वृत्रः पूर्वो मुख्यो येषां ते वृत्रपूर्वाः। वृत्रपूर्वान् वृत्रादीन् अभिव्याप्य इति आवृत्रपूर्वं। अभिविधावाङ्। आवृत्रपूर्वं यथा स्यात्तथा। अयमाशयः। वृत्रप्रभृतीनपि सुराणां शत्रून् अहत्वा न आवृत्तं न निवृत्तं पूर्वकाले। अधुना तद्वज्रं अहत्वा आवृत्तं निःफलं जातम्। तत् साधु न। तत् युक्तं न। किंभूतं वज्रं। देवानां अरिघाति। अरिघ्नं। अरीन् घातयतच्छीलं (घातयत् शीलं) अरिघाति। हे गरुत्मन्। तस्य वज्रस्य मानः सत्कारः क्रियताम्। यद्वा एवं पाठः। *आ(अना-?)वृत्तपूर्वमनिहत्य शत्रुं*। तस्मिन् पाठे अयमर्थः। इदं वज्रं शत्रुं अनिहत्य अहत्वा कदाचित् आवृत्तपूर्वं न। कदाचिदपि विफलं न आवृत्तं। पूर्वं पूर्वकाले। [यदद्य आवृत्तं] तत् सुराणां साधु न। हितं न। हे गरुत्मन् वज्रस्य मानः पूजा क्रियताम्, यद् इदं दधीच-ऋषेरस्थिस्वरूपम्।

एवमिन्द्रेणानुनीतः सन् सामवाक्यपूर्वकं प्रार्थितश्च सन् गरुडोऽपीन्द्रमनोरथं प्रमाणयिष्यन्नाह॥ गरुड उवाच इन्द्रं प्रति –

औ॒र्वं त॒नू॒जं॑ वि॒सृं॒जा॒म्य॒नि॒न्द्य॒
तच्छिं॑न्धि वज्रे॑ण भव॒ त्वमीड्यः॑।

हि॒तं दे॒वानां॑ प्रि॒यमे॒व तु॒भ्यं॒
साम्नां॑ऽस्मि कु॒र्ता न बले॑न शक्र॥५॥

॥ *पदपाठः* ॥

और्वं॑। तनूं॑जं। वि। सृ॒जा॒मि॒। अ॒निं॒द्य॒। तत्। छिं॒धि॒। वज्रे॑ण। भ॒व॒। त्वं। ईड्यः॑। हि॒तं। दे॒वानां॑। प्रि॒यं। ए॒व। तु॒भ्यं॑। साम्नां॑। अ॒स्मि॒। कु॒र्ता। न। बले॑न। श॒क्र॒॥

॥ *भाष्यम्* ॥

हे अनिन्द्य इंद्र। त्वत्कामनासिद्धये अहं और्वं ऊरौ भवं तनूजं विसृजाम्येकं। उत्सृजामि। मुंचाम्यधुना। हे इंद्र त्वं स्ववज्रेण तत् च्युतं मदीयं पिच्छं छिंधि। खण्डय। खण्डितं कुरु। तथा सति त्वं च ईड्यो भव। स्तुत्यो भव। कृतकृत्यो भव। पूर्णमनोरथो भव। एवं करणं देवानां हितं। तुभ्यमपि प्रियमेव। एतदपि पुच्छविमोचनं तु अहं साम्ना सामवाक्येनैव प्रियवाक्येनैव अनुनयेन प्रार्थितः सन् कर्त्ताऽस्मि। परं तु बलेन कोऽपि चेत् पिच्छमपि मोचयितुमिच्छति तर्हि अहं एतत् पत्रविमोचनकर्त्ता नास्मि।

गरुड उवाच –

ऋषेर्मानं करिष्यामि वज्रं यस्यास्थिसम्भवम्।
वज्रस्य च करिष्यामि तव चैव शतक्रतो॥६॥

॥ *पदपाठः* ॥

ऋषेः। मानं। करिष्यामि। वज्रं। यस्य। अस्थि॰सम्भवं। वज्रस्य। च। करिष्यामि। तव। च। एव। शतक्रतो इति शत॰क्रतो॥

॥ *भाष्यम्* ॥

हे शतक्रतो। अहं तस्य ऋषेर्दधीचेः मानं करिष्यामि। दास्यामि। मानं सत्कारं पूजां करिष्यामि। आज्ञास[म्पाद]नं करिष्यामि। तस्य कस्य ऋषेः? यस्य अस्थिसंभवं इदं वज्रं हस्ते धारयसि। अस्य वज्रस्य आयुधस्य च मानं पूजां करिष्यामि। गौरवं सम्पादयिष्यामि। तव च मानं गौरवं करिष्यामि। पिच्छं त्यक्ष्यामीत्यर्थः। अन्यथैतेषां त्रयाणां लघुत्वं भवेत्॥ इति सप्तविंशतितमोवर्गः॥

॥ अथ अष्टाविंशो वर्गः ॥

वामदेव ऋषिरुवाच –

छिन्नं त्रिधा तत्कुलिशेन पत्रं
तस्याग्रखण्डादभवन्मयूरः।
मध्ये द्विवक्त्रा भुजगेन्द्रराजी
मूले च शत्रुर्नकुलस्त्वहीनाम् (नकुलः फणीनाम्)[८५]॥७॥

॥ *पदपाठः* ॥

छिन्नं। त्रिधा। तत्। कुलिशेन। पत्रं। तस्य। अग्र॰खण्डात्। अभवत्। मयूरः। मध्ये। द्वि॰वक्त्रा। भुजगेन्द्र॰राजी। मूले। च। शत्रुः। नकुलः। फणीनां॥ [तु। अहीनाम्।]

॥ *भाष्यम्* ॥

तत् पत्रं। पिच्छं इन्द्रेण कुलिशेन वज्रेण त्रिधा छिन्नं। त्रिखण्डं कृतं। तस्य अग्रखण्डात् मयूरः शिखी अभवत्, उत्पन्नः। मध्ये इति मध्यखण्डात् भुजगेन्द्रराजी

---

[८५] 'अहीनाम्' इति भाष्यकारधृतपाठः। पदपाठे तु 'फणीनाम्' इति विद्यते। एतदेव ग्रूबेमहाशयेनाप्यंगीकृतम् ('नकुलः फणीनाम्)।

नाम काचिज्जातिरभवत्। शलको नाम प्राणी उत्पन्नः। मूले इति मूलखण्डात् नकुलजातिरभूत्। नकुलो रक्तमुखः जातिविशेषः। स च अहीनां सर्पाणां शत्रुर्हन्ता। एवं जाते सति ततः इन्द्रः सुपर्णमिदमपृच्छत्।

पृच्छामि त्वा शकुने किंबलोऽसि
कस्ते भागः समु सह्यो[८६] द्विजेन्द्र।
आ चक्ष्व मे वीर्यमसह्यसाहं
सख्यं च नो भवति शाश्वतीभ्यः॥८॥

॥ *पदपाठः* ॥

पृच्छामि। त्वा। शकुने। किं०बलः। असि। कः। ते। भागः। सं। ऊँ इति। सह्यः[८६]। द्विज०इन्द्र। आ। चक्ष्व। मे। वीर्यं। असह्य०सहं। सख्यं। च। नः। भवति। शाश्वतीभ्यः॥

॥ *भाष्यम्* ॥

इन्द्र आह। हे शकुने विहग। हे द्विजेन्द्र, द्विजाः पक्षिणस्तेषामिन्द्र, पक्षिराज। हे असह्यसाहं। सहं एवं साहं। आदन्तत्वमार्षं। सोढुं शक्यं सह्यं। न सह्यमसह्यं। असह्यं साहं बलं यस्यासावसह्यसाहः। त्वा त्वां प्रति अहमिदं पृच्छामि। किं? त्वं किंबलः असि। किं इति कियत् बलं यस्यासौ स किंबलः। तव बलं कियदस्ति। हे शकुने। ते तव कः भागः अंशः देहोद्भ[वः] संसह्योऽस्ति। सम्यक् सोढुं शक्योऽस्ति। त्वं हि प्रकृत्या सर्वात्मना दुःसह एवासि। त्वच्छरीरे तु को विभागः अंशः किमंगं कस्मिन्नवसरे वा केनोपायेन वा कोऽप्यंशः सह्यः सोढुं शक्योऽस्ति तद्वद। त्वं स्ववीर्यं स्वसामर्थ्यं मह्यमाचक्ष्व। नः अस्माकं त्वया सार्धं शाश्वतीभ्यः समाभ्यः शाश्वतीनां समानार्थेव निरन्तरभावीनि वर्षाणि अक्षयं भवितुं सख्यं सखित्वं मित्रत्वं भवति भविष्यति। अतः सखित्वात्स्वशक्तिं मदग्रे कथ[य]। तव शक्तिः कियती। 'शाश्वतीभ्यः समाभ्य' इति चतुर्थीबहुवचनादयमर्थो लभ्यते। आचंद्रार्ककालाय। आचन्द्रार्कस्थायि आवयोः सख्यमस्तु। इति। गरुडः प्रत्युत्तरं अब्रवीत् –

अष्टौ भूमीर्नवदिशस्त्रीन्त्समुद्राञ्छचीपते।
परस्सहस्त्रं पर्वतान्वहेयं कामयेयं चेत्॥९॥

---

[८६] 'सह्यः' इति पदस्य सर्वानुदात्तत्वं चिन्त्यम्। 'सह्यः' इत्येवं रूपं शुद्धं स्यात्।

॥ *पदपाठः* ॥

अ॒ष्टौ। भूमीः॑। नव॑। दिशः॑। त्रीन्। स॒मु॒द्रान्। श॒ची॒०प॒ते। पर॑ःऽसहस्रं॑। पर्व॑तान्। व॒हे॒यं॒। का॒मये॑यं। चे॒त्॥

॥ *भाष्यम्* ॥

गरुड आह। हे शचीपते। अहं चेत् कामयेयं इच्छेयं एवं कर्तुमिच्छामि तत्सर्वं वहेयं। वो(ढुं अ)हं शक्नोमि। अष्टौ भूमीः। इमाः पातालानि सप्त। अष्टमी इयमेव पृथिवी। एताः अष्टौ भूमीः। तथा त्रीन् समुद्रान्। एको लवणोदकः। एको मृष्टोदकः। विचित्ररसानां पंचानां सागराणानां समुदायः सर्वोऽपि एक एव समुद्र इत्येकत्वेन समूहो विवक्षितः। अनेनाकूतेन त्रित्वं निर्दिष्टम्। ९ नव दिशः। इमाः प्राच्यादयः सकोणाः ८ अष्टौ। नवमी ऊद्ध्र्वा दिक्। तदुक्तं शांखायनकल्पे –'*अथ यन्नवविधं तन्नवरात्रेण चतस्रो दिशश्चतस्रोऽवान्तरं दिश ऊद्ध्र्वेयं नवमी दिक् नवाक्षरा बृहतीति*'॥ ननु अधस्तनादिदिक् सत्यपि कथं नोक्ता। दश दिश इति सत्यं। अष्टौ भूमीरित्यत्र पाताललोकानां सर्वेषामन्तर्भावात् पौनरुक्त्यं स्यात् तस्मान्नवेत्युक्तम्। परः सहस्रान् पर्वतान् वहेयं। वोढुं शक्नोमि। सहस्रात् परे अधिकाः परःसहस्राः तान् परःसहस्रान्। अष्टौ भूमीरित्यत्र पृथिव्या अन्तर्भावो पृथिव्यां तु पर्वतानामन्तर्भावे सत्यपि तेषां महाभारव[त्त्वा]त् पृथगुपादानं न पुनरुक्तिदोषमावहति। अहं निजेच्छया एतत्सर्वं समुच्चितमेव युगपद्धेलामात्रेण वहामि। एतावत् मे वीर्यं। इत्येवं गरुडेन स्ववीर्ये यथार्थवाक्येनाविष्कृते, इंद्रः 'हे सुपर्ण, त्वमिमं मदीयममृतकलशं गृहाण। गृहीत्वा चेष्टस्थानं प्रति नीत्वा स्वकार्यं साधय। परं तु इमं समयं मया क्रियमाणं पालयेथाः। अनेन समयपरिपालनेन गृहाण। सत्यवचनेन एतं समयं प्रथममंगीकुरुष्व। पश्चात्सोमकलशमादत्स्व। आदाय च यथेष्टं याहि'। कोऽयं समय इत्याशङ्कायां समयव्यापिनीमृचमिंद्र आह –

इन्द्र उवाच –

इन्दु᳚ चेत्स॒र्पाः पा॑स्यन्ति॒ त्वया॑ द॒त्तं वि॑हङ्गम।
अर्ज॑न॒ं ते क॑रिष्या॒मि[87] तन्न सा॒धु भ॑विष्यति॥१०॥

---

[87] 'करिष्यामि' इति क्रियादं स्पष्टतया 'करिष्यन्ति' इत्यस्यापपाठः। अमरत्वं प्राप्ताः विषधराः क्रमशः सकलं प्राणिजातं दष्ट्वा यमलोकं प्रापयिष्यन्तीत्याशयः। 'ते'-पदस्य उदात्तत्वादत्र भाष्यकारेण कृतः 'तव' अर्थः नैव संगच्छते। तत्-शब्दस्यैवैतत् पुंल्लिंगे प्रथमाबहुवचनान्तम्। (अपरपृष्ठेऽपि द्रष्टव्यम्)

॥ *पदपाठः* ॥

इन्दुं। चेत्। सर्पाः। पास्यंति। त्वया। दत्तं। वि० हंगम।
अजनं। ते। करिष्यामि[८७]। तत्। न। साधु। भविष्यति॥

॥ *भाष्यम्* ॥

पाठान्तरं तु। '*हेलनं ते करिष्यामि यन्न साधु भविष्यति*' इति। '*अमानं ते करिष्यामी*' ति वा। इन्द्र आह। हे विहंगम हे सुपर्ण। चेत् सर्पाः इममिन्दुं सोममममृतं पास्यन्ति। अस्य पानं करिष्यन्ति तर्हि अहं ते तव गृहं अजनं जनशून्यं हीनं करिष्यामि। सर्वान् गृहवासिनः हत्वा॥ अथवा। ते तव अमानं अवमानं धिक्कारं करिष्यामि। न मानः अमानः। तं अमानं सन्मानविपर्ययं। यद्वा हेलनं प्रकोपं ते करिष्यामि। तत्तु नव (तव) साधु श्लाघ्यं न भविष्यति। हितं न भविष्यति। कीदृशमिन्दुं। त्वया दत्तमर्पितं संतं। अथ गरुडः अविरोधार्थीदमिन्द्रं प्रत्युत्तरमाह।

नाहमिन्दुं परास्यामि सर्पेभ्यः शत्रुबाधन।
हृत्वा तु दर्शयिष्यामि शंक्र मा सौम्य मे कुपः॥११॥

॥ *पदपाठः* ॥

न। अहं। इंदुं। परास्यामि। सर्पेभ्यः। शत्रु० बाधन। हृत्वा।
तु। दर्शयिष्यामि। शक्र। मा। सौम्य। मे। कुपः॥

॥ *भाष्यम्* ॥

गरुडो वदति। हे शक्र। हे शत्रुबाधन। शत्रूणां बाधाकर। शत्रून् बाधते इति शत्रुबाधनः। अहं सर्पेभ्यः इन्दुं सोमं न परास्यामि न प्रक्षिपामि न दास्यामि। किं तर्हि करिष्यामि। इतः सोमं हृत्वा सर्पेभ्यो दर्शयिष्यामि। हे शक्र हे सौम्य। प्रसन्नमूर्ते। त्वं मे मह्यं मा कुपः। कोपं मा कार्षीः। '*क्रुधद्रुहेर्ष्यासूयार्थानामि*'ति (पा० १.४.३७) चतुर्थी। इति अष्टाविंशतितमोवर्गः॥

॥ पञ्चदशं सूक्तम् ॥

॥ एकोनत्रिंशो वर्गः ॥

तत इंद्रेणानुमतो वैनतेयः सोमकलशं हृत्वा समातृकाणां नागानां दर्शयामास एवं वदन्। किं?

अयं वं आहृतः सोमस्तं पंश्यन्त्विह पार्थिवाः।
अहं चं मुक्तोंऽस्म्यरुणश्चं मुक्तो
मुक्ता चं शुङ्गा विनंता सुपर्णी॥१॥

॥ *पदपाठः* ॥

अयं। वः। आ०हृतः। सोमः। तं। पश्यन्तु। इह। पार्थिवाः।
अहं। च। मुक्तः। अस्मि। अरुणः। च। मुक्तः। मुक्ता। च।
शुंगा। वि०नंता। सु०पर्णी॥

॥ *भाष्यम्* ॥

हे नागाः। वः युष्मभ्यं अयं सोमः आहृतः मया स्वर्गादानीतः। वः युष्मदर्थे पार्थिवाः कद्रूसुताः सर्वेऽपि भवन्तः तं सोमं पश्यन्तु। पृथिवी कद्रूः। सा हि कद्रूः पृथिव्या अवतारः अत एवमुच्यते। पृथिव्याः अपत्यानि पार्थिवाः। मया निवेदितं सोमममृतं पश्यंतु। एनं गृह्णंतु। यथासुखं पिबन्तु। अनेन भवद्भ्योऽमृतार्पणेन अहं दासीपुत्रोऽपि दासत्वात् मुक्तोऽस्मि। च अपरं। अरुणः मद्भ्राता पंगुः सूर्यसारथिश्च प्राक् दासीपुत्रत्वाद्दासत्वं प्राप्तः। सोऽपि अधुना दास्यान्मुक्तः। च अपरं विनता मे माता शुंगेत्यपरपर्याया दास्यात् स्वयंकृतदोषोत्पादितात् मुक्ता। अमीषां सर्वेषामस्माकं दासत्वं गतम्।

सुपर्ण ऋगंतरेण स्वदास्यविमोक्षणं विशदयन् स्वस्य दौर्जन्यमपमार्ष्टुं सर्पेभ्यो हितमुपदिशति। गरुड उवाच सर्पान् प्रति,

अयं सोमः काद्रवेया मया स्वंस्-
तृतीयांत् पृष्ठाद्रजंसो विमानांत्।

आनीत इन्दुस्तदु वो ब्रवीमि
संपश्यथैनं प्र जिंघाति राजा॥२॥

॥ *पदपाठः*॥

अयं। सोमः। काद्रवेयाः[88]। मया। स्वरितिं स्वंः। तृतीयांत्। पृष्ठात्। रजंसः। वि०मानांत्। आ०नींतः। इंदुः। तत्। ऊँ इतिं। वः। ब्रवीमि। सं। पश्यथ। एनं। प्र। जिघाति[89]। राजां॥

॥ *भाष्यम्* ॥

हे काद्रवेयाः मया स्वर् इति स्वर्गलोकात् अयं सोमः आहृतः आनीतः। किंलक्षणात् स्वः स्वर्गलोकात्। तृतीयाद्रजसः। रजःशब्दो लोकपर्यायः। *'लोका रजांस्युच्यंत'* इति यास्कः (४.१९)। तृतीयात् लोकादित्यर्थः। किंलक्षणात् तृतीयलोकात्। विमानात्। विमानमयात्। स्वर्गे हि सर्वेऽपि सुरगणाः वैमानिकाः एव वसन्ति। ते च विमानारूढा एव यान्ति। एवं विमानत्वं तृतीयत्वं। भूर्लोक-भुवर्लोक-स्वर्लोक इति क्रमात्। किं लक्षणात्। पृष्ठात्। स्वर्गस्य पृष्ठात्। सेव्यप्रदेशात्। यद्वा स्वः इति षष्ठ्येकवचनं। स्वःपृष्ठात्। नाकस्य पृष्ठात्। उक्तं च श्रुतौ मन्त्रभागे। *'नाकस्य पृष्ठे अधितिष्ठति श्रितो यः पृणातीति'* (ऋ० १.१२५.५)। तथा *'तृतीये पृष्ठे अधिरोचने दिवः'* (ऋ० ९.८६.२७) च। पृष्ठत्वं प्रसिद्धं। तत् तस्मात् कारणात् अहं वः युष्मान् प्रति ब्रवीमि। एनं सोमं सम्यक् यूयं पश्यथ? काकूक्त्या क्रियापदं प्रश्नार्थत्वात्। *प्रजिघाति* राजा। [पाठान्तरे] *प्रतिहाति* राजा। राजा इंद्रः एनं सोमं प्रजिघाति प्रेरयति। स्वकीयं नाकलोकं प्रति प्रेरयिष्यति। नेष्यति। तस्मात् रक्षणे यत्नं कुरुत। यद्वा एनं प्रति इं(द्रो) हाति जहाति त्यजति त्रपां [कृपां ?]। दयालुरपि निर्दयो भविष्यति। अथ [आदि-] वर्णलोपेन जहातीत्यर्थे हातीत्येवमेव। राजा सुराणां पतिः। अथवा *प्रतिहन्तीति* पाठः। सुरराजः एनं सोमं प्रति ये आकांक्षां कुर्वंति। ये तृष्णां कुर्वंति तान् तान् आकांक्षां कुर्वतः इंद्रोः हंति नाशयति। तस्मात् अमृते स्वप्राणरक्षणे च प्रयत्नं कुरुत। इंद्राद्भयं शंकनीयं।

---

[88] 'काद्रवेयाः' (हे कद्रूपुत्राः) इति संबुद्धिपदं सर्वानुदात्तत्वं विहाय कथमत्र 'वैनतेय'वद् अन्तोदात्तत्वं बिभर्ति, इत्यस्य कारणं चिन्तनीयम्। तदेव परस्यामृचि 'उरोगमाः' इत्यत्र।

[89] 'प्र-जिघाति' इत्यस्य स्थाने भाष्यकारः 'जिहीर्षति' इत्यपि संहितापाठे पाठान्तरत्वेनोल्लिखति, किन्तु नैतत् पदं कुत्रापि भाष्ये व्याख्यातं वर्तते। अपरे च पाठान्तरे 'प्रति-हाति' 'प्रति हन्ति' च, ये व्याख्याते।

इत्थं सुपर्णेन सोमकलशे नागेभ्यो दत्ते आत्ममातुः सपुत्रायाः दास्यमोक्षे सम्पादिते, पुनः पुनः प्रमाणवाक्यैर्दृढीकृते च, ततो दास्यविनिर्मुक्तकुटुंबे गरुडे यथेष्टगते सति, सपदि शक्रस्तत्रागत्य नागान् प्रति निःशंकमेवमुवाच। इंद्र उवाच नागान् प्रति।

अहं हरामि वः सोमं(मः)[१०] सर्वेषामनु धावताम्।
यो वीरः सोऽनु सदतु सर्वे वा वीरयध्वमुरोगमाः॥३॥

॥ *पदपाठः* ॥

अहं। हरामि। वः। सोमं। सर्वेषां। अनु। धावतां। यः। वीरः।
सः। अनु। सदतु। सर्वे। वा। वीरयध्वं। उरःऽगमाः॥

॥ *भाष्यम्* ॥

इंद्रः कथयति। 'अहं हरामि वः *सोमः*' हे नागाः अयं सोमः। वः युष्मभ्यं। गरुडेन दत्तं(:), तमिमं सोममहं हरामि। अथवा *अहं हरामि वः सोम*मिति पाठः। वः युष्माकं सोममहं हरामि। युष्माकं सर्वेषामेनं सोममनु लक्ष्यीकृत्य धावतां मध्ये यः कश्चिद्वीरः शूरो भवति। सः एनं सोमं अनु लक्ष्यीकृत्य सदतु। उपविशतु। सोमसमीपे तिष्ठतु। सीदतु इत्यस्य स्थाने सदत्विति छांदसः प्रयोगः। वा अथवा। हे उरोगमाः उरगाः यूयं सर्वेऽपि यदि शूराः भवथः। तर्हि सर्वे यूयं वीरयध्वं वीरत्वं कुरुत। शौर्यं दर्शयत। पराक्रमं कुरुत। अहं प्रसिद्धवृत्त्या सोमं हरामि। यदि शक्तिर्भवति तर्हि मया सह युध्यध्वं। इत्यर्थः। एवमुच्चैर्ब्रुवन्निंद्रः सोमकलशं हृत्वा दिवं गतः। ते नागास्तु निराशा बभूवुः। गरुडः प्रागेव यथेष्टं क्वापि गतवान्। गरुडस्यासंभिधाने(? अभिसंधानेन) इन्द्रो हृत्वा स्वर्गं गतः। इदं वृत्तं ज्ञात्वा गरुडः स्वर्गे इंद्र-समीपे गत्वा इंद्रं प्रति इत्थमुवाच –

अयं तं आहृतः सोमो यं तेऽहमंहरम्पुरेन्दुमिन्द्र[११]।
अहं चं मुक्तोऽस्म्यरुणश्चं मुक्तो
मुक्ता चं शुंगा विनंता निरोधात्॥४॥

---

[१०] 'सोमः' इत्येष भाष्यकारेण धृतोऽशुद्धः पाठः। मूले, पदपाठे च 'सोमम्' इत्यस्यैव निरवद्यपाठस्य स्वीकृतिः।

[११] 'पुरा'पर्यन्तमेवेयमनुष्टुप्पंक्तिः। 'इन्दुमिन्द्र'इत्यरिक्तान्यनपेक्षितानि पदानि। अग्रिमा पंक्तिस्त्रिष्टुप्।

॥ *पदपाठः* ॥

अयं। ते। आ० हृतः। सोमः। यं। ते। अहं। अहरं। पुरा।
इंदुं। इंद्र। ०। निरोधात्॥

॥ *भाष्यम्* ॥

गरुड उवाचेन्द्रं प्रति –

गरुडो ब्रूते। हे इंद्र। ते त्वया अयं प्रत्यक्षं दृश्यमानः सोमः आहृतः नागानां समीपात् आनीतः। अयं कः। यं ते त्वदीयमिंदुं सोमं। पुरा पूर्वस्मिन् मुहूर्ते अहं स्वयमेव अहरं स्वर्गात् हृतवानस्मि। अनेन त्वदीयेन सोमेन नागेभ्यो निवेदितेन अहं अस्मि मुक्तः निरोधात्। दासत्वात् दास्यात्। अरुणश्च निरोधात् मुक्तः। मम माता विनता च मुक्ताः। शुंगेति नाम्नी सा च निरोधात् मुक्ता॥ इत्थं त्वया उपकृतमिति भावः। अथेंद्रः स्वर्गे आगतं समीपस्थं गरुडं प्रति किंचित्प्रष्टुकामः प्रसंगोत्पादनाय प्रथमं स्वपराक्रमान् वर्णयति द्वाभ्यामृग्भ्यां।

इन्द्र उवाच गरुडं प्रति –

अहं पिप्रुन्नमुंचिं शंबरं च
हत्वा पुरेमं विप्रचित्तिं विजित्यं।
द्यावांपृथिवी परिं दधे
वासंसीव वृत्रहा॥५॥

॥ *पदपाठः* ॥

अहं। पिप्रुं। नमुंचिं। शंबरं। च। हत्वा। पुरा। इमं। विप्र०चित्तिं।
वि० जित्यं। द्यावां० पृथिवी इतिं। परिं। दधे। वासंसीऽइव।
वृत्र०हा॥

॥ *भाष्यम्* ॥

इन्द्रो वदति। हे गरुड। पुरा पूर्वस्मिन् काले अतीतकाले अहं ऋगादावुक्तांस्त्रीन् असुरान् हत्वा इमं प्रसिद्धं विप्रचितिं नामानं दानवं जित्वा इमे द्यावापृथिवी परिदधे परिधानीयं कृतवान्। कटिवेष्टनं कृतवान्। के इव। वाससी इव। '*अर्द्धमिदस्य प्रतिरोदसी उभे*' (ऋ० ६.३०.१) इति श्रुतेः। कीदृगहं। वृत्रहा। वृत्रं नाम असुरं हतवान् इति वृत्रहा॥ इंद्र उवाच गरुडं प्रति॥

अहं बलेनात्यंतरं सपत्नान्
सर्वं भवामीदमहं बलेन।
एवं बलस्यातिबलस्य मे स्वतः(सुतः)[१२]
कथं स्विदिन्दुं सहसा जहर्थ॥६॥

॥ *पदपाठः* ॥

अहं। बलेन। अति। अतरं। स॰पत्नान्। सर्वं। भवामि। इदं।
अहं। बलेन। एवं॰ बलस्यं। अति॰ बलस्य। मे। सुतः।
कथं। स्वित्। इंदुं। सहसा। जहर्थ॥

॥ *भाष्यम्* ॥

हे गरुड। अहं बलेन शक्त्या सपत्नान्। रिपून् अतिशूरानपि अतरं। तीर्णः। अहं बलेन शक्त्या इदं सर्वं विश्वं जगत् स्वयं भवामि। पृथिव्यादिरूपैः अहमेव भवामि विलसामि। तादृशस्य मे इंदुं सोमं, हे गरुड, त्वं कथं जहर्थ। केन प्रयोजनेन हृतवानसि। किमर्थं हृतवानसि? तद् ब्रूहि। कीदृशः(स्य) मे। मम एवं बलस्य। एवं पूर्वोक्तं पिप्रुनमुच्यादिहननसाधकं बलं यस्यासावेवंबलः। तस्य एवंबलस्य। तथा अतिबलस्य अति उत्कटं द्यावापृथिव्योः परिधानकरणादिकं बलं यस्यासावतिबलः। अस्य अतिबलस्य। स्विदिति प्रश्ने वितर्के च। कथमित्यनेन प्रयोजनं पृच्छति। तव सोमस्य ईदृग्दुःखाहरस्य प्रयोजनं किं? तदेव ब्रूहि। केन आहरणसाधनेन जहर्थ हृतवानसि। इत्याशंक्य स्वयमेव तद्वर्णयति। स्वतः सहसेति। स्वतः समुत्पन्नेन सहसा बलेन। स्वतः शरीरादुत्क्षिप्तेन सहसा बलेन। अनन्योत्पाद्येन। तवेदं सहः बलं कस्या[प्या]राधितस्य देवस्यानुग्रहात् त्वया न लब्धं। किंतु स्वत एवोत्पन्नं। तपश्चरणादिनिरपेक्षतया। यद्वा *'एवं बलस्याति बलस्य मे सुतः'* इत्ययमेव पाठः समीचीनः। मे मम सुतः। कनीयान् भ्राता। 'सूनुर्भ्रातरि पुत्रे चे'त्यभिधानग्रंथे सूनुर्लघुभ्रातेत्युक्तं। लघुरेव मंतव्यः। पुत्रे चेति पुत्रसाहचर्यात्

[१२] पदपाठकारेण, ग्रूबेमहोदयेनापि स्वीकृतस्य 'सुतः' इत्यस्य स्थानेऽत्र विद्यमानो यः 'स्वतः' इति पाठः, स तु लिपिदोषादुत्पन्नः। उकारस्य मात्रायाः वकाररूपेण पठनात्। भाष्यकारस्तु 'स्वतः' इत्यस्य स्थाने 'सुतः' इत्यपि पाठान्तरं स्वीकरोति, किन्तु 'अनुजः' इति रूपेण तद् व्याख्याति। वस्तुतः सवनार्थकस्य 'सु'-धातोर्निष्पन्नमेतन्निष्ठान्तं पदं सोमस्य विशेषणम्। 'मे सुतः[सोमः]' मदर्थे लताभ्यः सुतः निष्पीडितः इत्यर्थः। पदपाठे प्रथमं 'स्वतः' इति विलिख्य तदनन्तरं तत् 'सुतः' इति रूपेण परिवर्तितम्। किन्तु शुद्धं तु वस्तुतः 'सुतम्' (. . . . मे सुतमिन्दुम्) इत्येव।

सूनुरित्यस्याभिधेये तात्पर्यं न शब्दे। अतः सुतोऽपि सूनुपर्यायत्वात् कनीयान् भ्राता भवति। इति एकोनत्रिंशत्तमोवर्गः।

॥ अथ त्रिंशो वर्गः ॥

कथं जहर्थेति पृष्टस्योत्तरं प्रत्यर्पयति –

माता मम विनंता सुपर्णी
दास्याद् दुःखमंगमत् स्पर्द्धयेन्द्र।
तस्यै निष्क्रयस्तव सोमं आसीत्
तमाहरं ते न विंघृष्टमन्यैः॥७॥

॥ *पदपाठः* ॥

माता। मम। वि०नंता। सु०पर्णी। दास्यात्। दुःऽखं। अगमत्। स्पर्द्धया। इन्द्र। तस्यै। निःऽक्रयः। तव। सोमः। आसीत्। तं। आ। अहरं। ते। न। वि० घृष्टं। अन्यैः॥

॥ *भाष्यम्* ॥

हे इंद्र, मम माता विनता दुःखं अगमत् प्रापत्। कस्मात्? दास्यात्, दासभावात्। कया दास्यमुत्पन्नं? स्पर्द्धया। असूयया। संघर्षेण। द्वेषेण। तस्यै मात्रे तवायं सोमः त्वदीयः सोमः निःक्रयः आसीत्। दासत्वनिःकृतये आसीत्। सोमार्पणेन दास्यात् निःकृतिः सर्पैरंगीकृता। अतः ते त्वदीयं तं सोममहमाहरं। आहृतवानस्मि। सोमहरणं कृतवानस्मि। किंलक्षणं सोमममृतं। अन्यैः परैः विघृष्टं स्पृष्टं न। केनापि न स्पृष्टः। केनचित् अधुनापि स्प्रष्टुं न शक्यत एव।

गरुड उवाचेन्द्रं प्रति -

तवं सुपर्णो मंघवंस्तवेन्दुंर्
भूतोंऽसि भव्यंश्च भवंश्चं शक्र।
त्वं गोप्तासि शरंणं त्वं संमुद्रस्
तवेदं विश्वं भुवंनं सं सुशांधि॥८॥

॥ *पदपाठः* ॥

तवं। सु०पर्णः। मघ०वन्। तवं। इंदुंः। भूतः। असि। भव्यंः।

च। भवन्। च। शक्र। त्वं। गोप्ता। असि। शरणं। त्वं। समुद्रः। तव। इदं। विश्वं। भुवनं। सं। सु० शाधि॥

॥ *भाष्यम्* ॥

गरुड आह। हे मघवन्। अयं सुपर्णो वैनतेयो मल्लक्षणो जनः तवैव। तावक एव। त्वद्दासः। इंदुः सोमश्च अमृतमयः तवैव। त्वदीय एव। यद्यपि मया आहृतः तथापि त्वत्स्वामिक एव। त्वं भूतोऽसि। अतीतकालोऽसि। भव्यो भविष्यंश्चासि। भविष्यत्कालोऽसि अनागतकालात्मासि। च अपरं भवन् वर्तमानकालोऽप्यसि। हे शक्र। त्वं सर्वस्य लोकस्य गोप्तासि। त्वं विश्वस्य शरणमसि। त्वं समुद्रोऽसि। असूयारहितोऽसि। मुत् हर्षः। आनंदः। मुदा सानंदेन सह वर्त्तंत इति समुदः पूर्णकामाः लोकाः। तान् राति[= लाति, *ला* आदाने] आदत्ते गृह्णाति अनुगृह्णातीति समुद्रः। सुखितेषु अनुग्रहमेव करोषि। न स्पर्द्धां। मत्सरं वा। इति समुद्रः। किंच इदं विश्वं तव। तावकमेव। विश्वस्य स्वामी त्वमेव। विश्वस्मिन्ममाप्यंतर्भावात्। तव सुपर्ण इत्युक्त्या विशेषतो मदीयप्रभुत्वाच्च मां सुतरां सं इति सम्यक् शाधि शिक्षय। आदिश। आज्ञापय नियुंक्ष्व। यतस्तवाहं नियोज्योऽस्मि। त्वं तु प्रभुत्वात् नियोक्तासि। अतः मां शाधि। *शासु* अनुशिष्टौ। अस्य धातोर्लोटि परस्मैपदं मध्यमपुरुषैकवचनं।

इत्थमिंद्रगरुडयोः संवादे प्रवर्तमाने पुत्रविरहं क्षणमात्रमप्यसहमाना विनता तद्दिदृक्षया स्वर्लोकमाजगाम। आगत्य च सविनयेन वचसा पुत्रस्यापराधमपमार्ष्टुमाह द्विपदामृचमिंद्र प्रति॥ विनतोवाचेंद्रं प्रति –

शूरं सुपर्णमरुणात्कनिष्ठ-
मन्नं प्रतीयाभि वदेममिन्द्र॥९॥

॥ *पदपाठः* ॥

शूरं। सु०पर्णं। अरुणात्। कनिष्ठं। अन्नं। प्रतीय। अभि। वद। इमं। इन्द्र।

॥ *भाष्यम्* ॥

शूरं सुपर्णमरुणात्कनिष्ठमन्नं प्रतीयामिवदेममिंद्र॥ इत्येषा द्विपदा।

अन्नमत्रामृतमेव। हे इंद्र। इमं सुपर्णं अन्नममृतमुद्दिश्य स्वर्लोके प्रागागतं, मातुर्दास्यविमोक्षणायामृतमाकांक्षन्तं, अमृतार्थे कृतापराधं प्रतीय ज्ञात्वा एनं अभि। अभिलक्ष्य। अभिमुखो भूत्वा सानुग्रहो भूत्वा वद। वात्सल्योपेतं वाक्यं वद। अनेन गर्वाहंकारादिदोषतो नापराद्धं। यत्तवामृतमाहृतं। किंतु आपन्निवारणार्थं

अपराद्धं। तस्मादस्मिन् कृपा विधेया। अत्र सोपयोगपदाध्याहारो युक्तो ज्ञेयः। अरुणादपि कनिष्ठमित्येतद्द्योत्पादनार्थं। बालत्वान्नास्य दोषः। बालत्वादौद्धत्यमपाम्रष्टुं अस्मिन् वत्सलो भवेत्यर्थः। अथेंद्रो विनतां विनीतामालक्ष्य सानुग्रहमना अमुष्यै वरं दित्सुराह। इंद्र उवाच विनतां प्रति॥

वरं॑ ददामि ते सौम्ये[१३] यं कं च मन॑सेप्ससि।
मत्सं॑ख्यादन्नं॑ममृतं॑त्वं वाचि त्वमेतदुभयं॑ वृणीष्व[१४]॥१०॥

॥ *पदपाठः* ॥

वरं॑। ददामि। ते। सौम्ये। यं। कं। च। मन॑सा। ईप्ससि।
मत्०सं॑ख्यात्। अन्नं॑। अमृतं॑०त्वं। वाचि। त्वं। एतत्। उभयं॑।
वृणीष्व॥

॥ *भाष्यम्* ॥

'*त्वमेतदुभयं तवेहेति* [तव इह इति]' केचित्पठन्ति।

हे सौम्ये, अक्रूरे क्षांते दांते विनते। तं वरं ते तुभ्यमहं ददामि। तं कं च वरं [यं] मनसा ईप्ससि वांछसि। मम सख्यात् स्नेहात् अन्नममृतं लभ्यते। वाचि वाण्यां च अमृतत्वं माधुर्यं लभ्यते। त्वं हे विनते, एतदुभयं वृणीष्व याचस्व। सुधां पानार्थं। वाङ्माधुर्यं सकलार्थसिद्धये। त्वमेतदुभयं [प्राप्स्यसि]। 'तवेहेति' पाठे एवं योजना। हे विनते हे सौम्ये प्रसन्नमुखि अहं, ते तुभ्यं तं वरं इष्टं ददामि। तं कं वरं? यं कं च वरं त्वं मनसा ईप्ससि वांछसि। मम सख्यं मत्सख्यं। मैत्रे (मैत्रं) प्रसन्नत्वं। मत्प्रसादात् अन्नं पायसमोदकमंडकापूपौदनादिकविधं लभ्यते। वाचि अमृतत्वं। अपशब्दादिदोषराहित्येन दिव्यत्वं च लभ्यते। दिव्यवाक्त्वं प्राप्यते। तव इहैतस्मिन्प्रत्यक्षशरीरे त्वदीये पक्षिणीदेहे, एतदुभयमपि प्रागेव सिद्धं वर्तते। उभयं किं? यथेष्टमन्नमोदनादिकं। दिव्यवाक्त्वं च। अतः प्रसादातिशयादुत्फुल्ल-मनसा मया 'वरं ददामि ते सौम्ये मत्सख्यादन्नममृतत्वं वाची'ति यदुक्तं तन्न क्षोदक्षमं। अविचारितत्वात्। अतस्तव पुत्राय वरं दा[दित]सामि। तदेव तवेष्टतमम्।

अपरया द्विपदयेंद्रो वैनतेयाय वरदित्सया ब्रूते॥ इंद्र उवाच गरुडं प्रति –

---

[१३] 'सौम्ये' इत्येतन्निश्चप्रचं 'सौम्य' (सौम्य) इत्यस्यापपाठः (गरुडस्यकृते)। भाष्यकारस्तु 'सौम्ये' एव शुद्धं मन्यमानः, एतत्संबोधनपदं विनतया संबध्नाति, यत्तु प्रसंगविरुद्धम्॥

[१४] 'वृणीष्व' इत्यस्य स्थाने मातृकाद्वयं "तवेह" इति पठति।

ताक्ष्यर्पुत्र त्वं ब्रूंहि मनसेप्सितं। वरं वृणीष्व वैनतेय॥११॥

॥ *पदपाठः* ॥

ताक्ष्यं० पुत्र। त्वं। ब्रूहि। मनसा। ईप्सितं। वरं। वृणीष्व। वैनतेय॥

॥ *भाष्यम्* ॥

'ताक्ष्यर्पुत्र त्वं ब्रूहि मनसेप्सितं वरं वृणीष्व वैनतेय', इति द्विपदा। हे ताक्ष्यर्पुत्र। सुपर्ण। त्वं ब्रूहि वद। मनसा वांछितं वरं वृणीष्व, हे वैनतेय।

गरुड उवाचेंद्रं प्रति –

नागांन्वृणे [१५]भक्ष्यंमहं शंचीपते
वहेंयं यज्ञं प्र विंशेयं वेदांन्।
अधींयीरन् मा ब्राह्मणाः स्वर्गकांमास्
ते चांप्नुयुस्त्रिदिवे संसदं नौ॥१२॥

॥ *पदपाठः* ॥

नागांन्। वृणे। भक्ष्यं। अहं। शची०पते। वहेंयं। यज्ञं। प्र। विशेयं। वेदांन्। अधींयीरन्। मा। ब्राह्मणाः। स्वर्ग०कांमाः। ते। च। आप्नुयुः। त्रि० दिवे। सं० सदं। नौ॥

॥ *भाष्यम्* ॥

हे शचीपते यदि त्वं प्रसन्नोऽसि, यदि मह्यं वरं दित्ससि तर्हि अहं इमं वरं वृणे। इमं कं वरं? नागान् सर्वानपि भक्षं वृणे। भक्षत्वेन वृणे। नागाः मम भक्ष्याः सन्तु। तथा यज्ञं इति जात्यभिप्रायेणैकवचनं। यज्ञान् सर्वान् वेदरूपेण वहेयं। वेदाः खलु मन्त्रब्राह्मणाभ्यां यज्ञान् वहंति। तथा वेदान् चतुरोऽपि प्रविशेयं। वेदानां मध्ये प्रविशामि तदात्मत्वेन। स्वर्गकामाः विप्राः मां सुपर्णाध्यायात्मकं अधीयीरन्। अधीयंतु। पठंतु। ते च विप्राः त्रिदिवे स्वर्गे नौ आवयोः संसदं सभां सुधर्मानामिकां आप्नुयुः प्राप्नुवंतु। इत्यमुं वरमहं वृणोमि।

[इतः परं ऋग्द्वयस्य मूलं भाष्यं च मातृकायां नास्ति]

---

[१५] भाष्यकारस्तु 'भक्ष्यम्' इत्यस्य स्थाने 'भक्षम्' इति मूलपाठत्वेनाङ्गीकुरुते। पदपाठेनापि एतत् संपुष्यते। 'भक्षः–भक्ष्यम्' इत्दुभयोः समानार्थत्वात् वाक्याशये न किमपि अन्तरम्।

नागा॑स्ते भ॒क्षाः॑ सन्तु विहङ्गमेन्द्र
वह॑ य॒ज्ञं प्र वि॑श शू॒र वेदा॑न्।
अध्यै॑ष्यन्ते त्वा ब्राह्म॒णाः स्व॒र्गार्था॑[१६]
प्राप्स्य॑न्ति च त्रिदि॒वे स॒सद॑ नौ॥१३॥

॥ *पदपाठः* ॥

नागाः॑। ते॒। भ॒क्षाः॑। स॒न्तु। वि॒ह॒ङ्ग॒म॒०इ॒न्द्र॒। वह॑। य॒ज्ञं। प्र। वि॒श। शू॒र। वेदा॑न्। अध्यै॑ष्यंते। त्वा॒। ब्रा॒ह्म॒णाः। स्व॒र्ग० अ॑र्थाः। प्राप्स्यं॑ति। च॒। त्रि॒०दि॒वे। स॒० सद॑। नौ॒॥

[*भाष्यमनुपलभ्यते*]

"[हे विहंगम, आकाशचारिन् गरुड, नागाः सर्पास्ते तव भक्षो भोज्यं भवन्तु इति मदीया आशिषः। हे शूर वीर, त्वं यज्ञं वह, सुपर्णरूपायां वेदिकायां देवेभ्य उत्सृज्यमानं द्रव्यं देवान् प्रति वह, प्रापय। देवतार्थे द्रव्यत्यागो यज्ञः। स्वर्गार्थाः स्वर्गकामाः, स्वर्गमुद्दिश्य प्रवर्तमानाः प्रयतमानाः वा ब्राह्मणास्त्वां अध्येष्यन्ते, त्वं च सर्वत्र वेदेषु छन्दोरूपेण प्रविष्टः स्थास्यति। 'छन्दांसि एव सुपर्णः' इति पूर्वे उक्तत्वात्। ऐहिकीं लोकयात्रामतीत्य एतादृशाः ब्राह्मणाः स्वर्गम् आगत्य अस्माकं संसदं सान्निध्यं प्राप्स्यन्ति।]" (*सम्पादकः*)

उद॑श्रयन्तु[१७] स॒र्पाः हर्ष॑माणाः सु॒प॒र्णं दृ॒ष्ट्वा त्रिदि॒वे पत॑न्तम्।
तान्भ॑क्षयि॒त्वा बल॑वाञ्छकुन्तो व॒र्द्धय॒न्बल॑म॒स्याध्य॑वर्द्धत॥१४॥

॥ *पदपाठः* ॥

उत्। अ॒श्र॒यं॒तु॒[१७]। स॒र्पाः। हर्ष॑माणाः। सु॒०प॒र्णं। दृ॒ष्ट्वा। त्रि॒०दि॒वे। पत॑न्तं। तान्। भ॒क्ष॒यि॒त्वा। बल॑०वान्। श॒कुं॒तः। व॒र्द्धय॑न्। बलं॑। अ॒स्य॒। अधि॑। अ॒व॒र्द्ध॒त॒।

---

[१६] 'स्वर्गार्थाः' इत्यस्य स्थाने 'स्वर्गकामाः' इति साधीयान् पाठोऽपि हस्तलेखेषु प्राप्यते।

[१७] 'उदश्रयन्तु' इति पाठश्चिन्त्यः। 'उदाश्रयन्त' (लङि), 'उदाश्रयन्तु' यदि वा 'उच्छ्रयन्तु' इति साधीयांसः पाठाः अभविष्यन्। 'उदाश्रयन्त' इति पाठे स्वीकृते 'उदतिष्ठन्' इति निर्गलितोऽर्थः ऋच उत्तरार्धेनानायासं संगच्छते।

॥ *भाष्यम्* ॥

"[उदश्रयन्तु उत्तिष्ठन्तु व्याकुलिता, भयेन रोमहर्षिताश्च सर्पाः सुपर्णम् आकाशे भ्रमन्तमुड्डीयमानं दृष्ट्वा तस्य स्वोपरि पातमुत्प्रेक्षमाणाः। तान् सर्पान् भक्षयित्वा शकुन्तो गरुडः पूर्वापेक्षया बलवत्तरो जातः, एवं क्रमशश्च तस्य बले महती वृद्धिरभवत्॥]" (*सम्पादकः*)। इति त्रिंशत्तमो वर्गः॥

॥ अथैकत्रिंशो वर्गः ॥

सुषूंपर्वण्यंवसानं महाद्रौं
कृत्वा नीडं शंल्मलौ तं महान्तंम्।
गुरुत्मंन्तं गरुडं वैनतेयं
पतंत्रिराजमवंसे जोहवीमि॥१५॥

॥ *पदपाठः* ॥

सु। सु०पर्वणि। अव० सानं। महाद्रौं। कृत्वा। नीडं। शल्मलौ। तं। महांतं। गरुत्मंतं। गरुडं। वैनतेयं। पतंत्रि० राजं। अवंसे। जोहवीमि।

॥ *भाष्यम्* ॥

अथ वामदेव ऋषिर्गरुडाराधनकामस्तमेवानयार्च्चा आह्वयति। वामदेवो ब्रवीति। अहं महाद्रौ हिमालये नीडमावासगृहं आश्रमं कृत्वा तस्मिन् आश्रममध्यवर्तिनि नीडे पर्णकुटीरे अवसानं विश्रामं निवासं कृत्वा तत्र आसीनः सन् सुपर्वणि शोभनपर्वणि पुण्यकाले सूर्योपरागादौ तं गरुडं सुजोहवीमि। सुष्ठु यथा स्यात् तथा जोहवीमि। आह्वयामि। किंलक्षणे महाद्रौ पर्वते। शल्मलौ। '*शल्मलिः सुशरो भवति शरवान्वेति*' यास्कः (१२.१.९)। सुशरे। शोभनशरवणोपेते। शरवति। कीदृशं तं गरुडं, महांतं। शरीरेण गुणैश्च। गरुत्मंतं सुपक्षं। वैनतेयं पतिव्रता [विनता-]तनयं पक्षीन्द्रं अवसे स्वरक्षणार्थम्।

वामदेव उवाच –

स मैं स्तुतश्छन्दंसा त्रैष्टुंभेन
होत्रेंव घर्मः प्र जिंहाति वाचंम्।

शुभं सुषीमं च सुखं च धेहि
वैनतेयो[९८] जह्येनः सपत्नान्॥१६॥

॥ पदपाठः ॥

सः। मे। स्तुतः। छंदसा। त्रैस्तुंभेन। होत्राऽइव। घर्मः। प्र। जिहाति। वाचं। शुभं। सु०सीमं। च। सु०खं। च। धेहि। वैनतेयः। जहि। एनः। स० पत्नान्॥

॥ भाष्यम् ॥

स गरुडः मे मया त्रैष्टुभेन छन्दसा त्रिष्टुप्छन्दसा स्तुतः सन् वाचं वरप्रदानस्वरूपां वाणीं प्रजिहाति आविष्करोति प्रकटयति। केन क इव? होत्रा घर्म इव। यथा होत्रा यज्ञे स्तुतः घर्मः, महावीरः प्रवर्ग्यः, ज्वालां प्रजिहाति आविष्करोति। '*शतयोजनेह वा एष इतस्तपतीति*' श्रुतेः वाचं प्रजिहाति प्रेरयति प्रकटयति, वरदानं वाणीं श्रावयति इत्यर्थः। किंच अहं वामदेवः एनं गरुडं एवं प्रार्थये। हे वैनतेय। मह्यं शुभं कल्याणं धेहि देहि। सुषीमं। सुष्ठु वर्णाश्रमधर्ममर्यादापालने शक्तिं च धेहि देहि। सीमा मर्यादा। सुखं संतोषं धेहि देहि। किंलक्षणस्त्वं? वैनतेयः विनता पतिव्रता तस्याः सुतः। तादृशस्त्वं एनः पापं जहि नाशय तथा मे सपत्नान् रिपून् जहि नाशय। वामदेव उवाच –

यद्यप्यंस्तोकं यदि वाप्यहाऽशिंखं[९९]
सुपर्णं (वै?) मनसा श्रद्दधानः।

स एव नो मृळतां दीर्घमायुर्
ददातु नश्चक्षुर्बलेन चिरायं॥१७॥

॥ पदपाठः ॥

यदिं। अपिं। अस्तोकं। यदिं। वा। अपिं। अहं। अशिंखं[९९]। सु०पर्णं। मनसा। श्रत्०दधानः। सः। एव। नः। मृळतां। दीर्घं। आयुः। ददातु। नः। चक्षुः। बलेन। चिरायं॥

---

[९८] अत्र वैनतेय-पदं संबुद्धौ एव (आद्युदात्तं 'वैनंतेय' इति) साधु स्यात्, जहि-धेहि-क्रियापदयोः तेनैव संगतिः।

[९९] 'अहासिषं' (त्यक्तवानस्मि) इत्यस्य विकारः प्रतीयते।

॥ *भाष्यम्* ॥

वामदेवो ब्रूते। अहं श्रद्दधानः श्रद्धालुः सन् मनसा सुपर्णं इति याचे। इतीति किं। स एव सुपर्णः नः अस्मभ्यं दीर्घं आयुर्ददातु। तथा बलेन सह चक्षुर्ददातु। नेत्रतेजो ददातु। चिराय चिरकालं दीर्घमायुर्ददातु। तथा स एव सुपर्णः नः अस्मान् मृळतां सुखयतु। किंलक्षणं आयुः। यद्यपि प्रकृत्या विधातृलिखित-ललाटरेखायां, अस्तोकं बहुलम्। अ इति खेदे। यदि वा मम आयुः प्रकृत्या अशिखं अल्पमेवास्ति चेत्। तथापि स एव चिराय दीर्घं ददातु। न विद्यते शिखा वृद्धिर्यस्य तत् अशिखं वृद्धिहीनं अल्पं ह्रस्वमित्यर्थः। विधातृलिखितकपालरेखायां यद्यपि ह्रस्वमेव चेत् तथापि स एव सुपर्णो दीर्घं चिराय आयुर्ददातु।

[अथ फलश्रुतिः]

अथ वामदेवक्रियमाणेन गरुडाराधनेन स्तवनेन च संतुष्ट इंद्रो वामदेवाश्रम आगत्य तस्यैवर्षेः सन्निधौ सुपर्णाध्यायाध्ययनफलश्रुतिं वामदेवं श्रावयति स्वयमेव मघवा॥ इंद्र उवाच वामदेवं प्रति –

य: सौपर्णमंधीयीत नित्यं पर्वणि-पर्वणि।
वीरोऽस्यं पुत्रो जांयेत मेधावीं ब्रह्मवर्चसी[१००]॥१८॥

॥ *पदपाठः* ॥

यः। सौपर्णं। अधि० ईयीत। नित्यं। पर्वणि० पर्वणि। वीरः।
अस्य। पुत्रः। जायेत। मेधावीं। ब्रह्म०वर्चसी॥ ०॥

॥ *भाष्यम्* ॥

हे वामदेव नित्यं निश्चितं यः पर्वणि२ पुण्यकाले युगादिप्रभृतौ संक्रमणव्यतीपात-द्वादशीप्रभृतौ चेदं सौपर्णं सुपर्णसंबंधि श्रौतमाख्यानमधीते अस्य अध्येतुश्चेत्पुत्रकामना स्यात् तर्हि अचिरात्पुत्रो जायते। कीदृक् मेधावी ग्रन्थग्रहणधारणशक्तः। ब्रह्मवर्चसं ब्राह्मं तेजः। स्वधर्मानुष्ठानसंभवं यत्तेजः तदस्य। तेजस्वीति ब्रह्मवर्चसी॥

इंद्र उवाच –

य: सौपर्णमंधीयीत नित्यं पर्वणि-पर्वणि।
अनंन्त(तं)[१०१]–स्वर्गमारोहेद् गच्छेन्ममं सलोकंताम्॥१९॥

॥ *पदपाठः* ॥

०॥ अनंन्तं। स्वर्गं। आरोहेत्। गच्छैत्। ममं। स० लोकंतां॥

---

[१००] अस्मिन् मन्त्रे फलसंसूचिका क्रिया 'जायेत' सर्वानुदात्ता किन्तु अग्रिमे मन्त्रे उभयमपि क्रियापदं (आरोहेत्, गच्छैत् च) सोदात्तमिति विसंगतिः।

[१०१] सर्वास्वपि संहितापाठमातृकासु 'अनन्त'-पदमनुस्वारविरहितमसमस्तं च प्राप्यते। पदपाठमातृकास्तु 'अनन्तम्' इति पठन्ति।

॥ भाष्यम् ॥

हे वामदेव शृणु। यः त्वद्दृष्टमिदं सौपर्णं सुपर्णमाहात्म्यं सदा पर्वकाले स्वर्गकामः अधीते, असौ अनंतं अंतरहितं पुनःपातवार्जितं स्वर्गमारु(रो)हेत्। ननु स्वर्गाः नानाविधाः श्रूयंते। तेषां मध्ये कं लोकं प्राप्नोतीत्यत आह। ममेंद्रस्य सलोकतां गच्छेत्। समानो लोको यस्येति सलोकः। तस्य भावः सलोकता तां। अमरावतीं दिव्यनगरीं लभेतेत्यर्थः।

इंद्र उवाच –

अस्तिक्यादिह सौपर्णं यः शृणोति प्रणामवान्।
आपद्भ्यः सर्वाभ्यो मुच्येत द्विषद्भ्यश्च प्रमुच्यते॥२०॥

॥ पदपाठः ॥

आस्तिक्यात्। इह। सौपर्णं यः। शृणोति। प्र०नामवान्।
आपत्०भ्यः। सर्वाभ्यः। मुच्येत्। द्विषत्०भ्यः। च। प्र० मुच्यते।

॥ भाष्यम् ॥

हे वामदेव। यः इदं त्वया दृष्टं एकत्रिंशद्वर्गमयं सौपर्णं सुपर्णदेवताप्रधानं वैदिकं आख्यानं आपन्निवारणकामः इह पर्वकाले पठेत्। कथं? आस्तिक्यात् वेदे विश्वासपूर्वकं। अस्ति वेदप्रामाण्यबुद्धिर्यस्य, वेदविरुद्धे मार्गे दृढतरमप्रामाण्य-निश्चयवती च बुद्धिर्यस्यासावास्तिकः। आस्तिकस्य भावः आस्तिक्यं। तस्मात् आस्तिक्यात्। प्रणामवान् भक्तिनम्रः। सुपर्णभक्तः। असौ सर्वाभ्यः आपद्भ्यः मुच्येत। तथा यः शत्रुपीडानिवृत्तिकामः पठति। असौ द्विषद्भ्यः शत्रुभ्यः। मुच्यते। शत्रुपीडाभ्यः मुच्यते।

इंद्र उवाच –

आख्यानं गर्भिणी येदं शृणुयात् प्रतिपर्व चेत्।
पुमांसं जनयेत् पुत्रं बलिनं शत्रुतापनम्[१०२]॥२१॥

॥ पदपाठः ॥

आख्यानं। गर्भिणी। या। इदं। शृणुयात्। प्रति०पर्व। चेत्।
पुमांसं। जनयेत्। पुत्रं। बलिनं। शत्रु०तापनं।[१०२]

---

[१०२] भाष्यकारस्त्वत्र 'शत्रुतापनमुत्तमम्' इति पठति।

॥ *भाष्यम्* ॥

या पुत्रकामा स्त्री प्रतिपर्व सर्वेषु पर्वकालेषु पूर्वोक्तेषु इदं सुपर्णाख्यानं अमृताहरणाख्यं आदितः आन्तं शृणुयात्। पर्व पर्व प्रति इति प्रतिपर्व। सा प्रथमं गर्भं धारयति, ततः गर्भिणी सती चेत् शृणोति तर्हि पुत्रं जनयेत्। प्रसूते। कीदृशं पुत्रं। पुमांसं पुरुषार्थसाधनसमर्थं। शत्रुतापनं च। शत्रून् तापयति संतापयतीति शत्रुतापनस्तं शत्रुतापनं। उत्तममित्युत्कृष्टं। निर्दोषं सर्वगुणाधिकरणं च।

इंद्र उवाच गरुडं प्रति –

सौपर्णं चक्षुर्भवति श्रोतॄणामनंसूयताम्[१०३]।
स्वर्गांश्च लोकान् गंच्छेयुरावयोः कीर्त्तनात्सदा॥२२॥

॥ *पदपाठः* ॥

सौपर्णं। चक्षुः। भवति। श्रोतॄणां। अनंसूयतां[१०३]। स्वर्गान्।
च। लोकान्। गच्छेयुः। आवयोः। कीर्त्तनात्। सदा॥

॥ *भाष्यम्* ॥

इंद्रः गरुडं वामदेवाश्रमे आगतं दृष्ट्वा तं प्रति हर्षितः प्रसन्नोऽब्रवीत्। हे गरुड। ये ज्ञानकामाः इदं वामदेवदृष्टमेव त्रिंशद्वर्गात्मकं त्वदाख्यानं अध्येतुमक्षमाः शृण्वंति तेषां श्रोतॄणां शृण्वतां अवश्यं सौपर्णं चक्षुर्ज्ञानं भवति सर्ववेदसकलशास्त्रविषयं। ब्रह्मविषयमात्मज्ञानं ये [इ]च्छंति तेषां तदेव। ये तु त्रैकालिकं ज्ञानं वांछंतः शृण्वंति तेषां तदेव भवेत्। चक्षुः शब्दो ज्ञानवाची। अंधानां नेत्रविकलानां आंध्यनिवृत्तिकामनया शृण्वतां चक्षुरिन्द्रियं पटुतरं भवति। कीदृशां श्रोतॄणां। अनसूयतां असूयारहितानां। परगुणेषु द्वेषः असूया। न असूयं। परेषां गुणान् द्विषंतीत्यसूयंतः तेषां अनसूयतां। शत्रंतमेतत्। न असूयंतीत्यसूयंतः। न असूयंतः। अनसूयंतः। तेषां अनसूयतां। ईदृशाश्चेद्भवंति तर्हि सिद्धिं प्राप्नुवन्ति। नेतरे। हे गरुड, आवयोर्युष्मदस्मदोः अस्मिन् अध्याये वामदेवेन ऋषिणा यत्कीर्तनं कृतं तस्मात्कीर्तनात् तत्पठनाच्छ्रवणाद्वा तेन केवलमंधत्वान् न मुच्यंते। लोचनबलं लभंते। ते तु स्वर्गान् लोकांश्च गच्छंति। तेषां स्वर्गप्राप्तिरानुषंगिकी भवति। इमं इंद्रगरुडसंवादं श्रुत्वा हर्षितो वामदेव एतावुभौ द्विपदया नमस्कुरुते। तस्यां च वाक्याभ्यासो भक्तेरतिशयाद् ग्रंथसमाप्तिनिर्मितिश्च। सैषा द्विपदा। तामेव वामदेव उवाच –

---

[१०३] ग्रूबेमहाशयोऽत्र 'अनुसूयताम्' इति पठति यत्तु 'अनुश्रूयताम्' इत्यस्य विकृतिः प्रतीयते।

नमं इन्द्रसुपर्णयोर्नमं इन्द्रसुपर्णयोः॥२३॥

॥ *पदपाठः* ॥

नमः। इंद्र०सु पर्णयोः। नमः। इन्द्र०सुपर्णयोः॥

॥ *भाष्यम्* ॥

चतुर्थ्याः व्यत्ययेन षष्ठी। इंद्रसुपर्णाभ्यां नम इत्यर्थः। 'अभ्यर्हितं पूर्व'मिति वक्तव्यादिंद्रशब्दस्य पूर्वनिपातः। यद्वा षष्ठी स्वतंत्रा। अध्याहारेण योजना च। इंद्रसुपर्णयोः पद्भ्यां नम इति।

अथ वामदेवो ग्रंथस्य श्रुतिसमं प्रामाण्यं प्रतिपिपादयिषुः साक्षादृक्संहितांतर्गतां नेमेनर्षिणा दृष्टां सौपर्णीमृचमेवात्रोदाजहार ग्रंथांते। वामदेव उवाच –

मनोजवा अयमान आयसीमंतरत्पुरम्।
दिवं सुपर्णो गत्वाय सोमं वज्रिण आ भरत्॥२४॥

॥ *पदपाठः* ॥

मनःऽजवाः। अयमानः। आयसीं। अतरत्। पुरं। दिवं। सु०पर्णः।
गत्वाय। सोमं। वज्रिणे। आ। अभरत्॥

॥ *भाष्यम्* ॥

सुपर्णः इंद्रेणामृतरक्षणार्थं निर्मितामायसीमयोमयीं पुरं नगरीं अतरत्। अत्र लक्षणया पूः शब्देन प्राकार एवानुल्लंघ्योऽथ [तस्य] भंगश्च लक्ष्यते। तं प्राकारमतरत् तीर्णः। अतिचक्राम। उल्लंघितवानित्यर्थः। कीदृशः सुपर्णः मनोजवाः सन् अयमानः गच्छन् व्योम्नि। '*अय*' गतौ। किं कृत्वा आयसीं पुरं आयसं प्राकारमतरत्। उल्लंघितवान्। दिवं द्युलोकं, गत्वा इति गत्वा[य]। '*क्तो यक्*' (पा० ७.१. ४७) इति सूत्रेण। ततो वज्रिणः इन्द्रस्य सोमं इंद्रस्वामिकममृतं आ अहरत्। आहृतवान्। आहार्षीत्। षष्ठी शेषे। संबंध इत्यर्थः। इति एकत्रिंशो वर्गः॥

॥ *इति सुपर्णाध्यायभाष्यं समाप्तं* ॥

॥*श्रीरस्तु*॥

Section II
The Restored Text

A Short Note on the Restored Text

As has been mentioned in the Introduction, the text of the *Suparṇādhyāyaḥ* has come down to us in a highly unreliable form. There are obvious lacunae (*pāṭha-bhraṁśāḥ*), somewhere even big gaps, then additions and interpolations, and on the top of all that, highly corrupt and distorted readings. Disarrangement of the textual material at some stage also seems to have taken place. The restoration of the text, therefore, throws up a great challenge to the scholars. Till now seven outstanding Indologists have endeavoured to bring about some sort of consistency in the text by examining the readings delivered by the manuscripts and suggesting their own emendations and variants.

I have critically examined all the suggestions of the previous scholars, accepts some, rejects some and suggests some of my own. Further, I propose a different placement for certain verses which he thinks have drifted to a wrong place sometimes in the past due to reshuffled state of the folia in the archetype of all the existing copies.

It goes without saying that a lot of "subjective element" plays an important, or even the major role in such an effort and much of what an editor considers right or wrong depends upon his individual perspective, although every scholar tries to be as objective and as critical as humanly possible for him.

None of the previous scholars, nor the present editor, claims that he has finally restored the text to its pristine original form. Many future scholars are expected to come up with other, more brilliant and more acceptable suggestions for the solutions of the *grantha-granthis* (to borrow a word from the poet Śrīharṣa!) which have formed themselves due to the incapacities of the ignorant scribes. However, every scholar-editor has tried to be honest to himself and has given his best according to his intellectual capacity.

Not every bird can sore so high in the sky as Suparṇa; some fly low, some move in the mid-region and some rise very high, "up above the world". "*Nabhaḥ patanty ātmasamaṁ patatriṇaḥ*", says the Ādikavi Vālmīki and we all agree with him.

A list of scholars who have critically examined and edited the text of *Suparṇādhyāya* is given herewith, with the bibliographical details of their works. Many of their views on the *emendationes* of the text have been given a "second thought" by me and discussed in the footnotes ensuing the text of each *sūkta*.

***Please understand that in order to take note of and to fully appreciate the emendations in the following Restored Text, one has to constantly refer to the original accented text along with its* padapāṭha.**

List of Authors and their Works discussed in the Notes

Caland, Willem, 1927, "Vedische Religion (1915-27), a Review", in *Archiv für Religionswissenschaft*, 25: 283-94.

Charpentier, Jarl, 1920-22, *Die Suparṇasage; Untersuchungen zur alstindischen Literatur und Sagengeschichte*, Uppsala-Leipzig.

Grube, Elimar, 1875, "Suparṇâdhâyaḥ", Suparṇī Fabula; Dissertatio Inauguralis ad summos in Philosophia honores in Alma litterarum Universitate Friderica Guilelma, Berolini (Berlin).

Hertel, Johannes, 1909, "Der Suparṇāadhyāya, ein Vedisches Mysterium", *Wiener Zeitschrift für die Kunde des Morgenlandes*, 24(3-4): 273-346.

——, 1919, *Indische Märchen* (A complete German translation of the *Suparṇādhyāya* is included in this collection of Indian stories by the same author), Jena, pp. 344-66.

Johansson, Karl F., 1910, *Solfågeln i Indien*; *En religionshistorisk-mythologisk Studie*, Uppsala: Uppsala University.

Negelein, Julius von, 1924, A Review Article (in German) on the *Suparṇasage* of Charpentier, in *Goettingische Gelehrte Anzeigen* (Annual Number), 186: 65-72 & 87-119, Berlin.

Oldenberg, Hermann, 1883, "Das altindische Ākhyāna, mit besonderer Rücksicht auf das Suparṇākhyāna", *Zeitschrift der Deutschen Morgenländischen Gesellschaft*, 37: 54-86.

——, 1919, "Zur Geschichte des altindischen Erzählungsstils", in *Nachrichten von der Königl. Gesell. der Wissenschaften zu Göttingen*, Phil.-hist. Klasse, of the year 1919, Berlin, pp. 61-94.

Rau, Wilhelm, 1967, "Zum Text des Suparṇādhyāya", *Zeitschrift der Deutschen Morgenländischen Gesellschaft*, 117: 353-62.

॥ सुपर्णाध्यायः ॥

Critically Restored Text with Notes

सविमर्श समीक्षितः पाठः

॥ प्रथमं सूक्तम् ॥

प्रथमो वर्गः (१)

[*आख्यानप्रशस्तिः*]

सौपर्णानि पवित्राणि सूक्तान्येकादशाभ्यसेत्।[१]
वाञ्छन् पुत्रान् पशून् वित्तं स्वर्गमायुरनन्धताम्॥१॥

[*मङ्गलाशंसनम्*]

सौवर्णवर्णममितद्युतिमप्रमेयं
छन्दोमयं विविधयज्ञतनुं वरेण्यम्।
पक्षौ बृहच्च भवतो रथवच्च यस्य
तं वैनतेयमजरं प्रणमामि नित्यम्॥२॥

ये बालखिल्या मुनयः प्रसिद्धा-
स्तेषां तपोऽर्धेन विवृद्धतेजाः।
जातो गरुत्मान् परमेश्वरांशः
स नोऽनिशं रक्षतु पक्षिराजः॥३॥

यन्मङ्गलं सुपर्णस्य विनताऽकल्पयत् पुरा।
अमृतार्थं प्रयातस्य तन्मे भवतु मङ्गलम्॥४॥

[*ऋषिच्छन्दोदेवतादि*]

सुपर्णाख्यानमेकत्रिंशद्वर्गसूक्तम्, वामदेव ऋषि-

गरुडेन्द्रतार्क्ष्यविनातकद्रूसर्पादेवाः देवतास्त्रैष्टुभ[२] छन्दः, पर्वण्यध्ययने ब्राह्मणाभिश्रावणे च विनियोगः॥५॥

द्वितीयो वर्गः (२)

[प्रस्तोता सूत्रधारो वा]

द्यावापृथिव्यौ भवतो भगिन्यौ
ते मूर्त्तिमत्यौ चरतस्तु लोकान्।
द्यौरासीत् तत्र विनता सुपर्णी
भूमिस्तु नाग्यभवत् कद्रुनाम्नी[३]॥६॥

ते देवसत्रे अपराद्धवत्यौ[४]
ततो देवैर्जपहोमैः प्रबाधिते[५]।
प्रापद्येतां[६] तार्क्ष्यमृषिं भयार्ते
दृष्ट्वाक्षि कद्र्वा हुतिभिर्विनाशितम्[७]॥७॥

पलाशपर्णवृन्तांस्तु[८] समिदर्थे गृहाणकौ[९]।
तरन्तौ गोष्पदे कौचित् पङ्कमग्नावुभावृषी॥८॥

पङ्के सन्नान्[१०] ऋषीन् दृष्ट्वा बालखिल्यांस्तु गोष्पदे।
इन्द्रेण हसितं, क्रुद्धास्ततस्तार्क्ष्यमृषिं[११] गताः॥९॥

[बालखिल्याः तार्क्ष्य प्रति]

तपोऽर्द्धं तव दास्यामः सुतमुत्पादयाण्डजम्[१२]।
इन्द्रस्य विनयेद् दर्पमात्मसम्भावितस्य यः॥१०॥

[प्रस्तोता]

तपोऽर्द्धं बालखिल्यानां तार्क्ष्यः[१३] पीत्वा महायशाः।
विनतायां दधौ गर्भमण्डजानामनुत्तमम्[१४]॥११॥

Notes on the Restored Text vis-à-vis the Original One

१ The opening verse explicitly mentions that the text consists of *eleven* hymns whereas in the present (extended?) form it has *fifteen* hymns. It is obvious that the text has been expanded with additional material and, possibly, some hymns may also have been split and rearranged. I suspect that the first two *sūktas*, composed for the most part in Anuṣṭubh, which provide the background of the story (i.e. the plot of this dramatic work) and the fully irrelevant, long description of devouring the Niṣādas by Garuḍa, which form the bulk of the 8th and 9th *sūktas* constitute some such material.

२ The MSS read "त्रिष्टुभं", but the actual word is त्रिष्टुभ् in feminine gender. Hence the *padapāṭha* renders it as त्रैष्तुभं, modified by us into त्रैष्टुभम्, to go with छन्दस्.

३ The MSS read कद्रुनामा which has been emended by Negelein 92.8 into ०नाम्नी.

४ The MSS uniformly provide the uncomfortable reading अपराध्नुवन्त्यौ (present participle?), hence this emendment by the present editor. We need a perfect participle here.

५ The text originally reads प्रबाधितैः qualifying the word देवैः. But in this context we expect a Locative in जपहोमैः (०होमे/होमेषु) which is not there and unless there is a previous mention of some harm/injury done to either कद्रु or विनता, the rationale of approaching the Sage Tārkṣa is not there. Hence I prefer to read प्रबाधिते (harmed), Fem. dual. Nom.

६ The text in the MSS and in Grube's edition had प्रपद्येतां which was correctly restored to its intended past tense (प्रापद्येताम्) by Negelein 92.9.

७ The text has कद्र्वाहुतिभिः. Both Caland 288, n. 4 and Rau think that there is a double *sandhi* between the two words and that the second word in आहुतिभिः (कद्र्वाः + आहुतिभिः >कद्र्वा आहुतिभिः > कद्र्वाहुतिभिः). This might be correct because there are several instances of this phenomenon in our text. But we can very well operate with हुतिभिः without distorting the intended sense.

८ वृन्तस्य[गृहाणकौ] is what has been handed down in the text which is grammatically problematic. I presume that the word वृन्त was originally in Accusative case (वृन्तान्, वृन्तांस्तु/वृन्तं तु). However, it must be granted that the Genetive in वृन्तस्य may denote "a part of the वृन्त" according to Vedic linguistic usage (cf. सोमस्य

पिबति=सोमस्य कञ्चिद् अंशं पिबति। वृन्तस्य गृह्णाति=वृन्तस्य कञ्चिदंशम् गृह्णाति).

९ The MSS, so also Grube, read actually गृहाननौ which does not make sense. Rau suggests amendment of the reading in form of गृह्णानकौ which is metrically impossible (if not also on other counts) making the 5th syllable of an Anuṣṭubh heavy. I, therefore, prefer the simpler and grammatically unproblematic गृहाण:, गृहाणकः (addition of the suffix कप् in स्व-अर्थ).

१० पङ्के सन्नान् is the reading delivered by MSS. Charpentier 210.26 suggests changing of सन्नान् into मग्नान् which is plausible in view of the readings of the previous verse and of the fact that from eleventh century onward, the formation of the letters स and म is very similar and म is liable to be misread as स. However, सन्न (originally meaning "sunk deep") in the sense of "smeared" has come down right up to modern Hindi: सना हुआ (पंक में), hence also not bad.

११,१३ All MSS read here तार्क्ष्य. But since Garuḍa himself has been referred to as such in the text (as well as in the *Ṛgveda* I.79. स्वस्ति नस्तार्क्ष्यो अरिष्टनेमिः), his father could only be तार्क्ष (= belonging to the clan of तृक्षु) whereas the patronym तार्क्ष्य does not make sense in this context.

१२ Rau strangely wants to change the correct अण्डजम् (सुतम्) into a vocative अण्डज (meant for तार्क्ष-कश्यप). This is unacceptable.

१४ All MSS read आण्डजानाम् instead of the correct अण्डजानाम्।

॥ द्वितीयं सूक्तम् ॥

तृतीयो वर्गः (३)

[*प्रस्तोता*]

लब्ध्वा बीजवरं पुण्यं शौनकी तु गुरूदरी।
शुद्धक्षेत्रे, च सम्पूर्णे कालेऽमुक्त त्रिरण्डकम्[१]॥१॥

आतुरा सा तु सुश्रोणी क्षतं कृत्वाऽग्रजाण्डके।
भिद्यमानोर्ध्वनिष्क्रान्ता[२] विद्युन् मेघसखाऽम्बरे॥२॥

ह्रिया सा परयाऽऽपन्ना[३] चिन्तयन्ती मुहुर्मुहुः।
मध्यमं निर्बिभेदाण्डं जातोऽर्कस्य सखाऽरुणः॥३॥

अरुणेन जातमात्रेण शप्ता माता तपोधना।
दुष्कृतं किं महाऽपुण्यं पादहीनोऽस्मि चण्डि हे!॥४॥

तस्मिन् प्रसूते रविराजगाम
ब्रुवन् वाक्यं देवि देहीति मह्यम्।
तव सुतोऽयं मम वाजिवेगान्[४]
धर्तुं शक्तो, भव च मोदमाना॥५॥

चतुर्थो वर्गः (४)

[*प्रस्तोता*]

गरुडस्य जातमात्रस्य त्रयो लोकाः प्रकम्पिताः।
प्रकम्पिता मही सर्वा सशैलवनकानना॥६॥

गगनं नष्टचन्द्रार्कं न ज्योतींषि चकासति[५]।
देवता भयवित्रस्ता नष्टचेष्टाश्च मारुतः॥७॥

नार्यो गर्भं न गृह्णन्ति समुद्राः शोषमागताः।
गावः क्षीरविवर्जिता विद्रवन्ति भयातुराः॥८॥

ब्राह्मणा वेदविभ्रष्टाः सर्वे त्रेसुरुरोगमाः[७]।
सर्वतो गरुडं ज्ञात्वा तमेव शरणं गताः॥९॥

ततः सर्वे यथास्थानं तत्क्षणेनोरुगा गताः[८]।
गरुत्मत्संभवे नष्टा पुनः सृष्टाः स्वयंभुवा॥१०॥

मघानक्षत्रजातानां सर्ववेदशरीरिणाम्।
सहस्त्रवर्षगर्भाणामग्निष्टम्भः स्म जायते[९]॥११॥

Notes on the Restored Text vis-à-vis the Original One

१ The MSS read अण्डजम् which could hardly be correct. अण्डजम् means "egg-born", "a being who has slipped out of an egg", i.e. birds, etc. Vinatā did not "release" (अमुक्त) *egg-borns* but *eggs*, hence my *emendatio* into अण्डकम्। Charpentier 211.8 likes to change it into (त्रिः) अण्डजान् which is unacceptable due to that fact that Vinatā does not release thrice, and each time, "egg-borns" in multiple number, but only one egg at a time.

२ The *emendatio* of Negelein 937 into [अण्डे?] भिद्यमाने + ऊर्ध्वं is unwarranted and grammatically problematic. भिद्यमाना clearly refers to विद्युत्.

३ The text of the MSS has ह्रिया सा परमापन्ना. Since a badly written य can be misread as म and we expect an instrumental feminine qualifying ह्रिया, hence I have emended it into परया. Another possibility could be ह्रिया परमयाऽऽपन्ना which is less preferable because we are then forced to delete the सा.

४ The text has महापुण्ये (महा + अपुण्ये) which is not a good reading in view of the accent (i.e. *udātta* on ये) because a vocative in the midst of a sentence is not supposed to carry the acute (cf. the next vocative चण्डि which is accentless). "You have done a bad and very sinful deed."

५ वाजिनेयान् Charpentier 213 n. 1, वायुवेगान् Rau. Both suggested readings are unwarranted. The text is in order.

६ च काशन्ते Negelein 93.36. This *emendatio* in the text suggested by Negelein is not acceptable since the text is perfectly in order. The suggestion of Negelein. further disturbs the metre since it makes the 7th syllable long whereas it ought to be short.

७ सर्वत्रासुरुरोगमाः is the reading in the MSS which does not yield any good sense (though grammatically justifiable). The *emendatio* is by the present editor who thinks that taking in view the events described at the birth of गरुड, the त्रास (fear) of serpents is not only justified but is most likely the only feature need to be mentioned. Rau suggests सर्वे त्रेसुरुरोगमैः which is unacceptable.

८ Charpentier corrects उरुग into उरग. However Rau points out that उरुग is also a doublette for उरग and refers to *Altindische Grammatik* of Wackernagel, vol. I, p. 65.7ff.

९ A verse which appears to be out of context. It is a general statement, although valid only for Garuḍa, since Garuḍa consists of the entire corpus of Vedic *mantras*, he is born after having been gestated in the womb of his mother for one thousand years and is born in the constellation of Maghā. The author generalizes these characteristics and states that the one with these traits has the capacity to remain unscathed in the midst of fire.

॥ तृतीयं सूक्तम् ॥

पञ्चमो वर्गः (५)

[*प्रस्तोता*]

ओजस्विनं वीरमसह्यसाहं
स्तोष्याम्यहं गरुडं वैनतेयम्।
मातरं यो निरक्रीणात्
कद्र्वा दास्ये पराजिताम्॥१॥

तदस्य कर्म वक्ष्यामि वैनतेयस्य श्रीमतः।
पृथिव्यां प्रथितयशसः[१] सोमाहरणजं महत्॥२॥

कद्रूश्च वै सुपर्णी च पस्पृधाते स्वरूपयोः[२]।
सा कद्रूः सुपर्णीमजयत्।
साऽब्रवीत्–(३)

[*सुपर्णी*]

सत्यं किलैतदपरे वदन्ति
दुरात्मका[३] दीर्घजात्याः[४] सदैव।
अप्रज्ञाना कलहे या सुतं मे
काणा घोरैर्वचनैर्निकृन्तसि[५]॥४॥

[*कद्रूः*]

यावत्त्वं[६] द्वाभ्यां विनते सुपर्णि,
चक्षुर्भ्यां पश्यस्यरुणस्य मातः।
तावच्चेन्नाहमेकेन पश्ये
[तद्][७]दासी तव स्यां त्वमु वा मम स्याः॥५॥

षष्ठो वर्गः (६)

[*कद्रूः*]

प्रेक्षस्व पारं[८] विनते सुपर्णि,
सौपर्णं चक्षुरिति वै श्रुतं मे[९] [ते?]।
अश्वः श्वेतो न्यकषिष्ट[१०] स्थाणौ
तस्यासौ कृष्णस्तिर्यङ्ङववाति बालः[११]॥६॥
[-कृष्णो अववाति बालः?]

[*विनता*]

(गद्यम्)

आ नु दीदिहीषे,[१२] उन्नु[१३] मदेन माद्यसि?
न बालं पश्यामि।

[*कद्रूः*]

किम् आपश्यसि[१४]?॥७॥
यद्यश्वः श्वेतो,[१५] यदि वाऽपि कृष्णः?
किन्नु केन नु कथं न[१६] पश्यसि?॥८॥

[*विनता*]

अनृतं वै त्वं वदसि कद्रु,[१७] काणे प्रतिघृष्टदर्शने[१८]।
सर्वश्वेतमहं[१९] मन्ये नास्य कृष्णोऽस्ति[२०] कश्चन॥९॥

दासी ते [तव?] स्यामिह[२१] सर्पमातर्-
यद्ध्येतदेवं,[२२] न मृषा ब्रवीषि।
मम वा त्वमदिते,[२३] दास्यमद्य
करिष्यसि हन्त चेदावगत्वा[२४]॥१०॥
दूतं प्र हिण्वो[२५] मातरिश्वानमाशुम्[२६]
आशास्वहे[२७] वक्ष्यति तद्यथातथम्।
उभे वा स्वयमेव गच्छाव कद्रु,
वहामि त्वा वाजी चरति यत्रासौ[२८]॥११॥

Notes on the Restored Text vis-à-vis the Original One

१ The nine syllables of the third *pāda* of this verse have led some scholars to suggest some *emendationes* which reduce the number of syllables to eight: प्रथितयशः Hertel 303 n. 3, पृथिव्यां प्रथितं यशः Rau. I do not see any compelling reason to amend the text as the Vedic Anuṣṭubh is not so strictly structured. However it must be admitted that the existence of two acutes (*udātta*) in *práthitayaśásaḥ* poses difficulty in construing these two words as a Bahuvrīhi compound.

२ The MSS read सरूपयोः। स्वरूपयोः is an *emendatio* by Oldenberg (1). 68.37 to which I agree, although I would also willingly accept सुरूपयोः (who is comparatively more beautiful?).

३ Ed. *emendatio*, MSS read दुरात्मकं.

४ This word (*dīrghajātyāḥ*) poses difficulty of comprehending its correct sense. Although in some way or the other, it should refer to the serpents, yet the formation is not clear (*dīrghajātyāḥ* = longbodied?). Oldenberg (1) 69.18 suggests तिर्यग्जात्याः or तिर्यग्गताः. The second suggestion is good though it disturbs the metre considerably. गताः for जात्याः is quite acceptable but an initial long and the following short syllables (– ˘) in the first word of the compound would suit better. Can we have तिर्यग्गताः or perhaps तूर्य or तूर्ण (= fast) गताः instead?

५ काणा घोराणि वचनानि कृन्तति is the reading in the MSS which is certainly wrong somewhere. Hertel 304.5 translates कृन्तति as if it were कृन्तसि, but घोराणि वचनानि (Nom. or Acc.?) still remains in the air. I think that only an instrumental could have stood here and have emended it accordingly.

६ यावद् यद् is an unnecessary emendation of यावत्त्वं by Charpentier 213, fn. 3 (perhaps in view of the तद् appearing in the *pāda* "d" (4th)).

७ The word तद् appears to be a redundant and lengthens the *pāda* unnecessarily. In order to accommodate it, Rau suggests replacement of the following तव by ते which corrects the number of syllables (11) in this *pāda*, although I would think that it disturbs the natural rhythm of the *pāda*.

८ The text reads प्रेक्ष्यः सुपारं, which in a very far-fetched manner may be related to अश्वः श्वेतः. However it may not be admissible, since अश्वः, etc. occurs in the next sentence. I accept here the reading suggested by Oldenberg (1) 69.35 which has all the likelihood of being correct and original because first we expect an imperative here, second सुपारं does not give any sense and further the orthographic corruption of स्व into सु is very easily possible. In a number of Nāgarī MSS the sign of उ below has great similarity with व joined with the letter.

९ Instead of मे, perhaps the *enklitikon* ते would give a better sense, but I resist the temptation of changing it into ते, though Oldenberg would like to have it that way.

१० The text is corrupt at this place and reads अनगसिष्ट (= अनक् + असिष्ट) which does not seem to give any sense and poses great difficulty of interpretation. Oldenberg very ingeneously suggested an *emendatio* in the form of न्यकषिष्ट which I find brilliant and would like to go with it. न्यकषिष्ट would be an aorist (लुङ्) form of 3rd p.s. *ātmanepada* derived from the root कष् (to scratch); conjoined with नि (under, beneath); it may therefore mean "the white horse has rubbed against the stem (of a tree) or a pole".

११ This fourth *pāda* has two syllables more (i.e. 13) than what is required. Either कृष्णः or तिर्यङ् would normally should have been there. Of these the word कृष्ण is indispensable because the whole bet is about whether the hair remains (of the white horse) are black or white. But तिर्यङ् also conjures up the image of the hair tuft tossing about slantingly in the wind. I therefore do not dare to drop it either. In the Vedic texts such sudden increase in the number of syllables is not in common. Charpentier would prefer कृष्णो अववाति बालः 217.21ff. whereas the *padapāṭha* prefers to drop असौ altogether.

१२ The text originally reads दीदिहीषोन्न. Already Grube found it difficult to understand. He wanted to suggest *anu dīdihi iṣe* (*'dīdihīṣe est obscurum; anu dīdihi-iṣe scribendum'*?), but could not find sufficient justification for *iṣe* (the Dative sing. of इष्) (*Sed quid hoc loco sibi velit ishe* (*dat.vocis ish*) *difficillime intelligitur*). The *padapāṭha* bifurcates these conjunct words as [आ + अनु] दीदिहीषे + उत् + न. It means that the final *e* of दीदिहीषे is first dropped in view of the vowel उ following it and then a double *sandhi* is effected by joining दीदिहीष and उत्. Though such "double" *sandhis* are not rare in an archaic language, it is not obligatory here, as it is a piece of prose. I have restored the verb form दीदिहीषे for the sake of clarity. Now, this is really a word which is not easy to handle or to explain. I derive it from root दिह् (= to smear) and perceive in it the Ātmane. Perfect (*liṭ*) form of 2nd person singular. May be the lengthenning of *i* in the initial syllable is unwarranted (दिदिहिषे?). The meaning would be something like: "Are you (= your eyes) greased/ smeared (so that you cannot see properly)"? आ is to be taken in the sense of ईषत्। Oldenberg 70.75 and Rau are in favour of changing दीदिहीष into दीधीष, but what meaning do they assign to it, I am not sure.

१३ As stated above, the text has न for our नु. नु is a particle which converts a simple statement into an interrogative (or strengthens it). Since this second half of the sentence seems to be structured like the first half, नु is certainly a better choice.

१४ Chapter 218.8 suggests emendation of the expression आपश्यसि into त्वं पश्यसि because आपश्यसि is very unusual. Oldenberg would like to have किं पश्यसि त्वम्। I do not see much difficulty in accepting the text as it is. The prefix आ denotes perhaps ईषत् (or समन्तात्?): "What kind of (horse) do you see" in the sense "How does it appear to you"?.

१५ In place of यद्यश्वः Rau would like to suggest: यद्येष [= बालः] श्वेतो . . . because the dispute is over the colour of hair and not of the colour of the horse.

१६ Oldenburg changes न into नु which is certainly wrong.

१७ The same scholar (Oldenberg 70.70) finds this vocative कद्रु as totally redundant and is in favour of dropping it. It is true that the word appears to be dispensable and disturbs the metre (Anuṣṭubh) by lengthening the *pāda* into 10 syllables but in such archaic texts we often have to put up with such a phenomenon.

१८ Charpentier does not feel comfortable with the expression प्रतिघृष्ट (218.8) and suggests निघृष्ट or विघृष्ट as substitutes. I have no difficulty in accepting it as genuine; प्रतिघृष्ट is "rubbed against" "rubbed off" hence denotes the state of an object which has lost its original form, shape or characteristic. प्रतिघृष्टदर्शना is therefore someone (f.) whose vision/sight is impaired.

१९ The text originally reads सर्वश्वेतं ह्यहं. Which I have been amended for good reasons. The particle हि is not only accented (i.e. has *udātta* on it) in the Vedic language but it also makes the verb following it accented. However the verb मन्ये in our verse is totally unaccented. The *anudātta* on ह्य॒ cannot be correct unless we separate it into हि + अ॒हं where *hi* is accented and अ of *aham* has the *anudātta* preceding an *udātta* (on हं॑), but it shall pose at least three problems: the rule of obligatory *sandhi* in a verse is violated, the number of syllables gets increased by one and the verb मन्ये remains unaccented.

[२०] In place of कृष्णो Hertel (304) suggests बालो which is not accepted by Rau.

[२१] The shortage of one syllable leads Charpentier 219.17 to suggest the pronunciation of स्याम् as सि–आम् (or सियाम्) and Rau to suggest insertion of one more syllable in the form of particle वा (दासी वा ते स्याम्). Another possibility is to replace ते with तव.

[२२] एतदेव for एतदेवं, Charpentier 219.17.

[२३] अदिति denotes here "the earth" in which sense it often occurs in the Vedic literature (see my *Vaidika Devatā: Udbhava aur Vikāsa,* 2nd edn, pp. 608-09) and as कद्रू represents the earth, she is addressed as such, not to be confused with the mother of the Ādityas.

[२४] The *padapāṭha* separates it into आ + वगत्वा. There is no problem in taking वगत्वा as अवगत्वा which is common in Sanskrit (वष्टि भागुरिरल्लोपम् अवाप्योरुपसर्गयोः cf. पूर्वापरौ तोयनिधी वगाह्य for अवगाह्य in *Kumārasambhavam* 1.1), but the additional आ poses problem of interpretation unless it is taken as an irregular (i.e. *ārṣa* lengthening of the initial अ of अव). अवगत्वा (अवगत्या?) probably means "in case you are defeated" (अवगति = downfall, defeat). अवगत्या could be a better reading.

[२५] प्र–हिन्वः is written in the text as two separate words, hence the र in प्र has not caused any cerebralization of न् in *hinvaḥ*. In classical Sanskrit, the correct form is always with cerebral *ṇ* (i.e. ण) and is joined with प्र (i.e. प्रहिण्वः), however in the Vedic language both forms are met with, I have opted for the common one.

[२६] The text reads मातरिश्वन only without any ending which cannot be correct. Of course, the *padapāṭha* renders it as मातरिश्वने (dative) with loss of final *e* because of a vowel following, but we cannot go along with a Dative here, because we need a direct object (Accusative) for the verb प्रहिन्वः which can only be the मातरिश्वन् (god of wind and messenger of gods esp. of Vivasvān). The conjectural reading मातरिश्वानम् is therefore correct. Āśu (आशु) is an adjective (meaning "swift") which very often accompanies the word मातरिश्वन् in the *Ṛgveda*. I therefore conjecture that here stood most probably the adjective आशुं which got dropped due to haplology since we have practically the same syllables in the *pāda* following (आशास्वहे).

२७ The traditional text has the form आशासाव: which cannot grammatically be justified, nor does it (or a similar form in some other person) appear anywhere else. Hence this *emendatio*.

२८ The metre of this verse is Jagatī which consists of 12 syllables in each *pāda*.

॥ चतुर्थं सूक्तम् ॥

सप्तमो वर्गः (७)

[*कद्रूः*]

एष बालो लम्बते वृक्षशङ्कौ
कच्चिदेनं पश्यसि लम्बमानम्?
जिता मेऽसि समुद्रसाक्ष्याच्-
छूद्रा[१] मे भव त्वमाश्रमात्[२]॥१॥

[*नागाः*]

समुद्रे रमणीयकं द्वीपं शुश्रुम शाश्वतम्।
नागानामालयं पूर्वं तत्र नो विनते वह॥२॥

[*विनता आत्मगतम्*]

अहं वहामि परि तान् (ताम्?)[३] वहामि
सर्पान् वहामि यथा दुष्कृतकारिणी[४]।
दीपान्तसमुद्रस्य वहामि दुष्कृत्-
कद्रूं सपुत्रामुदकं स्पृशन्ती[५]॥३॥

अष्टमो वर्गः (८)

[*कद्रूर्विनतां प्रति*]

यस्ते कुमारस्तरुणः[६] सुपर्णि,
यस्य शाखाः[७] पततः खं[८] नुदन्ति।
तं प्रेषयस्व बलिनं स एतु[९]
सर्वानस्मान् नयतु यत्र सूर्यः॥४॥

[*सुपर्णो गरुडः सर्पान् प्रति*]

अहं सुपर्णः प्रहितोऽरुणेन
सर्पाः, करिष्यामि यथाह शुङ्गी।

आरोहत श्लिश्यत[१०] मे शरीरं
वोळ्हास्मि सर्वानचिरेण सूर्यम्॥५॥

[*नागाः गरुडं प्रति*]

तीक्ष्णाः सुपर्ण,[११] बहुधा मरीच्यः
सूर्यस्य ता नः प्रदहन्ति भोगान्।
नमः पतङ्गाय, निवर्त साधु [साधो?]
यत्र माताऽदितिस्तत्र[१२] गच्छ॥६॥
अलं सूर्यस्य सदनं गतेन
दग्धा नस्तन्वः सवितुः शिखाभिः।
विहाय वा त्वा प्रपताम भूमौ
निवर्त वा शकुने नोद्यमानः[१३]॥७॥

[*कद्रूः सुपर्णीं प्रति*]

इदं न साधु यदयं[१४] सुपर्णि,
सुतान् ममैनानवहत् सधस्थे[१५]।
विचेष्टमानानुरगानशक्तान्[१६]
जवेन सूर्यं प्रति दह्यमानान्॥८॥

Notes on the Restored Text vis-à-vis the Original One

१ Grube reproduces the text as "समुद्रसाक्ष्या छूद्रा" which is certainly based on the misreading of the letter छ in the MSS which is a combined form of च् + छ, i.e. च्छ (*cch*). Except in the beginning of a word, the letter *cha* (छ) is always combined with a च् (cf. Pāṇ. 6.1.73) and the form of छ has actually developed out of a Brāhmī *ca* combined with *cha*. At present this letter in Nāgarī script denotes only *cha* devoid of *c* which is additonally added to it, if and when required. Already Charpentier (220.14) corrected साक्ष्या into साक्ष्यात्।

२ This line represents two *pāda*s of a lengthened Anuṣṭubh (of 9 syllables each, instead of 8). In order to restore its "pristine" Anuṣṭubh character, therefore, Rau suggests the following amendment: "जिता समुद्रसाक्ष्येऽसि, शूद्रा मे भव आ श्रमात्" which is totally unnecessary (also faulty: साक्ष्ये should be साक्ष्येण and the hiatus between भव and आ is also unacceptable). Already Oldenberg (71.11) was in favour of separating आ from श्रमात् although the *padapāṭha* treats it as one single word with an accent on ॰मा. Note the sudden deviation from the Triṣṭubh of the previous half.

३ Negelein 95.22 would like to have ताम् here (referring of course to Kadrū, since the serpents are mentioned separately). A good suggestion indeed.

४ This *pāda* (सर्पान् . . . कारिणी) is rather too long and contains 13 syllables which has disturbed many a scholar. Negelein (95.21) is in favour of deleting the word सर्पान् which is obvious from the context, Rau suggests सर्पान् वहामि कृतकारिणीव (p. 356) and refers to the *Mahābhārata* 12.130.60 for the word "कृतकरी" (in the sense of "evil-doer"). I think there is some misunderstanding (or misprint) of the text and the word in question in the *Mahābhārata* could only be अकृतकारिणी/अकृतकरी since अकृत is synonymous with दुष्कृत. I would rather like to amend the text as सर्पान् वहामि यथाऽकृतकारिणी or rather: सर्पान् वहाम्यकृतकारिणीव।

५ The text originally reads here कद्रून्त्सपुत्रां which is accepted as such by Grube. But it is an impossible *sandhi* and insertion of a त् after the *anusvāra* of Accusative case (कद्रूं) is not prescribed by any rule (cf. also Caland).

Further, Grube gives the reading as स्पृशन्तीम् which is certainly wrong since in that case it can only refer to कद्रू which is not the intended meaning of the text. It is the Vinatā who is flying too close to the surface of the oceanic water since she is old and feeble and cannot fly very high due to weight on her back. This is also the reason, why next time the serpents want to fly with Garuḍa who is young and who can sore much higher into the sky, "right up to the sun".

६ Totally unsuitable amendment of this word into कुमारो अरुणः suggested by Rau (p. 356).

७ Rau unnecessarily suggests emendation of शाखा – which means "wings" (the two spread out hands or wings of Garuḍa) – into शिखः।

८ खं is our emendation of the original *khe* in the text, since the verb नुदन्ति requires a direct object (accusative) at this place.

९ "स एतु" is given in the text as सैतु which is a clear case of double *sandhi* (सः एतु > स > एतु > सैतु).

१० Charpentier 224.18 (seconded by Rau later) suggested this brilliant emendation in place of the original क्लिश्यत occurring here. Taking the situation and the context in view क्लिश्यत[मे शरीरं] (hurt/cause pain to my body) does not seem appropriate whereas "mount on me and get glued" and "stuck to my body" seem to be the only expressions intended.

११ The text reads सुपर्णा (with acute accent on र्णा) which makes this word an adjective to मरीच्यः. The reading is confirmed by the *padapāṭha* and has been accepted by Grube. I am, however, absolutely convinced that it is a corruption of the original सुपर्ण (vocative); cf. शकुने of the next verse.

१२ One expects the serpents to be impatient to get back to their mother (Kadrū) and not to Aditi, the mother of gods. But our *bhāṣyakāra* takes the word Aditi in the sense of the Earth which is supported by references in the *Ṛgveda* and Brāmaṇas (see my वैदिक देवता : उद्भव और विकास, pp. 608-09) and this identifies her with कद्रू. It may further be noted that though the *saṁhitāpāṭha* makes a *sandhi* between माता and अदिति leading to the elison of the अ of अदिति, one has to separate them in order to restore the metre.

१३ Unnecessary emendation of this word into चोद्यमानः by Charpentier (225.9).

१४ The text reads यदिदं which has no relevance since इदं has already occurred in the beginning and here the pronoun has to refer to Garuḍa.

[१५] For अवहत् सधस्थे Rau (p. 356) suggests अवहत् सुतस्ते which is unwarranted since we need an indication of some location or destination for the verb अवहत्, and सधस्थे (= in the sky) suits best the context.

[१६] The text has असक्तान् which has rightly been corrected into अशक्तान् by Charpentier (225.19) and Rau (p. 356).

॥ पञ्चमं सूक्तम् ॥

नवमो वर्गः (९)

[*कद्रूः अरुणं प्रति*]

एते सूर्यस्य तपसाऽभितप्ताः
क्षितौ वर्तन्तेऽरुण भोगवन्तः।
अहं न विन्दामि हितं[१] सुतानां
न चेह तार्क्ष्यः, स हि शर्म विद्यात्॥१॥

[*कद्रूः सुपर्णं प्रति*]

एतत्ते कर्म परुषं सुपर्ण,[२]
यत् सौरसेयानवहो बलात्त्वम्।

[*प्रस्तोता*]

आर्ता कद्रूर्वदति दग्धपुत्रा
नीचैर्वर्तेथाः प्रभवत्सु नित्यम्॥२॥

[*कश्यपस्तार्क्ष्यः*]
(*प्रविश्य पर्जन्यं स्तौति*[३])

"अभिक्रन्द स्तनयार्दयोदधीन्त्[४]-
समास्तास्ते[५] गिरिभिः सन्त्वापः।
आ हन्तु शेषः[६] शिखरं गिरीणां
गच्छन्तु सर्पाः सलिलस्य मध्यम्॥३॥
एकोदकं पारमपारमस्तु
मण्डूकिका वदतु सर्वरात्रम्।
उतादुघामपदी[७] गां दुहन्तु
मृग[८] एतु स्थलमिच्छमानः॥४॥"

दशमो वर्गः (१०)

[*सुपर्णी गरुडं प्रति*]

वर्षस्यश्रूणि किमिदं गरुत्मंस्-
तार्क्षस्य[९] पुत्रस्त्वमरिष्टनेमे[१०]।
न तादृशानां विहग, द्विजेन्द्र[११]
शोचत्यपत्यमिति वै श्रुतं मे॥५॥

[*गरुडः मातरं प्रति*]

आर्तिं वै मे विनते नयन्त्य-
पनतह्रिया त्वनपत्येव मातः।
यानाचारान् युवत्यो न चक्रु-
रित्थं वै तेऽश्रुमुक्ताः पतन्ति[१२]॥६॥

सर्वान्[१३] लोकान् चक्षुषाऽन्वेमि मातर्
अहमोजसा तरसा बलेन।

[गद्य]

अथ कथं दासोऽस्मि जातः?
किं स्वित् पापं चकर्थ?
अथो पिता मे दुश्चरितं चचार?[१४]॥७॥

[*विनता गरुडं प्रति*]

अहं तया स्पर्द्धमाना कद्रुवाऽऽशंस उपाददे।
अजानन्ती भयं क्रोधात्[१५] (मोहात्?) सा माऽजयत् सम्पराये[१६]॥८॥

[*गरुडः मातरं प्रति*]

कथं दास्यान्मोचये त्वां[१७] विषह्यान्[१८]-
मया दासेन यदि वा पृथिव्या[१९]।
आचक्ष्व शुङ्गे[२०] दृळ्हमस्मि आर्तो
अन्नेन वाप्युत वा धनेन॥९॥

गच्छानुयुङ्क्ष्व[२१] सर्पान् यदि मोक्षोऽस्ति केनचित्।
मया वा यदि वाऽरुणेन पशुभिर्वा धनेन वा॥१०॥

Notes on the Restored Text vis-à-vis the Original One

१ The text reads हतिं (injury) which does not yield sense with न विन्दामि. Oldenberg suggests गतिं (oc. [2] 84, n. 1) which is acceptable ("I do not know what will now happen to my sons", "I do not know how they are"). However, I go with Charpentier who emends हतिं into हितं (226.4) because it goes better with the latter half of the *pāda* ("I do not know how they will get well again, Tārkṣa is also not here, otherwise he would know how to help them").

२ The text has सुपर्णि but अवहः makes it clear that सुपर्ण is meant because it was he who carried the serpents (and brought them nearer to the sun against their wish: बलात्).

३ Kadrū laments (in 1d) that her husband is not there otherwise he would know what to do in order to revive the serpents with scorched skin. Ṛṣi Kaśyapa or Tārkṣa comes to know of the distress of Kadrū through his yogic powers and appears on the scene, something which is not mentioned in the text. But the following verses (ṛ*ks*) do not leave any scope for doubt.

४ The text reads स्तनयोऽदयोऽदधीन् which is emended by Oldenberg (2) 90, n. 2 on the basis of *AV* 4.15.6 and 11. I feel that it is in order and accept it. Cf. *ṚV* V.83.7: अभिक्रन्द स्तनय गर्भमा धा उदन्वता परिदीया रथेन, etc. which is the basis of this verse.

५ After ते the text has an additional word पर्जन्य (in vocative) which, I feel, is redundant (समाः ताः ते [पर्जन्य] गिरिभिः सन्तु आपः).

६ The reading, if correct, poses difficulty of interpretation, we expect here a word for cloud (मेघः/ओघः) could शेषः be "accumulated water"?

७ "उप दुग्धपदीं" is what the text reads. The *emendatio* is by me: "Even those cows which cannot walk (i.e. are too old) and dry, may yield milk", cf. सुप्रपाणं भवतु अघ्न्याभ्यः, *ṚV* V.83.8.).

८ The text reads मृळ which is a common Vedic verb form (Imperative, 2nd person, singular) meaning "be kind", "be compassionate" (cf. *ṚV* II.33.14 मीढ्वस्तोकाय तनयाय मृळ). If we take it as an adjective मृळः (kind) it hardly gives any sense in conjunction with the verb एतु which requires a subject, i.e. a noun. The *emendatio* of Oldenberg into मृगः (meaning "wild animals" in general) is therefore acceptable although the *pāda* still poses difficulty with its only ten syllables. Rau suggests मृदुल which according to him means a "sea monster" on the basis of the testimony of *Āpastamba Dh.S.* I.5.39 and *Hiraṇyak. Dh.S.* I.5.70, however does not yield any good sense. Could we think of the word मृगयुः (a hunter)?

९ The MSS read here तार्क्ष्य but as observed earlier, the correct word could only be तार्क्ष, since it refers to the father of Garuḍa who is referred to with his patronym as तार्क्ष्य. Tārkṣa is the father (belonging to the gotra of Tṛkṣa) and Tārkṣya is his son, Garuḍa.

१० Oldenberg takes this Vocative as a Genitive and would like to have it emended into अरिष्टनेमेः because the word does not lose its accent (*udātta* on the initial *a*) which ought to be the case with a Vocative. However, Tārkṣya is often referred to as Garuḍa Ariṣṭanemi (cf *ṚV* I.89.6 . . . . स्वस्ति नस्तार्क्ष्यो अरिष्टनेमिः) and the accent on *a* is unreliable. Mother Vinatā encourages her son by reminding him of his attribute अरिष्टनेमि which could mean something like "of unimpeded/unchecked flight or speed" (lit. "the felly of whose wheel is not worn out").

११ Rau would like to have विहगद्विजानां in order to let it grammatically correspond with तादृशानां which I find totally unwarranted since the unaccented character of विहग and द्विजेन्द्र or, taking it as one word विहगद्विजेन्द्र, speaks against it. However, one must admit that the occurrence of these two more or less synonymous words pose some difficulty of interpretation unless one of them, especially विहग, is taken as an adjective (विहायसा गच्छति, highflying).

१२ Almost all scholars who have worked on सुपर्णाध्याय have suggested some amendments of this verse. First of all, I wish to change the ते of the text into मे because the sentence is an answer of Garuḍa to Vinatā telling her why he is shedding tears. Oldenberg ([1] 7 fn. 2) prefers नियन्ति for नयन्ति. अपनतह्रिया has troubled many. Charpentier (222.7ff.) suggests अनपत्या (which I wish to emend further into तु अनपत्येव "as if you have no children/sons"), Negelein (95.6) has अनपत्यत्वात् तु, whereas Rau changes it into नता ह्रिया. I do not see any difficulty in interpreting the verse if we take अपनतह्रिया as an adverb going with अश्रुमुक्ताः पतन्ति, i.e. "weeping while 'casting aside the sense of grace, indecently', something which young ladies endowed with such great children are not supposed to do". Now see how Charpentier and Rau would like to have the verse:

आर्तिं वै ते विनते नयन्ति अनपत्या त्वमरुणस्य मातः।
य आचार्यान् युवानो च चक्रुर् (चक्रिरे) इत्थं वै तेऽश्रुमुखाः पतन्ति॥ (Ch. 222.7)

आर्तिं वा एते विनते नियन्ति नता ह्रिया ते अरुणस्य मातः।
य आचार्यान् योयुवतो न चक्रुरित्थं वै ते अश्रुमुखाः पतन्ति॥ (Rau 356)

For यानाचारान्, Negelein has ये शरणानि (?). Needless to say that these emendations are much worse than the original!

This and the preceding verse (i.e. nos. 5 and 6 of this hymn) appear in the original text as nos. 3 and 4 of the 4th hymn where they are totally out of context. Such misplacements, occur quite often in the text due to reshuffled or misarranged folia in the source *exemplar*.

१३ The text has स्वर्गान् [लोकान्] which has been emended by me into सर्वान् which better suits the context. स्वर्ग is usually not used in plural. Further it limits the capacity of Garuḍa to scan and examine only the heavenly worlds.

१४ Not realizing that it is a prose piece some scholars (notably Charpentier) have tried to emend it by deleting supposedly spurious words. The last two lines would then have to appear as: पापं चकर्थाथो पिता चकार with किंस्वित् joining the previous *pāda*.

१५ Vinatā perhaps means to say that she accepted the challenge or bet of Kadrū (आशंसस् = utterance) in a fit of rage because the latter had remarked that she sees less with her two eyes than what Kadrū sees with a single eye. However, it is tentalyzing to replace क्रोधात् with मोहात् ("out of ignorance", "not realizing the consequences").

१६ Rau suggests संपणने instead of संपराये.

१७ This is a restoration of the manuscript reading मोचयतु विषह्या.

१८ All MSS deliver here the text as विषह्या which is corroborated by the *padapāṭha*: "वि०सह्या". The commentator curiously explains विषह्या as शक्या ("केनोपायेन मोचयितुं विसह्या असि = शक्या भवसि"). I consider it as an obvious mistake for विषह्यात् (unbearable) which qualifies दास्यात् as an adjective and of which the final letter न् (emerging out of त् being followed by मो) got dropped already at an early stage. This indicates, further, that all our present MSS go back basically to one single source.

१९ Rau would like to see the word पृथिव्या replaced by अरुणेन in view of the similar expression in the following verse.

२० Hertel (*Indische Märchen*, 1919, p. 351 fn. 6) prefers the Vocative शुंगि because the adjective शुंगी for Vinatā is more common than शुंगा.

२१ अनुयुक्ष्व of the MSS has been rightly corrected by Charpentier (228.31) into अनुयुङ्क्ष्व (अनु + युञ्ज् = To ask), so also has he added an additional वा between पशुभिः and धनेन.

॥ षष्ठं सूक्तम् ॥

एकादशो वर्गः [११]

[*विनता सर्पान् प्रति*]

"न पुत्रान् वेद न पतिं तथाहं
युष्मान् वहन्ती अबला कृशाऽस्मि।
क्षीणो मे[१] धातुर्न जवो ममास्ति
कथं दास्यात् परिमुच्येय वृद्धा॥१॥"

[*प्रक्षेपः?*]

किमाहृत्वा[२] किं विजित्वा[२] किमु कृत्वा तु पौरुषम्।
दास्याद् वो विप्रमुच्येय[३] तदु शंसत लेलिहाः॥२॥[४]

[*नागाः विनतां प्रति*]

इन्द्रस्य सोमो निहितो गुहायां
तृतीये पृष्ठे रजसो विमाने[५]।
तमाहृत्य तरसा, शंतमेन
तेनात्मानं निष्क्रीय शं चर त्वम्॥३॥

वारं[६] वरीयो[७] दिवि उत्तमायां
रहः श्रृणुमो बृहदिन्द्ररक्षितम्।
[८]तमाहृत्यामृतमुपोर्णुवेम[९]
दास्यान् मुच्यस्व यदि शक्तिरस्ति ते[१०]॥४॥

द्वादशो वर्गः [१२]

[*विनता गरुडं प्रति*]

सोमं सर्पाः पिपासन्ति अस्माभिर्दिव आहृतम्।
दुराहरो दिवश्चेन्दुर्गरुत्मंत्स च निष्क्रयः॥५॥

[गरुडः मातरं प्रति]

आ ते श्रृणोमि विनते सुपर्णि
यदि ब्राह्मणं न जघन्थ मातः।
पतिष्यामि तव कामाय दूराद्[११]
दिवस्पृष्ठात् सोममाहर्तवा उ॥६॥

[विनता गरुडं प्रति]

न ब्राह्मणं जघनाहं गरुत्मन्
न सत्रघ्नाप्यभवम्[१२] द्वितीया[१३]।
नानेन (नान्येन?) समेनसा प्रोर्णुवीमि[१४]
नागस्स्पृशो अपहरामि एनः॥७॥

[गरुडो मातरं प्रति]

इन्द्रस्य सोमं निहितं गुहायां
तृतीयात् पृष्ठाद् रजसो विमानात्[१५]।
निहत्य रक्षांस्तरसा[१६] प्रणुद्या-
ऽऽहरिष्यामि च तवेन्दुं, नु नैव[१७]?॥८॥

[विनता गरुडं प्रति]

सर्वे देवा दिवि रक्षन्ति सोमं
भूतानि चान्यानि महन्ति तात।
तस्य जानीष्व, यदि ते विषह्यं[१८]
श्रेयोऽभौजिष्यात् तव जीवितं मे॥९॥

[गरुडो मातरं प्रति]

छन्दांसि वै स्मो विनते सुपर्णि,
यज्ञं यानि विततं धारयन्ति।
असकृद् वै यज्ञमहे पुरस्तान्[१९]
मा नो धाता[२०] निदधे[२१] माऽवमंस्थाः[२२]॥१०॥

यानि छन्दांसि चतुरुत्तराणि
यज्ञं वहन्ति[२३] विततं सप्ततन्तुम्।
तान्यहमस्मि विनते सुपर्णि,
मां देवताः प्राहिण्वन्त[२४] सोममच्छ[२५]॥११॥

Notes on the Restored Text vis-à-vis the Original One

१ Charpentier (229.15) suggests an insertion of मे after क्षीणः in order to make the *pāda* complete with 11 syllables, which is acceptable.

२ आहृत्वा and विजित्वा are non-Pāṇinian archaic form (for आहृत्य and विजित्य) taken over from older strata of the language.

३ For विप्रमुच्येय Charpentier has an unnecessary emendation वि वो प्रमुच्येय for which I see no reason.

४ This verse appears almost in this very form (except विदित्वा for our विजित्वा) in the "Āstīka" Upaparvan of the first book (Ādiparva) of the *Mahābhārata* (I.23.11, cr. ed) which again proves the dependence of *Mahābhārata* on the *Suparṇādhyāya* for its narration of the story. Or should we postulate here in our text a later contamination from the *Mahābhārata*?

५ The sense of the words रजसो विमाने does not seem to go well with other words of the sentence and the twin words appear to be totally redundant. These two words have been taken verbatim from *ṚV* X.121 (Hiraṇyagarbhasūkta) where they appear as an adjective to हिरण्यगर्भ who is said to encompass the whole universal space (रजस्) from one end to the other.

६ वारं in older language means "water". The weaker form of this word वार् is commonly used in the classical Sanskrit. वारं with the following adjective वरीयं (chosen, distinguished) refers to *soma*, the water of immortality.

७ The MSS read here वरीयं which is an inconvenient form unless we let it pass as an archaic (आर्ष) formation parallel to वरीयस् (वर + ईयसुन्). One would have, of course, felt more comfortable with this regular comparative degree of वरम् as already suggested by Charpentier (231.22).

८ The MSS here reads आहृत्वा but I believe the author repeats here the expression of the previous verse.

९ The original reading is अमृतपोर्णुवेम which has baffled a number of scholars. अमृतपाः (pl.) ऊर्णुवेम (Charpentier 231.24, पा joined with ऊ after dropping the *visarga*), अमृतमपोर्णुवानो or अपोर्णुवन् नो (Oldenberg [2] 84 fn. 2) are the emendations suggested. I find that the text of this *pāda* containing 10 syllables is short by one, namely a म between त and पो। अमृतम् उपोर्णुवेम (so that we attain immortality). The root is ऊर्णुङ् आच्छादने = to cover, joined with उप = to achieve.

१० Charpentier finds ते (12th syllable) as redundant.

११ Rau (p. 357) thinks that here दूरम् would have been more appropriate. However, दूरात् is obviously not an adverb to पतिष्यामि but an adjective to दिवस्पृष्ठात्।

१२ The MSS read अभवद्, but since Vinatā speaks in first person all through, this emendation seems justified.

१३ द्वितीया poses some difficulty of interpretation. द्वितीयम् (and second. . . , "Besides also not . . . .") could have been meant.

१४ "I do not cover myself — am not tainted — with this or a similar sin, nor do I have taken over the sin of someone else for expiation."

१५ "रजसो विमानात्" is used here perhaps in the sense of "the top of the world (heaven)", cf. "लोका रजांसि उच्यन्ते" *Nirukta* IV.19.39; or "across the expanse of the universe" विमानः = measured from one end to the other.

१६ The MSS read here निहत्य रक्षस्तरंसा . . . The word रक्षंस् with accent on the first syllable stands for "injury" whereas with acute on the second syllable (रक्षस्) it means "one who causes injury". Further, there is a word रक्षः (masc.) too with accent on क्ष (रक्षः) meaning "protector". I prefer that word here since it appears again in the first verse of the *sūkta* 14 (रक्षान् धर्षितवान्). The absolutive निहत्य (after killing) can only refer to persons, not to obstacles. The accent is also to be emended accordingly.

१७ The MSS have च वा इन्दुं नु मैव which causes difficulty and does not appear to be correct. The reading accepted by us has been suggested by Charpentier, except that he prefers तत (from there) for तव (232.3). He is also in favour of dropping च and splitting the *sandhi* between प्रणुद्य and आ हरिष्यामि (in order to get eleven syllables for the 4th *pāda*). तव stands here for तुभ्यं (for you) and नु नैव with *Kāku* means "is not it so?", "don't you think so?". Other suggestions for emendation are तवेन्दुं ममैव by Negelein (97.1) and च वा इन्दुं नु नैव by Rau (p. 357). It is to be explored whether मैव or मेव (मा-इव) could have the same meaning as नैव. In some of the dialects of Hindi (e.g. Bundelī) a similar word माव has this meaning (mostly in negatively interrogative sentences).

१८ Charpentier (232.26) would like to read अविषह्यं here which is unwarranted as Rau has rightly pointed out. Vinatā simply means: "Think it over well; in case it endangers your life, I would rather have you alive than to get rid of my slavery."

१९ पुरस्तान् is bifurcated in the *padapāṭha* as पुरस् and तान् and both words carry their own accents. It has to be construed with नः (previously [also] those us). However Johansson (48 fn. 2) and Rau would like to see it as one word पुरस्तात् to be construed with यज्ञमहे।

२०-२१ धाता (= Prajāpati) is my emendation for the word दाता which I fail to understand in this context. This last *pāda* has left almost all previous scholars guessing for the correct wordings and their meaning. Charpentier suggests मा नो दानानि दमेऽवमंस्थाः (233.2), whereas Rau (p. 357) is in favour of emending the text as मा न एतानि इदम् अवमंस्थाः and would like to translate it as "Do not despise these now which belong to us" (*Verachte diese, die uns gehören, jetzt nicht!*). I find the suggestion of Rau rather far-fetched and am in favour of emending only दाता into धाता and निर्दमे (split as नि + दुमे with no accent on the noun दमे = in house) into निदधे. This seems totally justified as the adverb असकृत् needs a verb and, further, since दमे is devoid of accent, it could not be a noun. Even with a proper accent on दमे it would be rather clumsy to interpret the expression निर्दमे as "in-house", "within family" as the prefix नि would not have any function.

२२ Although suffering from the poetic blemish विप्रकृष्टत्व, मा is to be taken definitely with the aorist form अवमंस्थाः, with नः as object of the sentence ("do not underestimate us").

२३ The suggestion of Rau (p. 357) to replace वहन्ति with वयन्ति (weave) citing the authority of *Ṛ̣V* II.38.4 is unnecessary. The metres are quite often mentioned as "carrying" the sacrifice to gods. This is also the reason why Garuḍa is the carrier of Viṣṇu who is frequently identified with sacrifice in the Brāhmaṇas.

२४ MSS read प्राहिन्वन्त without cerebralization which is grammatically not fine.

२५ अच्छ (towards) is often found, or is supposed to be read, as अच्छा in the *Ṛgveda* (cf. अच्छा वद तवसं गीर्भिराभिः, *ṚV* V.83.1, and also at another 23 places in the beginning of a verse). In this case also it would facilitate the chanting of the verse.

॥ सप्तमं सूक्तम् ॥

त्रयोदशो वर्गः [१३]

[गरुडो मातरं प्रति]

नानश्नतो वीर्यं किञ्चनास्ति
अस्मिन्[१] लोके चरतः सुपर्णि।
पृच्छामि त्वा विनतेऽहमेतत्
किं स्विद् भुक्त्वा पथामि[२] देवलोकम्॥१॥

[विनता गरुडं प्रति]

एष महान् पर्वतस्तस्य कूटे
महान् ह्रदस्तत्र भूतं महान्तम्।
तद् हस्तिनं चावतीर्णं ग्रहीष्यसि
स ते भक्षस्तावुभौ पश्य पुत्र॥२॥

महानागो घोषवान् नाम, पद्मी[३]
महादन्तो मेघ इवावभासते।
तं तेऽददात् सह सख्येन धाता
तौ भक्षयित्वाऽथ पथासि[४] देवलोकम्॥३॥

[गरुडः सहर्षमात्मगतम्]

अहमिमावशिताऽस्मि[५] सुपद्म[६]-
नागौ मतङ्गानुचरौ प्रभिन्नौ।
अग्रहैषं प्रमुदितो महान्ता-
वध्वानमेतं पतैतद्[७] जिघित्सन्[८]॥४॥

[गरुडो मातरं प्रति]

वयांसि वै स्मो विनते सुपर्णि
नास्मान् भूमौ भक्ष्यमाणं धिनोति।

वृक्षं नो ब्रूहि, यदि वेत्थ कञ्चिद्
यत्राधिरुह्याद्याम[9] रुच्याऽम्ब भक्ष्यम्॥५॥

[विनता गरुडं प्रति]

यत्र ऋषयो बालखिल्याः सुपर्ण
वैखानसाश्च मुनयो वसन्ति।
यस्य शाखाः प्रथिता[10] योजनानि
तमारोह शाखिनं भोजनाय॥६॥

नगश्रेष्ठं रौहिणं गच्छ शीघ्रं
बृहच्छाखं जनयितुः सखायम्।
तमारुह्य भक्षयेथाः सुपर्ण
स चेद् गरुत्मन् मृषयेन्न[11] चान्यः॥७॥

चतुर्दशो वर्गः [१४]

[*रौहिणो नाम वृक्षः, आत्मगतम्*]

महावीर्यं हस्तिनं मेरुमात्रं
सहग्राहं धारयन्नन्तरिक्षे।
जवेन वायुं बलवन्तमीरयन्
उपैत्यसौ कम्पयन् मा सुपर्णः॥८॥

[*गरुडो रौहिणं प्रति*]

प्रतितिष्ठ रौहिण[12] धारयस्व
श्रमेण वै मो[13] (नो?) मुमुहुर्भवानि[14]।
छन्दोभिर्मिश्रः सह देवताभिर्
आ त्वा रोक्ष्यामि सहसाऽहं[15] गरुत्मान्॥९॥

[*रौहिणो गरुडं प्रति*]

एषा प्राची गरुड तां श्रयस्व
यस्यां वैखानसा ऋषयो[16] बालखिल्याः।
परस्यां नमति तावत्तिरश्ची[17]
स[18] चेद् गरुत्मन् वृजिनाद् बिभेषि॥१०॥

(शाखा भज्यते)

अभाङ्क्षीः शाखां वृजिनं करिष्यसि
हनिष्यसि ब्राह्मणान् ये पृथिव्याम्।
अतूर्त[१९] तमो रजो विनशिष्यसि[२०]
नाहरिष्यसि सोममेतं गरुत्मन्॥११॥

Notes on the Restored Text vis-à-vis the Original One

१ Rau adds the particle उ to अस्मिन् (अस्मिन्नु) to make up for the deficiency of one syllable.

२ The root *path* is rather uncommon; Rau therefore is in favour of reading पतामि (I shall fly), so also Hertel (308.3) in the 3rd verse of this *sūkta* (पतासि). One may refer to the article of Karl Hoffmann in *Kuhnische Zeitschrift* (*KZ*), vol. 79 (1965), pp. 180-83 for discussion on this root which is used here in the sense of "to travel", "to go on way".

३ All MSS read पत्मी (पतनशीलः?). The formation is difficult to explain, but it seems to be a genuine regular Vedic word. पत् + मन् (like, स्तोमन् or कर्मन्) + इन् (the suffix forming possessive adjectives) = पत्मिन्, or according to the rules of consonantal combination, पद्मिन्/पद्मी which turns into सुपद्म in later texts (e.g. *Mahābhārata*). It remains unresolved, however, whether the "actual" name of the elephant is घोषवान् (trumpeter) or पत्मी (a dasher)! Which one is adjective and which one the noun?

४ पथामि is what the MSS read which is certainly not correct since it is not Garuḍa who is speaking these words, but his mother. It seems that at some stage the archetype of all the present MSS confused स for म which are quite similar in the Devanāgarī script. पथासि is a Vedic Subjunctive (लेट्) 2nd person, singular of पथ्. We may also accept the verb form पतासि in case we are not comfortable with the root पथ्. In lieu of पथासि, पथ (Imperative) could also be a good reading. Delete also the redundant अथ to rectify the metre.

५ This verse (7.4) has come down to us in a very bad shape. इमौ वाशितायामिव is the reading of the manuscripts which Charpentier tries to emend as वाशिताऽऽयम्येव (वाशिता आयम्य इव = वाशिता इव आयम्य, "bound/overpowered as if they were cows/female elephants") which I do not find very convincing. Negelein (98.18) has the best and the most acceptable suggestion in अहमिमावशिता शुद्धपद्मौ where अशिता (going to eat) is definitely correct but शुद्ध does not seem to make any sense. I have chosen to change it into सुपद्म which occurs as the name of the elephant in later texts. अशिता further needs an अस्मि to complete the verb form (लुट्) which I have added.

६ Charpentier is also in favour of dropping the word मतङ्ग (शुद्धपद्मौ नागानुचरौ for which I see no reason. Perhaps he meant मातङ्गनागानुचरौ.

. . .

७ पतैतत् is to be understood as formed by double *sandhi*, not so uncommon in epics and ancient narrative texts [पते–एतत् > पत-एतत् > पतैतत् (द्)].

८ जिघित्सन् is my conjecture. The text originally has ध्रजिष्यन्, the meaning or formation of which I am unable to grasp. That it is a future participle, is clear, but the verb? With my "restoration", the *pāda* would mean "I am flying on this track with the desire to devour them one by one".

९ All MSS have अधिरुह्याद्म where अद्म is a difficult form to explain (an archaic unreduplicated Perfect with Present meaning analogous to विद्म? Cf. उभे ते विद्म रजसी पृथिव्या विष्णो . . . *ṚV* VII.99.1). One expects here either an Optative or an Imperative (1st p. pl.) अद्याम or अदानि. I have opted for Optative. Other suggestions which have been advanced are ०रुह्याम्ब अद्याम भक्ष्यम्, Charpentier; ०ह्य ममाद्यं तु भक्षम्, Negelein; and ०ह्य रुच्याद्म भक्षम्, Rau.

१० The MSS have पतिता: which does not yield any good sense. प्रथिता: (spread out) is a brilliant suggestion by Charpentier (235.25).

११ The text originally reads वृषयेत् which is certainly wrong. Charpentier (236.3) suggested मर्षयेत्, Negelein (98.14) धर्षयेत् and finally Rau मृषयेत् which is the best of all. He also quotes (pp. 357-58) *Kṣīrataraṅgiṇī* to substantiate this form. With this amendment the meaning would be: "It is only he who could withstand you, if at all, none else".

१२ MSS read रौहिणम् which is certainly wrong. Charpentier has it correct.

१३ For मा (मा + उ) some scholars have suggested नो which is equally good.

१४ मुमुहु: is a rare formation from the root मुह् in the sense of "unconscious", "fainted", "swooned". Rau draws our attention to Wackernagel"s *Altindische Grammatik*, vol. II, pt. 2, p. 472, 35ff. where the word is discussed. Hertel (309 fn. 2) pedantically suggests the variant मुमुक्षु:(!) at which one can only wonder.

१५ Charpentier (238.10) would like to delete अहं in order to bring back the *pāda* to its actual length (eleven syllables). I think it is dramatically important that Garuḍa introduces himself to Rauhiṇa before asking him for support. Although Rauhiṇa is said to know it beforehand, Garuḍa cannot take it for granted.

१६ Charpentier (238.17) is in favour of an emended reading वैखानसर्षयो which eliminates the excess twelfth syllable. I feel this double *sandhi* is not necessary. The author often takes the liberty of extending the *pāda* by one or even two syllables.

१७ Hertel suggests the reading शाखा तिरश्ची which is not bad since a word denoting "branch" is needed here which appears only in the next verse. Charpentier's *emendatio* is रहस्यं तपन्ति (for परस्यां नमति) which is meant to refer to the ascetic practice of the sages Bālakhilyas (as well as Vaikhānasas).

१८ The text reads स चेद्, which is not bad, but I think न चेद् could even be better. "If you are not afraid of committing a sin (in case the eastern branch is broken, from which Bālakhilyas are suspended)." The western branch is not suitable for settling down since it is slantingly bent.

१९ अतूर्तं is a rare Vedic word used at a few places in the *Ṛgveda*. Its etymology is not certain but the contexts show that it means "boundless", "limitless" or "unsurpassed" cf. अतूर्तो राजा श्रव इच्छमानः (*ṚV* I.126.1), i.e. "the unsurpassed (*unübertroffen*: Geldner) king craving for fame"; अन्तरिक्षमतूर्तं . . . समुद्रम् (*ṚV* X.149.1) "The sky placed in boundless space", etc. Rauhiṇa means to say that by killing the brāhmaṇas Garuḍa will fall into the limitless darkness of sin. The commentary explains अतूर्तं as शनैः शनैः = "slowly", "gradually". "Because of this grave sin, you will slowly descend into dark nether worlds, (रजस्)."

२० A form not preferred in usage, although allowed by grammarians. The normal and the more regular form is विनंक्ष्यसि which would also set the *pāda* right which has presently one syllable in excess. But the main problem is not the form, but the verb itself which does not go well with तमो रजस्. Looking at the syntax these two words can only be direct objects (Accusative case) of the verb. Construed together ([त्वं] तमो रजो विनंक्ष्यसि), the words do not make sense. What is meant by the author is perhaps: "You will sink deep into the darkness [of sin]". पतिष्यसि instead of विनशिष्यसि would therefore have been more to the point. तमो रजस् in accusative (द्वितीया, कर्म) would also go well with पतिष्यसि according to the rule कालाध्वनोरत्यन्त-संयोगे (Pāṇ. II.3.5).

Additional Note

It appears that the first two verses of the next *sūkta* (VIII) सव्येन शाखां . . . and अहं . . . संहरस्व belong to this very *sūkta* as the final verses and that the *sūkta* VIII starts actually with "को नु", etc. (verse 3).

॥ अष्टमं सूक्तम् ॥

पञ्चदशो वर्गः (१५)

[*नेपथ्ये प्रस्तोता, जनसंकुलो वा*]

सव्येन शाखां धारयति दक्षिणेनेतरा उभौ[१]।
बलं पश्य सुपर्णस्य न वाचा परिमाय्यम्[२]॥१॥

[*गरुडो हिमवन्तं प्रति*]

अहं वै ते [३]हिमवन्त्संवत्सलः[४]
पृष्ठेऽधि मात्रा प्रहितोऽयमस्मि[५]।

[*हिमवान् गरुत्मन्तं प्रति*]

पदाऽनु शाखामधरं प्रवृङ्ग्धि[६]
बिलिन्थे[७] पक्षावपि संहरस्व॥२॥

(गरुडो भुक्त्वा, प्रतिनिवृत्य, आकाशे उड्डीयमानो मातरम् आकारयति, विनता सौत्सुक्यम्, आत्मगतम्)

[*विनता आत्मगतम्*]

को नु वाचमीरयत्यन्तरिक्षे महोदयाम्।
एकः स्वपिति मे सुतो द्वितीय उपजीव्यति[८]॥३॥

शब्देनासौ पृथिवीं दिवं च
संनादयन्नेति नभो दिशश्च।
मन्ये शौङ्गेयो गरुडोऽरुणो वा
प्रियः पुत्रो भवति मे क्षयेऽद्य[९]॥४॥

[*गरुडो अवतीर्य मातरं प्रति*]

नैनां (न तां?) बद्धः[१०] परिहरेच्छतचर्मा[११] अनुच्छिदः[१२]।
याममम्ब रौहिणस्याहं श्रान्तः शाखामधारयम्॥५॥

न हस्तिनं भक्षयित्वा बिलिन्थे
सहग्राहं, भुक्तवानस्मि शुङ्गे।
दिश भूयो भक्ष्यमन्यं महान्तं
यथा तृप्तः स्वः पथेयं क्षणेन॥६॥

षोडशो वर्गः (१६)

[*विनता गरुडं प्रति*]

जङ्गमः[१३] स्थावराण्यत्तीत्येषा[१४] वृत्तिः सनातना।
वयांस्युभयमश्नन्ति स्थावरं जङ्गमं च यत्॥७॥

निषादराष्ट्रं बहु नैकभेदं[१५]
तदद्धि त्वं मम कामाय शूर।
नाश्रावयन्ति[१६] न यजन्ति एते
अन्नं शिवं शुश्रुमैतद् गरुत्मन्॥८॥
ब्राह्मणं स्म तु मा हिंसीश्चरन्तं जनतामनु।
देवं क्षमापरं[१७] शूर स मृत्युर्न तवापरः[१८]॥९॥

[*गरुडो मातरं प्रति*]

एकशीर्षा ते[१९] द्विपादा द्विहस्ता
अवगृहीता मम चेत्[२०] सुपर्णि।
पृच्छामि त्वा विनतेऽहमेतत्
किं स्विद् रूपं भवति ब्राह्मणस्य॥१०॥

Notes on the Restored Text vis-à-vis the Original One

१ The text has come down with a hiatus between these two words. I have not disturbed it.

२ परिमाय्यम् "that which can be measured", other more common word with the same meaning is परिमेयम्, also परिमाप्यम्। परिमाय्यम् belongs to the older strata of the language as क्रय्य and जय्य, etc. cf. Pāṇ. VI.1.81-82.

३ The text reads here मघवन् which is totally out of context. Indra is nowhere in the scene. I follow the *Mahābhārata* and replace it with हिमवत्. Charpentier (240.20) prefers भगवन्त्.

४ The text has संवत्सर: a word which is commonly used in the sense of "year", also a calf; extended meaning a "son". There is no doubt as to the fact that the word intended to be used here is वत्सल (affectionate, beloved one) with dialectical change of ल into र "O Himavān, sitting on your back (top, summit, high plateau), this am I, your beloved son, who has been sent by his mother. . . ."

५ प्रहित: is an *emendatio* for निहित: of the text.

६ प्रवृङ्ग्धि = cast aside, throw away (the root is वृज्-वृञ्ज् (रुधादि, वर्जति-वृणक्ति, वृङ्क्ते).

७ बिलिन्थे, No one knows what it exactly means. Hertel has taken it to mean "deep valley" (*Abgrund*). Rau is in favour of translating it with "nest" or "perching place" (*Horst*). A few scholars like Georg V. Simson have surmised that it is a rare word of Indo-European origin meaning "flat surface", "brick platform" and connect it with the Greek "plinthos" (πλινθος) which survives in Latin as "plinthus" and in English as "plinth" (cf. *Greek Etym. Dictionary of H. Frisk*, Heidelberg 1970, 562f.). However it is difficult to agree with this interpretation since Garuḍa explicitly mentions in *sūkta* 7.4 that he being a bird does not like to consume its prey sitting on the ground (नास्मान् भूमौ भक्ष्यमाणं धिनोति), instead would like to perch on a tree.

८ The text has उपजायते (is coming into being) which is perplexing. Rau (p. 358) has given a good suggestion that it may mean "approaching", "coming back". I like to take the root जीव् with the prefix उप as meaning "to make living from", "to be alive on the basis of" (cf. *ṚV* I.164.42. तद् विश्वमुपजीवति). In the later semantic development, the root also acquires the meaning of "to eat", "to take food" (cf. the Hindi word जीमना). I suppose that the expression उपजीवति is used in this very sense here as well. "One of my two children (the charioteer of the sun-god) is asleep (because it is night), the other is busy taking his food; who is then this calling me from above in such a pleasing voice"?

९ Charpentier (245.17) has difficulty with मे क्षयेऽद्य and suggests alternative readings like मोक्षायाद्य or मोक्षे मेऽद्य since he wrongly understands the word क्षयः as meaning "doom", "destruction" (*Verderben*) whereas it is obviously used in the sense of "home", "house". "I think, one of my dear sons is now coming back home."

१० बद्ध्रः is to be understood as meaning "rope" (from the root बन्ध् = to bind), may be also "measuring tape". From references in the Brāhmaṇas we know that such tapes were made from the fine stripes of bovine hide joined together (therefore also referred to as औक्ष्णं चर्म cf. *ŚBr.* I.2.5 तां [पृथिवीम्] औक्ष्णैश्चर्मभिः पश्चात् प्राञ्चो विभजमाना अभीयुः।"). Garuḍa says that the length (or girth) of the broken branch could not be measured even with a hundred leather tapes joined together. The word बद्ध्रः (rather बद्ध्री) has survived in Hindi in the from of बद्धी which means "a binding device", a strap.

११ परिहरेत् (परि + हरेत्) = "to go around" therefore "to measure". The *Mahābhārata* has a similar verse in this context in which the परिहरेत् appears as परिणहेत् (परि + नह् = to wrap around), परिणाह (m.) is girth, circumference, volume of something round in shape (cf. स्तनयुगपरिणाहाच्छादिना वल्कलेन", *Abhijñānaśākuntalam* I.18). The verse of *Mahābhārata* under reference is as follows:

न तां वध्रः परिणहेत् शतचर्मा महानणुः।
शाखिनो महतीं शाखां यां प्रगृह्य ययौ खगः॥ — I.26.19

MSS, Grube and the *Mahābhārata* all render the word बद्ध्रः as वध्रः which connects it with the verb वध् which is not correct. वध् means to injure, to damage, to kill, वध्रः, वध्रिः is a castrated bull, known in Hindi as बधिया (बैल).

१२ अनुच्छिदः, I take it to mean "joined together", "joined in a series by making holes at the end", अनु = the following). The *Mahābhārata* discards this rare word in favour of a simpler expression महान् अणुः (exact sense of which is equally incomprehensible !). The reading अनुच्छदः (covering each other at the ends) could also be plausible.

१३ The MSS as well as the printed text of Grube has जङ्गमम् which is certainly wrong.

१४ Particle इति has been supplied by me and it is definitely required for the sake of completion of the sentence and for the metre, unless we concede a hiatus between त्ति and ए. It has been dropped in the MSS, obviously due to haplology.

१५ The text has एकभेदम् which has been explained by Rau as meaning "uniform", "without having group or caste division" (*von einerlei Art, d. h. ohne Kasten*). Not bad. But how to explain बहु preceding it? I therefore emend it into नैक which is the same as अनेक (although a little tautological in conjunction with बहु!), "many multiple groups, therefore not united", "having differences with each other, quarrelling with each other". भेद cannot go with एक. It should be रूप (एकरूपम्), if the intended meaning suggested by Rau is to be accepted.

१६ आश्रावयन्ति has been understood by Rau to mean "to invoke in sacrifice" on the authority of the *Kaṭha Saṁhitā* 25.1, 27.6, 31.13, etc. However, to be precise: आश्रावणं is that particular rite in the sacrificial ceremony in which the "Adhvaryu" asks the "Āgnīdhra" whether all the preliminaries for invocation of deities are fulfilled and whether the "Hotā" can now proceed to invoke the deities by reciting *mantras*, lit. whether he can now "make the *mantras* be heard" (Causative of the root *śru*)? Upon receiving the consent of "Āgnīdhra", the Adhvaryu asks the "Hotā" to recite the prescribed *mantras* for invocation of deities to the sacrificial altar.

A good conjectural reading for न यजन्ति (to avoid the repetition of the sense of the previous statement) could be न पठन्ति, i.e. "they neither learn the Vedas nor recite them".

१७ Oldenberg [(2) 92 fn.1] would like to have here the word क्षमाचरं which is hardly common in Sanskrit. There is no need to replace or emend the original.

१८ All MSS read तव परः. I am absolutely sure that the original text had तव-अपरः (not anyone else for you). A long sixth syllable is also the demand of the metre.

१९ ते is added by me. Without it not only the sentence looks incomplete, but also the *pāda*. ये could be equally good.

२० The text has ते which does not seem to serve any purpose. I find that instead we need चेत् (in case). "All of them have one head, two legs and two hands. In case I catch one, how to distinguish a brāhmaṇa from the others?"

Additional Note

२१ Note that the *sūkta* ends here quite abruptly which is very unusual. Garuḍa raises a question and the answer of Vinatā appears only in the next *sūkta* whereas it could have been easily accommodated in this very hymn which is rather short. This would also have done justice to the principle of "सन्निधि" of Indian hermeneutics.

॥ नवमं सूक्तम् ॥

सप्तदशो वर्गः (१७)

[विनता गरुडं प्रति]

[१]रजस्वलो जटिलः पङ्कदन्तो-
न्नीतशिखो[२] वदति सत्यमेव।
अमित्रमध्ये न बिभेति मृत्योः
स ब्राह्मणस्तं स्म मा हन् गरुत्मन्॥१॥

षळग्नयो[३] यं पुरुषं तपन्ति[४]
जैह्वो हार्द औदरो रैतसश्च।
तप्तश्च घर्मः शिशिरञ्च शीतं[५]
स ब्राह्मणस्तं स्म मा हन् गरुत्मन्॥२॥

मत्स्य इव[६] बिलिशं[७] जग्रसानो
गुरूदरो भवति ब्राह्मणेन।
अङ्गारेव[८] विदहन्नेति कण्ठं
स ब्राह्मणस्तं स्म मा हन् गरुत्मन्॥३॥

[गरुडो मातरं प्रति]

आहरिष्यामि ते सोमं ज्ञातो भक्षः सनातनः।
माऽन्ततो भक्षयिष्यामि उभयं स्थाष्णु[९] जङ्गमम्॥४॥

[प्रस्तोता]

अष्टादशो वर्गः (१८)

ततः सुपर्णः समयाद्[१०] बुभुक्षितो
मात्राऽऽज्ञप्तो[११] भक्षयन्[१२] वै निषादान्।
आकृष्य पक्षावनुगम्यमानान्
संप्राप्यमानांस्तु[१३] मुखे[१४] प्रयच्छते॥५॥

उत्प्लुत्योत्प्लुत्य भक्षाणो[१५] निषादान् वै विहङ्गमः।
गते कण्ठे तु चैकस्मिन् दहते[१६] स्माग्निराशिवत्॥६॥

निर्धूमे निष्फुलिङ्गे च[१७] आर्तः शुङ्गावचः स्मरन्।
"अहो वीर्यं द्विजातीनां ज्ञातिमात्रोपजीविनाम्[१८]"॥७॥

[*गरुडो ब्राह्मणं प्रति*]

निष्क्रमास्मद्[१९] (०आस्याद्?) द्विजश्रेष्ठ
न भक्षस्त्वं[२०] हि मे भवेः।
एते भक्षा मयात्रोप्ता[२१]
न त्वं शोचितुमर्हसि॥८॥

[*ब्राह्मणो गरुडं प्रति*]

न मन्ये जीवदात्मानं[२२] भार्यापुत्रैर्विवर्जितः।
द्विजस्तु सनिषादीकः ससुतस्त्वन्मुखे विषम्॥९॥

[*पुनः प्रस्तोता*]

सजनं तं द्विजं त्यक्त्वा
तीर्त्वा चाज्ञां विहङ्गमः।
इतरान् भक्षयित्वैव
सिद्धिं (स्वर्गं, तृप्तिं?) यातस्ततो ध्रुवम् (द्रुतम्?)[२३]॥१०॥

Notes on the Restored Text vis-à-vis the Original One

१ This verse appears in the MSS as the last verse of the previous hymn. I have brought it here as the first verse of this *sūkta* for good reasons. The identical refrain of the 4th *pāda* (स ब्राह्मणः . . .) of this verse makes it a part of the Kulaka (group) formed by verses 1-3. Making verse 1 as part of the last hymn interrupts the answer of Vinatā on the query of Garuḍa.

२ पङ्कदन्तोन्नीतशिखः is again a case of double *sandhi* (पङ्कदन्तः + उन्नीतशिखः) with the drop of *visarga* in the first stage and thereafter *a+u* giving rise to an ओ. The formation of the compound उन्नीतशिखः and its sense are both quite clear. I, therefore, fail to understand why Charpentier (243.11) wants to change it into उष्णीषी स, Negelein (100.21) into उष्णीषी च and Rau (with a question mark) into ऊर्ध्वशिखः (p. 359)? Perhaps they all have the appearance of traditional south Indian brāhmaṇas in mind. A hundred years ago every adult man wore turban in India, not only brāhmaṇas.

३ All MSS read a dental ल (षलग्नयः) here, being of north Indian origin; but the only correct Vedic form demands a cerebral one (ळ) or a ड if the *sandhi* rule is properly applied.

४ Rau draws our attention to a similar idea expressed in *AB* 8.24.6.

५ The text has शिशिरश्च शीतः, but as शीतं is neuter gender, I have emended it accordingly.

६ Quite often the rules of *sandhi* in our text adjust themselves to the demand of the metre. Whereas we have a regular *sandhi* (drop of *visarga*) in मत्स्य इव, in अङ्गारेव the process of *sandhi* has been carried out twice: अङ्गारः इव > अङ्गार + इव > अङ्गारेव. Both *pādas* have the prescribed number (11) of syllables.

७ The word बिलिशं denotes the "hook" of a fishing rod. A fish is doomed when it tries to swallow it, so is a Brāhmaṇa for Garuḍa. The word appears as बडिशं in the *Vālmīki Rāmāyaṇa* (झषवद् बडिशं गृह्य शीघ्रमेव विनष्यति. . . .) and also in the *Mahābhārata* II.24.6 (निगीर्णं बडिशं यथा). The ड of the *Rāmāyaṇa* and *Mahābhārata* seems to presuppose a cerebral ळ. It was probably a dialectical word taken from fishers' language and had more than one form (बडिश, बळिश, बिलिश, बिडिश, etc.).

८ अङ्गारेव is yet again an incidence of double *sandhi* which takes place after the drop of the *visarga* (अङ्गारः + इव = अङ्गार इव). Instead of the recommended *hiatus* between the two in this instance, the words are made to coalesce with each other.

९ Charpentier (244.15) finds स्थास्नु to be grammatically more correct.

१० The *padapāṭha* splits this word as सं-अयात् (went, went on) where the prefix सं (= together) does not seem to carry any meaning unless we take it just as a reinforcement of अयात् (सं = सम्यक्). This verb form is related to भक्षयन् in the sense of past continuous: भक्षयन् (सं) अयात् = went on devouring. For similar expression cf. "तत् त्वा यामि ब्रह्मणा वन्दमानः" (*RV* I.24.11) = "I go on praising you with my verses"; "यत्सत्यं विरतेऽपि गीतसमये गच्छामि शृण्वन्निव" (*Mṛcchakaṭikam* III.5) = "I still go on as though listening to it even after the song is over". Another (better?) possibility is to take समयाद् as an ablative sing. form of समयः = agreement, covenant (derived from Latin *co-venire* = to come together; समयः has the same formation सं + इ = to go together). समयाद् भक्षयन् = devouring as per agreed upon.

११ मात्राऽऽज्ञप्तः was first suggested by J. Hertel (p. 311 fn. 1) which I fully endorse. The text originally has मात्रा आज्ञातः according to *padapāṭha*. Rau (359) finds it in order and would like to leave it as an ablative of the word आज्ञा (आज्ञा + तसिल्) in the sense "on account of 'or' because of, the permission (or order) of the mother". However, it is not convincing, since in this case we would expect the word for the mother in genetive, i.e. मातुः .

१२ भक्षयन् is an *emendatio* of the original भक्ष यान् of the text which has caused headache to many scholars, except Charpentier (245.31ff.) who accepts it as it is. Negelein (101.30) has भक्षय वै निषादान् and Rau suggests (359) भक्षितवै निषादान् where भक्षितवै is the Vedic infinitive for भक्षयितुं which is to be syntactically taken with मात्राज्ञातः (acc. to Rau मातृ + आज्ञातः). The other good possibility is [अ]भक्षयत् (मात्राऽऽज्ञप्तोऽभक्षयद् वै . . .) = devoured.

१३ संप्राप्यमानान् appears in the text as संप्राप्यान् which also renders the *pāda* short by one syllable. Negelein (101.30) suggests संप्राप्य तान्. Rau is satisfied with adding just a स्म at the end (सं प्राप्यांस्तु मुखं प्रयच्छते स्म) which however brings the metre in doldrums. Further, the addition of स्म with the verb in present tense makes it a form of the past which is not required. I have emended this unsatisfactory reading into a parallel Present Participle Passive form in order to go along with अनुगम्यमानान्. My second choice would be संप्राप्तान् (add तान् before तु, if necessary, i.e. संप्राप्तांस्तांस्तु).

१४ मुखं of the text is grammatically incorrect. We do not need a direct object but a locative ('puts in mouth'). Further, one expects rather प्रयच्छति.

१५ The text has a problematic reading भक्षाणां which is syntactically not connected with any other word. Hertel's brilliant emendation (311 fn. 2) भक्षाण: is quite acceptable, contrary to, भक्षान् तान् of Negelein (102.6) and भक्षानान् निखादन् of Charpentier (246.11ff.). According to the latter निषादान् is a hyper-Sanskritization of निखादन्!

१६ The MSS read दह्यते स्म (विहङ्गम:). Though grammatically not problematic, I consider this passive form unnecessary in the absence of any Instrumental (तृतीया) in the sentence and especially in view of the fact that the root दह् is both transitive (अग्निस्तृणं दहति) and instransitive (वनं दहते, the forest is on fire). विहङ्गमोऽग्निराशिवद् दहते is therefore equally correct. A good example of the use of दह् (*ātmanepada*) in intransitive sense is the following verse from the *Rasamañjarī* of Bhānudatta (verse 12):

लोलालिपुञ्जे व्रजतो निकुञ्जे स्फारा बभूवु: श्रमवारिधारा:।
दहे, समीहे भवता विधातुं धीरं समीरं नलिनीदलेन॥

१७ For the original reading निर्धूमे विष्फुलिङ्गे च Charpentier suggests (246.26) निर्धूमविष्फुलिङ्गेन. I would rather prefer निर्धूमे नि:स्फुलिङ्गे च.

१८ The MSS read जाति which since many hundred years is used in the narrow sense of "caste". I think that ज्ञाति (= ज्ञानं, knowledge) suits better the context. The brāhmaṇas do not "make a livelihood" by simply having been born as such but, as the last verse of *varga* 16 and the first verse of 17 suggest, "because they indulge in severe penance and practice high moral values". In the present context stress is laid on their being knowledgeable.

१९ अस्मद् is ablative, "from us", but the text has अस्माद् which does not give any relevant meaning. Rau draws attention to a similar verse occurring in this story in the *Mahābhārata* I.25.2, which has the excellent reading आस्याद् (द्विजोत्तम विनिर्गच्छ तूर्णमास्यादपावृतात्). We ought to read hence निष्क्रमास्याद् "get out of my mouth".

२० The text always prefers भक्ष: even where भक्ष्य: could be more appropriate. The word भक्ष: means "food" and it appears often in the *Ṛgveda* in this sense.

२१ अत्र = here, before you. उप्ताः originally "sown"; here most probably "thrown out" and "planted on earth", "made to stand on ground". If ०त्रोप्ता is allowed to change into न्युप्ताः (*ni* + *vap* = "to bury") which occurs in the *Ṛgveda* in the sense of "to kill" (cf. अन्यं ते अस्मन् नि वपन्तु सेनाः, *ṚV* II.33.11), it would simply mean, "Whatever was [to become] my food (*bhakṣaḥ*), I have already swallowed down the gullet. *You* ought not to become my food."

२२ जीवदात्मानं is grammatically problematic: We expect जीवन्तमात्मानं which may not have been there since it makes व, the 5th syllable heavy (*guru*).

२३ The language of this *pāda* is not impressive; भक्षयित्वा च and तृप्तिं यातस्ततः पराम्, स्वः प्रयातस्ततः परम् (or स्वर्गंयातः . . .) is expected in view of the context. The emendation of Charpentier (247.27):

सजनं तद् द्विजं त्यक्त्वा . . . विहङ्गम। इतरान् भक्षमापन्नो (!)
सिद्धिर्भवति ते ध्रुवम्॥

is much worse than the original.

As far as ध्रुवम् (for sure) is concerned, I find its use at this place quite unusual and not much contributing to the intended sense. There is a strong likelihood of its being a corruption of द्रुतम्.

॥ दशमं सूक्तम् ॥

एकोनविंशो वर्गः (१९)

[खे उत्पतन्तं गरुत्मन्तं प्रति प्रस्तोतुः स्तुतिः, सर्वेषां वा समवेततया]

वयसां राजानमभिमातिषाहं[1]
दिव्यं सुपर्णं वचसा[2] बृहन्तम्।
शूरं [3]सुवर्णमभियत्प्रतीपम्[4]
तार्क्ष्यं शौङ्गेयं नमसोपतिष्ठे॥१॥

[विहायसा स्वः प्रत्युत्पतन्तं गरुत्मन्तं वीक्ष्य देवगुरुबृहस्पतिकृते प्रश्ने उत्तरयति गरुत्मान्]

अहं सुपर्णः पततां वरिष्ठो
मात्रा शिष्टः[5] सोमहारश्चरामि[6]।
भौजिष्यमृच्छत्यरुणस्य माता
तन्मा [7]शिवेनाभिवद[8] द्विजेन्द्र॥२॥

[बृहस्पतिः]

अभ्यायुषा वर्चसा त्वा वदामि
कच्चिद् वस्तात् कुशलं गृहेषु।
कच्चिद् गरुत्मन्नरुणस्य[9] माता
न शोचति स्पर्द्धनं मानसे[10] वा॥३॥

[गरुडः]

वेदाहमन्यत्[11] कुशलं गृहेषु,
दास्याद् दुःखं वेदयते सुपर्णी।
आमन्त्रये त्वा वदतां[12] वरिष्ठ
पताम्यहं त्रिदिवमिन्दुमच्छा[13]॥४॥

[बृहस्पतिर्गरुत्मन्तम् आशिषा योजयति]

यज्ञस्तु[१४] त्वा रक्षतु दक्षिणा[१५] च
वारं वरीय:[१६] पतत: पूर्वमस्तु[१७]।
ऋचो यजूंषि परित:[१८] सुपर्ण
सर्वाणि हौत्राण्यभित:[१९] (अभि त्वा?) श्रयन्ताम्॥५॥

(नेपथ्ये)

[सर्वे समवेतस्वरेण गरुत्मतो वर्चोबलवर्धनार्थं तम् ऋग्युगलेन स्तुवन्ति]

स्वस्त्यंनं ताक्ष्यर्मरिंष्टनेमिं
महद्भूतं वायसं देवतांनाम्।
असुरघ्नमिन्द्रंसखं समत्सुं
बृहद्यशो नावंमिवारुंहेम॥६॥
अंहोमुचंमाङ्गिरंसं गयंञ्च
स्वस्त्यांत्रेयं, मनंसा च ताक्ष्यंम्।
प्रयंतपाणि: शरणं प्र पंद्ये
स्वस्ति संबाधेष्वभंयं नो अस्तु॥७॥ *

विंशो वर्ग: (२०)

[इन्द्राबृहस्पती स्वर्लोके परस्परं संलपत:]

[इन्द्रो बृहस्पतिं प्रति]

अपि स्वित् किञ्चिदिह भूतमस्ति
भूतं[२०] भविष्यद्वाऽपि बृहस्पते।
यन्मे रक्षां निहितामतीत्य[२१]
वीर्येण सोमं सहसा हरेदित:॥८॥

[बृहस्पति: इन्द्रं प्रति]

षष्टिं सहस्राणि रजसश्चितीनां
नवनवतीर्नद्या: शतानि।
आहरिष्यति गरुडो वैनतेय:
प्रासहा सोमं निहितं जिहीर्षु:[२२]॥९॥

---

* ऋक्परिशिष्टान्तर्गतं चतुर्थाष्टकस्य तृतीयेऽध्याये सप्तमवर्गानन्तरं स्थितमृग्द्वयम्। खिलाध्याये सप्तमसूक्तान्तर्गतम्।

[इन्द्रस्य बृहस्पतिं प्रति प्रश्नः]

कुतः स्विज्जातः?
कस्माल्लोकात्?
कतरस्याः पृथिव्या?
भौवनं यो युयुत्सति धनुर्ग्राहमनुत्तमम्॥१०॥

[बृहस्पतिः]

सुपर्णी विनता नाम तपोऽतप्यत दुष्टरम्।
तस्यां जातो गरुडो वैनतेयो,
यश्च सोमं हर्ता शकुनिः, तस्य विद्धि॥११॥

Notes on the Restored Text vis-à-vis the Original One

१ अभिमातिषाहम्, षाह्/षाट्/षाढ् are the Vedic forms derived from the root सह् = to withstand, to conquer. अभिमाति is insidious, inimical, enemy.

२ The text originally has वयसा ("through the bird"?, "by virtue of age"?) which is a repetition of the opening word of this verse. It does not give any sense in conjunction with बृहन्तम्. वचसा is my conjecture which is not only nearest to the handed down reading but also has a strong case of being correct. It is a common aspect of the Vedic world-view that glorification of a god through hymns or words of praise increases his power (cf. *ṚV* 2.12.14 यस्येदं [इन्द्रस्य] ब्रह्म वर्धनम् . . .). The dwarf Viṣṇu assumes a gigantic form when gods surround him and sing his praise (cf. *ŚB* I.2.5.6-7). Even in the Kiṣkindhā-Kāṇḍa of the *Rāmacaritamānasa* of Tulasīdāsa, Hanumān recollects his real power and assumes a gigantic form before crossing the ocean to Laṅkā when other monkeys, especially Jāmavanta start singing his glory:

कवन सो काज कठिन जग माहीं, जो नहिं होत तात तुम्ह पाहीं।
राम काज लगि तव अवतारा, सुनतहिं भयउ पर्वताकारा॥ — *RCM* IV.29-30

By the way, the Hindi word बधाई [देना] which means to "congratulate" also comes from वर्धापनम् (बढ़ाना = "to increase [the self-confidence of someone and to let him feal great]".

३ The text had once more the word सुपर्णं here with which I feel uncomfortable. No poet would use the same word (or name) twice in the same verse in the same sense. Since Garuḍa is said to have wings and feathers of gold or golden colour I have replaced this second सुपर्णं with सुवर्णं, the nearest, possible alternative (which also simply means "of nice appearence", "of good colours").

४ अभियत्प्रतीपम् an *emendatio* from अभियत्प्रतीकम्। अभियत् is a person who is marching against someone, an adversary, enemy (cf. the word अभियान = campaign, attack). प्रतीप (etym. "against the current") is the one who is capable of repelling him. प्रतीक is more commonly used in the sense of "sign", "symbol".

५ मात्रा–आदिष्टः or मात्रादिष्टः (मातृ+आदिष्टः), मात्रा दिष्टः and मात्रा-आशिष्टः are all possible conjectures. मातृ (or मात्रा) आदिष्टः or दिष्टः ("as ordered", "as directed") may not be that good because it was not the mother who asked or suggested him to go. शिष्टः (or

आशिष्टः) would mean "as instructed", "well instructed", "under instructions from", etc.

६ Rau (359) suggests सोमहरः which is not as good as the सोमहारः of our text. सोमहारः is the one who "carries" *soma* (cf. स्थाणुरयं भारहारः किलाभूद् अधीत्य वेदं न जानाति योऽर्थम् — *Nirukta*), whereas सोमहरः is the one who "steals", "snatches", "takes away" *soma*. Even though it might have happened so later, Garuḍa would not have thought of himself as so, or at least avoid to admit it before Bṛhaspati from whom he seeks blessings. And if we argue that सोमहरः means the same as सोमहारः, why then disturbs the traditional text?

७ मा शिवेनाभिवद is an emended reading of मा अशिवेनाभिभवः = "do not weaken (let me down) with your inauspicious words (curse)", "do not rob me of my powers with your magical formulae". But, in fact, what Garuḍa actually wants, is to get blessed by Bṛhaspati, the lord of magical words (ब्रह्मणस्पतिः), for his risky enterprise. Check the next verse in which Bṛhaspati blesses (अभि + वद्) him for long life (आयुष्), physical strength and glory (वर्चस्), and the same expression अभि + वद् is used (त्वा आयुषा वर्चसा [च] अभि-वदामि).

It is, therefore, absolutely reasonable to assume that Garuḍa requests Bṛhaspati for अभिवाद[नं] and he responses with अभिवदामि. Further, since मा is unaccented in the text, it cannot be a prohibitive particle but only an *enklitkon* (*mā* = *mām*). In the later part of the story, Bṛhaspati emerges as a supporter and admirer of Garuḍa, not surprising in view of the fact that Garuḍa is the personification of the Vedic metres and Bṛhaspati is of the holy word and hymns (ब्रह्मणस्पतिः).

८ The MSS read गरुत्मत्यरुणस्य (*padapāṭha*: गरुत्मती + अरुणस्य) which may be overstretched to yield the sense "the mother who has Garuḍa and Aruṇa as her sons", but the expression which is expected and needed here is a vocative addressing Garuḍa.

९ The text has मानसं with which I cannot operate. Bṛhaspati seems to say "[I know that she has lost bet and has to serve a life-term of servitude to Kadrū] but I do hope that she is not too depressed and has not taken it so seriously to her heart (मानसे), because, after all, she has two competent and worthy sons like you and Aruṇa".

१० The text reads एतत् but the demand of the context is अन्यत्.

Bṛhaspati knows about the slavery of Vinatā (told by Garuḍa), he asks further whether otherwise all is well in the family and hopes that the mother of Aruṇa does not feel excessively distressed in her heart due to being a slave. Garuḍa replies that as far as he knows everything else is in order, only his mother feels aggrieved and unhappy about her servitude.

११ Garuḍa is in a hurry, he takes leave of Bṛhaspati (आमन्त्रये त्वाम्) whom he addresses as "the senior-most of all poets" (वदतां वरिष्ठ). The text has पततां वरिष्ठ which seems to be corrupt because it would become a vocative addressed to Garuḍa in 2nd person, whereas it is Garuḍa who is flying "towards" (अच्छ) Soma and wants Bṛhaspati to utter blessings for success in his endeavour which he also actually receives in the next verse.

१२ अच्छा < अच्छ. Lengthening *metri causa.*

१३ All MSS have the corrupt reading यज्ञस्य which does not go with रक्षतु. I do not accept यज्ञश्च of Hertel (312 fn. 1) because we already have a च with दक्षिणा and the very first word does not need it.

१४ It is tantalizing to change this original reading into दक्षिणेन. Soma is to protect Garuḍa from the front and the sacrifice from the right. To have divine protection in the front and on the right is believed to be auspicious and leading to success. (cf. सदा भवानी दाहिने सम्मुख रहें गणेश। तीन देव रक्षा करें ब्रह्मा विष्णु महेश", a Hindi benedictory verse). However, दक्षिणा (symbolically described as the "wife" of *yajña* in the Brāhmaṇas and Purāṇas) is so closely associated with sacrifice that I have not dared to change it.

१५ वारं वरीयः (वरीयं in the MSS) refers probably to Soma as in Hymn VI.4 which can here be understood as Moon. It is astrologically auspicious to have the planet Moon in one's front (calculated according to the clockwise movement of the signs of Zodiac) while going on a journey. Johansson (54.3) prefers वारो वरीयान्.

१६ There is a ते at the end of this *pāda* which Charpentier (249.14) has rightly deleted. As it is, the *pāda* still has twelve syllables. "तव पूर्वमस्तु" of Charpentier is not bad but it exludes पततः which is important.

१७ Grube has the reading पततः which, I think, is a mistake, either of the editor (Grube) or of some scribe, impelled by the first पतत: occurring in the second *pāda*. The *padapāṭha* very clearly reads परित: (all around).

१८ This is my *emendatio* for सर्वास्त्वाऽहोरात्रा which I do not find proper because अहोरात्रम् is neuter gender (cf. *Ṛ̣V* X.190.2). Further, it appears to be a *lectio simplicior* for our हौत्राणि (oblations/ invocations) which goes so well with Ṛcas and Yajūṁṣi, rather than "day and night". Charpentier and Rau find the text in order.

१९ The text has अभि चाश्रयन्ताम् (= अभ्याश्रयन्ताम् च). अभित: श्रयन्ताम् has first been suggested by Charpentier (249.14) which goes well with परित: . Rau, on the authority of Whitney (*Roots and Verb Forms*, Leipzig, 1885) suggests the formation of श्रयन्ताम् from a root शॄ meaning "to cover", "to protect" instead of श्रि = "to lean on for support").

२० This second *pāda* has only nine syllables, the expression for "past" is missing. Indra is bragging about the security of Soma and asks Bṛhaspati: "Is there a person, or ever will be . . . who could violently take away my Soma?" I feel that a word expressing "has there ever been" is missing which I have supplied with भूतं and which I believe was dropped at some stage due to haplology (twice भूतं). The suggestions of both Negelein (103.32) ०भूतमस्ति अस्ति भविष्यद् . . . and Rau . . . बृहस्पतेऽस्ति (p. 360) are senseless.

२१ For यन्मे रक्षां निहितामतीत्य Charpentier (250.27) suggests . . रक्षांसि निहिता अतीत्य or रक्षांसि निहितान्यतीत्य. Rau also does not want to lag behind and suggests (360) यन्मे रक्षान् निहितानतीत्य। Thus we have a choice of three words of three different genders: रक्ष: (m.). रक्षस् (n.) and रक्षा (f.). Honestly speaking, I see no reason to change the word रक्षा (= security arrangements).

२२ This eighth verse of our 10th hymn has come down to us in a very corrupt form. I have tried to reconstruct it on the basis of the further course of the story in this text as well as its detailed description in the *Mahābhārata* (Ādi-[āstīka]parvan). Some *emendationes* by me are: चितीनां for आचितानां, नद्या: for वेद्या: आहरिष्यति for आहरिष्यसि, प्रासहा for प्रसह्य in some MSS as well as in the *padapāṭha*, निहितं for निहितो and जिहीर्षु: for जिहीरिषु:। आहरिष्यति was suggested already by Oldenberg (2). 86, fn. 3; Rau is in favour of dropping आ (only हरिष्यति) not realizing that आहरिष्यति (will bring) refers to Garuḍa *bringing* sand and water from outside and not to carrying away Soma. निहितं जिहीर्षुः found favour with Johansson as well (54 fn. 5). निहितो जिहीर्षुः of Charpentier is useless (251.12).

॥ एकादशं सूक्तम् ॥

एकविंशो वर्गः (२१)

[इन्द्रो बृहस्पतिं प्रति]

अहं स्विदिन्द्र, उत वैनतेयः
कतरः शुश्राव, भुवनानि इच्छन्।
इन्दुं पराञ्चं निहितं विचक्षणो[1]
ममेत्तु सोमं सहसा हरेद् यः[2]॥१॥

[बृहस्पतिः]

तवेन्द्र जातमुत यज्जनिष्यत्
तवेन्द्र भूतमुत यद् भविष्यत्।
तव दिशः प्रदिश उद्दिशो बृहत्[3]
तवाशिषा प्रशिषा[4] सर्वमुच्यते[5]॥२॥

[आकाशे कोलाहलं श्रुत्वा विनता अरुणं प्रति]

महान् घोष उपरि श्रूयतेऽसौ
कथं पुत्र भ्रातरं नाभिधावसि?
एकः सुपर्णो बहवश्च देवा
न ह्येनमेकः प्रसहेत शक्रः[6]॥३॥

[अरुणो मातरं प्रति]

न हि मातररुणो याति नूनं
गच्छत्वयं[7] त्रिदिवं सोमहारः।

[विनता आत्मगतम्]

अभ्राता भ्रात्रा गरुडोऽरुणेन
अपुत्रा शुङ्गा विनता सुपर्णी॥४॥

द्वाविंशो वर्गः (२२)

[*विनता अरुणं प्रति*]

अपाद् भौवनो न हि शं [बट्?][८] करोति
अरिहा[९] त्वसौ, न नहुषि[१०] प्रमाद्यति[११]।
अन्धो जागृविर्न हि सः प्रमाद्यते
कथं सुपर्णो गरुडोऽतिमोक्ष्यते[१२]॥५॥

[*अरुणो मातरं प्रति*]

ओज इव सह इव बलमिव
नभ इवाभ्र[१३] इव[१४] भीरिव।
महद् बलमप्रधिष्यमेतद्
गरुत्मत उपमा नास्ति शुङ्गे॥६॥

[*पुनरप्यरुणो मातरमाश्वासयन्, विनताया आशिषो वा प्रथमार्द्धे,*[१५] *द्वितीयार्द्धेऽरुणस्योक्तिः*]

वातोऽस्य प्राणान् मरुतोऽस्य पक्षा[१६]-
वग्निः शिरो रक्षतु जातवेदाः।
अहं पुरस्तादहमस्मि पश्चाच्-
चन्द्रो ललामो[१७] [ललम्बे?] गरुडस्य पृष्ठे॥७॥
(cf *Mbh*. I.24.8)

[*स्वर्लोके इन्द्रो बृहस्पतिं प्रति*]

किन्नु घोषः श्रूयते यत्र सोमो
बृहस्पते हन्त वेदावगत्वा[१८]।
ज्या ह शिङ्क्तेऽपदाऽवसृष्टा[१९]
रोरूयते वधिरः[२०] सोमपालः॥८॥

[*बृहस्पतिरिन्द्रं प्रति*]

अहमेतं मघवन् वेद घोषं
सुपर्णस्यैष पततः शचीपते।
वैनतेयो हरति यत्र[२१] सोमं
निहत्य ते[२२] सोमपालान् गरुत्मान्॥९॥

Notes on the Restored Text vis-à-vis the Original One

१ The MSS read विचक्षणं (clever) which would refer to इन्दुं, or as an adverb to निहितं (विचक्षणं निहितं = cleverly or carefully deposited). However I feel that Indra wants to say something like: "who is this Vainateya about whom I am listening and who is so clever that he can carry away my Soma which I have deposited far away from the reach of the mortals"? I therefore have emended विचक्षणं into विचक्षण: to go with वैनतेय:.

२ हरेद् यत् is the original reading where यत् does not give any sense. य: goes smoothly with [सहसा] हरेत्.

३ According to Rau the word बृहत् is to be taken here in the sense of "heaven", "highest sky" (*höchster Himmel*) in which sense its use is attested in the *Ṛgveda* I.52.13 (त्वं बृहत: पतिर्भू:) and VII.18.20 (बृहत: शम्बरं भेत्). It is not clear why Johansson prefers to have बृहन् (55 fn. 2).

४ प्रशिषं = will, command; cf. उपासते प्रशिषं यस्य देवा: (*ṚV* X.121.2). Our commentator Jaya takes both these twin words in the sense of "blessing" but makes an interesting difference between the two. Blessings received from a respected person *upon ones own request* is आशी: and प्रशी: is the blessing which a respected person utters *of his own accord* without being asked or requested to do so: प्रार्थ्यमानात् प्राप्तं वरदानवाक्यमाशी:। अप्रार्थ्यमानाल्लब्धं वरदानवच: प्रशी:, इतीयान् भेद:। (comm. *ad* XI.2).

५ Taking the content of the first two verses of this *sūkta* in view, it appears that they too belong to the previous hymn and form part of the dialogue between Indra and Bṛhaspati. Such artificial grouping of the verses — ignoring the content and continuity — into hymns, each containing around ten verses is seen elsewhere also which seems to indicate that the text of the *Suparṇādhyāya* was originally in form of a continuous narration, split up later into hymns following the model of the Saṁhitās.

६ The *pāda* appears to mean: Since gods are in multiple number and the Suparṇa is alone, he is in danger. [If Indra alone were there, there wouldn't have been any problem], Indra alone cannot withstand him.

७ The MSS have गच्छ स्वयं which cannot be correct because it is a form of 2nd person(s) Imperative, whereas Garuḍa is not present before Aruṇa. Already Charpentier (254.18) corrected it rightly into गच्छतु अयं (let him go).

८ बद् occurring in the text defies all explanations. It also unnecessarily lengthens the *pāda*. Can we take it as an older or dialectical form of the indeclinable particle बत ("for sure", "obviously")? Not much is lost even if this word is removed.

९ The MSS have अतिहात्वा. The *padapāṭha* splits it into three words अति॰ हा। त्वा. The *bhāṣya* treats अति-हात्वा as one word and explains it as संग्रामांगणम् अतिक्रम्य, हात्वा = त्यक्त्वा च", (हात्वा = हित्वा) an archaic form of the root हा (जहाति).

अरिहा त्वसौ is a very good *emendatio* of Hertel (314 fn. 2) with which at least one can work. It is also acceptable to Charpentier (255.1). In हा of अरिहा or अतिहा one has to discover the root हन् (+ क्विप्) and should not operate with हा = to desert, to leave, to give up.

१० नहुषि is a relatively small *emendatio* for नहस:, a term which is very difficult to understand. It appears again in the next line. Charpentier changes it into नहुष: at both the places. I think that a better conjecture is नहुस् = [an approaching] stranger, neighbour. न नहुषि (= not in respect of a stranger). The *bhāṣya* takes it as a proper name (नहससंज्ञको देव:).

११ प्रमाद्यति is the normal form of the verb (cf. 6.2 above). The text has प्रमाद्यते (Ātmane).

१२ The text has अतिमोक्षते, but we need a passive form here ("how shall he get released" = how shall he get rid of all these adversaries).

१३ The text has ओज इव सह इव नभ इव बलमिव अभ्रमिव. . . . In order to avoid the blemish (*doṣa*) of पतत्प्रकर्ष, I have changed a little the order of words. For ओज इव, . . . etc. Negelein suggests (105.39) ओजस्वन्तं सहस्वन्तं नभस्वन्तं . . . which does not suit the grammatical construction.

१४ The text reads अभ्रम् इव but the word अभ्र is masculine as all synonyms of the word "cloud" are.

१५ There is a great deal of uncertainty as to who is the speaker of the following benedictory verse. It could be a continuation of the speech of Aruṇa, benediction of the elder brother to his younger one. The latter half is certainly uttered by him in which he promises that he (i.e. along with the sun-god) would support him from the front and the back. Hertel thinks that the speaker is Soma. Rau's opinion is more covincing who cites a parallel passage with almost similar words from the

Mahābhārata (Ādiparvan, Adh. 24.8-9) in which it is Vinatā who utters this benediction for her son. The wordings of the second half of our verse, however, appear differently in the *Mahābhārata,* and in verse 24.9 she assures Garuḍa that she shall always be praying for the well-being of him. In our version of the story Garuḍa has already left for Indra's heaven, whereas in the *Mahābhārata* he is still with his mother and receives her blessings in person which is more logical. The passage under reference in the *Mahābhārata* is as follows:

पक्षौ ते मारुतः पातु चन्द्रः पृष्ठं तु पुत्रक।
शिरस्तु पातु ते वह्निर्भास्करः सर्वमेव तु॥
अहं च ते सदा पुत्र शान्ति-स्वस्तिपरा यथा।
अरिष्टं व्रज पन्थानं वत्स कार्यार्थसिद्धये॥

१६ Rau's emendation of the personal pronoun of the first *pāda* into वातस्ते प्राणान् मरुतस्ते पक्षौ is unwarranted since Garuḍa is not present before them (Vinatā + Aruṇa).

१७ Instead of ललामो (beautiful) our text had just ललामः which hangs in the air and looks like a perfect form (not required in this context!) of some unkonwn or less known root. The nearest possibility could be (पृष्ठे) ललम्बे/ललम्ब (hung/hanging over the back). I have just added a *visarga* to ललाम and have made it an adjective to Candra (the beautiful moon).

१८ The archaic use of क्त्वा instead of ल्यप् although conjoined with a prefix as elsewhere in the text.

१९ The text has ज्या ह शिङ्क्ते (mistakenly printed as शिन्ते in Grube) यदाऽवसृष्टा which appears unproblematic on its face, but Rau (360) has brilliantly (and correctly) modified यदा into ऽपदा since the archer Bhauvana is lame (अपात्). This became perhaps his chief qualification for appointment as the protector of Soma since he cannot leave the spot (!). Rau was perhaps inspired by Charpentier (256.1ff.) who had suggested an additional यदा after यदा (यदा यदाऽव०) in order to make up for the two missing syllables of the *pāda*. Both Charpentier and Negelein suggest to read *jyā* as two syllabic *jiyā* for which, however, there is no grammatical or phonetic reason; also no justification.

२० Rau suggests अवधिरः, thinking that he is lame all-right, but he can hear very well. (Although both Charpentier and Rau reproduce this word as बधिर, I think it is better to read वधिर

since it is derived from the root वध्.)

२१ Rau suggests हरत्यस्य (?) for यत्र. तत्र could have been equally good. I retain the original.

२२ The text had तव. Rau's suggestion (p. 361) to replace it with ते reduces the *pāda* to its desired length, hence acceptable.

॥ द्वादशं सूक्तम् ॥

त्रयोविंशो वर्गः (२३)

[इन्द्रो बृहस्पतिं प्रति]

अपाद् भौवनः क्षिप्रधन्वा क्वासीद्[१]
यस्याग्निं बाणमुखं तिरस्यति[२]।
यस्य बाहुभ्यां वीयते सायकोऽवृथा[३]
त्रिंशत् स्तबकान्ययुतानि[४] षष्टिम्[५]॥१॥

[बृहस्पतिरिन्द्रं प्रति]

अपादं वै[६] भीषयमाणः सुपर्णः
क्षिप्रमध्वानं[७] चरति क्षेमेण[८] [शूरः][९]।
नैनं चरन्तं परि बाण आस[१०]
सोमं यदाऽर्च्छद्[११] दिवि उत्तमायाम्॥२॥

[इन्द्रो बृहस्पतिं प्रति]

क्वार्बुदो नहुषः काद्रवेयः
उलूको बल्बूलः श्वसनः क्वासीत्[१२]?
स्वपन्ननिमिषः[१३] प्रलिशः क्व आसीद्[१४]?
यन्म इन्दुं हरति वैनतेयः॥३॥

ककुब् भण्डश्च चक्रतुण्डः क्वासीद्?
अश्वमुखः कुण्डकर्णः क्व आसीत्?
विक्रोशनः खरकण्ठः क्व आसीद्?
यन्म इन्दुं हरति वैनतेयः॥४॥

[बृहस्पतिरिन्द्रं प्रति]

गतिं विज्ञाय शकुनस्य सर्पा-
स्तेजोबलेन गरुडस्य शक्र।

ते पन्नगा विहगेन्द्रस्य स्पर्शाद्
भीताः शिरांस्यप्यदधुस्तनूभिः॥५॥

चतुर्विंशो वर्गः (२४)

[पुनरपि इन्द्रः]

कशम्बूको वेणुकोऽश्वक्रन्दो-
ऽलगर्दः परुषः क्व आसीत्?
नभोरूप-सरूपौ क्व आस्तां?
यन्म इन्दुं हरति वैनतेयः॥६॥

उपतीरं वर्तमानः शशाक्षः
क्रोधेन मृत्यु[१५]रजनस्य कर्ता।
व्यादाय स्वापी विभिदः क्व आसीद्
यन्म इन्दुं हरति वैनतेयः॥७॥

[बृहस्पतिरिन्द्रं प्रति]

ता ग्रीवच्छिन्ना अपि च मूर्धभिन्नाः[१६]
कृत्ताः सचन्ते बहुलानि[१७] शक्र।
अपाद् भौवनो निहतस्तदासीन्[१८]
महद् वैशसमकरोत् सुपर्णः॥८॥

[इन्द्रो बृहस्पतिं प्रति]

ये विद्युतौ चरतः सर्वतो[१९] घ्नती
अन्नं रक्षन्ती अभया भया च।
[२०]चतुर्मुख्यावस्वपन्नीक्षमाणे[२१]
कथं स्विदेवाप्यतियाति[२२] गृध्रः[२३]?॥९॥

[बृहस्पतिरिन्द्रं प्रति]

ये विद्युतौ चरतः सर्वतो घ्नती
अन्नं रक्षन्ती अभया भया च।
ताभ्यां समख्यद्[२४] गरुडो वैनतेयो
विषूच्यावयातां[२५] स्वरभया भया च॥१०॥

Notes on the Restored Text vis-à-vis the Original One

१ Easier to recite the verse would be if we split this word into क्व आसीद्. Rau (p. 360) opines that the word भौवन: is to be pronounced as two-syllabic in Triṣṭubh metre (in the *vargas* 22.1, 23.1 and in 25.6) which will balance this excess of one syllable. (But how? भौव्न:, भौन:?)

२ The text has originally तिरश्चता which (if at all there is any such word and form!) is syntactically not related to the preceding words. In fact, we need a verb here. तिरस्यति is my conjecture ("the tip of whose arrow is more destructive than the fire, overcomes fire"). Negelein's curious explanation of तिरश्चता as a "corrupt form of the root त्रस्" (107.3) is not acceptable.

३ अवृथा is my conjecture for वृषा of the text. In older MSS थ is very likely to be misread as ष. वृषा has no meaning in this context. With अवृथा we get a sensible meaning: "Shot with whose arms every arrow hits [the target] without fail". Rau suggests अमृषा (truly) which I consider a second choice.

४ स्तबकानि is an emended form of स्तवन्यानि appearing in the MSS. I take it to mean "bunch" [of arrows: thirty at a time].

५ Negelein (103.34) wants to delete षष्टिं for incomprehensible reasons.

६ I find वै not of much use. However, I have not removed it, though it lengthens the *pāda* by one syllable.

७ The manuscripts uniformly read here क्षिप्रधन्वा. It has sneaked into this *pāda* from the first verse, as rightly pointed out by Negelein (107.6) and is of little use unless it has some other case ending (क्षिप्रधन्वानम्, etc., cf. Charpentier 247.10ff.). Rau (361) discovered the word अध्वन् in the compound and suggested क्षिप्रं स्म अध्वानम् which I find excellent, *sans* स्म, and have accepted it.

८ क्षिप्रेण is the handed down text which cannot be correct. क्षिप्र is an adjective, क्षिप्रं an adverb. क्षिप्रेण चरति would be very unusual. Rau (361) suggests क्षेपेण, not a bad reading, but I opt for क्षेमेण (without getting hurt).

९ Of not much avail is this शूर: of the second *pāda* which can easily be deleted without any loss to the sense and which unnecessarily lengthens the *pāda* by two syllables.

१० आस is the perfect form (लिट्) of the root अस्-अस्यति "to shoot", "to throw", to hurl the passive sense of "injuring", "hurling" which is to be taken in passive voice; आस = अविध्यत्. Rau's suggested reading आस्यत् is also good, but since we can very well operate with the available text, we need not change it. One can also take it as the Vedic perfect form of the root अस् ("to be", cf. तस्माद्धान्यन्नपरः किञ्चन आस — *ṚV* X.129.2). This verb form with the preposition परि (around) governing एनं चरन्तं [परि बाणः न आस] would then mean. No arrow sat itself (= reached, hit) on his body since he was flying round and round (परि + चरन्तं) while dashing against Soma (यदा आर्च्छद् सोमम्).

११ आर्च्छत् (kom ऋ > ऋच्छति + अ, Imperfect) was first suggested by Negelein (107.7) and I consider it an excellent reading to replace the original आर्चत् of the text. Rau later suggested (p. 361) आर्जत् which is not even half as good. Further the MSS and *padapāṭha* have यत् (आर्चत्) which I think must be construed as यदा-आर्च्छत् ("when he dashed against the Soma" or "when he snatched away the Soma").

१२ क्व आसीत् and क्वासीत् have been used side by side depending upon the requirement of syllables in the *pāda*.

१३ The text has सपन्निमिषः which the *padapāṭha* separates as सपत्-निमिषः, i.e. "Nimiṣa with feet". This and the following three verses enumerate the names of the serpents deputed to protect the Soma. Although a synonym for serpent is *guptapāda*, i.e. "the one whose feet are hidden" or "one who has no feet", in this case, we have to conceive of some animal looking similar to the Chinese dragon. However, I believe that it is a corrupted form of स्वपन् अनिमिषः and is used as an adjective to प्रलिश "who has the characteristic of sleeping with open eyes so that he is ever watchful on Soma". There is also a *vibhidaḥ* who sleeps with his jaws open.

The reading स्वपन्ननिमिषः of our text gives rise to a personal name (!) in the *Mahābhārata* I.28.18 which speaks of a snake called निमेष. The other four snakes mentioned in I.28.18-20 are उलूक, श्वसन (both appearing in our text too), प्रलिह (प्रलिश of SA) and प्ररुज. The warriors of the *Mahābhārata* are four in number: अश्वक्रन्द (also SA), रेणुक (वेणुक of SA), क्रथन and तपन.

१४ *Vide* fn. 12.

१५ The text has क्रोधेन मर्त्तः which does not yield any sensible meaning. Charpentier (259.33) changes मर्तः into मर्ता which is equally unappealing. Does he mean killer? But how can an intransitive verb like मृ be combined with an agentive suffix तृच्? It is possible only when the verb is turned into a causative (मार्-मारयिता). For "क्रोधेन मृत्युः" cf. the Vārttika on P.II.3.18 (प्रकृत्यादिभ्य उपसंख्यानम्). I think my *emendatio* suits the context and the meaning best.

All these four verses are blatant examples of the poetic blemish "अकाण्डे प्रथनम्" (unnecessary and useless expansion of a certain event).

१६ The metre would be set right either if we join छिन्ना + अपि (छिन्नापि) as suggested by Negelein (109.25) or delete च which is totally redundant in view of the existence of अपि. Charpentier (263.32) changes ताः into ते which I endorse in view of this new placement of the verse. It was originally the verse 13.6 and referred to the severed throats and smashed heads of Māyā and Lightnings, etc.

१७ For सचन्ते बहुलानि Charpentier (264.1) suggests शयते (he probably means शयन्ते which is misprinted, but even when we make this allowance, the form is terribly wrong. The correct form of third p. pl. Pres. Ind. is शेरते!). His suggestion to change बहुलानि into बहुधाऽपि or बहुधा हि also does not yield any good sense. Rau's interpretation of बहुलानि सचन्ते (without any alteration) is: ["cut apart कृत्ताः] they enter into thick darkness" (*geraten in dichte Finsternisse*). I think he is right and the darkness of death or hell is probably meant to which the warriors sink upon their death. In fact, "to enter into darkness" is an old expression for losing life, to embrace death. Apte's dictionary s.v. तमस् quotes the following hemistich from the *Rāmāyaṇa* which corroborates it: तया भिन्नतनुत्राणः प्राविशद् विपुलं तमः। This verse was originally placed in *sūkta* 13 at no. 6, where it referred to the severed heads of Māyā and Vidyuts!

१८ Rau (362) favours तत्र for तद् which is unnecessary. First of all because यत् and तत् can really be used as temporal adverbs in Vedic language ("when", "then") and second, we can also split the *sandhi* (against the *padapāṭha*) into तदा-आसीत् which would perfectly serve our purpose.

१९ Unnecessary and wrong "correction" of this word into सर्वदा by Charpentier (260.29).

२० This word appears as चक्षुर्मुखौ in the text. Both Charpentier (261.4) and Rau (361) perceive in चक्षुः the word क्षुर (क्षुरमुखौ

Ch, क्षुरमुख्यौ R.). Although we do hear of razors later in the text, they are unlikely to be connected with Lightnings.

२१ The text reads ईक्षमाणा: which has rightly been corrected into ईक्षमाणे by Charpentier and Rau.

२२ The MSS have अति पिपाति which does not give any sense. Since प and य look confusingly similar in the manuscripts, if not written very carefully, the first and the given choice for *emendatio* is अति यियाति (surpasses, bypasses, supersedes). However as the form is a grammatical impossibility unless we let it pass as some archaic or obscure Vedic form such as an *intensivum* (instead of यायाति/यायेति) or a present form of the third group (जुहोत्यादि). Charpentier suggests (261.4) अति पिपर्ति and Rau अतियाति (which make the *pāda* shorter by one syllable). अति-पिपर्ति certainly does not suit the context and अतियाति the metre. I am in favour of ०अप्यतियाति or *अतियियाय (an unusual perfect, analogous to इयाय, but one should actually decide in favour of अपि + अति + याति (अप्यति-याति) which not only yields the best sense but is corroborated later by the text itself in verse 13.8 (3rd verse of 26th *varga*). [Verse 13.5 is an editorial emendation.]

२३ Indra intentionally and purposefully uses the word गृध्र (vulture) for Garuḍa who is an Eagle. First he wants to express his contempt for him and further, since the word गृध्र is formed out of the root गृध् which means "to covet", "to be greedy", this secondary meaning of being greedy also gets suggested. It would, therefore, be better to understand the expression as "greedy vulture".

२४ Charpentier (261.11) changes समख्यद् into सम्-आखेद्, a form of the root खिद् imposing upon it the sense of "to snatch away" [from between the two Lightnings] and Negelein (108.24) would have समक्षत् for समख्यत्. Both suggestions are useless and grammatically unacceptable. समख्यत् is absolutely in order. "As soon as the two (*vidyuts*) discerned Garuḍa". A better possibility of interpreting ताभ्यां समख्यत् is "he made arrangement with them" (they being the manifestations his elder sister!). समाख्या = agreement, arrangement.

२५ The text delivered by the MSS reads विषूच्यौ ते अयाट् [स्वरभया भया च]. The grammatical form (singular) and the intended meaning of अयाट् are not clear. What is clear is that the text is corrupt. अयाताम् (विषूच्यौ अयाताम्) is my conjecture. Charpentier

(261.16f.) suggests विषूची तेऽस्तर् and Negelein (108.24) विषूच्यौ तेऽस्तार् [अभया भया च] operating with the root स्तॄ (to strew, scatter) and taking it in the sense of [intransitive] "they escaped aside, to the left and right". Both make the mistake of joining अ with the dual form ए of ते (f.) which is a *pragṛhya*, hence not subject to *sandhi*. I retain स्वर् which I think we need to clearly understand the statement although it extends the metre by two syllables.

॥ त्रयोदशं सूक्तम् ॥

पञ्चविंशो वर्गः (२५)

[इन्द्रो बृहस्पतिं प्रति]

या मे माया निमिषतो[१] जवीयसी
संकल्पज्योतिरनिवर्तमाना।
क्षुरपविर्ब्रह्मन्[२] क्व नु सा बभूव
यन्म इन्दुं हरति वैनतेयः॥१॥

[बृहस्पतिरिन्द्रं प्रति]

या ते माया निमिषतो[३] जवीयसी
संकल्पज्योतिरनिवर्तमाना।
तामात्मस्ताची गरुडो वैनतेयो
जवाद् जवीयान् न्यजहाद् बलेन॥२॥

[इन्द्रो बृहस्पतिं प्रति]

यन्मे चक्रं निमिषतो जवीयः
संकल्पज्योतिरनिवर्तमानम्।
क्षुरपवि[३] ब्रह्मन् क्व नु तद् बभूव
यन्म इन्दुं हरति वैनतेयः॥३॥

[बृहस्पतिरिन्द्रं प्रति]

यत्ते चक्रं निमिषतो जवीयः
संकल्पज्योतिरनिवर्तमानम्।
तदात्मसाची गरुडो वैनतेयो
जवाद् जवीयान् न्यजहाद् बलेन॥४॥

[इन्द्रो बृहस्पतिं प्रति]

पर्वताष्ठीराः[४] क्षुरपव्यः सुबुध्न्यो[५]

सोदा[6] ह्रदा ह्रादिनीः सूर्यवर्चसः[7]।
चन्द्र इव भान्तीर्बहुधा[8] विश्वरूपाः
कथं स्विदेवाप्यतियाति[9] गृध्रः॥५॥

षड्विंशो वर्गः (२६)

[*इन्द्रो बृहस्पतिं प्रति*]

आदित्या रुद्रा वसवोऽथ साध्याः
सोमं रक्षन्तो बहुधा निविष्टाः[10]।
मरुतो ब्रह्मन् क्व नु ते बभूवुर्
यन्म इन्दुं हरति वैनतेयः॥६॥

[*बृहस्पतिरिन्द्रं प्रति*]

प्राञ्च आयन् वसवः प्रेर्यमाणा[11]
उदञ्चो विश्वे मरुतोऽथ साध्याः।
दक्षिणा रुद्राः सह गन्धर्वसेनया
प्रतीच आदित्याननयद् वैनतेयः॥७॥

[*इन्द्रो बृहस्पतिं प्रति*]

वैश्वानरो जातवेदाः क्व आसीद्
यो म इन्दुं परिगृह्याधि तिष्ठति।
अर्चिर्ज्वलन्तमनिघृष्टतेजसं
कथं स्विदेवाप्यतियाति[12] गृध्रः॥८॥

[*बृहस्पतिरिन्द्रं प्रति*]

घृतस्य सिन्धूननयद् वैनतेयो
चञ्च्वा[13] बद्धानयुतानि[14] षष्टिम्।
तैस्तर्पयित्वा तव जातवेदसं
हिरणमयः[15] सोऽत्यपतच्छकुन्तः[16]॥९॥

[*बृहस्पतिः, प्रस्तोतृगणो वा*]

वैश्वानरं तर्पयित्वा घृतेन
सर्वानन्यान्त्सोमपालान् विजित्य।
महामेघ इव निम्नानि समानि[17] कुर्वन्
पराङ् गच्छद्[18] गरुडो वैनतेयः॥१०॥

Notes on the Restored Text vis-à-vis the Original One

१ The *padapāṭha* renders this word as अनिमिषत: but as the following verses clearly testify, it is निमिषत: (Ablative of comparison) which is to be read with जवीयसी or जवीय: (that which is faster than the blink of eye). अनिमिष:, is a term for gods since they are believed not to blink.

२-३ Charpentier would like to have this Vocative (*brahman*) deleted (262.12). I however think that क्षुरपवि: has slipped into this verse (no. 1) without any right, from the verse 3. The Māyā of Indra (of Ṛgvedic fame!) is not thunderbolt, for sure, and does not consist of razors or knives. The *cakra* mentioned in the verse 3, of course, could have them. The text pieces of the verses 1-4 seem to be jumbled up with one another. We do not have details of the function of the Māyā, nor do we know what was it supposed to do. The concept of Indra's पवि (bolt) having sharp razors has been influenced by its adjective "सहस्रभृष्टि" appearing in the *ṚV* I.85.9: त्वष्टा यद् वज्रं सुकृतं हिरण्ययं सहस्रभृष्टिं स्वपा अवर्तयत्.

४ The *padapāṭha* separates it as पर्वत + अष्ठीरा:. Rau cites *KS* 37.17, *JB* 3.360 and *ŚB* X.3.4.3, 5 where the word अष्ठीर/अष्ठील occurs in the sense of boulders, rocks (Rau renders it with the German word *Steinkugel,* i.e. stone balls or stone bullets. I would rather prefer the German word *Geröll*). A grammatically plausible explanation for the formation of the word would be difficult to furnish, but the root स्था > स्थिर is definitely in play. अष्ठील (अस्थिर) is perhaps that part of a mountain, i.e. those rocks which tumble/roll down during a landslide.

५ Rau's *emendatio* सुब्रध्न्यो. However सुबुध्न्य: in the sense of "deep valleys" is in order.

६-७ Charpentier has emended the original मोदा into सोदा (उदन्= water) and सूर्यवर्चस: into सुवर्चस:. सोदा: goes well with ह्रदा: (pools full of water), although tautological; but ह्रादिनी: सूर्यवर्चस: (streaks of lightning brilliant like sun) is perfectly in order.

८ Rau suggests बहुला for बहुधा. But how does it make the sense better?

९ Original text has अति पिपाति as before. Rau suggests again अति याति (p. 361) which is short by one syllable. I am confident that the original was अप्यतियाति (cf. 13.9). Hence have emended it accordingly.

१० बहुधा निविष्टा: = appointed/deputed posted at several [vantage] points, or in several ways (i.e. each one with a specific duty).

११ प्रेर्यमाणा: "impelled", "driven back" is my conjecture for the textual reading प्रेक्षमाणा: "witnessing", "in the process of watching", "while seeing". I think that we need some action on the side of Suparṇa to make them flee helter-skelter in all directions. प्रेक्षमाणा: is a pres. part. active (Ātmane) whereas we need a passive form.

१२ Rau (362) is in favour of dropping अपि and would like to have only अति याति. I think, अपि does not disturb at all, has full justification to be here (even then) and completes the metre.

१३ चञ्च्वा is a totally arbitrary *emendatio* of mine based on the course of the events as described in the *Mahābhārata*. The text has बद्धं in place of this word (बद्धं बद्धानि . . .) the meaning of which I fail to comprehend. बद्धं is syntactically not connected with any other word in the sentence in which it occurs. As for the बद्धानि, the only good possibility is बद्धान् (adj. to सिन्धून्) for which I have opted. The *Mahābhārata* narrates that Garuḍa brings water of rivers in his mouth (beak) to extinguish the fire. Here he brings clarified butter to "satisfy" fire (who is reported to be especially fond of Ghee; cf. the episode of the burning of Khāṇḍava forest in the *Mahābhārata* (Ādiparvan) for curing Agni oversatiated with Ghee).

१४ As noted, the MSS read बद्धानि which is to be construed with अयुतानि, but does not yield any sense. Hence this correction. This word also seems to have influenced/changed the previous [unknown] word into बद्धम्.

१५ According to a common belief gold is indestructible in fire. This belief finds its reflection not only in the ancient Indian philosophy of nature but also in Nyāya-Vaiśeṣika system of thought. Since Suparṇa is हिरण्मय he remains unscathed in fire. सुवर्णं तैजसम्। असति प्रतिबन्धके अत्यन्तानलसंयोगेऽपि अनुच्छिद्यमानजन्यद्रव्यत्वात् (*मुक्तावली*, तेजोनिरूपणखण्ड:)। "अग्नेरपत्यमेतद् वै सुवर्णमिति धारणा" (Mbh. XIII.85.147).

१६ The *padapāṭha* reads here हिरण्यमय: स्रोति [अपतत्] where स्रोति is a very hard nut to crack. Johansson (59) suggests ज्योतिर् [अपतत्] for स्रोति, but हिरण्मय: (m.) does not go with ज्योतिस् = (n). Charpentier (265.26) has हिरण्मयं (n.) with स: [अपतत्] which has the same problem. Our *emendatio* is the easiest way out, or should we operate with some unattested word like स्रुति (Loc. sing. of स्रुत्, formed from the root स्रु = to flow).

१७ Charpentier (266.3) corrupts the text by changing the correctly handed down reading into: महामेघेव निम्ना समीकुर्वन्. It could also refer to the manner of the flight of Garuḍa, his flapping of wings: up and down and flat or straight placed horizontally while gliding.

१८ गच्छत् is Vedic for अगच्छत्। पराङ्गच्छत् (पराञ्च् गच्छत् = पलायित:) in the sense "flew away" (and disappeared), "went to a yonder destination". "परागच्छद्" is a simplified reading in certain MSS by dropping the dot of *anusvāra* (transformed from ञ्च्) on the letter रा.

॥ चतुर्दशं सूक्तम् ॥

सप्तविंशो वर्गः (२७)

[*बृहस्पतिरिन्द्रं प्रति*]

एको बहून् भीमबलोऽध्यतिष्ठत्
तवैव शक्तः (शक्र)[१] सदृशो[२] बलेन।

[*इन्द्रो बृहस्पतिं प्रति*]

यन्मे रक्षान् धर्षितवाञ्छकुन्तस्
तेनास्य क्रुद्धः प्रहरामि वज्रम्॥१॥

[*वज्रप्रहरणानन्तरं पुनरपीन्द्रः*]

तपोमयं क्षुरपवि सुवीर्यं[३]
येन वृत्रस्य हृदयं निकृत्तम्।[४]
तन्मे वज्रं[५] प्रतिहतं शकुन्ते
बृहस्पते किन्नु भूतं सुपर्णः?॥२॥

[*बृहस्पतिरिन्द्रं प्रति*]

एष छन्दांसि सहितानि शक्र
यजुर्मयः सामतनुः सुपर्णः।
इन्दुं पीत्वा वीर्यवांस्तार्क्ष्यपुत्रस्[६]
तेन वज्रः प्रतिहतस्तवात्र॥३॥

[*इन्द्रो गरुत्मन्तं प्रति*]

इदं देवानामरिघाति वज्र-
मनावृत्तपूर्वमनिहत्य[७] शत्रुम्।
यदावृत्तं[८] तत् सुराणां न साधु
वज्रस्य मानः क्रियतां गरुत्मन्॥४॥

[*गरुत्मान् इन्द्रं प्रति*]

और्वं तनूजं विसृजाम्यनिन्द्यं[९]
तच्छिन्धि वज्रेण भव त्वमीड्यः।
हितं देवानां प्रियमेव तुभ्यं
साम्नाऽस्मि कर्ता न बलेन शक्र॥५॥

ऋषेर्मानं करिष्यामि वज्रं यस्यास्थिसंभवम्।
वज्रस्य च करिष्यामि तव चैव शतक्रतो[१०]॥६॥

अष्टाविंशो वर्गः (२८)

[*प्रस्तोता*]

छिन्नं त्रिधा तत् कुलिशेन पत्रं
तस्याग्रखण्डादभवन् मयूरः[११]।
मध्याद्[१२] द्विवक्त्रा भुजगेन्द्रराजी[१३]
मूलाच्च शत्रुर्नकुलः फणीनाम्॥७॥

[*इन्द्रो गरुत्मन्तं प्रति*]

पृच्छामि त्वा शकुने किंबलोऽसि
कस्ते भारः[१४] समु सह्यो द्विजेन्द्र।
आचक्ष्व मे वीर्यमसह्यसाहं
सख्यं च नो [१५]भवतु शाश्वतीभ्यः[१६](समाभ्यः)॥८

[*गरुत्मानिन्द्रं प्रति*]

अष्टौ भूमीर्नव दिशस्त्रीन्त्समुद्राञ्छचीपते।
परस्सहस्त्रं पर्वतान् वहेयं कामयेयं चेत्॥९॥

[इन्द्रो गरुत्मन्तं प्रति]

इन्दुं चेत् सर्पाः पास्यन्ति त्वया दत्तं विहङ्गम।
अजनं ते करिष्यन्ति[१७] तन्न साधु भविष्यति॥१०॥

[*गरुत्मानिन्द्रं प्रति*]

नाहमिन्दुं परास्यामि[१८] सर्पेभ्यः शत्रुबाधन।
हत्वा तु दर्शयिष्यामि शक्र मा सौम्य मे कुपः॥११॥

Notes on the Restored Text vis-à-vis the Original One

१ "तवैव शक्र" (Vocative) is a good suggestion of Hertel (p. 317 fn. 1); for शक्र Charpentier has शक्ते: (266.18) which is less convincing.

२ The *padapāṭha* reads सदश: (for सदृश:) which can yield a far-fetched meaning of "having the same state/condition" (समाना दश ययो:), but it is absolutely certain that the MSS deliver us a corrupt reading and the correct word is सदृश: which Hertel and Charpentier both have long since established.

३ The text has स्ववीर्यं, i.e. "that which operates with its own power/energy" for which Hertel suggests सुवीर्यं which is better and plausible since in many varieties of ancient north Indian scripts, the sign for *u* below can be misread for a *va*.

४ This past participle appears in most of the MSS and in Grube's edition as निकृन्तम्. The *padapāṭha* MS also seems to have it originally so which has been emended later *secunda manū* into निकृत्तम्, obviously after consulting the *bhāṣya* which has it correct.

५ Mark that whereas in verse 2 वज्रं is used in neuter gender, in the following verse, it is masculine. Usual usage is in neuter gender, but I have not changed the gender in verse 3 in order to give the reader an example of such promiscuity.

६ The MSS read, of course, तार्क्ष्य here as well. Of special interest in this *pāda* is the statement of the poet that Garuḍa already has a sip of *soma* before carrying the jar containing it. This fact is corroborated by *ṚV* IV.26.6 "ऋजीपी श्येनो ददमानो अंशुम् . . . सोमं भरद् दादृहाणो . . ." in which the weak bird (*śyena*) is depicted as deriving strength from the droplets of the juice oozing from the twig of Soma held in its beak.

७ The original reading is आवृत्रपूर्वम् where आ (prefix) and पूर्वं in the compound could have the same meaning and the same function although with different grammatical constructions. What we need here is an attribute (adjective) to वज्रम् and आवृत्रपूर्वम् is an adverb which needs a verb. There is no doubt as to the fact that वृत्र is a corrupted form of वृत्त which is also attested by its repetition in the next *pāda*. The meaning of the *pāda* is quite clear: "the thunderbolt has never come back without killing the enemy". Indra is facing this humiliation for the first time. If we read आवृत्रपूर्वम् with अनिहत्य शत्रुम् आवृत्तम् it means just the opposite. Four scholars working on the text have suggested four different emendations: आवृत्रतूर्यम् (Johansson 60 fn. 1), अवृत्तपूर्वम् (Oldenberg [2], 86 fn. 1) आवृत्यपूर्वम् (Charpentier 267.23ff) and finally नावृत्तपूर्वम् (Rau 362) which is the best, however to be taken as two words: (न + आवृत्तपूर्वम्). I prefer *one single compound* with negative meaning as an adjective qualifying वज्रं, have therefore suggested अनावृत्तपूर्वम्, although it lengthens the *pāda* by one syllable.

८ The MSS and *padapāṭha* have तदावृत्तम् (तत् + आवृत्तम्) which is not proper since we have one more तत् immediately following.

९ The text reads an unaccented अनिंद्य (not अनिन्द्यम्) which makes it a Vocative referring to Indra. However, it is to be taken with तनूजं (bodily hair) which is "irreproachable", "without blemish". और्वं is belonging to ऊरु, thigh.

१० This verse has been taken from the *Mahābhārata* (I.29.17) and also occurs *verbatim* in a Sāmavedic prose work on the story of Suparṇa titled अमृताहरणम् edited by me (Nag Publishers, Delhi, 2005) in paragraph 21, on page 16. The verse is obviously interpolated. If at all, it should come before the preceding verse.

११ The text has अभवन्मयूरः, the *padapāṭha* clearly restores it to अभवत् + मयूरः. However misled by न् Charpentier (268.15) turns मयूरः into मयूराः (!) whereas as a Collective Noun the single refers to the whole species.

१२ *Emendatio* of मध्ये which fails to yield the desired meaning.

१३ Hertel, unable to do much with the word राजी converts it into राज्ञी (318 fn. 1). The "double-headed" snake is called डुडुभः in Prākṛt (attested in the *Mṛcchakaṭikam* III.20) and दुमुही (द्विमुखी) in Hindi (feminine). दुमुही belongs to the class of reptilia but is not a snake. It is non-poisonous and has a thick gland at its tail evoking the impression that it has two heads. Snakes and दुमुही can often be seen entangled in fight with each other. The word राजी also occurs in Sanskrit and refers to a particular species of snakes, whether it is the same as द्विवक्त्रा-दुमुही, I am not competent to tell.

१४ The text and the *padapāṭha* provide us the reading भगः which is unsuitable to the context. It has rightly been corrected into भारः by Rau (p. 362) which suits very well to समु सह्यः.

१५ The text has भवति which can be modified a little to make it a form of Vedic Subjunctive: (लेट्) भवाति (in the sense of भवेत्), which would be most suitable to the context; but it does not fit into the metre, hence my preference for भवतु.

१६ शाश्वतीभ्यः is an adjective and needs a noun which I have supplied. समा (originally meaning "summer") is a feminine word for "year" and very frequently accompanies शाश्वती ("मा निषाद प्रतिष्ठां त्वमगमः शाश्वतीः समाः" — *Rām*. I.2.15), however in accusative case to denote a timespan (vide P. II.3.5: कालाध्वनोरत्यन्तसंयोगे") and not in Dative as here.

१७ A glaring example of the hopelessly corrupted state of the text is again provided by the reading करिष्यामि which appears at this place in the text. It is not Indra who is going to create अजनं by destroying the human population, but the venomous serpents who become immortal by imbibing a draught of Soma. करिष्यामि was already corrected into करिष्यन्ति by Johansson (60 fn. 5).

१८ Rau (p. 362) suggests a *lectio simplicior* प्रदास्यामि for परास्यामि. I stick to the original *lectio difficilior* which gives a much better sense: "Don't think that I am going to *throw away* the Soma to/at them."

॥ पञ्चदशं सूक्तम् ॥

एकोनत्रिंशो वर्गः (२९)

[गरुत्मान् सर्पान् प्रति]

अयं व आहृतः सोमस्तं पश्यन्त्विह पार्थिवाः!
अहं च मुक्तोऽस्म्यरुणश्च मुक्तो
मुक्ता च माता विनता सुपर्णी॥१॥

(सर्पाः उपसर्पन्ति)

अयं सोमः काद्रवेया मया स्वस्
तृतीयात् पृष्ठाद् रजसो विमानात्।
आनीत इन्दुस्तदु वो ब्रवीमि
संपश्यतैनं,[1] प्रजहाति[2] राजा॥२॥

अहं हरामि वः सोमं, सर्वेषामनुधावताम्।
यो वीरः सोऽनुसचतां,[3] वीरयध्वमुरोगमाः॥३॥

(गरुडः सोममादाय पलायते)

[स्वर्लोकमागतो गरुत्मानिन्द्रं प्रति]

अयं त आहृतः सोमो यत्तेऽहमहरं पुरा[4]।
अहं च मुक्तोऽस्म्यरुणश्च मुक्तो,
मुक्ता च माता विनता निरोधात्॥४॥

[इन्द्रस्यात्मस्तुतिः]

अहं पिप्रुं नमुचिं शम्बरं च
हत्वा पुरा[5] विप्रचित्तिं विजित्य।
द्यावापृथिवी परिदधे वाससी इव[6] वृत्रहा॥५॥

[इन्द्रो गरुत्मन्तं प्रति]

अहं बलेनात्यतरं सपत्नान्-
त्सर्वं भवामीदमहं बलेन।
एवं बलस्यातिबलस्य मे सुतं[७]
कथं स्विदिन्दुं सहसा जहर्थ?॥६॥

त्रिंशो वर्गः (३०)

[गरुत्मानिन्द्रं प्रति]

माता[८] मम विनता सुपर्णी
दास्याद् दुःखमगमत् स्पर्द्धयेन्द्र।
तस्यै निष्क्रयस्तव सोम आसीत्
तमाहरं[९] ते, न विघृष्टमन्यैः[१०]॥७॥

[गरुत्मत्कृता इन्द्रस्तुतिः]

तव सुपर्णो मघवन्स्तवेन्दुर्
भूतोऽसि भव्यश्च भवंश्च शक्र।
त्वं गोप्ताऽसि शरणं त्वं समुद्रः
तवेदं सर्वं भुवनं[११] सुशाधि॥८॥

[बृहस्पतिरिन्द्रं प्रति]

शूरं सुपर्णमरुणात् कनिष्ठम्
अन्नं प्रतीष्याभिवदेममिन्द्र[१२]।

[इन्द्रो गरुत्मन्तं प्रति]

वरं ददामि ते सौम्य[१३] यं कं च मनसेप्ससि॥९॥

[गद्यम्]

मत्सख्याद् अन्नम्, अमृतत्वं वाचि, त्वमेतदुभयं वृणीष्व।
तार्क्षपुत्र, त्वं ब्रूहि, मनसेप्सितं वरं वृणीष्व, वैनतेय![१४]॥१०॥

[गरुत्मान् वरं वृणुते]

नागान् वृणे भक्षमहं शचीपते
वहेयं यज्ञं प्रविशेयं वेदान्।

अधीयीरन् मा ब्राह्मणाः स्वर्गकामास्-
ते चाप्नुयुस्त्रिदिवे संसदं नौ॥११॥

[*इन्द्रो गरुत्मन्तं प्रति*]

नागास्ते भक्षः सन्तु विहगेन्द्र[१५]
वह यज्ञं प्रविश शूर वेदान्।
अध्येष्यन्ते त्वा ब्राह्मणाः स्वर्गार्थाः[१६]
प्राप्स्यन्ति च त्रिदिवे संसदं नौ॥१२॥

[*प्रस्तोता*]

उदाश्रयन्त[१७] सर्पा हर्षमाणाः
सुपर्णं दृष्ट्वा त्रिदिवः[१८] पतन्तम्।
तान् भक्षयित्वा बलवाञ्छकुन्तो-
वर्धितो[१९](ऽभ्यर्हितो?) बलमस्याभ्यवर्धत[२०]॥१३॥

[*अवसानमङ्गलम्*]

एकत्रिंशो वर्गः (३१)

सुषूपर्वण्यवसानं[२१] महाद्रौ
कृत्वा नीडं शाल्मलौ तं महान्तम्।
गरुत्मन्तं गरुडं वैनतेयं
पतत्रिराजमवसे जोहवीमि॥१४॥
स मे स्तुतश्छन्दसा त्रैष्टुभेन
होत्रेव सोमः[२२] प्रजिहाति[२३] वाचम्।
शुभं सुषीमं[२४] च सुखं च धेहि
वैनतेय[२५] जहि एनः, सपत्नान्॥१५॥
यदपि स्तोकं[२६] यद्वाप्यहाशिषं[२७]
सुपर्णं वै मनसा श्रद्दधानः।
स एव नो मृळतां, दीर्घमायुर्
ददातु नश्चक्षुर्बलम् चिराय॥१६॥

Notes on the Restored Text vis-à-vis the Original One

१ The text has संपश्यथ (Pr. Ind. II p. pl.) "you are (or, are you?) watching it". I think, we need an imperative here: "Behold it, [the king, i.e. Soma, is now leaving]", have therefore swapped the थ for त.

२ For प्रजिहाति occurring in the text many alternatives have been suggested: प्रतिभाति or प्रजिहीते (Charpentier 271.1ff.) प्र-जिघर्ति (wrongly printed as प्र-जिघ्रति, Negelein 113.25) and प्र-जिगाति (Rau 362) which he translates as "coming nearer", "approaching", "stepping forward" [*er tritt heran*], but what Garuḍa actually wants to say is that "it (Soma) is going away, leaving you in the next moment, so have a look at it". प्रजिहाति seems to be a hybrid form produced by a mixture of जहाति and जिहीते.

३ This is my *emendatio* for अनु सदतु which does not convey the intended meaning. Garuḍa while flying away with Soma challenges serpents to chase and catch him (which of course they cannot, being पार्थिवाः). The root सद् means "to sit" and not to "run behind" (अनु). सच्-सचते is a Vedic root meaning "to run after", "to follow", "to pursue" (cognate with Latin *sequi*). Rau suggests the reading अनु सश्चत् the meaning of which I fail to understand.

After सचतां there are two more words which, I think, have crept in from elsewhere or are insertion by some later scribe. They are सर्वे वा. These words disturb the character of अनुष्टुप् and are redundant, hence I have deleted them. We may as well include them and consider the line as a prose.

४ In the same way, after पुरा, there are again two words इन्दुमिन्द्र which are not required at all and disturb the metre by unnecessarily lengthening it, hence deleted, as already suggested by Rau (p. 362).

५ The text has an additional इमं following upon पुरा which appears with *sandhi* as पुरेमं [विप्रचित्तिं . . .]. It has been deleted because of its irrelevance.

६ The text combines वाससी with इव (वाससीव) which is not admissible as long ई of dual is प्रगृह्य and cannot undergo a *sandhi*; further it makes the metre short by one syllable.

७ The text has सुतः which is obviously wrong. We do not require a word for "son" but an adjective for इन्दुं in accusative "मे सुतं"

= "extracted" for me. Scholars took a long time to rectify this textual corruption till Rau (p. 363) set it right in 1967 (*ZDMG* 117). Johansson (61 fn. 1) had suggested स्वत: and Charpentier (272.8) सत: (मे सत:, "although I was there", "in my presence"). Negelein unnecessarily suggests deletion of मे disturbing the sense of the sentence and the cadence of the line. We need मे; मे सुत:/सुतम् = pressed out/extracted for me (इन्दुं).

८ Rau (362) suggests inclusion of या in the very beginning of this *pāda* (या माता), perhaps mainly to get eleven syllables. I do not find it necessary.

९ The reading तम् आहरम् is in order. I however, personally feel that the कथं (why) of Indra needs an answer with some parellel word denoting "therefore", "that is why", i.e. तेन or some similar expression. That which restrains us from changing तम् into तेन is the fact that तम् goes better with [न] विघृष्टम्.

१० न विघृष्टमन्यै: "that which has previously not been violated", i.e. robbed or snatched away by others (अन्यै:). But we may as well take "न अन्यै:" as meaning न अन्यै: [कारणै:] = "not for any other reasons" (except to redeem my mother).

११ The MSS read भुवनं संसुशाधि. I feel that सं is irrelevant, सुशाधि conveys the intended meaning ("rule well" [the whole world]) sufficiently well. सं seems to have crept in inadvertantly at some stage. In case we insist upon retaining सं, we have to throw out सु in order to connect this prefix with the verb. Rau wants (p. 363) to change सं into शं and delete सु. शं शाधि then according to him would mean "rule for the welfare of the world". I find the meaning far-fetched. शं कुरु, शं चर, शं भवेत्, etc. are all right but शं शाधि (with शं as an adverb) is an unlikely construction.

१२ "प्रतीष्य" appearing in this *pāda* is my *emendatio* for प्रतीय which has been handed down in all the MSS and has been accepted by tradition (पदपाठ, भाष्य) as well as by Grube. The *bhāṣyakāra* explains it as "ज्ञात्वा" (= having known, believed; प्रत्यय: = trust, faith, confidence): "having believed [in the statement] that he (Garuḍa) stole the ambrosia for the sake of the redemption of his mother, etc." But the immediately preceding word अन्नं as direct object of this Absolutive (or "gerund") does not allow this construction and this meaning. प्रतीष्य (प्रति + इष्, प्रतीच्छति) simply meants "to accept", "to receive (back)". It is attested in this sense in the *Ṛgveda* X.129.4 (हृदि प्रतीष्या कवयो मनीषा); cf.

also *Durgāsaptaśatī* 8.59 (= *Mārkaṇḍeya Purāṇa* 88.59): यतस्ततस्तद् (शोणितं) वक्त्रेण चामुण्डा संप्रतीच्छति। "अन्नं प्रतीष्य अभिवद इमम्" therefore simply means "accepts this Soma (from Garuḍa) and bless him (Indra!)".

Negelein (114.12) had great difficulty in understanding the text. He wanted to remove *annam* from the verse, to reconstruct a Causative verb form प्रत्यभिवादये from प्रतीयाभिवदे (!) and also would like to have इमं out, since he thinks that it has been taken from some commentary which had "इमं श्लोकमिन्द्र उवाच". I think that not only has he missed the true purport of the text but has also messed it up.

१३ The MSS have सौम्ये which makes little sense. The only right form is सौम्य, a very common address to a near and dear one, usually by an elder to his younger. The vocative character of the word is attested by its being totally unaccented. Johansson's (62 fn. 2) suggestion of converting it into सौम्यं (वरं) is also unnecessary.

१४ All previous scholars have been under the impression that it is a corrupted and mutilated verse. Rau (363) has also made an attempt — totally unsuccessful — to reconstruct it in form of a "verse":

मत्सखिआद् (= सख्याद् with *Svarabhakti*) अन्नम् अमृतत्वं वा, अपि त्वम् एतद् उभयं वृणीष्व।
तार्क्ष्यपुत्रं त्वं ब्रूहि मनसेप्सितं, वरं वृणीष्व . . . वैनतेय।

Negelein (114.25) wants to delete मनसेप्सितम् and Charpentier would like to add त्वं (तुवम्) between वरं and वृणीष्व. All are useless amendments.

१५ The text has विहङ्गमेन्द्र which does not fit into the metre. Charpentier (274.8) rightly opts for विहग in place of विहङ्गम. Rau (363) wants to change the order of सन्तु and विहगेन्द्र (i.e. "भक्षे विहगेन्द्र सन्तु") which undoubtedly reads better.

१६ It is difficult to say why Indra changes the expression स्वर्गकामाः of Garuḍa into स्वर्गार्थः except that it saves one syllable which is in excess of the previous verse. But स्वर्गार्थाः ब्राह्मणाः is not a good expression. It should either be स्वर्गार्थं or स्वर्गार्थिनः.

१७ उदश्रयन्तु is delivered by the text and the *padapāṭha* (उत् + अश्रयन्तु). There is no form like अश्रयन्तु. It could either be उच्छ्रयन्तु (better: उच्छ्रयन्ताम्) or उदाश्रयन्तु if imperative is meant. But I think that the thematic vowel अ in अश्रयन्तु of *padapāṭha* could be an indicator to the fact that the verb was in imperfect (past) tense. The verb of the main sentence is also in imperfect. Hence I have allowed myself this small *emendatio* उत् + आ + अश्रयन्त.

१८ The text has त्रिदिवे. I find ablative much better since the Garuḍa has to swoop down on the serpents from the sky. The locative in त्रिदिवे does not indicate the action of "coming down" involved in the root पत् in the present context.

१९ The text has a perplexing reading वर्द्धयन् [बलं] which cannot be correct. If we connect it with the main verb, it would read वर्द्धयन् बलम् अस्य अध्यवर्धत which does not make much sense. I have chosen a reading desperately which suits the context a little better. Not daring to go too far from the original, I have simply changed the present participle into past participle (वर्धयन् into वर्धित:) and take it in the sense of "became glorious" (cf. तेऽवर्धन्त स्वतवसो महित्वना . . . *Ṛ̣V* I.85.7).

२० The text has अध्यवर्धत which is certainly not correct. I believe firmly that it was अभ्यवर्धत. There is not much difference in the meanings of वृद्धि and अभिवृद्धि, whereas the prefix अधि has a meaning similar to locative case.

२१ सुषूपर्वणि is not easy to understand. As it stands now it can refer only to महाद्रौ (on a high mountain) with a number of cliffs or summits. Charpentier has a brilliant suggestion in सुपर्णवति referring to शाल्मली which has nice foliage (सुपर्ण), अवसानं is a resting place (originally, the spot where the journey ends (from the root "षो अन्तकर्मणि", दिवादि:). For the use of the word in the sense of final resting place, home, cf. *Ṛ̣V* X.14.9 (यमो ददात्यवसानमस्मै).

२२ It is very difficult to understand the use of the word घर्म: which originally appears in the text (for सोम) and means "heat", "hot sunshine" (etymologically: "that which causes to melt", from the root *ghṛ*, cf. घृतम् = melted butter). A [wild] guess could be सोम: . In that case, the verse may be construed in the sense: "Just as Soma praised by the *hotṛ/hotā* lets the speech flow from the mouths of *ṛṣis*, so may Suparṇa release speech [from our mouths too] and shower upon us well-being, happiness . . . etc."

२३ प्रजिहाति (lets run smoothly?), Hertel 337 fn. 1.

२४ *Padapāṭha* separates सुषीमं as सु-सीमं. Negelein thinks (115.2) that it was originally सुखी + इमं. I think, we may operate well with the word सीमन्/सीमा which means boundary, limit; सु-सीमं = wide space, boundlessness, fearlessness. Contrast it with Vedic अंहस् which means constriction, narrowness; hence misery, suffering (etymologically related to German *eng* = narrow, *Enge* = narrowness and *Angst* = fear, serious worry, trepidation).

२५ वैनतेय appears as वैनतेयः (-यो) in the *padapāṭha* with accent on यो, but the context shows that it can only be Vocative because of the following verb in Imperative II person.

२६ *Padapāṭha* has यदि + अपि = यद्यपि. But I think that in view of a parallel construction closely following, it could only be यत् अपि। अस्तोकं (much, in excess) is definitely a mistake for स्तोकं. The poet craves indulgence of Suparṇa for his deficiency (not for his over praise, see also the next note).

२७ For अहाशिषं ("whatever I have left", from the root हा-लुङ्-I person S.), the *padapāṭha* has a curious restoration, namely अह + अशिखं the meaning of which I fail to understand. I am not aware of any such form derived from the verb शिख्. Charpentier (275.31), Negelein (115.14) and Rau (364-65) have all suggested *emendationes* to the text in the following order:

a. यदप्यस्तोकं यदि वाऽपि कृच्छ्राद्, अदाशिषं मनसा श्रद्दधानः।

b. यद्यपि अस्तौषं यदि वाप्यहाऽऽशिषम्–सुपर्णं मनसा . . .।

c. यद्यतिस्तोषं यदि वाप्यहाशिषं – सुपर्णं मनसा श्रद्दधानः।

(अति-स्तोषं = praised too much, exaggerated [because of my strong and genuine faith in him]. The combination of अति + स्तु occurs according to Rau in *JB* I.356 and *PVB* 9.3.7-11.)

I find is difficult to agree with Rau because the emendation and its meaning are totally against the context. After the end of a *stuti,* one usually begs excuse for his shortcomings and not for his "over-praise" or "over-glorification" of the deity!

[फलश्रुतिः]

यः सौपर्णमधीयीत नित्यं पर्वणि पर्वणि।
वीरोऽस्य पुत्रो जायेत मेधावी ब्रह्मवर्चसी॥१॥

यः सौपर्णमधीयीत नित्यं पर्वणि पर्वणि।
अनन्तं स्वर्गमारोहेद् गच्छेन्मम सलोकताम्॥२॥

आस्तिक्यादिह सौपर्णं यः शृणोति प्रणामवान्।
आपद्भ्यः सर्वाभ्यो मुच्येत द्विषद्भ्यश्च प्रमुच्यते॥३॥

आख्यानं गर्भिणो चेदं शृणुयात् प्रतिपर्व चेत्।
पुमांसं जनयेत् पुत्रं बलिनं शत्रुतापनम्॥४॥

सौपर्णं चक्षुर्भवति श्रोतॄणामनुश्रूयताम्।
स्वर्गांश्च लोकान् गच्छेयुरावयोः कीर्तनात् सदा॥५॥

मनो॑जवा॒ अय॑मान आय॒सीम॑तरत् पुर॑म्।
दिवं॑ सुप॒र्णो ग॒त्वाय॒ सोमं॑ व॒ज्रिण॒ आ भ॑रत्॥
(ऋ० ८.१००.८)

॥ *नम इन्द्र सुपर्णयोः* ॥

Suparṇādhyāya
English Translation of the Restored and Rearranged Text

Sūkta I

Varga 1

Phalaśruti

1. The one, who wants to get progeny, cattle and wealth, wants to keep off blindness [in old age] and desires to reach heaven, should regularly recite these eleven sacred hymns related to [the glorification] of Suparṇa.

Prayer unto Suparṇa

2. I am forever full of reverence towards the immortal (lit. without decay) son of Vinatā who has golden wings, is of immeasurable brilliance and immeasurable powers, whose adorable person is made up of [Vedic] metres, consists of various sacrifices and whose wings are formed by the [Sāmavedic chants] *Bṛhat* and *Rathantara.*

3. That king of birds protect us forever who is born out of a part of the Supreme Being and whose powers got enhanced after receiving half of the [merits of the] austerities of the famous Bālakhilya sages.

Benediction

4. The benediction that [the mother] Vinatā uttered for Suparṇa when he proceeded to bring ambrosia [from

heaven], let that benediction also apply to us.

Details of the seer, deities, etc.

5. This *ākhyāna* of Suparṇa consists of thirty-one *vargas*; it has been visualized by the Sage Vāmadeva; the deities are Tārkṣya, Vinatā, Kadrū and Sarpas (snakes); it has Triṣṭubh [for its metre and it is meant] [also] to be recited on *parvans* (new-moon, full-moon, transit of sun into the next zodiac and other festive days) and is meant to be recited by the brāhmaṇas invited for dining [during the *śrāddha* ceremony].

Varga 2

Narrator

6. The Heaven and the Earth happen to be related to each other as sisters. Once they assumed the personal forms [of two ladies] and wandered through the worlds. The Heaven took the form of a Bird with beautiful wings named Vinatā and the Earth that of a female Serpent under the name Kadrū.

7. They committed the offence [of interrupting] the sacrifice of gods [by flying over the sacrificial altar] which disturbed the gods in performing the prescribed rites of *japa* (recitation of *mantras*) and *homa* (offering oblations in fire) whereupon casting spell on them by putting oblations into the sacrificial fire, they destroyed one of the eyes of Kadrū. Having seen one of the eyes of Kadrū destroyed by means of a sacrificial offering, both of them got scared and went to Sage Tārkṣa (Kaśyapa) [to get it redressed/or, to seek advice].

8. [Some time around that] two of the Bālakhilya sages who were carrying the stalks of *palāśa* leaves for using them as *samidhas* (faggots) for a sacrifice slipped into a

small pit created by a cow's hoof and while trying to swim across, both got stuck in its mud.

9. Having observed the Bālakhilya sages getting stuck up in mud inside a hoof's mark, Indra burst into laughter. On this [impudence] they became angry and went straight to Sage Tārkṣa.

Bālakhilyas

10. We shall give you half of the merit of our austerities; produce a son through (=born out of) an egg who should curb the pride of Indra, the conceited one, who thinks high of himself.

Narrator

11. After having imbibed half of the glow of the austerities of the Bālakhilyas, the highly glorious Tārkṣa placed a foetus of the highest order of the avians in [the womb of his wife] Vinatā [the Mother of all birds].

Sūkta II

Varga 3

Narrator

1. Having received the excellent and auspicious Seed, the Śaunakī (Vinatā) developed heavy belly and when the time of gestation in her pure womb was over, she released three eggs.
2. Out of her [excessive] impatience, the lady with a nice posterior made a hole in the first egg and lo! as soon as a crevice was formed, there rushed out the Lightning which flew straight upwards and became the friend of the clouds.

3. Upon this she (Vinatā) was taken over by a strong feeling of guilt and after prolonged contemplation she brought herself over to breaking open the middle egg, of which slipped out (lit. "born") Aruṇa, the companion of the Sungod.
4. As soon as Aruṇa came to the world, he scolded his highly sagelike (i.e. meritorious) mother with the words: "What a great sin have you committed, O you cruel one! I have [developed] no legs at all."
5. Just after he (Aruṇa) was born, the Sungod came [to Vinatā] and said these words: "[Do not feel sorry], be happy, O lady, deliver your son to me. Your son is quite capable of controlling the speed of my [impetuous] horses."

Varga 4

Narrator

6. As soon as Garuḍa was born, all the three worlds trembled. The entire earth shook along with its mountains, forests and groves.
7. The sun and the moon vanished from the sky, the stars and planets lost their shine, the gods got frightened and the winds stopped blowing.
8. Women stopped conceiving, the oceans dried up, the cows could not produce milk and started running helter-skelter apprehensively.
9. The brāhmaṇas forgot their Vedas, serpents got terrified imagining Garuḍa all around. They started praying to Garuḍa to spare them.
10. All the snakes immediately resorted to their hiding places. Those which succumbed to death out of fear at the birth of Garuḍa were brought back to life by the Creator god.

11. Those who have undergone a gestation period of one thousand years [in mother's womb] and are then born under the constellation of Maghā, and further, whose body consists of all the [four] Vedas, have the power to obstruct [the properties of] Fire (i.e. they remain unhurt in fire).

Sūkta III

(The actual beginning of the dramatic composition)

Varga 5

Narrator-cum-Stage Director

1. I am going to sing the glory of the valiant and energetic Garuḍa, the son of Vinatā, one who can withstand (= conquer) even the invincible ones, the one who bought back his mother from Kadrū who had enslaved her by defeating her in a wager (bet) mutually agreed upon.
2. I shall narrate that wondrous deed of the glorious son of Vinatā which is related to the fetching of Soma [from the heaven] and which has made him renowned all over the earth (world).
3. Kadrū and Suparṇī [once] rivalled with each other as to their [and their childrens'] physical appearance. The Kadrū thereby defeated Suparṇī [and emerged victorious]. Suparṇī thereupon uttered these words:

(Enter Suparṇī and Kadrū on the stage)

Suparṇī

4. "It is really true what the people commonly say, namely, that the longbodied ones (serpents?) are mostly of malicious nature, since whenever there is an argument between us, you, the non-prudent, who herself has only

one eye, pierces [the heart of] my son with your sharp remarks [about his being handicapped (i.e. "pedicapped")].

Kadrū

5. [The loss of one eye is of no disadvantage to me, let us bet:] If I don't see as much with my one eye (meant is: "much more") as you see with your two eyes, I shall become your slave, otherwise you become mine.

Varga 6

(*Kadrū and Suparṇī on the seashore*)

Kadrū

6. "O Vinatā, of nice feathers, look across [to the yonder shore], I have heard that you have the sight of an Eagle. There is a dried tree stem over there against which a white horse has scratched [his body] so that a tuft of black hair hangs down stuck to the stem which is tossing to and fro due to the blowing wind.

Vinatā

7. "[Tell me], are you (= your eyes) smeared up (due to swelling)? Or else, are you speaking under the effect of alcohol? I don't see any hair [over there]."

Kadrū

8. "What do you see then? [Tell me] whether the horse is white or is it black? How come, and what is the reason that you are not able to perceive [the reality]?"

Vinatā

9. "Kadrū, you are certainly telling an untruth. You have only one eye and your vision is impaired. I believe that it (the horse) is through and through white and no part of its body is black.

10. I agree to become your slave, O mother of serpents, in case the facts are exactly so as you state and you are not telling an untruth. On the other hand, if you suffer a defeat, be sure, you will serve me as my *ancilla* (maidservant) from now onward.

11. Let us send the fast-running Mātariśvan (the wind-god) as our emissary and hope that he will tell us exactly how the things stand. Or, Aditi (earth), [if you like] we both may ourselves go together [to check it personally]. I shall carry you [on my back] to the spot where the horse is grazing."

Sūkta IV

Varga 7

(On the opposite shore of the ocean)

Kadrū

1. "Here it is! Look, the tuft of black hair hangs down from the peg-like [branch] of the tree. Do you [now] see it hanging [or don't you]?"

   "This Ocean is witness that I have won [the bet]. You now become my bonded maidservant executing physical labour to the maximum of your bodily capacities."

(At the residence of Vinatā)

The serpents to Vinatā

2. Since long we have been hearing about a picturesque island in the midst of the ocean which is the ancient abode of the serpents. Vinatā, carry us over there.

Vinatā (to herself, flying in the sky)

3. "I am carrying, carrying them around, carrying these [wretched!] serpents as if I had committed some crime. I

am carrying this wicked Kadrū along with her sons from one island of the ocean to the other, flying so low that my wings touch the water due to their weight."

(Kadrū and her sons do not enjoy the ride, the flight, being too low. All descend ending the flight.)

Varga 8

Kadrū to Vinatā

4. [You are weak and are flying too low] Suparṇī, send your strong son, that young boy [Garuḍa] whose wings scratch the sky when he flies. Let him come and take us all to those heights where the sun shines.

(Suparṇa/Garuḍa appears on the scene)

Suparṇa to the snakes

5. "I am Suparṇa, O Snakes. My [elder brother] Aruṇa has sent me [to you]. I undertake to do what [my mother] Śuṅgī has asked me [to do]. Come, climb on me and get properly stuck to my body. I am going to take you all to the sun within no time."

(Suparṇa takes to flight, sores higher and higher)

Snakes to Suparṇa

6. "The rays of the sun are excessively scorching, O Suparṇa. They are burning our hoods. We respectfully bow to the sun-god [from here itself]. Noble soul, turn around and take us back to the place where our mother Aditi (personified Earth) is present."
7. "[Hey!] Stop going to the place of the Sun! Singed are our bodies with the rays of the sun. Either you turn back now at our behest or else we are going to jump off your body and let ourselves fall on ground."

(Suparṇa does not oblige, snakes jump off the body of Suparṇa)

Kadrū complains to Vinatā

8. It was not nice of this [your son], Suparṇī, that he continued to carry with great speed these sons of mine always higher and higher up in the sky towards the sun even though these [poor] snakes were burning with heat, feeling weak and convulsing in agony.

Sūkta V

Varga 9

Kadrū to Aruṇa

1. Look Aruṇa, scorched with the heat of the sun, these snakes are lying here on the ground. I do not know, how to help them. [My husband, the Sage] Tārkṣa is also not around. He could perhaps know how to comfort them.

Kadrū to Suparṇa

2ab. This was indeed cruel of you, Suparṇa, that you forcibly continued to carry the snakes [against their wish].

Narrator

2cd. Overwhelmed with grief upon seeing her sons with sunburn, Kadrū admonishes Vinatā [and her son] to always remain servile towards their masters.

(*Tārkṣa/Kaśyapa appears and utters mantras invoking Parjanya to induce rains*)

3. "Roar, thunder, agitate the oceans! Let the level of your waters achieve the height of mountains. May the [serpent] Śeṣa (i.e. streaks of lightning resembling the white Śeṣanāga) strike the summit of the mountains and the serpents get submerged in waters."

4. "May this whole stretch of land right across be filled up with water and water only. Let the female frog quack

the whole night, the deer run around looking for a [dry] place and even those cows which [are so old that they] can hardly walk should yield milk [due to lavish growth of grass later]."

Varga 10

Vinatā to Garuḍa

5. "What is this Garutman? You are shedding tears! [Remember] You are a son of the Sage Tārkṣa and have the byname 'Ariṣṭanemi' [i.e. the one who can fly to any destination without getting tired]. O skydiver, the progeny of such [eminent] persons does not have any cause to be worried, as the people say."

Garuḍa's answer to mother

6. "O mother, I feel distressed not because of me, but because of *your* plight. You are [often] shedding pearl-like tears without any reservation {*apagatahriyā* = without feeling embarrassed about it} like a childless woman [who has nobody to support her], something which the young women of your age are not known to have ever done [i.e. are not supposed to do].
7. Mother, I am capable of surveying every nook and corner of the worlds, thanks to my eyesight, energy and strength. [But even after having done so,] I fail to find any fault in any one of us. Why have I been born as a slave? What sin have you committed? Or did my father made himself guilty of some misdeed?"

Vinatā to Garuḍa

8. "While once betting with Kadrū, I accepted her condition [of the wager] due to my stupidity (*mohāt*) {v.l., in a fit of rage (*krodhāt*)}, without realizing the risk it involved. And she won me [as her slave] in the competition."

Garuḍa to Vinatā

9. "How can I make you free from this unbearable slavery? Should I offer my own self in lieu of yours, or offer her a piece of land instead? Or would the gift of [a large quantity of] foodgrains or money would do the required? Tell me forthwith [O mother] Śuṅgā; I am greatly disturbed.

10. Please go and ask the serpents whether there is a way to get relieved [of this bondage]; whether through me, through my brother Aruṇa, through a gift of cattle or by offering [a certain amount of] money."

Sūkta VI

Varga 11

Vinatā to the serpents

1. "Carrying you [on my back] all around [since long], I have now become weak and frail. [Over these years] I have not even been aware of [the whereabouts and the well-being of] my sons and my husband. My bodily substances have now dissipated and I do not have any energy in me. [Tell me], how can this old lady be relieved of the bondage?

2. Tell me serpents, what having been brought, what having been conquered, what having been achieved with valour, can I be made free from serving you?"

[Identical with *Mahābhārata*, Adiparvan, 23.11]

Serpents to Vinatā

3. "The Soma of Indra is kept safely in a cave on the top of the third sphere of the space. Let that, the most beneficent substance [for the creatures of the world], be brought down promptly [for us] and get yourself with that be

bought back, going about happily wherever you like.

4. We hear that this exquisite elixir has been kept well protected by Indra in the highest of heaven. Getting access to that we shall gain immortality. Bring that [for us] if you have capability [and means] to do so and get yourself be released [from bondage]."

Varga 12

Vinatā to Garuḍa

5. "The serpents wish to drink Soma which they want to be brought by us from the heaven, O Garutman. It is very difficult to bring Soma from the heaven, but it is the [only] ransom [which they shall accept]."

Garuḍa to mother

6. "I give my word to you, Mother Vinatā, of nice wings, that in case you have never killed any brāhmaṇa in your life, I shall fly for your sake to a great distance, right up to the top of the heaven, to bring Soma."

Vinatā to Garuḍa

7. "Garutman, I have never killed a brāhmaṇa, nor have I ever caused any disturbance in the performance of a sacrifice as an outsider. I am not guilty of (lit. 'covered with') any such or similar sin, also not have I taken over the sin of someone else upon myself for expiation."

Garuḍa to mother

8. "That Soma of Indra which is kept hidden in a cave, I shall [certainly] bring for you from the top of the third sphere of the space after violently pushing its protectors away and striking them down; don't you think so (i.e. don't you believe)?"

Vinatā to Garuḍa

9. "All the gods in heaven unite in protecting the Soma, along with several other dreadful creatures. Keep it in mind [and think it over]. If you are not able to withstand (i.e. to fight with) them, I would rather prefer to continue with my slavery than to risk your life."

Garuḍa to mother

10. "[O Mother] Vinatā of nice feathers, I am the Metres incarnate, which lend [their] support to the sacrifice when it is carried out. On several occasions during the sacrificial festivals, God Brahmā has spoken of our paramount importance. Do not underestimate us.

11. My person consists of those *four* foremost Metres of the [total] seven which uphold (or, sustain) the sacrifice and through which a sacrifice is 'extended' (i.e. 'elaborated', or carried out in minute details). In the past too, gods have [often] sent me towards Soma (i.e. to fetch Soma from the heaven, cf. *TS* VI.1.6.1f., *MS* III.7.3, etc.)."

Sūkta VII

Varga 13

Garuḍa to mother

1. "Mother Suparṇī, in this world, one who is engaged in [physical] activities, but does not eat [properly] has hardly any bodily strength [to carry out the job]. [Therefore] Vinatā, I wish to ask you, what should I eat before I proceed to the world of gods?"

Vinatā to Garuḍa

2. "Look my son, there is a great mountain [over there]. On the summit of it there is a large lake. There [in the

lake] lives a huge water-monster (alligator). [Besides it] catch also that elephant which has descended in the lake. These two [creatures] shall serve you as your food.

3. This enormous *nāga* (alligator) as well as the *padmin* (speckled with red dots on skin) {or, v.l. *patmin,* the dashing} elephant called *ghoṣavān* (loud trumpeting) endowed with large tusks who looks like a huge [dark] cloud; him and his counterpart, these two have been offered to you by the creator god. Eat them [both] and thereafter proceed to the world of gods."

Garuḍa to himself (flying in the sky with animals in his clutches)

4. "I am [soon] going to eat this Supadma and the *nāga* both of which, followers of {or, looking like} Mataṅga(?) and are inimical to each other (*prabhinnau*). I am very happy at having caught these huge [creatures] and now I am flying [back] on the very same track with the desire to consume them [at a proper place]."

Garuḍa asks his mother

5. "[As you know, my mother] Vinatā of nice feathers, we are avions [of high sky], and as such it does not suit us (i.e. we do not like) to take our food sitting on ground. Tell me about a proper tree, if you know one, perching on which I may relish my meals."

Vinatā to Garuḍa

6. "Alight on that [particular] tree, Suparṇa, which is a resort of the sages Bālakhilyas and the wise saints Vaikhānasas and whose long branches extend for many *yojanas*.

7. Go swiftly to that best of the trees, the Rauhiṇa, which has big branches and which is a friend (favourite) of your

father. Perching on that take your food. If at all any tree can withstand you (i.e. your weight combined with the weight of these animals), it is he, and none else."

Varga 14

The tree Rauhiṇa to himself

8. "Here approaches me this Suparṇa carrying in the air a mighty elephant so huge as the mountain Meru along with a water-monster (lit. alligator) impelling a strong gust of wind by his speed which is shaking me up."

Garuḍa to the tree Rauhiṇa

9. "Be steady, Rauhiṇa, lend me support so that I do not faint out of exhaustion! I, Garutman, who (i.e. whose person) consist(s) of metres mixed with deities, am going to land on you with great force."

Rauhiṇa to Garuḍa

10. "Here is this branch extending towards east which is a resort of the Bālakhilya and Vaikhānasa sages; you may alight on it. The other one projecting towards west is slanting and is bent down [hence not very suitable for a comfortable 'dining space']. [However] if you are afraid of committing a possible transgression [by sitting on the eastern branch], you may choose the other one."

(Garuḍa chooses to sit on the eastern branch which instantly snaps)

11. "Oh, you have broken the branch! You shall [now] incur [a great] sin; shall kill the brāhmaṇas who will fall on the ground [as a result of which] you will sink into the limitless, dark space [of sin] and shall not be able to bring Soma, Garutman!"

Sūkta VIII

Varga 15

Narrator, or the voices of the people from the back of the stage

1. "Holding the [broken] branch in the left [claw] and both [the creatures] in the right, look at the strength of Garuḍa which cannot be measured (= described) in words."

Garuḍa to the mountain Himavān

2ab. "Here am I, your affectionate child, O Himavān, on your summit sent by my mother. . . ."

Himavān to Garuḍa:

2cd. "Cast away the branch from your foot (claw) [carefully] in the valley deep down and close your wings (i.e. descend)."

(Garuḍa returns home after finishing his food and gliding in the sky calls out to his mother)

Vinatā to herself

3. Who could be uttering these pleasing words in the sky? One of my sons must be sleeping [at this hour of the day] and the other is presently [busy elsewhere] taking his food.
4. This one [up there] is coming [down] resounding the sky and the directions with his voice. I think, it must be [one of] my own dear sons coming home, either Garuḍa or Aruṇa!

(*Garuḍa descends and narrates to his mother what has happened recently*)

Garuḍa to his mother

5. "Mother, I got [really] tired holding a branch of the Rauhiṇa which was so long that not even one hundred leather straps joined together could have measured it out.
6. Even after eating the elephant together with the alligator, I do not feel like having eaten to my fill. Tell me of some other eatable of large quantity, having eaten which I leave immediately for heaven [on my mission] fully satiated."

Varga 16

Garuḍa (or Vinatā)

7. "The moving ones (i.e. animals) eat the static ones, this is an eternal practice. The birds [however] eat both moving and unmoving (i.e. grains, fruits, etc.) objects."

Vinatā to Garuḍa

8. "There is a nation of tribals divided into many groups warring against each other. That you can consume for the sake of fulfilling my wish. These do not recite [religious texts], nor do they perform sacrifices. I think that is a good food for you.
9. Do not, however, my brave son, kill any godly brāhmaṇa endowed with forbearance moving among them. He will be a virtual death for you, nothing else."

Garuḍa to mother

10. "They all have one head, two legs and two hands. In case I catch some of them, I like to ask you, [mother] Vinatā, how does a brāhmaṇa look like?"

Sūkta IX

Varga 17

Vinatā to Garuḍa

11. "One who has dusty appearance, matted hair, unclean (?) teeth, with hair tied upwards [in a knot], one who always speaks truth and is not afraid of death even amidst enemies, he is a brāhmaṇa. Do not kill him, Garutman.
12. The one who is tormented by six kinds of fire: of tongue, heart, belly and genitals (lit. 'semen'), of hot summer and biting cold; he is a brāhmaṇa. Don't kill him, Garutman.
13. Having devoured a brāhmaṇa, one gets heavy belly (i.e. cannot digest it) as a fish gets after swallowing a hook. It goes down the throat burning the gullet like heated charcoal. Such is a brāhmaṇa. Don't kill him, Garutman."

Garuḍa to mother

14. "I shall [surely] bring Soma for you, now since my food has been [exactly] identified. [I feel so hungry at this moment that] I could have perhaps eaten up both the mobile and the immobile creation to its end!"

Varga 18

[According to the conventions of the Nāṭyaśāstra, *this scene cannot be presented on the stage, hence the narrator takes over and describes the event verbally.]*

Narrator

1. The hungry Suparṇa then went on eating the Niṣādas as [suggested and] allowed by his mother. He would [repeatedly open] and close the wings and put those in his mouth who got trapped [within his wings] from amongst the ones who were following him in the gust of the wind.

2. While the Bird was thus devouring the Niṣādas hopping from one place to the other, one entered his throat which started burning him as a heap of fire.
3. Since there were no sparks and no smoke, the suffering Garuḍa was reminded of the words of Śuṅgā [and said to himself]: "Oh, what a vigour these brāhmaṇas possess who have only the knowledge as the source of their excellence (lit. 'sustenance, livelihood')!"

Garuḍa to brāhmaṇa [narrator's voice]

4. "Come out of myself, O nice brāhmaṇa, you need not become my food! Look, here I have [thrown out and] planted (placed erect) whatever I had swallowed. You need not feel scared (lit. 'sorry')."

Brāhmaṇa to Garuḍa [narrator's voice]

5. "I do not consider myself alive without my wife and children. Just as a brāhmaṇa, so also his wife of Niṣāda clan and the children born out of this wedlock are equally harmful for you to ingest."
6. Having emitted the brāhmaṇa with his family members, thus carrying out the orders of his mother, and having swallowed the others, Garuḍa thereafter quickly left for heaven.

Sūkta X

Varga 19

Narrator or chorus in the background

(Glorification of Garuḍa)

1. "I pay obeisance to Tārkṣya, the son of Śuṅgā and the king of the birds, the divine Suparṇa of nice appearance, the brave one whose strength increases with words

uttered in his praise, who is superior to his adversaries, pushes them back and conquers them."

(Flying up towards heaven, Garuḍa is intercepted by Bṛhaspati, the Priest and the Chief Advisor of Indra, who wants to know his identity and the purpose of his going to heaven.)

Garuḍa identifies himself to Bṛhaspati

2. "I am Suparṇa, the foremost among the flying ones and am on my way to fetch Soma (ambrosia/*amṛta*) with the blessings of my mother. My mother is presently bonded in slavery [and the Soma is supposed to redeem her]. O the best of the brāhmaṇas (priests), please bless me and wish my welfare!"

Bṛhaspati to Garuḍa

3. "May you be blessed with long life and vigour, [my] son! Is otherwise all well in your home? I hope, Garutman, that the mother of [such capable sons as] Aruṇa [and you] does not take her setback in the rivalry [with Kadrū] too much to heart."

Garuḍa to Bṛhaspati

4. "The humiliation which is being suffered by Suparṇī in slavery *does* torment her; except that all else is well in our family (lit. home).

   I wish now to take leave of you, the foremost among the orators (or, poets), and am flying to heaven towards Soma."

Bṛhaspati blesses Garuḍa

5. "Let the sacrifice and its gifts protect you. While flying let the exquisite water (Soma/Moon) be in front of you.

The *Ṛks* and the *Yajus* should surround you [from all sides] and the divine hymns be on your right and left flanks."

Chorus

6. "We pronounce benediction to Tārkṣya, of unobstructed speed (lit. 'the felloe of whose wheel is never worn out'), of huge stature, the bird of gods, Indra's friend and the slayer of *asuras* in the battles. Let us take refuge in his glory [to save ourselves] as one climbs a ship [at the time of high waters]."
7. "With folded hands I take refuge in the sin-redeeming [sages] Āṅgirasa, Gaya and Svastyātreya; also bow with devotion to Tārkṣya. Let us remain unharmed in adversities and let there be well-being all around."

Varga 20

(Venue: heaven; Indra and Bṛhaspati talk to each other)

Indra to Bṛhaspati

8. "Tell me Bṛhaspati, is there [presently] any Being, was there any, or shall there be any who could undermine and surpass the security installed by me and forcibly take away the Soma by dint of his valour?"

Bṛhaspati to Indra

9. "[Yes], even if sixty thousand hillocks are to be flown over, and even if ninety-nine hundred rivers [are to be crossed], there is One, Garuḍa, the son of Vinatā, who intends to seize the concealed Soma and *he* is going to take it away by force."

Indra's query to Bṛhaspati

10. "From whom is he born? Which world he belongs to? Which earth he comes from, this one who wants to fight with [our] outstanding archer Bhauvana with bow in his hands?"

Bṛhaspati's reply

11. "There is a [Birds' mother] with nice feathers called Vinatā. She performed severe austerities. Of her is born this Garuḍa, [hence known as] 'Vainateya'. This Bird is going to carry away the Soma. Learn this about him."

Sūkta XI

Varga 21

Indra to Bṛhaspati

1. "[Tell me, whether] is it I who am 'Indra', or is this Vainateya 'Indra' about whom I hear that this clever one wants to carry away my Soma with force which is deposited at a yonder place, flying across all the worlds [in between]?"

Bṛhaspati

2. "[Yes] Indra, You are the overlord of all that which is created and which is going to be created. Everything which has been and is to be, belongs to you. All the directions, intermediate directions, upper directions and the heavens belong to you. People say that it is due to your blessings and your orders that everything takes place."

(There is commotion, noise and battle cry in the sky)

Vinatā to her elder son Aruṇa

3. "A great noise is being heard, up there in the sky. Why don't you run to [the help of] your brother, my son? The Suparṇa is alone and the gods are many. Indra alone cannot withstand him."

Aruṇa to his mother

4ab. "Mother, [your] Aruṇa cannot go [being lame and also unable to leave the chariot of the Sungod]. Let the bringer of Soma go alone to the heaven. [He is fully capable of taking on his adversaries]."

Vinatā to herself

4cd. "[Alas,] with Aruṇa as his brother, Garuḍa is [as good as] not having any brother and with Aruṇa as her son, the mother Śuṅgā/Vinatā/Suparṇī is as good as not having any son at all!"

Varga 22

Vinatā to Aruṇa

5. "The lame Bhauvana, for sure, is not going to do any good to him (Garuḍa). He (Bhauvana) is a slayer of enemies and is never negligent [towards his duties]. [After all] it is a matter of [protecting] the [divine] drink of exhilarating Soma; he certainly won't be careless. How can [your younger brother] Garuḍa secure himself from him?"

Aruṇa to Vinatā

6. "Mother Śuṅgā, Garuḍa is energy, courage and strength in person. He is intangible like sky, subtle like clouds and fear incarnate for his enemies. He has unassailable physical strength. Nobody is a match to Garutman."

(*Aruṇa blesses Garuḍa*)

7. "Let the God Vāta protect his life-breaths, thc gods Maruts his wings and the God Agni his head. I shall be in his front and back (i.e. all around wherever required) and the shining Moon shall give support to Garuḍa from the rear."

(*Indra and Brihaspati talking in heaven*)

Indra to Bṛhaspati

8. "What sort of noise is this where Soma is deposited? Bṛhaspati, please go down and enquire about it. The string of the bow of the Lame [Bhauvana] is humming being [drawn back] and let loose. The deaf protector of Soma is also roaring and crying aloud, on the other hand."

Bṛhaspati to Indra

9. "I know the source of this sound, Maghavan. It is that of Suparṇa falling upon [the protectors of Soma]. This [noise] is emerging from the place where the son of Vinatā is carrying away the Soma after striking down your guards of Soma."

Sūkta XII

Varga 23

Indra to Bṛhaspati

1. "Where was [our] lame Bhauvana, that quick sharp-shooter whose arrow-points surpass the burning fire and whose arms are capable of shooting thirty bunches of arrows [at a time] across sixty thousand [*yojanas*] which do not miss their target?"

Bṛhaspati to Indra

2. "Instilling fear in the mind of the lame one, Suparṇa moved ahead quickly and safely on his way. Since he was moving in a circle while falling upon Soma in the highest heaven, the arrow could not hit him."

Indra to Bṛhaspati

3. "Where were [the serpents] Arbuda, Nahuṣa and Kādraveya; where Ulūka, Balbula and Śvasana? And where was Praliṣa who keeps his eyes wide open even when he sleeps, so that the son of Vinatā has managed to carry away my Soma?
4. Where were Kakubh, Bhaṇḍa and Cakratuṇḍa? Where were Aśvamukha and Kuṇḍakarṇa? Where were Vikrośana and Kharakaṇṭha so that the son of Vinatā is carrying away my Soma [with impunity]?"

Bṛhaspati to Indra

5. "Having anticipated the swoop of the Bird and overwhelmed by the [reputed] force and strength of Garuḍa, O Indra, these serpents got scared of the touch of the king of the birds and hid their heads under their bodies."

Varga 24

Indra

6. "Where were Kaśambūka, Veṇuka, Aśvakranda, Alagarda and Paruṣa and where were Nabhorūpa and Sarūpa so that the son of Vinatā is carrying away my Soma [without resistence]?
7. [Where was] this Śaśākṣa who keeps watch [on the Soma] being present at the very entrance [of the spot], the one who, when enraged, is Death in person wiping

out whole masses of people; and further, this Vibhida who sleeps with his jaws wide open? Where were these all so that the son of Vinatā is carrying away my Soma?"

Bṛhaspati

8. "Some of these with their severed throats and some with their smashed heads fell as mutilated bodies into the depths of darkness, Indra. The lame Bhauvana got killed in the broil. Suparṇa perpetrated a great carnage."

Indra

9. "And those two lightnings, Bhayā and Abhayā, which protect the [divine] food, wakefully looking in all directions and capable of striking all around, how could this greedy vulture (*gṛdhra*) surpass them?"

Bṛhaspati

10ab. [Repetition of 9ab].

10cd. These two lightnings, Bhayā and Abhayā, which have the property of spreading all over (*viṣūcī*), Garuḍa [amicably] talked to them [and when they discerned that he is their younger brother, cf. *supra* II.2], they [immediately] left for heaven.

Sūkta XIII

Varga 25

Indra

1. "And what happened to my Māyā which is more nimble than the wink of an eye, has the potency of flaring up at her will and which never comes back [without fulfilling her assignments], and, *Brahman*, also to my missile (*pavi*) fixed with razors that this son of Vinatā is running away with my Soma?"

Bṛhaspati

2ab. [Repetition of 1ab].

2cd. "As to your Māyā which is more nimble . . . etc., this Garuḍa, the son of Vinatā, who moves with the speed of thought [lit. 'at his will', cf. *manojavā ayamānaḥ* in *ṚV* VII.100.8], the one who is faster than the fastness itself, [easily] outmanoeuvred her with his deftness and she was let down."

Indra

3. "And, *Brahman*, where was my discus [at that time] which is fixed with sharp razors, that has the potency of flaring up at its will, is swifter than the wink of an eye and which never bounces back [without smiting the enemy], that this Vainateya is absconding with my Soma?"

Bṛhaspati

4. "That your discus which is fixed with sharp razors . . . etc., the son of Vinatā, who moves with the speed of thought, the one who is faster than the fastness itself, [easily] dodged it with his competence [of speeding ahead of it, leaving it trailing behind]."

Indra

5. "Those rocky mountains, the sharp-edged missiles, the deep [unfordable] moats filled with water and the lightnings — some bright like the sun, the other shining like the moon and changing their forms [and colours] in myriads of ways [to dazzle and blind the invader], how could [after all], this greedy 'vulture' overcome all these and get away?"

(Bṛhaspati's answer missing)

Varga 26

Indra

6. "[Many groups of gods and demi-gods like] the Ādityas, Rudras, Vasus, Maruts and Sādhyas were posted by me at various points to keep vigil on the Soma and to protect it. What happened to them, *Brahman*, that this Vainateya is making good with my Soma?"

Bṛhaspati

7. "Repelled by Garuḍa the Vasus were pushed towards the east, all Maruts together with the Sādhyas towards the north, the Rudras with the battalion of the Gandharvas towards the south and the Ādityas were thrown back {thwarted} towards the west.

Indra

8. Where was this Jātavedas /Vaiśvānara fire which keeps burning constantly encircling the Soma. . . . How could this greedy vulture pass unhurt through the burning flames of this excessive heat?

Bṛhaspati

9. The son of Vinatā brought six hundred thousand streams of clarified butter in his beak and satiated your (Firegod) Agni with that. Thereafter this Bird whose body is made of gold (which is indestructible in fire), easily crossed through it and flew away.

Bṛhaspati (or, the Narrator)

10. Having [thus] satisfied the Fire with clarified butter and defeated all your guards of Soma, the son of Vinatā brought all the variously [high] and low-lying areas to a common ground level [with the rubble and the dust

which was whirled up as a result of his vehement flight], much like a large cloud which brings high and low areas of the earth to a common level [through inundating rains] and flew away to a yonder destination.

Sūkta XIV

Varga 27

Bṛhaspati to Indra

1ab. Terribly strong, [although] alone, he overpowered the multitude of them. He is as mighty as you and is equal to you in strength.

Indra to Bṛhaspati

1cd. Since the Bird has attacked my guards and mauled them up, I am [greatly] enraged, and [here], I hurl my thunderbolt at him.

[*Indra again, after smiting Garuḍa with his Vajra which springs back*]

Indra to Bṛhaspati

2. "This my thunderbolt which is replete with ascetic power, has sharp razors and has strong striking force {or, *svavīryam*, 'operates with its own energy'}, the one which split apart the chest of Vritra, this has bounced back colliding against the body of the Bird! Bṛhaspati, tell me, what sort of a creature is this Suparṇa?"

Bṛhaspati to Indra

3. "Indra, this Suparṇa is a conglomerate of all [Vedic] metres taken together, he consists of *Yajus* and his body is constituted of Sāmans. The son of Tārkṣa has [now] become [even more] powerful after having taken a sip

of Soma, that is why your thunderbolt has bounced off him."

Indra soliciting Garuḍa

4. "This is the [ultimate] weapon of the gods, Garutman, for killing their adversaries. It has never come back without killing the enemy. [The fact] that it has come back [today without fulfilling its mission], does not augur well for the gods. [Please] give due respect to it!"

Garuḍa to Indra

5. "I am releasing a faultless (lit. 'irreproachable') feather from the upper part of my leg. Cut it with your thunderbolt and remain respectable [in the eyes of the people]. The welfare of gods is also agreeable to me, Indra, but that I am going to do only upon a friendly request and not under duress."
6. "[By dropping this feather] I shall be paying due respect to the Sage (Dadhyañc) of whose bones this *vajra* is formed, shall be doing honour to the *vajra* itself and also to you, O 'Śatakratu' (*of hundredfold activities*)!"

Varga 28

The Narrator

7. [Indra] cut that feather into three pieces with his thunderbolt. The piece that comprised the front part of the feather, became Peacock; the middle one became the bi-headed reptile Rājī, the dominator of snakes and from the last portion originated mongoose (*nakula*), the [arch-]enemy of the snakes.

Indra to Garuḍa

8. "O Bird, I wish to ask you how much strength do you have and how much weight can you withstand. Tell me

about your capabilities and let there be friendship between us for all the times to come."

Garuḍa to Indra

9. Eight Earths [with their] nine directions, three oceans and more than one thousand mountains can I carry, should I wish to do so.

Indra to Garuḍa

10. In case the snakes [are allowed to] drink the Soma (= *amṛtam*) [brought by you and] given to them, they will make a clean sweep of all human beings [on earth]. This [surely] wouldn't be nice.

Garuḍa to Indra

11. O slayer of enemies, I am not going to throw away the Soma to the serpents. Having taken it from here, I shall merely *show* it to them, dear Indra, [please] don't get angry with me!

Sūkta XV

(*Garuḍa flies back to earth and arrives at the serpents' dwellings with the vessel of Soma*)

Varga 29

Garuḍa to serpents

1ab. "O ye Children of Earth, the Soma has been brought for you, look at it [well]!

1cd. [As per our agreement] I am now free, Aruṇa is free as well, free is also our mother Vinatā, the Suparṇī!"

(*Serpents eagerly start crawling towards the vessel of Soma*)

Garuḍa again to serpents

2. "This here is Soma, O the sons of Kadrū, I have brought it for you from the third sphere of heaven. Look at it attentively [for once], I tell you, because this king [of herbs] is going to leave you [in the next moment]!

(***As the Snakes run towards the Soma, Garuḍa picks up the vessel***)

3. All of you would be running after me while I carry the Soma away from you. Let someone who considers himself to be brave, chase [and try to catch] me; or all of you, the earth-crawlers, show your bravery collectively!"

(***Garuḍa disappears from the scene with the vessel containing Soma and reaches heaven***)

Garutmān to Indra

4ab. "[Here], I have brought back this Soma which I had previously snatched [from your guards] and made away with.

4cd. I have [now] been set free, [my brother] Aruṇa is similarly set free and the mother Vinatā also has become free from her bondage."

Indra alone (bragging about himself)

5. "After slaying [the *asuras*] Pipru, Namuci and Śambara and having vanquished Vipracitti, I, the slayer of Vṛtra, now cover myself with the Earth and the Sky as my lower and upper garments."

Indra turning towards Garuḍa

6. "I have excelled all my enemies in might. Because of my might I am all in this (i.e. overlord of this) world. How did you [dare to] take away by force the Soma which is

pressed [especially] for such a mightier than mighty [person] like me?"

Varga 30

Garuḍa to Indra

7. "Indra, My mother [known as] Vinatā *alias* Suparṇī was leading a miserable life due to slavery into which she [unwittingly] had slipped because of [entering and losing in] a rivalry. Your Soma was the only ransom fixed for buying her back [into freedom]; that is why I had to snatch it from you [i.e. your guards] which had till now remained untouched [lit. unscratched] by others."

Glorification of Indra by Garuḍa (or collectively)

8. "O Maghavan, [not only] the Soma is yours [but] this Suparṇa is [also] yours. Śakra (= the mighty), you are what has been, is presently there and shall come into existence [in future]. You are the protector and [the ultimate] refuge [of human beings and gods]. The oceans (?) belong to you and the world belongs to you. Rule it well!"

Bṛhaspati to Indra

9ab. Indra, bless this brave Suparṇa, younger brother of Aruṇa, after having provided (= fixed, decided) food for him.

Indra to Garuḍa

9cd. "I grant a boon to you, O gentle one. Ask [me] for whatever you have in your heart.

10. Having me as your friend, choose [any desired] food and also immortal existence in speech, both.

[Or], Son of Tārkṣa, you tell. Ask for any boon whatever moves your heart, you, the son of Vinatā."

Garuḍa to Indra

11. "I choose snakes for my food, Indra (lit. 'husband of Śacī', i.e. power). Let me carry the sacrifice [unto gods] and enter into the Vedas. The brāhmaṇas desirous of attaining heaven should recite me [over and over again] and let them achieve the company of us two when they come to heaven."

Indra to Garuḍa

12. "Let the snakes be your food, O the king of the birds! carry the sacrifice, enter into the Vedas, you brave-heart. The brāhmaṇas shall read you for the sake of attaining heaven and they will enjoy the company of us two."

The Narrator

13. [Since then] the snakes have been seeking to hide themselves trembling with fear (lit. with horripilated bodies) whenever they see Suparṇa diving down from the sky and the free-flying Bird has become constantly stronger after devouring them.

Varga 31

(*Glorification of Suparṇa-Garuḍa*)

14. I invoke that great Garuḍa, the son of Vinatā and the king of birds, for [my] protection who has made his resting place in a nest on a *śālmalī* tree standing on the great mountain (Himalayas) with beautiful summits.

15. When praised with Triṣṭubh metre, he makes my speech flow freely as a draught of Soma does in the case of a Hotā (= invoker of gods). O son of Vinatā, impart us bliss, all round welfare and make us fearless; remove our sins and destroy our enemies.

16. Whatever I have understated or left out while praising

Suparṇa with great reverence in my heart, may he be kind to us (i.e. forgive us for deficiencies) and bless us with long life and strong vision till old age.

Phalashruti of the Text

(Put into the mouth of Indra)

1. Whoever would regularly read [this] glorification of Suparṇa on [the days of] each *parvan* (new moons, full moons, solstices, eclipses, etc.), to him will be born a son who would be brave, intelligent and a scholar of the Vedic lore.
2. Whoever shall regularly recite [this] glorification of Suparṇa on [the days of] each *parvan*, he would ascend to heaven, come to my world and shall live here eternally.
3. Whoever would listen to the [recitation of this] Sauparṇa with faith and reverence, will get relieved of all calamities and will become free of his enemies.
4. If a pregnant lady listens to this *ākhyāna* on each *parvan*, she would give birth to a male child who would develop into a mighty person, tormenter of his foes.
5. Those who listen to the recitation of this text, develop sharp eyesight like that of an eagle and those who propagate our glory, come to the heavenly worlds, for sure.

> "Moving ahead with the speed of thought, [he] glided over the metallic walls of the fort. Having gone to heaven, Suparṇa fetched Soma for the wielder of thunderbolt." — *Ṛgveda* VII.100.8

[Obeisance to Indra and Suparṇa]

श्री सुपर्णाध्यायः

हिन्दी भावानुवाद

॥ प्रथम सूक्त ॥

प्रथम वर्ग

[*आख्यान का महत्त्व*]

जो व्यक्ति सन्तान, धन, पशु, अन्धेपन से बचाव, दीर्घ-जीवन एवं स्वर्ग की कामना करता है उसे सुपर्ण-गरुड के यशोगान से सम्बन्धित इन ग्यारह सूक्तों का निरन्तर पारायण करना चाहिए॥१॥

[*मंगलाचरण*]

मैं विनता के पुत्र उन गरुड को नित्य प्रणाम करता हूँ जिनके पंख स्वर्णमय हैं, जो अतुलनीय तेजस्वी हैं, जिनके सामर्थ्य की कोई सीमा नहीं है, जिनका शरीर छन्दों से युक्त यज्ञों से निर्मित होने के कारण परम महनीय है और जिनके पंख बृहत् और रथन्तर सामन् से बने हुए हैं॥२॥

वे पक्षिराज गरुड सदैव हमारी रक्षा करें जो परमेश्वर के अंश से उत्पन्न हुए और जिनका तेज और बल तब और बढ़ गया जब उन प्रसिद्ध बालखिल्य मुनियों ने अपनी तपस्या के फल का आधा तेज उन्हें प्रदान कर दिया॥३॥

जो मंगलकामना विनता ने सुपर्ण-गरुड के लिए उस समय की थी जब वे अमृत लेने के लिए प्रयाण कर रहे थे, वही मंगलकामना हम सबके लिए भी फलदायी हो॥४॥

[*ऋषि-छन्द-देवता आदि का उल्लेख*]

यह सुपर्णाख्यान इकतीस वर्गों से युक्त स्तुति है, इसके ऋषि वामदेव हैं, इसमें देवता (मन्त्रों में वर्णित पात्र) गरुड, इन्द्र, तार्क्ष (कश्यप) विनता, कद्रू, सर्प, तथा देवगण

हैं, इसकी निर्मिति त्रिष्टुभ् छन्द में है तथा इसका विनियोग अमावास्या-पूर्णिमादि पर्वों पर स्वयं पाठ करने एवं ब्राह्मणों से सुनने (को सुनाने?) के लिए है॥५॥

द्वितीय वर्ग

[*प्रस्तोता*]

आकाश एवं पृथ्वी ये दोनों बहनें हैं। एक बार ये शरीर धारण करके लोकों में विचरण कर रही थीं। उस समय आकाश का रूप एक सुन्दर पंखों वाली पक्षिणी की भाँति था और भूमि का रूप, एक नागिन के समान। पहली का नाम "विनता" था और दूसरी का "कद्रू"॥६॥

एक बार जब देवगण यज्ञ कर रहे थे तो उनके यज्ञ-मण्डप के ऊपर उड़ते हुए उन्होंने यज्ञ में विघ्न डाल दिया जिससे देवों का जप एवं होम बाधित हो गया। इस पर देवों ने मन्त्रपूर्वक अग्नि में आहुति डालकर कद्रू की एक आँख विनष्ट कर दी। इस दण्ड से भयभीत होकर दोनों उसके निराकरण के लिए अपने पति तार्क्ष (कश्यप) ऋषि के पास गईं॥७॥

[पूर्वकाल में] एक बार बालखिल्य वर्ग के कोई दो ऋषि पलाश के पत्तों के वृन्तों को समिधा के रूप में होम के उद्देश्य से ला रहे थे कि वे गाय के खुर से बने हुए एक गड्ढे में फँसकर कीचड़ में सन गए॥८॥

इतने छोटे से गड्ढे में डूबकर कीचड़ में सने हुए उन बालखिल्य ऋषियों की दशा को देखकर इन्द्र उनकी लघुता का उपहास करता हुआ हँस दिया जिससे वे क्रोधित हो गए और तार्क्ष ऋषि (प्रजापति महर्षि कश्यप) के पास पहुँचे॥९॥

[*बालखिल्यगण*]

"हम आपको अपनी तपस्या का आधा तेज प्रदान करते हैं। उस तेज के सम्मिलित प्रभाव से आप एक तेजस्वी पुत्र को पक्षी के रूप में उत्पन्न कीजिए जो इन्द्र के दर्प को चूर कर सके जिसे अपने ऊपर इतना घमण्ड है"॥१०॥

[*प्रस्तोता*]

महान् यशस्वी महर्षि कश्यप ने बालखिल्य ऋषियों की तपस्या का आधा तेज आत्मसात् कर अपनी विनता नामक पत्नी में एक ऐसे गर्भ को स्थापित किया जो समस्त पक्षियों में सर्वोत्कृष्ट था॥११॥

॥ द्वितीय सूक्त ॥

तृतीय वर्ग

[*प्रस्तोता*]

अपनी विशुद्ध देह (गर्भाशय) में महर्षि कश्यप के उस पवित्र बीज को धारण कर विनता गर्भवती हो गई और जब समय पूर्ण हो गया तो उसने अपने शरीर से तीन अण्डों को निःसृत किया॥१॥

अण्डों से बच्चों के शीघ्र निकलने की प्रतीक्षा में व्याकुल होकर उस सुन्दरी ने सबसे पहले उस अण्डे में छेद कर दिया जो उसने सबसे पहले दिया था। जैसे ही अण्डा फूटा उसमें से एक ज्योतिपुञ्ज निकलकर आकाश की ओर उड़ गया जिसे आज मेघों की सहचरी विद्युत् के नाम से जाना जाता है॥२॥

अपनी इस उतावली पर उसे अत्यन्त ग्लानि हुई और बहुत सोचते-सोचते कुछ समय तक और प्रतीक्षा करने के उपरान्त उसने बीच वाले, दूसरे अण्डे को भी तोड़ दिया जिससे सूर्यदेव का सखा अरुण बाहर निकला॥३॥

अरुण ने उत्पन्न होते ही अपनी तपस्विनी माता को बुरा-भला कहा और बोला – "माँ, तुमने घोर पापपूर्ण यह कितना बुरा काम किया! तुम कितनी क्रूर हो, देख नहीं रही हो कि अभी मेरे पैरों का ही निर्माण नहीं हो पाया है?"॥४॥

जैसे ही सूर्यदेव को अरुण के जन्म का पता लगा वे विनता के पास आए और बोले – "देवी, बच्चे की विकलांगता पर दुःख मत करो। अपने इस बालक को मुझे दे दो, तुम्हारा यह पुत्र मेरे ओजस्वी अश्वों के वेग को नियन्त्रित करने में पूर्ण समर्थ है"॥५॥

(महाभारत के अनुसार अरुण के कहने पर विनता तीसरे अण्डे के स्वतः फूटने की प्रतीक्षा करती है जिसमें एक सहस्र वर्ष लगते हैं।)

चतुर्थ वर्ग

[*प्रस्तोता*]

जैसे ही गरुड का जन्म हुआ तीनों लोक काँप उठे। पर्वतों एवं वनों समेत समस्त पृथ्वी थर्रा गई॥६॥

आकाश से सूर्य एवं चन्द्रमा लुप्त हो गए। तारों की ज्योति बुझ गई। हवाओं का चलना बन्द हो गया और देवगण एक अज्ञात आशंका से घबरा उठे॥७॥

गभर्वती नारियों का गर्भ धारण किए रहना कठिन हो गया। समुद्रों का जल सूख

गया। गायों के थनों में दूध नहीं रहा और वे भय से व्याकुल होकर इधर-उधर भागने लगीं॥८॥

वेदपाठी ब्राह्मण वेद भूल गए। सभी प्रजातियों के सर्प भयाक्रान्त हो गए। उन्हें अपने चारों ओर [अपना विनाशक] गरुड ही दिखाई देने लगा जिससे वे [भयभीत होकर, अपने प्राणदान के लिए] गरुड की ही शरण में गए॥९॥

गरुड द्वारा अभय प्रदान किए जाने पर वे तत्काल अपने-अपने स्थान पर चले गए (= जाकर छिप गए) और [जिनके] गरुड के जन्म से [भयत्रस्त होने के कारण] प्राण-पखेरू उड़ गए थे, उन्हें स्वयंभू-ब्रह्मा ने पुनः जीवन प्रदान कर दिया॥१०॥

जिनका शरीर सम्पूर्ण वेदों से निर्मित है, जो एक सहस्र वर्ष तक गर्भ में रहने के उपरान्त मघा नक्षत्र में उत्पन्न हुए हैं, उनमें अग्नि का स्तम्भन करने की शक्ति होती है (अग्नि का प्रभाव उनके शरीर पर नहीं होता)॥१२॥

॥ तृतीय सूक्त ॥

पञ्चम वर्ग

[प्रस्तोता]

हम विनता के पुत्र उन गरुड की स्तुति करते हैं जो असीम ओजस्वी हैं, अप्रतिम वीरों का भी सामना करने में समर्थ हैं और जिन्होंने अपनी उस माता को दासता से मुक्त कराया जिसे उसकी सपत्नी कद्रू ने [एक शर्त में] पराजित करके अपनी दासी बना लिया था॥१॥

अब मैं उन शोभाशाली विनता-पुत्र गरुड के उस महान् कृत्य का वर्णन करूँगा जो स्वर्ग से पृथ्वी पर सोम को लाने से सम्बन्धित है और जिसके कारण उनका यश सम्पूर्ण विश्व में फैला हुआ है॥२॥

[कथारम्भ]

एक बार कद्रू एवं सुपर्णी में विवाद हुआ कि पक्षि-स्वरूप एवं सर्प-स्वरूप में कौन-सा स्वरूप अधिक उत्तम है। विवाद में कद्रू ने सुपर्णी (सुन्दर पंखों वाली) विनता को हरा दिया। इस पर विनता कद्रू से बोली॥३॥ –

[विनता]

“लोग सच ही कहते हैं कि लम्बे शरीर वाले ये साँप हृदय से ही सदैव दुष्ट होते

हैं। स्वयं तो तू कानी है कद्रू, किन्तु जब भी कोई विवाद होता है तो मेरे पुत्र (अरुण)[१] [की विकलांगता] के विषय में कठोर वचन कहकर मेरे हृदय को छेदती रहती है"॥४॥

[*कद्रू*]

"अरुण की माता, विनता, [आ, शर्त लगाते हैं कि] जितना तू दोनों आँखों से देखती है अगर मैं अपनी एक आँख से उतना (उससे अधिक) न देख पाऊँ तो तेरी दासी बन जाऊँगी नहीं तो तुझे मेरी दासी बनना पड़ेगा"॥५॥

छठा वर्ग

[*कद्रू*]

"विनता, समुद्र के उस पार देख। मैंने सुना है कि तेरी दृष्टि आकाशचारी पक्षियों की भाँति तेज़ है। देख, उधर वृक्ष का एक ठूँठ खड़ा है। वहाँ [इन्द्र के] श्वेतवर्णी अश्व (उच्चैःश्रवा) ने आकर अपना शरीर रगड़ा है जिससे उसके कुछ काले बालों का एक गुच्छा उसमें अटककर नीचे लटक रहा है और हवा के झोंकों से वह दाहिनी-बाईं ओर हिल रहा है"।

[*विनता*]

"अरी, तेरी आँखें धुँधली हो गई हैं, क्या? या मदिरा के नशे में पागल हो रही है? मुझे तो कोई [काले] बाल नहीं दिखाई दे रहे"!

[*कद्रू*]

"तो फिर तुझे क्या दिखाई दे रहा है? बता कि घोड़ा श्वेत है या काला? क्या बात है, क्यों और किस कारण से तू देख नहीं पा रही है?"

[*विनता*]

"अरी कानी कद्रू, तुझे ठीक प्रकार से दिखाई नहीं देता। तू झूठ बोल रही है। मैं समझती हूँ, घोड़ा पूरा का पूरा सफ़ेद है, उसके शरीर का कोई भाग काला नहीं है"॥९॥

"अगर ऐसा है, सर्पों की माता, जैसा कि तू कह रही है और तू झूठ नहीं बोल रही तो मैं तेरी दासी हो जाऊँगी। अन्यथा, धरती-स्वरूपिणी कद्रू, यदि तू हार गई तो तुझे मेरी दासता स्वीकार करनी पड़ेगी"॥१०॥

---

[१] अभी गरुड का जन्म नहीं हुआ है।

"ऐसा करते हैं कि हम दोनों तीव्रगामी मातरिश्वा (वायु का अधिष्ठाता देवता) को दूत के रूप में वहाँ भेजें और प्रतीक्षा करें कि वह आकर बताए कि यथार्थ क्या है। या ऐसा कर सकते हैं कि हम दोनों स्वयं वहाँ चलें, मैं तुम्हें अपनी पीठ पर बैठाकर वहाँ ले चलती हूँ जहाँ वह घोड़ा विचरण कर रहा है"॥११॥

॥ चतुर्थ सूक्त ॥

सातवाँ वर्ग

[*कद्रू*]

"यह देखो, बालों का यह गुच्छा सूखे वृक्ष के इस शंकु (ठूँठ) से लटक रहा है। इसे लटकता हुआ देख रही हो, कि नहीं? यह समुद्र साक्षी है[२] कि मैंने शर्त जीतकर तुम्हें हरा दिया है। अब तुम मेरी दासी होकर रहोगी और मेरी आज्ञा से सभी प्रकार का शारीरिक श्रम तुम्हें करना होगा"॥१॥

[*कद्रू एवं नागगण*]

"हमने सुना है कि समुद्र के बीच में एक अत्यन्त मनोरम द्वीप है जहाँ नाग पहले निवास किया करते थे, विनता, तुम हम सबको वहाँ ले चलो"॥२॥

[*विनता स्वगत*]

"मैं अपनी पीठ पर बैठाकर इसे (कद्रू को) ले जा रही हूँ, इन नागों को ले जा रही हूँ, जहाँ इनका मन होता है, वहाँ इधर-उधर घुमा रही हूँ, मानों मैंने कोई पाप-कर्म कर डाला हो जिसका प्रायश्चित्त मुझे भोगना पड़ रहा है। इस दुष्ट कद्रू को उसके पुत्रों सहित, उनके भार से झुकी हुई मैं, समुद्र के जल को लगभग स्पर्श-सी करती हुई एक द्वीप से दूसरे द्वीप तक उड़ी चली जा रही हूँ"॥३॥

---

[२] जल में (विशेषतः समुद्र में) वरुण का वास है और वैदिक मान्यता के अनुसार वरुण ऋत-सत्य के रक्षक हैं, वे प्राणियों के सत्यानृत को देखते रहते हैं और तदनुसार उन्हें अनुशासित करते हैं (तु. की., "यासां राजा वरुणो याति मध्ये सत्यानृते अवपश्यन् जनानाम् . . ." — ऋ.वे. ७.४९.३ आदि)। जल हाथ में लेकर शपथ लेने की परम्परा प्राचीनकाल से आज तक चली आई है ("गंगाजली उठाना") हमारी धार्मिक परम्परा में चौदह देव साक्षी माने गए हैं – आदित्यचन्द्रावनिलोऽनलश्च द्यौर्भूमिरापो हृदयं यमश्च। अहश्च रात्रिश्च उभे च सन्ध्ये धर्मश्च जानाति नरस्य वृत्तम् (पञ्चतन्त्र)॥

आठवाँ वर्ग

[कद्रू विनता से]

"विनता, वह जो तुम्हारा युवा पुत्र [गरुड] है, उसको भेजो। जब वह पंख फैलाकर उड़ता है तो जिसके डैने आकाश को भेदते हैं। वह बलवान् है, उससे कहो, कि वह आए और हम सबको वहाँ तक ऊँचा उड़ाकर ले जाए जहाँ पर सूरज चमक रहा है"॥४॥

(गरुड का प्रवेश)

[सुपर्ण-गरुड सर्पों से]

"मैं गरुड हूँ। मुझे बड़े भाई अरुण ने यहाँ भेजा है। हे सर्पों, जैसा मेरी माता शुंगी ने वचन दिया है, मैं वैसा ही करूँगा। आओ मेरे शरीर से लिपट जाओ। मैं अभी तुरन्त तुम सबको सूर्य के पास ले चलता हूँ"॥५॥

(गरुड नागों को लेकर सूर्य के समीप तक पहुँचते हैं)

[नागगण गरुड से]

"हे सुपर्ण, सूर्य की ये किरणें अत्यधिक तीक्ष्ण हैं। ये हमारे फनों को जलाए डाल रही हैं। सूर्य को हम प्रणाम करते हैं। हमें भली-भाँति (सुरक्षित) नीचे ले चलो वहाँ, जहाँ हमारी माता अदिति (कद्रू) विराजमान हैं"॥६॥

"हम सूर्य के घर नहीं जाना चाहते। सूर्य की ज्वालाओं से हमारा शरीर झुलस गया है। गरुड, या तो हमारे कहने से लौट चलो, या फिर हम तुम्हें छोड़कर नीचे पृथ्वी पर कूद पड़ते हैं"॥७॥

(नाग पृथ्वी पर गिर पड़ते हैं)

[कद्रू की सुपर्णा से शिकायत]

"विनता, यह बहुत ही अनुचित है कि तुम्हारा पुत्र आकाश में उड़ाकर बलात् मेरे पुत्र नागों को सूर्य के समीप ले गया जबकि वे पीड़ा से छटपटा रहे थे और निर्जीव से हो चुके थे"॥८॥

॥ पञ्चम सूक्त ॥

नवाँ वर्ग

[कद्रू की अरुण से शिकायत]

"यह देखो अरुण, ये फणधारी नाग सूर्य की उष्णता से झुलसकर पृथ्वी पर पड़े हुए हैं। मैं नहीं जानती कि ये अब कैसे ठीक होंगे। इनके पिता तार्क्ष (कश्यप)

भी इस समय यहाँ नहीं हैं, वे ही सम्भवतः इनके कल्याण के लिए कुछ कर सकते थे"॥१॥

[कद्रू की गरुड से शिकायत]

"गरुड, जो तुम [मेरे बेटों के लगातार मना करने पर भी उनको] बलपूर्वक सूर्य के समीप तक ले गए, यह तुमने बहुत ही कठोर काम किया है"।

[प्रस्तोता]

बेटों के झुलस जाने से अत्यन्त संतप्त कद्रू [विनता-गरुड आदि से बार-बार] कह रही है कि तुम लोग दास हो और दासों को अपने स्वामियों के आगे सिर झुकाकर रहना चाहिए॥२॥

[तार्क्ष्य-कश्यप आकर पर्जन्यदेव की स्तुति करते हैं]

"गरजो पर्जन्य, बिजली कड़काओ, [अपनी बूँदों से] समुद्रों के जल को ताड़ित करो, [इतना बरसो कि] तुम्हारे जल पहाड़ों की ऊँचाई छू लें। शेषनाग [की भाँति श्वेत, लम्बी और चमकीली विद्युत्] पर्वतों की चोटियों पर प्रहार करे और सर्पों के शरीर जल में डूब जाएँ"॥३॥

"यहाँ से वहाँ तक, आर-पार, केवल जल ही जल दिखाई दे। पूरी रात मेंढकियाँ टर्राती रहें। जल से पृथ्वी ऐसे डूबे कि हरिण अपने लिए सूखी भूमि खोजते फिरें और [फिर इतनी घास उत्पन्न हो जाए कि] चलने-फिरने में असमर्थ वृद्ध गाएँ भी दूध देने लग जाएँ"॥४॥

दसवाँ वर्ग

(विनता गरुड को आँसू बहाते हुए देखकर पूछती है)

[विनता गरुड से]

गरुड, ये [चुपचाप बैठे] आँसू क्यों बहा रहे हो? तुम महर्षि तार्क्ष्य (कश्यप) के पुत्र हो, तुम्हारी सर्वत्र निर्बाध और सतत गति है जिसके कारण तुम्हें "अरिष्टनेमि"[३] की संज्ञा मिली हुई है। पक्षियों के तुम सम्राट् हो, आकाशचारी हो। ऐसे कुल में जन्मे [और इतने सामर्थ्यवान्] पुत्र के लिए दुःखी होने का कोई कारण नहीं है, ऐसा मैं समझती हूँ॥५॥

---

[३] रिष्ट (रिष् = घिसना, रिष्ट = घिसा हुआ), अरिष्ट = बिना घिसा हुआ। नेमि = पहिए का बाहरी गोलवृत्त या उसमें पड़ा हुआ लोहे का गोल घेरा। अरष्टिनेमि = लगातार चलते रहने पर भी जिसके रथ के पहिए की नेमि न घिसे। आलंकारिक अर्थ – कभी न थकने वाला।

[गरुड माता से]

माँ विनता तुम [मेरी ही नहीं, अपितु सूर्य के सारथी तेजस्वी] अरुण की भी माता हो। [मुझे अपने लिए नहीं अपितु तुम्हारे लिए शोक है]। जिस प्रकार बिना किसी संकोच के तुम्हारी आँखों से आँसुओं के ये मोती झरते रहते हैं वैसा मैंने किसी भी युवती माँ को करते हुए नहीं देखा॥६॥

सभी लोक मेरी आँखों के सामने हैं, माँ! मैं सबको देख रहा हूँ और अपने ओज, बल और अपने वेग के कारण इन सभी को पछाड़ सकता हूँ।[४] आखिर, मैं कैसे दास के रूप में उत्पन्न हुआ? तुमने क्या पाप किया था? या कि फिर मेरे पिता ने कोई बुरा काम किया था?॥७॥

[विनता गरुड से]

एक बार उस कद्रू से स्पर्धा करते हुए रोष में आकर मैंने एक शर्त लगा ली थी। उस समय मुझे पता नहीं था कि इसका परिणाम इतना भयानक होगा। और उसने मुझे इस विवाद में [दासी के रूप में] जीत लिया॥८॥

[गरुड माता से]

कैसे मैं तुम्हें इस दुःसह दासता से मुक्ति दिलाऊँ? मैं स्वयं तुम्हारे स्थान पर दास बन जाऊँ या कि फिर कोई बड़ा सा भू-भाग उसे देकर तुम्हें छुड़ा लूँ? शुंगे माँ, शीघ्र बताओ, मैं बहुत व्याकुल हो रहा हूँ। बहुत सा अन्न (भक्ष्य पदार्थ) उसे देने से तुम्हारी मुक्ति सम्भव होगी या प्रचुर धन उसे देने से?॥९॥

जाओ, जाकर सर्पों से पूछो कि क्या किसी प्रकार से तुम्हारी मुक्ति सम्भव है – मेरे द्वारा, अरुण के द्वारा, अथवा पशुओं के या धन के प्रतिदान से?॥१०॥

॥ छठा सूक्त ॥

ग्यारहवाँ वर्ग

(विनता सर्पों के पास जाती है)

[विनता सर्पों से]

"न मेरे पुत्रों का पता है, न मेरे पति का [मेरा कोई सहायक नहीं]। तुम लोगों को पीठ पर ढोती-ढोती मैं अबला दुर्बल हो गई हूँ। अब मेरे शरीर में न तो उतना बल रह गया है, न ही उड़ान में तीव्रता। यह वृद्धा तुम लोगों की दासता से कैसे मुक्त होगी, बताओ"॥१॥

---

[४] अन्वेमि (अनु+एमि)=भागते हुए [शत्रु का] पीछा करना।

बताओ सर्पो, क्या लाकर, क्या जीतकर, या तुम्हारे लिए कौन-सा पौरुषपूर्ण कार्य करके मैं तुम लोगों की दासता से मुक्त हो सकती हूँ?॥२॥

[*सर्पगण विनता से*]

"इन्द्र का अमृत आकाश के [उच्चतम] तीसरे पृष्ठभाग पर एक गुफा में रखा हुआ है, जहाँ स्वर्गलोक का अन्तिम छोर है। उस कल्याणकारी अमृत को लाकर हम लोगों को दे दो, तुरन्त दास्यभाव से मुक्त हो जाओ और सुख से रहो"॥३॥

"हमने सुना है कि उस सर्वोत्तम पेय को इन्द्र ने अत्यन्त कड़ी सुरक्षा में सर्वोच्च आकाश में स्थापित कर रखा है। उसको पाकर हम सब अमरत्व प्राप्त कर लेंगे। यदि तुम्हारे पास क्षमता है तो उसे मँगवाओ और दासीभाव से मुक्त हो जाओ"॥४॥

बारहवाँ वर्ग

[*विनता लौटकर गरुड से*]

हे गरुड, सर्पगण अमृतपान करना चाहते हैं, जिसको वे चाहते हैं कि हम उनको स्वर्ग से लाकर दें। अमृत को स्वर्ग से लाना बहुत कठिन है जिसके कारण मुझे अपना निष्क्रय (अमृत देकर अपनी स्वतन्त्रता प्राप्त करना) कठिन लग रहा है॥५॥

[*गरुड माता से*]

मैं तुम्हें वचन देता हूँ, सुन्दर पंखों वाली माँ, विनता, कि यदि तुमने कभी ब्रह्म-हत्या नहीं की है तो तुम्हारे लिए (तुम्हारी इच्छा पूर्ण करने के लिए) आकाश की सर्वोच्च भूमिका से अमृत लाने के लिए उस सुदूर स्थान तक, उड़कर जाऊँगा॥६॥

[*विनता गरुड से*]

"मैंने कभी किसी ब्राह्मण की हत्या नहीं की, साथ ही न ही कभी किसी यज्ञ में विघ्न डाला।[५] इस प्रकार के पाप से मैं सर्वथा मुक्त हूँ और किसी अन्य का पाप भी मैंने उसका प्रायश्चित्त करने के लिए अपने ऊपर नहीं ले रखा है॥७॥

[*गरुड माता से*]

[तो फिर] इन्द्र ने जो सोम [अमृत] आकाश के उच्चतम तृतीय फलक पर गुफा में छिपा रखा है, वहाँ तक जाकर और उसके रक्षकों को मारकर तुम्हारे लिए वह सोम (अमृत) लेकर मैं त्वरित गति से शीघ्र वापिस आ जाऊँगा। तुम्हें इसमें कोई सन्देह है, क्या?॥८॥

---

[५] "ब्रह्म" शब्द का एक अर्थ यज्ञ भी है अतः ब्रह्म-हत्या, का तात्पर्य किसी यज्ञ में विघ्न डालना, उसको नष्ट कर देना भी हो सकता है (जैसा कद्रू ने किया था)।

[*विनता गरुड से*]

बेटे, उस सोम की रक्षा न केवल सारे देवता मिलकर करते हैं, अपितु और भी अनेक बड़े-बड़े विविध प्रकार के जन्तु उसकी रक्षा में तत्पर हैं, यह समझ लो। यदि तुम्हारे लिए यह कार्य कठिन है तो विचार छोड़ दो। मेरे लिए अपनी दासता से तुम्हारा जीवन अधिक प्यारा है॥९॥

[*गरुड माता से*]

हे सुन्दर पंखों वाली माँ विनता, हम वे छन्द हैं जो यज्ञ-कर्म के समस्त विस्तार को अपने अन्दर धारण किए रहते हैं। ब्रह्मा ने न जाने कितनी बार यज्ञ सम्पादन के अवसर पर हमको सबसे आगे रखा है। इस प्रकार तुम हमारी शक्ति को कम करके मत आँको॥१०॥

जिन चार प्रमुख,[६] छन्दों से युक्त कुल सात छन्द, "सप्ततन्तु" संज्ञा से प्रसिद्ध यज्ञ के समस्त विस्तार को अपने में समेटे रहते हैं, मैं वही हूँ। मुझे देवगण सोम लाने के लिए (सोम की ओर) प्रायः भेजा करते हैं॥११॥

॥ सप्तम सूक्त ॥

[*गरुड माता से*]

तेरहवाँ वर्ग

हे सुन्दर पंखों वाली माँ, जो भोजन नहीं करता, उसके शरीर में इस जगत् में इधर-उधर भ्रमण करने की भी शक्ति नहीं होती। इसलिए माँ विनता, मैं तुमसे यह पूछना चाहता हूँ कि क्या खाकर मैं देवलोक को प्रस्थान करूँ?

[*विनता गरुड से*]

देखो, यह सामने एक विशाल पर्वत है, इसकी चोटी पर एक बड़ा सा सरोवर है, उसमें एक बहुत बड़ा जन्तु रहता है। इस समय उसमें एक हाथी उतर रहा है, अब वह [जन्तु] उसे पकड़ लेगा। वही तुम्हारा भोजन है। इन दोनों को देखो, बेटे!॥२॥

यह पद्म जाति का घोषवान् नामक विशाल हाथी है। बहुत लम्बे-लम्बे इसके दाँत हैं। [अपने विशाल डील-डौल और अपने धूम्रवर्ण के कारण] यह दूर से एक

---

[६] ऋग्वेद के प्रमुख चार छन्द गायत्री, त्रिष्टुप्, जगती तथा उष्णिक् (या पंक्ति) हैं। शेष तीन का स्वरूप भी इन्हीं के ऊपर आधारित है। अनुष्टुप् ऋग्वेद में प्रधान नहीं, किन्तु उसका महत्त्व निरन्तर बढ़ता गया।

मेघखण्ड जैसा जान पड़ता है। विधाता ने इसे और इसके सहचर [उस जलीय जन्तु को] तुम्हारे लिए उपलब्ध कर दिया है। इन दोनों का भक्षण करके तुम देवलोक के लिए प्रस्थान कर सकते हो॥३॥

[*गरुड स्वगत, दोनों जन्तुओं को पकड़ने के बाद*]

मैं इन दोनों बड़े जन्तुओं को पकड़कर बहुत प्रसन्न हूँ – एक सुपद्म हाथी और दूसरा उसका यह साथी। इन दोनों को लेकर मैं अपने मार्ग पर [घर की ओर] उड़ा चला जा रहा हूँ और जाकर इन दोनों को खाऊँगा॥४॥

[*गरुड माता से*]

हम लोग पक्षी हैं, माँ सुपर्णी। इसलिए हमको भूमि पर बैठकर खाना अच्छा नहीं लगता। यदि तुम्हें किसी उपयुक्त वृक्ष का पता हो, तो बताओ जिस पर बैठकर मैं रुचिपूर्वक इस भोजन का आनन्द ले सकूँ॥५॥

[*विनता गरुड से*]

सुपर्ण गरुड, जल्दी से वृक्षों में श्रेष्ठ इस रौहिण नामक वृक्ष की ओर चले जाओ। तुम्हारे पिता का यह एक प्रकार से सखा है (उनका प्रिय है)। इसकी शाखाएँ बहुत लम्बी हैं और अनेक योजनों तक फैली हुई हैं। बालखिल्य और वैखानस ऋषिगण इस पर निवास करते हैं। इसी पर चढ़कर भोजन करो। यही एक वृक्ष है जो सम्भवतः तुम्हारा [और तुम्हारे भक्ष्यों का] भार सह सकता है, कोई अन्य वृक्ष नहीं॥६ एवं ७॥

(*गरुड रौहिण वृक्ष की ओर उड़ते हैं*)

[*रौहिण वृक्ष, स्वयं से*]

चौदहवाँ वर्ग

मेरु पर्वत के समान एक अतीव बलशाली हाथी को और एक विशाल ग्राह को पकड़कर अन्तरिक्ष में उड़ता हुआ और अपने पंखों से उद्भूत वायु के तेज़ झोंकों से मुझे प्रकम्पित करता हुआ यह सुपर्ण मेरी ही ओर उड़ा चला आ रहा है॥८॥

[*गरुड रौहिण से*]

हे रौहिण, स्थिर हो जाओ, ऐसा न हो कि मैं [तब तक] थकान के मारे मूर्च्छित हो जाऊँ। मैं गरुत्मान् हूँ जिसका शरीर छन्दों और देवताओं के सम्मिश्रण से बना हुआ है। अब मैं, गरुड, बलात् तुम्हारे ऊपर चढ़ने वाला हूँ॥९॥

[*रौहिण वृक्ष गरुड से*]

गरुड, यह जो पूर्व की ओर फैली हुई शाखा है, और जिसमें बालखिल्य ऋषि और वैखानस मुनि अवस्थित हैं, उसी पर आकर बैठ जाओ। यह जो शाखा पश्चिम की ओर जा रही है वह नीचे की ओर झुकी हुई है (अतः बैठकर भोजन करने के लिए उपयुक्त नहीं है), किन्तु यदि तुम्हें (बालखिल्यों से युक्त) पूर्व की शाखा पर बैठने में कोई दोष लग रहा है और डर रहे हो (तो पश्चिम की शाखा भी ठीक है)॥१०॥

(गरुड पूर्व की शाखा पर बैठने का निर्णय लेते हैं, किन्तु उनके बैठते ही शाखा टूट जाती है)

[*रौहिण वृक्ष गरुड से*]

अरे, तुमने शाखा तोड़ डाली ! [अब] इन ब्राह्मणों को पृथ्वी पर गिराकर मार डालोगे ! बहुत बड़ा पाप लगेगा ! गहन अन्धकार से युक्त लोक (नरक) में गिरोगे गरुड, और उस सोम को तो अब ला ही नहीं सकते॥११॥

॥ अष्टम सूक्त ॥

पन्द्रहवाँ वर्ग

(गरुड शाखा को बाएँ पंजे से पकड़कर गिरने से रोकते हुए आकाश में चक्कर लगाते हैं)

[*नेपथ्य से प्रस्तोता अथवा जनसंकुल, समवेत स्वर में*]

"बाएँ पंजे से शाखा को पकड़े हुए और दाहिने से अन्य दो [जन्तुओं] को! ज़रा गरुड का बल तो देखो, इसके बल का वर्णन तो वाणी से परे है॥१॥

(गरुड हिमालय की ओर उड़ते हैं)

[*गरुड हिमालय से*]

हे हिमवान्, तुम्हारी चोटी पर उड़ता हुआ यह मैं तुम्हारा प्यारा बेटा [गरुड] हूँ। माँ ने मुझे यहाँ भेजा है॥१-१/२॥

[*हिमालय पर्वत गरुड से*]

इस शाखा को पैर (पंजे) से काटकर नीचे की ओर [घाटी की गहराई में] फेंक दो और पंखों को समेटकर किसी समतल शिला पर बैठ जाओ॥२॥

(गरुड भोजन करके वापिस लौटते हैं और आकाश से ही माँ को पुकारते हैं)

[*विनता स्वगत*]

यह कौन मुझे इतना हर्षित करने वाली वाणी में आसमान से पुकार रहा है? मेरा एक बेटा (अरुण) तो इस समय सोया हुआ होगा और दूसरा इस समय [अन्यत्र] भोजन करने गया है॥३॥

दूर से ही यह अपनी आवाज़ से आकाश, अन्तरिक्ष, दिशाओं के छोर तथा पृथ्वी को निनादित करता हुआ इधर ही चला आ रहा है। लगता है, यह मेरे, शुंगी के पुत्रों में से ही कोई एक है, अरुण या गरुड, जो घर वापिस आ रहा है॥४॥

(गरुड उतरकर माँ से)

माँ, रौहिण वृक्ष की एक शाखा को पकड़कर उड़ता हुआ मैं बहुत थक गया जो इतनी मोटी थी कि चमड़े के एक साथ जुड़े हुए सौ फ़ीते भी उसकी पूरी मोटाई को नापने के लिए[७] कम पड़ते॥५॥

माता शुंगी, मैंने हिमालय की एक शिला पर बैठकर ग्राह सहित उस हाथी को तो खा लिया, परन्तु लगता है, अभी कुछ खाया ही नहीं है। अतः कुछ और खाने योग्य बड़ी वस्तु बताओ जिसे खाकर और पूर्ण तृप्त होकर फिर मैं तुरन्त स्वर्ग के लिए प्रस्थान करूँ॥६॥

[विनता के 'और क्या खाना चाहते हो' इस प्रश्न पर गरुड]

सोलहवाँ वर्ग

जो [गो आदि] जंगम प्राणी हैं वे प्रायः (तृण, घास आदि) स्थावर वस्तुओं का भक्षण करते हैं, ऐसी उनकी सदा से चली आ रही [प्राकृतिक] जीविका है। किन्तु [हम] पक्षियों के लिए स्थावर एवं जंगम दोनों प्रकार के भक्ष्य निर्धारित हैं॥७॥

[*विनता गरुड से*]

निषादों की एक बस्ती है जिसमें बसने वाले परस्पर झगड़ते रहते हैं। न तो ये लोग वेदादि सुनते हैं और न ही यज्ञादि करते हैं। मेरे कार्य की सिद्धि के लिए तुम जाकर

---

[७] मूल में प्रयुक्त शब्द है "परिहरेत्"। "परि" उपसर्ग गोलाई, वर्तुलता को आवृत्त करने की ओर इंगित करता है। "परिहरति" का अर्थ है किसी वस्तु के चारों ओर गोलाई में घूमकर जाना (बिना उसे स्पर्श किए हुए, इसीलिए "परिहार" का अर्थ है छोड़ना, त्याग करना), महाभारत इस स्थान पर परिणहेत् (परि+नह्) का प्रयोग करता है, जिससे निष्पन्न "परिणाह" शब्द गोलाई या मोटाई का वाची है।

उन्हीं का भक्षण कर लो, वह तुम्हारे लिए उचित भक्ष्य है, गरुड॥८॥

हे वीरवर [बस यह ध्यान रखना कि उस बस्ती में रहने वाले और] निषादों के बीच में विचरण करने वाले ब्राह्मणों की हिंसा मत करना, वे देव-स्वरूप होते हैं और उनका भक्षण तुम्हारे लिए मृत्यु होगा, और कोई नहीं॥९॥

[*गरुड माता से*]

माँ विनता, मैं तुमसे यह पूछना चाहता हूँ कि वहाँ सभी तो एक सिर, दो पैर और दो हाथों वाले होंगे, उनको यदि मैंने पकड़ लिया तो मैं कैसे समझूँगा कि उनमें से कौन-सा ब्राह्मण है? ब्राह्मण का स्वरूप किस प्रकार का होता है?॥१०॥

॥ नवमं सूक्तम् ॥

सत्रहवाँ वर्ग

[*विनता गरुड से*]

ब्राह्मण होता है धूल-धूसरित, जटाएँ रखने वाला, मलिन दाँतों वाला और अपनी शिखा को ऊपर की ओर ले जाकर बाँधने वाला। वह सदैव केवल सत्य ही बोलता है, शत्रुओं के बीच में पड़कर भी वह मृत्यु से नहीं डरता [जो व्यक्ति तुम्हें ऐसा मिले] वह ब्राह्मण है। उसे कभी मत मारना, गरुड!॥१॥

[*विनता*]

जिस व्यक्ति को छः अग्नियाँ निरन्तर तपाती रहती हैं – ग्रीष्मकालीन धूप, शिशिरकालीन शीत, जिह्वा की अग्नि (स्वादरहित भोजन के कारण), अपमान आदि का बदला न लेने के कारण हृदय की अग्नि, निरन्तर उपवास करने से जठराग्नि और ब्रह्मचर्य धारण करने से उत्पन्न आन्तरिक तेज। वह ब्राह्मण है, उसे मत मारना, गरुड॥२॥[८]

जैसे काँटे में लगा चारा निगलकर मछली का उदर भारी हो जाता है वैसे ही ब्राह्मण को खाकर [अन्य हिंस्र प्राणियों का]। वह अंगारे की भाँति गले को जलाता हुआ नीचे (उदर में) उतरता है। ब्राह्मण इस प्रकार का होता है। उसे गरुड, मत मारना॥३॥

---

[८] इस वर्ग का प्रथम मन्त्र षोडश वर्ग के अन्त में अनूदित।

[गरुड माता से]

मुझे अपने सनातन भोजन का पता चल गया। अब मैं तुम्हारे लिए सोम ले आऊँगा। भूखा तो इतना हूँ कि लगता है कि कहीं सम्पूर्ण स्थावर और जंगम दोनों को ही न खा जाऊँ!॥४॥

अठारहवाँ वर्ग

[प्रस्तोता दर्शकों से]

इसके पश्चात् माता को दिए गए वचन के अनुसार उनकी आज्ञा से भूखे गरुड ने निषादों का भक्षण प्रारम्भ कर दिया। वे पंख फैलाकर समेट लेते थे और जितने झोंकों के साथ खिंचकर पंखों के अन्दर आ जाते थे उन्हें मुँह में डाल लेते थे॥५॥

उछल-उछलकर निषादों को खाते हुए पक्षिराज के मुख में अकस्मात् एक [पुरुष] आ पड़ा जिससे उनका कण्ठ अग्नि की ढेरी के समान जलने लगा॥६॥

न तो मुँह से धुआँ निकल रहा था और न ही चिनगारियाँ [अतः कण्ठ में अंगारों का होना तो सम्भव नहीं था] फिर भी वे दाह से व्याकुल थे। ऐसी स्थिति में उन्हें माता शुंगा के वचनों का स्मरण हो आया [और मन ही मन उन्होंने सोचा] "बहुत ही विस्मयकारी है द्विजों का यह तेज, जो अपने ज्ञान एवं विद्या मात्र से अपनी जीविका अर्जित करते हैं (अथवा, केवल ज्ञानार्जन या तपस् मात्र के लिए अपना जीवन धारण किए रहते हैं)"॥७॥

[गरुड, ब्राह्मण से]

"हे ब्राह्मणश्रेष्ठ, दुःख मत करो। मेरे अन्दर (उदर में) में जितने भी भक्ष्य (मनुष्य) थे उन सबको निकालकर मैंने पृथ्वी पर खड़ा कर दिया है तुम इनमें से निकल जाओ।" (अथवा "मेरे मुख से निकल जाओ"।)॥८॥

[ब्राह्मण गरुड से]

"अपनी [निषाद-] पत्नी और बच्चों के बिना, जीते हुए भी मैं अपने को जीवित नहीं मानता। एक द्विज के साथ-साथ उसकी निषाद-पत्नी और बच्चे भी तुम्हारे मुख में विष के समान हैं"॥९॥

[प्रस्तोता]

सपरिवार उस ब्राह्मण को छोड़, माता की आज्ञा का पालन करते हुए शेष का भक्षण कर, पक्षिराज का [बुभुक्षा शान्त करने का] प्रयोजन सिद्ध हो गया। (अथवा, उन्होंने शीघ्रता से स्वर्ग की ओर प्रस्थान किया [द्रुतं स्वर्गं यातः])॥१०॥

॥ दशम सूक्त ॥

उन्नीसवाँ वर्ग

(गरुड आकाश में उडान भरते हैं)

[*आकाशचारी गरुड की स्तुति, समवेत स्वर में नेपथ्य से*]

शत्रुओं के लिए अपराजेय, पक्षियों के राजा, सुन्दर पंखों वाले दिव्य सुपर्ण (गरुड) की हम नमस्कारपूर्वक वन्दना (उप-स्था = उपासना) करते हैं जो अत्यन्त शौर्यशाली हैं और इस समय अपने विरोधियों के विरुद्ध अभियान पर निकले हुए हैं॥१॥

[***देवगुरु बृहस्पति का प्रवेश***, *स्वर्ग की ओर आकाश में उड़ते हुए गरुड को देखकर उससे देवगुरु का प्रश्न। गरुड का उत्तर*]

हे ब्रह्मर्षि, मैं उड़ने वाले प्राणियों में सर्वश्रेष्ठ "सुपर्ण" हूँ और इस समय माता के आदेश से सोम लाने जा रहा हूँ क्योंकि अरुण की माता[१] दासता में पड़ी हुई [जीवनयापन कर रही] है। इसलिए हे द्विजराज, आप मुझे कार्य की सफलता के लिए आशीर्वाद दीजिए॥२॥

[*बृहस्पति गरुड से*]

बेटे, मैं तुम्हारी आयु और तुम्हारे वर्चस्व की वृद्धि हेतु आशीर्वाद प्रदान करता हूँ। तुम्हारे घर में सब कुशल तो है? हे गरुत्मन्, कहीं अरुण की माता [दिति से की गई] अपनी स्पर्धा के कारण मन में बहुत दु:खी तो नहीं रहती?॥३॥

[*गरुड बृहस्पति से*]

जहाँ तक मुझे ज्ञान है, शेष सब तो कुशल है केवल माता सुपर्णी ही अपनी दासता के कारण दु:ख व्यक्त करती रहती है। हे वैदिक मन्त्रज्ञों में शिरोमणि, अब मैं आपसे विदा लेता हूँ और सोम लेने के लिए स्वर्ग की ओर उड़ रहा हूँ॥४॥

---

[१] गरुड से बृहस्पति की यह पहली भेंट है। गरुड के जन्म को अभी कुछ ही दिन हुए हैं। "मैं माता के आदेश से सोम लेने जा रहा हूँ" गरुड के इस कथन पर बृहस्पति का प्रश्न सम्भावित है कि तुम्हारी माता कौन है? अत: गरुड अगले वाक्य में ही उनका परोक्षतया परिचय दे देते हैं "अरुण की माता दासता में पड़ी हुई है"। अरुण बड़े भाई हैं, बहुत पहले उनका जन्म हो चुका है, वे सूर्य के सारथी हैं। बृहस्पति पहले से उन्हें तथा उनकी माता विनता को जानते हैं, अत: गरुड भी उनके पुत्र हैं, यह बृहस्पति को स्पष्ट हो जाता है।

[बृहस्पति गरुड को आशीर्वाद प्रदान करते हैं]

"यज्ञ एवं दक्षिणा तुम्हारी रक्षा करें। चन्द्रमारूपी वह श्रेष्ठ पेय सोम [स्वर्ग की ओर] उड़ते हुए तुम्हारे सम्मुख रहे। सारे हौत्र कर्म तुम्हारे दाहिने और बाएँ रहें तथा ऋचाएँ और यजुष्-मन्त्र तुम्हें चारों ओर से आवृत्त कर तुम्हारी सहायता करें।"॥५॥

[गरुड का तेज और बल बढ़ाने के लिए नेपथ्य से समवेत स्वर में उनकी स्तुति]

"हम कभी क्लान्त न होने वाले (अपूर्व ओजस्वी), तार्क्ष ऋषि के पुत्र उन विशालकाय गरुड की स्तुति करते हैं जो देवताओं के पक्षी हैं, जो इन्द्र के सखा हैं और युद्धों में उनके साथ असुरों का विनाश करते हैं। हम [अपने शब्दों के द्वारा] उनके विस्तीर्ण यश पर ऐसे आरूढ हों जैसे व्यक्ति नाव पर चढ़ते हैं (हमारे शब्द उनके महान् यश पर आरूढ होकर, उसका उपयुक्त वर्णन करें)"॥६॥

"पापविनाशक ऋषिगण अङ्गिरस, गय और आत्रेय कल्याण करें। हाथ जोड़कर मन ही मन मैं तार्क्ष्य-गरुड की शरण में जाता हूँ, हमारा कल्याण हो, युद्धों में हम सदैव निर्भय रहें (हत या आहत न हों)"॥७॥

बींसवाँ वर्ग

[स्वर्ग में इन्द्र एवं बृहस्पति का पारस्परिक संलाप]

[इन्द्र बृहस्पति से]

बृहस्पति, यह बताओ कि क्या सृष्टि में कोई ऐसा प्राणी है, हो चुका है, या होगा, जो सोम की सुरक्षा के लिए नियत मेरे सभी उपायों को अपने पराक्रम से लाँघकर अचानक मेरे सोम का अपहरण कर ले जाए?॥८॥

[बृहस्पति इन्द्र से]

विनता का पुत्र गरुड सोम ले जाना चाहता है। वह साठ हजार रेत के टीलों (या पर्वतों) एवं नौ हजार नौ सौ नदियों को पार करके भी बलपूर्वक तुम्हारे सोम को उठा ले जाएगा॥९॥

[इन्द्र का बृहस्पति से प्रश्न]

यह [प्राणी] कहाँ से उत्पन्न हो गया? किस लोक से आया? कौन-सी पृथ्वी में जन्म लिया? जो [सोम के रक्षक] अद्वितीय धनुर्धारी भौवन के साथ युद्ध करना चाहता है?॥१०॥

[बृहस्पति इन्द्र से]

विनता नाम की एक सुपर्णी (सुन्दर पंखों वाली) है जिसने अत्यन्त कठोर तपस्या की। उस तपस् के प्रभाव से विनता के पुत्र के रूप में यह गरुड उत्पन्न हुआ है जो पक्षी की आकृति में है और वही [तुम्हारे] सोम को ले जाएगा, यह जान लो॥११॥

॥ एकादश सूक्त ॥

इक्कीसवाँ वर्ग

[इन्द्र बृहस्पति से]

[लोकों का सम्राट्] इन्द्र तो मैं हूँ और यह वैनतेय [मेरे आगे] कौन होता है जिसके विषय में सुन रहा हूँ कि वह विचक्षण सम्पूर्ण लोकों को पार करता हुआ सुदूर, दुर्गम स्थान में सुरक्षित मेरे ही सोम को बलात् उठा ले जाएगा?॥१॥

[बृहस्पति इन्द्र से]

इन्द्र, [तुम ठीक कह रहे हो], जो कुछ भी [चेतन प्राणी] अभी तक उत्पन्न हुए हैं या होंगे उन सबके तुम ही स्वामी हो। ऐसे ही जो कुछ भी जड पदार्थ अभी सृष्टि में है या भविष्य में कभी होगा वह भी तुम्हारा ही है। मुख्य दिशाएँ, उपदिशाएँ और ऊपर-नीचे की दिशाएँ भी तुम्हारी ही हैं। तुम्हारे ही आशीर्वाद और निर्देशों के द्वारा जगत् का व्यापार चल रहा है, ऐसा सभी कहते हैं॥२॥

[आकाश में कोलाहल सुनकर विनता अपने बड़े पुत्र अरुण से]

ऊपर आकाश में यह भयंकर कोलाहल सुनाई पड़ रहा है। पुत्र, तुम अपने भाई की सहायता के लिए क्यों नहीं दौड़ पड़ते। सुपर्ण-गरुड अकेला है और देवता हैं अनेक। अकेले इन्द्र तो उसका सामना नहीं कर सकता था॥३॥

[यदि तुम इस विपत्ति में उसके काम नहीं आए तो समझो] अरुण के रहते हुए भी गरुड बिना किसी भाई के है, तुमको उत्पन्न करके भी सुपर्णी-विनता मानों निपूता ही रह गई।

[अरुण माता से]

माता, अरुण के जाने की बिल्कुल आवश्यकता नहीं है (गरुड स्वयं समर्थ है। अथवा, निरन्तर गतिशील सूर्य के रथ में सारथी होने के कारण मेरा रथ छोड़कर जाना सम्भव नहीं है)। गरुड को अकेले ही स्वर्ग जाने दो॥४॥

बाइसवाँ वर्ग

[*विनता चिन्तित होकर पुनः अरुण से*]

[सोम का रक्षक] वह पंगु भौवन उसका कल्याण नहीं करेगा। वह शत्रुओं का विनाशक है, बाहरी व्यक्ति (नहुष्) को पहचानने में उससे कोई भूल नहीं होती। जिस पेय का वह रक्षक है, वह प्राणियों में चैतन्य का संचार करने वाला (जागृवि) सोम है, उसकी रक्षा में कैसे प्रमाद किया जा सकता है। यह तो बताओ, वहाँ से सुपर्ण-गरुड कैसे बचकर आएगा?॥५॥

[*अरुण माँ को आश्वस्त करते हुए*]

माँ शुङ्गे, गरुड का कोई सानी नहीं है, वह अतीव बलशाली है, उसका कोई सामना नहीं कर सकता, उसे कोई हरा नहीं सकता। वह साक्षात् ओज है, शक्ति है, बल है। वह आकाश और मेघ के समान है जिनसे कोई लड़ नहीं सकता। शत्रुओं के लिए वह मूर्तिमान् भय है॥६॥

[*अरुण का गरुड को आशीर्वाद*]

वात-देव इस गरुड के प्राणों की रक्षा करें, मरुद्गण इसके पंखों की रक्षा करें, सभी उत्पन्न (=जीवित) प्राणियों में प्रविष्ट अग्नि उसके सिर की रक्षा करे। मैं उसके आगे और पीछे रहता हुआ उसकी सहायता करूँगा, मनोरम चन्द्रमा सदैव उसके पीछे रहकर [अपनी अमृतमयी किरणों से उसकी क्लान्ति दूर करता रहेगा]॥७॥

[***दृश्य परिवर्तन**, स्वर्गलोक में इन्द्र बृहस्पति से*]

अरे, जहाँ पर सोम रखा हुआ है, वहाँ यह कैसा शोर सुनाई पड़ रहा है? बृहस्पति, ज़रा जाकर पता लगाइए। उस पंगु (भौवन) के [द्वारा बाण चलाए जाने पर उसके] धनुष की प्रत्यञ्चा की टंकार सुनाई पड़ रही है और वह बहरा सोमरक्षक निरन्तर चिल्ला रहा है॥८॥

[*बृहस्पति, इन्द्र से*]

हे शचीपति इन्द्र, इस घोष के विषय में मुझे पता है। यह विनता के पुत्र गरुड के उड़ने का शब्द है जो वहाँ पर तुम्हारे सोमरक्षकों को मारकर सोम को लेकर उड़ा जा रहा है॥९॥

॥ बारहवाँ सूक्त ॥

तेईसवाँ वर्ग

[इन्द्र, बृहस्पति से]

तो फुर्ती से बाण चलाने वाला वह पंगु भौवन कहाँ था जिसके बाणों से फूटती हुई चिंगारियाँ अग्नि की भीषण ज्वालाओं का भी तिरस्कार करती हैं, जिसके बाहुओं से निरन्तर बरसते हुए अमोघ बाण तीस योजन की दूरी तक साठ अयुत (=छः लाख) सैनिकों को एक साथ बेध सकते हैं?॥१॥

[बृहस्पति, इन्द्र से]

उस लँगड़े को डराकर वीर सुपर्ण अपने मार्ग पर सुरक्षित आगे बढ़ता चला गया। उच्चतम आकाश में सोम का चक्कर लगाते हुए जब वह सोम पर झपटा तो भौवन का कोई भी बाण उसे बेध नहीं सका॥२॥

[इन्द्र, उत्तेजना में बृहस्पति से]

ये अर्बुद, नहुष, काद्रवेय, उलूक, बल्बूल, श्वसन आदि सर्प [उस समय] कहाँ थे? और बिना पलक झपकाए (=आँखें खोलकर) सोने वाला वह प्रलिश कहाँ था जो आज मेरे सोम को विनता का पुत्र हरे लिए जा रहा है?॥३॥

ककुब्, भण्ड, चक्रतुण्ड कहाँ थे? अश्वमुख और कुण्डकर्ण कहाँ थे? विक्रोशन और खरकण्ठ कहाँ थे, जो मेरे सोम को विनता का पुत्र हरे लिए जा रहा है?॥४॥

[बृहस्पति का इन्द्र को उत्तर]

इन सब सर्पों ने जब गरुड को इतने तेज और बल के साथ झपटते हुए देखा तो उसके स्पर्श (=प्रहार) से भयभीत होकर उन सभी ने अपने-अपने सिर शरीर के अन्दर छिपा लिए॥५॥

चौबीसवाँ वर्ग

कशम्बूक, वेणुक, अश्वक्रन्द, अलगर्द और परुष कहाँ थे? नभोरूप-सरूप कहाँ थे जो मेरे सोम को विनता का पुत्र हरे लिए जा रहा है॥६॥

प्रवेश सीमा पर नियुक्त वह शशाक्ष कहाँ था जो क्रुद्ध होने पर लोगों का विनाश करने के लिए साक्षात् मृत्यु है? और वह [अजगर] विभिद् कहाँ था जो मुँह खोलकर ही सोया करता है, जो इस प्रकार मेरे सोम को विनता का पुत्र हरे लिए जा रहा है?॥७॥

[बृहस्पति, पुनः इन्द्र से]

हे इन्द्र, उन [सर्पों] में से किसी की गर्दन कट गई, किसी का सिर फूट गया, कुछ के अंग क्षत-विक्षत हो गए, वे सब-के-सब [संज्ञाहीन होकर] इधर-उधर छितराए पड़े हैं। पादविहीन रक्षक भौवन [भी] उस युद्ध में मारा गया। सुपर्ण ने भीषण मार-काट मचाई॥८॥

[इन्द्र, बृहस्पति से]

भया और अभया नाम की जो दो विनाशक बिजलियाँ सोम की रक्षा करते हुए उसके चारों ओर निरन्तर भ्रमण करती रहती हैं, जो कभी सोती (रुकती) नहीं और चारों ओर जिनकी दृष्टि रहती है, आखिर उनको भी यह गीध कैसे लाँघ गया?॥९॥

[बृहस्पति इन्द्र से]

भया और अभया नाम की जो दो विनाशक बिजलियाँ सोम की रक्षा करते हुए उसके चारों ओर निरन्तर भ्रमण करती रहती हैं, जैसे ही वैनतेय गरुड उनकी दृष्टि में आया वैसे ही तितर-बितर होकर वे आकाश की ओर पलायन कर गईं[१०]॥१०॥

॥ तेरहवाँ सूक्त ॥

पचीसवाँ वर्ग

[इन्द्र, बृहस्पति से]

ब्रह्मन्, मेरी जो माया पलक झपकने से भी अधिक तीव्र है और जिसे [किसी के सोम अपहरण के] संकल्प मात्र से उसकी चेष्टा का पता चल जाता है और जो कभी सोम के पास से हटती नहीं, और साथ ही वह [तेज़ धार वाले] छुरों से युक्त वज्र, वे दोनों कहाँ थे जो मेरे सोम को वैनतेय हरे लिए जा रहा है?

[बृहस्पति इन्द्र से]

तुम्हारी जो माया पलक झपकने से भी अधिक तीव्र है और जिसे अपहर्ता के संकल्प मात्र से उनकी चेष्टा का पता चल जाता है, उसे मन के समान गतिशील (अथवा अपनी आन्तरिक दिव्य शक्ति से पतनशील), तीव्रता से भी अधिक तीव्र, गरुड अपने बल से तिरस्कृत कर पीछे छोड़ गया।

---

[१०] इसका कारण सम्भवतः यह है कि "विद्युत्" गरुड की बड़ी बहन है। प्रथम सूक्त के बारहवें मन्त्र में उसे विनता के प्रथम अण्डे से उत्पन्न बताया गया है (*भिद्यमानोर्ध्वनिष्क्रान्ता विद्युन्मेघसखाम्बरे*)।

[इन्द्र, बृहस्पति से]

और मेरा जो चक्र पलक झपकने से भी अधिक तीव्र है, जिसे [किसी के सोम अपहरण के] संकल्प मात्र से उसकी चेष्टा का पता चला जाता है, जो कभी सोम के पास से हटता नहीं (और निरन्तर उसके चारों ओर भ्रमण करता रहता है) वह कहाँ था जो मेरे सोम को वैनतेय हरे लिए जा रहा है?

[बृहस्पति, इन्द्र से]

तुम्हारा जो चक्र पलक झपकने से भी अधिक तीव्र है और जिसे अपहर्ता के संकल्प मात्र से उसकी चेष्टा का पता चल जाता है, उसे मन के समान गतिशील (अथवा अपनी आन्तरिक दिव्यशक्ति से पतनशील), तीव्रता से भी अधिक तीव्र गरुड अपने बल से तिरस्कृत कर पीछे छोड़ गया (=पीछे छोड़कर अन्दर प्रविष्ट हो गया)॥४॥

[इन्द्र, बृहस्पति से]

पर्वतों के समान वे शिलाखण्ड, छुरों से युक्त वे भयानक वज्र, गहरी घाटियाँ, जल से भरे हुए विशाल तालाब और ह्लादिनी नामक सूर्य सी तेजस्वी वे बिजलियाँ जो हर समय चन्द्रमा की भाँति चमकती हुई अपना रूप बदलती रहती हैं और जिनकी चकाचौंध से आक्रमणकारी को आगे का मार्ग नहीं सूझता, आखिर कैसे वह गीध उन सबका भी अतिक्रमण कर गया?॥५॥

[*संभवतः उत्तरस्वरूप एक ऋचा यहाँ और रही होगी* – सं०]

छब्बीसवाँ वर्ग

[इन्द्र, बृहस्पति से]

मैंने [द्वादश] आदित्य, [एकादश] रुद्र, [अष्ट] वसु, [ऊनपञ्चाशत्] मरुत् और साथ ही साध्य-गणों को भी सोम की रक्षा करने के लिए कई प्रकार से नियुक्त किया था। वे सब कहाँ चले गए जो मेरे सोम को वैनतेय हरे लिए जा रहा है?॥६॥

[बृहस्पति, इन्द्र से]

वैनतेय के [पंखों की वायु के झोंको] द्वारा ठेले जाने पर वसुगण पूर्व की ओर जा पड़े, सारे साध्य एवं मरुद्गण उत्तर की ओर, गन्धर्वों की सेना के साथ रुद्रगण दक्षिण दिशा की ओर गए और गरुड ने आदित्यों को पश्चिम की ओर ढकेल दिया॥७॥

[इन्द्र, बृहस्पति से]

वह वैश्वानर अग्नि कहाँ था जो सदैव मेरे सोम को घेरकर वहीं उपस्थित रहता है। उसकी जाज्वल्यमान भीषण लपटों को, जिनका तेज कभी कम नहीं होता, आखिर कैसे वह गीध उनको भी पार कर गया?॥८॥

[बृहस्पति, इन्द्र से]

वैनतेय अपनी चोंच में घृत की छः लाख नदियाँ भर-भरकर लाया और उनसे उसने तुम्हारे जातवेदा अग्नि को संतृप्त कर दिया। उसके पश्चात् [अग्नि में प्रवेश करके और बाहर निकलकर] स्वर्ण से निर्मित शरीर वाला वह पक्षी [सोम लेकर] उड़ गया॥९॥

[बृहस्पति]

वैश्वानर अग्नि को घी से तृप्त कर, सभी अन्य सोम-रक्षकों को [युद्ध में] जीतकर, जैसे कोई महामेघ आकर [अचानक अपनी भीषण वृष्टि से गड्ढे आदि] ऊँचे और निचले स्थानों को जलभराव से समतल करते हुए फिर उसी प्रकार से दूर चला जाता है, [वैसे ही गरुड आया, कुछ ही पलों में अपने वेग से पर्वतों और घाटियों को एक समान करके उत्पात मचाया, और सोम [पात्र] लेकर, [जिस प्रकार आया था वैसे ही] दूर जाकर आँखों से ओझल हो गया]॥१०॥

॥ चौदहवाँ सूक्त ॥

सत्ताइसवाँ वर्ग

[बृहस्पति, इन्द्र से]

वह भीषण पराक्रमी एक अकेला ही अनेक [शत्रुओं] के ऊपर हावी रहा। वह तुम्हारे ही समान शक्तिशाली एवं बल-सम्पन्न है॥१/२॥

[इन्द्र, बृहस्पति से]

क्योंकि इस पक्षी ने मेरे सोम-रक्षकों [के ऊपर आक्रमण करके उन सब] को पराजित और अपमानित किया है, इसलिए मुझे उसके ऊपर क्रोध आ रहा है और अब मैं उस पर वज्र से प्रहार कर रहा हूँ॥१॥

(इन्द्र गरुड पर वज्र प्रहार करते हैं, तदनन्तर)

[इन्द्र, बृहस्पति से]

अरे, बृहस्पति, यह सुपर्ण आखिर कौन-सा जन्तु है? मेरा यह अनेक छुरों से युक्त,

अमित बलशाली वज्र, जिसका निर्माण तपस् के तेज से हुआ है और जिसने वृत्र जैसे असुर का हृदय विदीर्ण कर दिया, वह इस पक्षी के शरीर से टकराकर [उसका बाल बाँका किए बिना] वापिस आ गया!॥२॥

[बृहस्पति इन्द्र से]

हे इन्द्र, यह सुपर्ण समस्त वैदिक छन्दों का समवेत रूप है। इसका शरीर [बृहद्, रथन्तर आदि] सामन् से बना हुआ है और यजुस् इसमें ओत-प्रोत हैं। साथ ही तार्क्ष ऋषि का यह पुत्र सोम पीकर अब और अधिक बलशाली हो गया है, यही कारण है कि तुम्हारा वज्र इसके शरीर से टकराकर लौट आया॥३॥

[इन्द्र, गरुड से]

शत्रुओं का विनाश करने वाला देवताओं का यह वज्र आज तक शत्रु का वध किए बिना लौटकर नहीं आया है। आज इसका व्यर्थ होकर लौट आना देवताओं के लिए शुभ संकेत नहीं है। हे गरुत्मन्, तुम इसका मान रखो॥४॥

[गरुड, इन्द्र से]

मैं अपनी जंघा का एक दोष-रहित [या सुन्दर] पंख विमुक्त कर देता हूँ। तुम अपने वज्र से उसका छेदन कर दो और प्रतिष्ठा प्राप्त करो। यदि तुम्हें देवों का हित अभीष्ट है तो वह मैं तुम्हारे मृदु व्यवहार से कर दूँगा, किन्तु बलात् मैं करने वाला नहीं (बल प्रयोग द्वारा तुम मुझसे वह नहीं करवा सकते)॥५॥

मैं उस ऋषि का मान रखूँगा जिसकी अस्थियों से यह वज्र निर्मित किया गया है। साथ ही वज्र अस्त्र का मान रखूँगा, और तुम्हारा भी॥६॥

अट्ठाइसवाँ वर्ग

[प्रस्तोता]

उस पंख को इन्द्र ने अपने वज्र से तीन भागों में विखण्डित कर दिया। उसके अगले भाग से मयूर उत्पन्न हुआ, मध्य भाग से दो मुँह वाले साँपों की प्रजाति और मूल भाग से नेवले का जन्म हुआ जो सर्पों का घोर शत्रु है॥७॥

[इन्द्र, गरुड से]

हे पक्षिराज, मैं तुमसे यह पूछना चाहता हूँ कि तुम्हारे अन्दर कितना बल है, तुम कितना भार सहन कर सकते हो (=उठा सकते हो)। तुम्हारा जो यह असह्य को भी सहन करने का पराक्रम है, उसके विषय में मुझे बताओ और हम दोनों में अनन्त काल के लिए मैत्री हो जाए॥८॥

[गरुड, इन्द्र से]

हे शचीपति, यदि मैं चाहूँ तो आठ धरतियाँ, नौ दिशाएँ, तीन समुद्र और एक सहस्र से अधिक पर्वतों को [पीठ पर] उठाकर ले जा सकता हूँ॥९॥

[इन्द्र, गरुड से]

पक्षिराज, यदि तुम्हारे द्वारा दिया गया यह सोम सर्पगण पी लेंगे तो [वे अमर हो जाएँगे और पृथ्वी से] मनुष्यों का अस्तित्व मिटा देंगे, यह ठीक नहीं होगा॥१०॥

[गरुड, इन्द्र से]

हे शत्रुविनाशक इन्द्र, मैं यह सोम सर्पों को समर्पित करने वाला नहीं हूँ। मैं तो इसे ले जाकर केवल उन्हें दिखाऊँगा। हे सौम्य (दयालु), मेरे ऊपर क्रोध मत करो॥११॥

॥ पन्द्रहवाँ सूक्त ॥

उन्तीसवाँ वर्ग

[गरुड, सर्पों से]

"हे पृथ्वी (कद्रू) के पुत्रगण (सर्प), लो यह सोम तुम्हारे लिए आ गया। इसे यहाँ आकर [भली-भाँति] देख लो। अब मैं [दासता से] मुक्त हूँ। अरुण भी मुक्त हो गया, और साथ ही माता सुपर्णी विनता भी मुक्त हुई॥१॥

(*सर्प चारों ओर से सोम के पास आते हैं*)

[गरुड, पुनः सर्पों से]

हे कद्रू-पुत्रों, मैं तुम सबसे घोषणा कर रहा हूँ कि शून्य आकाश को नापते (चीरते) हुए[११] स्वर्ग के तृतीय धरातल से मैं यह सोम ले आया हूँ। सब मिलकर भली-भाँति इसको देख लो और [साथ ही] यह भी देखो कि अब यह तुमको छोड़कर जा रहा है॥२॥

मैं तुम सबके देखते-देखते और तुम लोगों का मेरा पीछा करते-करते, तुमसे

[११] "रजसो विमानात्" का इस प्रंसग में ठीक अर्थ करना कठिन है। ये दो शब्द "रजसो विमानः" के रूप में ऋग्वेद में प्रायः साथ-साथ आए हैं। हिरण्यगर्भ प्रजापति के लिए भी (ऋ. १०.१२१.५) "सम्पूर्ण लोक में व्याप्त", "लोक को नापने वाले" इस अर्थ में विशेषण के रूप में ये शब्द प्रयुक्त हैं। अव्यय होने के कारण "स्वर् (स्)" को षष्ठी या पञ्चमी के अर्थ में भी ले सकते हैं।

यह सोम छीनकर ले जा रहा हूँ। तुम में से जो अपने को वीर समझता है, वह आए और मेरा पीछा करे। आओ सर्पों, अपना पराक्रम दिखाओ!"॥३॥

(गरुड सोम लेकर उड़ जाते हैं)

[*गरुड, इन्द्र से*]

यह लो, तुम्हारे जिस सोम का मैंने पहले अपहरण किया था, उसे मैं तुम्हारे लिए वापिस ले आया हूँ।

अब मैं मुक्त हूँ, अरुण भी मुक्त है और माता विनता भी बन्धन से मुक्त हुई॥४॥

[*इन्द्र द्वारा आत्मस्तुति*]

मैंने पूर्वकाल में पिप्रु, नमुचि और शम्बर नामक असुरों का वध किया था और विप्रचित्ति को पराजित किया। वृत्रासुर का विनाश करके मैंने पृथ्वी और आकाश को अपने चारों ओर ऐसे लपेट रखा है जैसे कोई दो वस्त्रों (अधोवस्त्र, उत्तरीय) को अपने शरीर पर धारण करता है (पृथ्वी = अधोवस्त्र, आकाश = उत्तरीय)॥५॥

[*इन्द्र, गरुड से*]

अपने अमित बल के कारण मैंने अपने शत्रुओं को नीचा दिखाया। अपने बल की इस उत्कृष्टता के कारण इस सृष्टि में जो कुछ भी है, वह मैं ही हूँ। विश्व में जो भी बलशाली है उससे मैं अधिक बलशाली हूँ। ऐसे मेरे बलशाली के लिए निकाले (=निचोड़े) गए सोमरस को कैसे तुम अचानक बलपूर्वक ले भागे?॥६॥

तीसवाँ वर्ग

[*गरुड, इन्द्र से*]

हे इन्द्र, सुन्दर पंखों वाली मेरी माता विनता एक स्पर्धा के फलस्वरूप दासता में पड़ी हुई बहुत कष्ट भोग रही थी। उसको [दासता के बन्धन से मुक्त करके] वापिस क्रय करने का [एकमात्र] साधन (फिरौती) तुम्हारा सोम ही था, इसीलिए मुझे उसका अपहरण करना पड़ा जो अब तक किसी अन्य ने नहीं किया था।॥७॥

[*गरुड द्वारा इन्द्र की स्तुति*]

हे उदार हृदय (मघवन्), सोम तुम्हारा ही है, और यह सुपर्ण भी तुम्हारा है, तुम सब कुछ हो जो अभी तक सृष्टि में उत्पन्न हुआ है, हो रहा है और होगा। तुम सबके रक्षक हो, [संकटग्रस्त की] शरण हो और समुद्र के समान [विशाल हृदय?] हो। तुम्हारी ही यह सम्पूर्ण सृष्टि है, इस पर भली-भाँति शासन करो॥८॥

[बृहस्पति, इन्द्र से]

हे इन्द्र, अरुण के छोटे भाई, इस पराक्रमी सुपर्ण से अपना सोम लेकर इसको आशीर्वाद दो।

[इन्द्र, गरुड से]

हे सौम्य, मैं तुमको वर प्रदान करता हूँ, जो कुछ भी तुम अपने मन में अभिलाषा रखते हो, माँग लो। मेरी मैत्री के फलस्वरूप सोमपान के अधिकारी होने के साथ-साथ [वेदों की] वाणी में निरन्तर निवास, ये दोनों तुम प्राप्त करो। तार्क्ष ऋषि के पुत्र, तुम स्वयं बताओ [और क्या चाहते हो]? जो भी तुम्हारे मन में इच्छा हो उसे, वैनतेय, मुझसे माँग लो॥१० एवं ११॥

[गरुड, इन्द्र से]

हे शचीपति, मैं अपने भोजन के रूप में सर्पों का वरण करता हूँ। मैं यज्ञ का वाहक बनूँ [और उसे देवों तक ले जाऊँ]। मैं वेदों में प्रवेश करूँ जिससे जो भी ब्राह्मण [=वेदज्ञ] स्वर्ग प्राप्ति हेतु वेदों का पारायण करें वे स्वर्ग आकर हम दोनों की संगति प्राप्त करें॥१२॥

[इन्द्र गरुड से]

हे पक्षिराज, सर्प तुम्हारे भोजन बनें। तुम यज्ञ का वहन करो। हे वीर, तुम वेदों में प्रविष्ट हो जाओ। जो ब्राह्मण स्वर्ग की कामना से वेदों का पारायण करेंगे वे स्वर्ग में आकर हम दोनों की संगति (गोष्ठी) प्राप्त करेंगे॥१३॥

[प्रस्तोता]

गरुड को आकाश से पृथ्वी पर उतरते देख भय से सर्पों के रोंगटे खड़े हो गए। गरुड अब दासता से मुक्त थे। सर्पों का भक्षण कर उस बलवान् पक्षिराज का बल और बढ़ गया॥१४॥

अवसान-मंगल मन्त्र

इकतीसवाँ वर्ग

सुन्दर शिखरों वाले महापर्वत [हिमालय] के ऊपर विद्यमान सेमल के वृक्ष पर अपने आवास के लिए एक विशाल नीड बनाकर रहते हुए पक्षियों के सम्राट्, विनता के पुत्र, उन गरुत्मान्, गरुड का मैं अपनी रक्षा के लिए आह्वान करता हूँ॥१॥

यह जो मेरे द्वारा त्रिष्टुभ् छन्द में की गई गरुड की स्तुति है, इसके पारायण से वाणी उसी प्रकार फूट निकलती है जैसे वह सोमपान के पश्चात् प्रस्फुटित होती है और मुख से मन्त्र [स्वतः] निःसृत होने लगते हैं। हे वैनतेय, तुम हमें मांगल्य, निर्भयता तथा सुख प्रदान करो, हमारे पापों को दूर करो तथा शत्रुओं का विनाश करो॥२॥

अपने हृदय में सुपर्ण के प्रति अत्यन्त श्रद्धा से आपूरित होकर रचित इस [स्तुति] में जो कुछ भी कमी रह गई हो, या जो कुछ भी मुझसे छूट गया हो, [उस पर ध्यान न देकर] वे हमारे ऊपर कृपा करें, हमको दीर्घ आयु प्रदान करें तथा साथ ही चिरकाल तक हमारे नेत्रों को देखने की शक्ति प्रदान करें॥३॥

फलश्रुति

(इन्द्र के मुख से)

जो नित्यप्रति प्रत्येक पर्व (पूर्णिमा, अमावास्या) पर इस सौपर्ण (सुपर्णाख्यान) का पाठ करेगा, उसके मेधावी, ब्रह्मतेज सम्पन्न तथा वीर पुत्र उत्पन्न होगा॥१॥

जो नित्यप्रति प्रत्येक पर्व में सौपर्ण का पाठ करेगा, वह स्वर्ग पहुँचकर मेरे लोक में आकर अनन्त काल तक रहेगा॥२॥

जो विनीत भाव से अत्यन्त श्रद्धा एवं विश्वासपूर्वक सौपर्ण का श्रवण करता है वह सभी प्रकार की आपत्तियों से एवं अपने शत्रुओं से मुक्त हो जाता है॥३॥

यदि कोई गर्भवती नारी प्रत्येक पर्व में इसको सुने तो उसके एक ऐसा बलवान् पुत्र उत्पन्न होगा जो शत्रुओं को संतप्त करेगा॥४॥

जो व्यक्ति इस सौपर्ण (सुपर्णाध्याय) को साथ में बैठकर सुनते हैं उनकी नेत्र दृष्टि सुपर्ण पक्षी के समान तीक्ष्ण हो जाती है। हम दोनों (इन्द्र एवं गरुड) की कीर्ति का गायन करने वाले स्वर्गलोक को प्रयाण करते हैं॥५॥

> मन की गति से उड़ते हुए सुपर्ण ने लौह-निर्मित प्राचीर को पार किया और स्वर्ग जाकर वज्रधारी इन्द्र के लिए सोम ले आया। — ऋग्वेद ८.१००.८

॥ *इन्द्र एवं सुपर्ण को प्रणाम* ॥

परिशिष्टम्

सुपर्णाध्यान्तर्गताः केचन शब्दाः येषां स्वराङ्कनम् ऋग्वेदादिभ्यो भिन्नम्

(कोष्ठगतं रूपम् प्राचीनतरं संहितादिषु प्रयुक्तम्)

अनन्त (अनन्त) १५.१९

अनेनस् (अनेनस्) ६.४

अन्ततः (अन्ततः) ९.३

अपत्य (अपत्य) ४.३

अपुत्रा (अपुत्रा) ११.४

अबला (अबला) ५.९

अयुत (अयुत) १२.१, १३.१०

अर्चिः (अर्चि) १३.९

अश्रुमुखाः (अश्रुमुखाः) ४.४

अहोरात्राः (अहोरात्रा) १०.४

आख्यान (आख्यान) १५.२१

आङ्गिरस (आङ्गिरस) १०.६

आचार्य (आचार्य) ४.४

आदित्याः (आदित्या) १३.७

आर्त (आर्त) ५.२, ९.८

आस्तिक्य (आस्तिक्य) १५.२०

उपतीरं (उपतीर) १२.६

उलूकः (उलूक) १२.३

एनान् (एनान्) ४.१०

काणा (काणा) ३.४

जनता (जनता) ८.८

तनूज (तनूज) १४.५

तर्पयित्वा (तर्पयित्वा) १३.११

तार्क्ष्यपुत्र (तार्क्ष्य, ऋ०) १४.३

त्रिधा (त्रिधा) १४.७

दक्षिणा (दक्षिणा) १०.४, १३.८

दुष्टरम् (दुष्टर) १०.१०

द्वीप (द्वीप) ४.२, ४.५

नकुलः (नकुलः) १४.७

नित्यं (नित्य) १.२ (अन्यत्र ५.२, १५.१८, १९ शुद्धम्)

पौरुषं (पौरुषं) ६.५

मध्यमं (मध्यमं) १.१४

मरुत् (मरुत्) ११.७, १३.७, ८

मर्तः (मर्तः) १२.६

मानस (मानस) १०.२

मुनिः (मुनिः) ७.४

मुहुः (मुहुः) १.१४

मृषा (मृषा) ३.९

मेधाविन् (मेधाविन्) १५.१८

मोदाः (मोदाः) १३.५

रथवत् (रथवत्) १.२

रविः (रविः) १.१६

रैतस् (रैतस) ९.१

लब्ध्वा (लब्ध्वा) १.१२ (मन्त्रादौ स्थितत्वादाद्युदात्तत्वम् ?)

वक्ष्यामि (वक्ष्यामि) ३.२

वरेण्यम् (वरेण्यम्) १.२

विघृष्ट (विघृष्ट) १५.७

वीर्यवान् (वीर्यवान्) १४.३

शकुनिः (शकुनिः) १०.१०

शिखा (शिखा) ४.९

श्वसनः (श्वसनः) १२.३

सनातनः [०तना] (सनातनः) ९.३

सरूपयोः (सरूपयोः) ३.३

सर्पमातर् [संबुद्धौ] (सर्पमातर्) ३.९

सलोकता (सलोकता) १५.११

(समु-)सह्यः (सह्यः) १४.८

स्वर्ग (१.१), स्वर्ग (५.५) ('स्वर्ग' इत्येव शुद्धम्)

मन्त्रानुक्रमणिका

(मूलपाठगतस्थानात् कस्यचिन्मन्त्रस्य स्थितिः संशोधितपाठे क्वचिदन्यत्र चेत्, तर्हि तस्याः कोष्ठकगता निर्दिष्टिः)